HISTORIC PHOTOS OF
CUBAN MIAMI

TEXT AND CAPTIONS BY JENNIFER ORTIZ

TURNER
PUBLISHING COMPANY

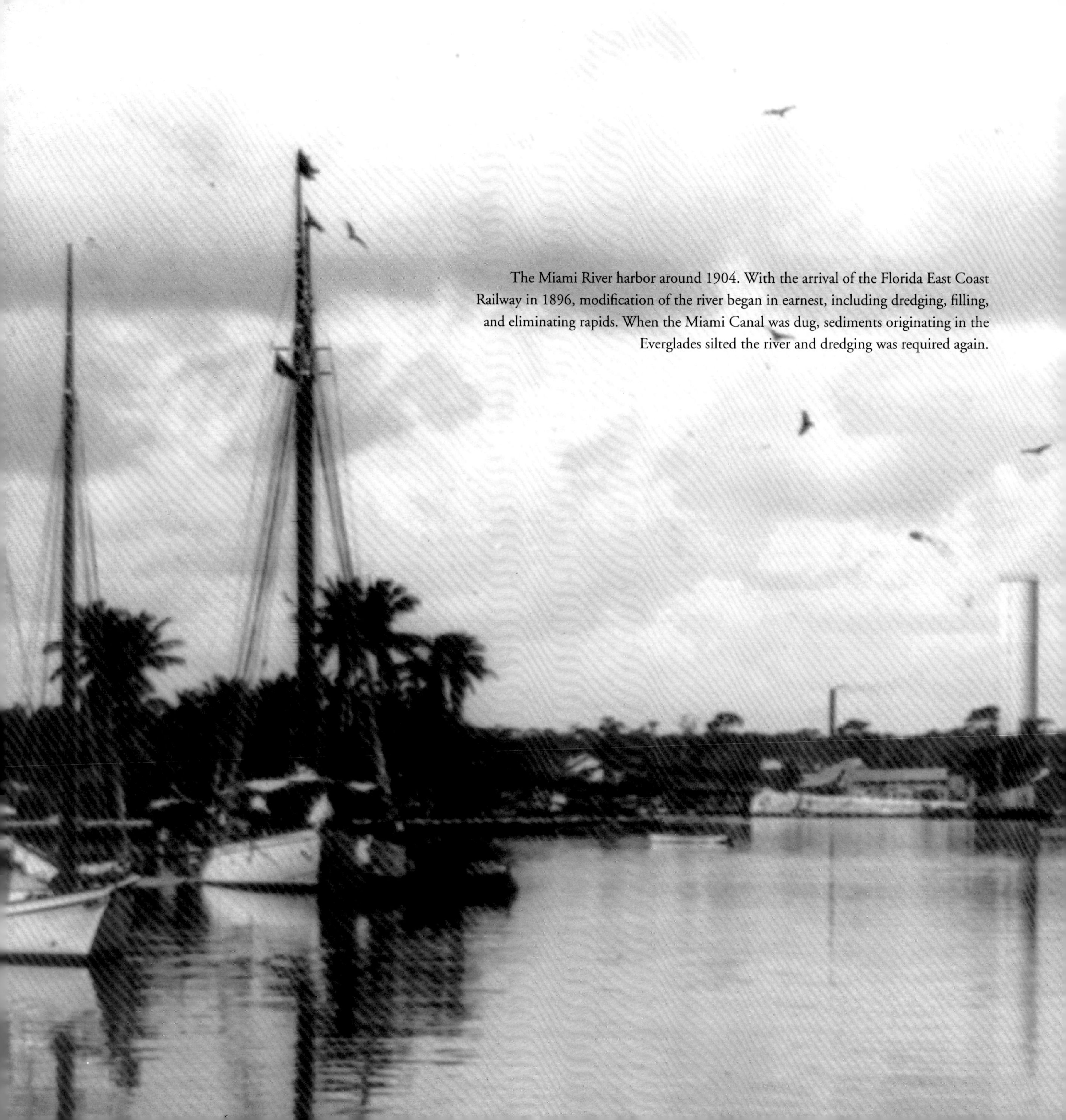

The Miami River harbor around 1904. With the arrival of the Florida East Coast Railway in 1896, modification of the river began in earnest, including dredging, filling, and eliminating rapids. When the Miami Canal was dug, sediments originating in the Everglades silted the river and dredging was required again.

HISTORIC PHOTOS OF
CUBAN MIAMI

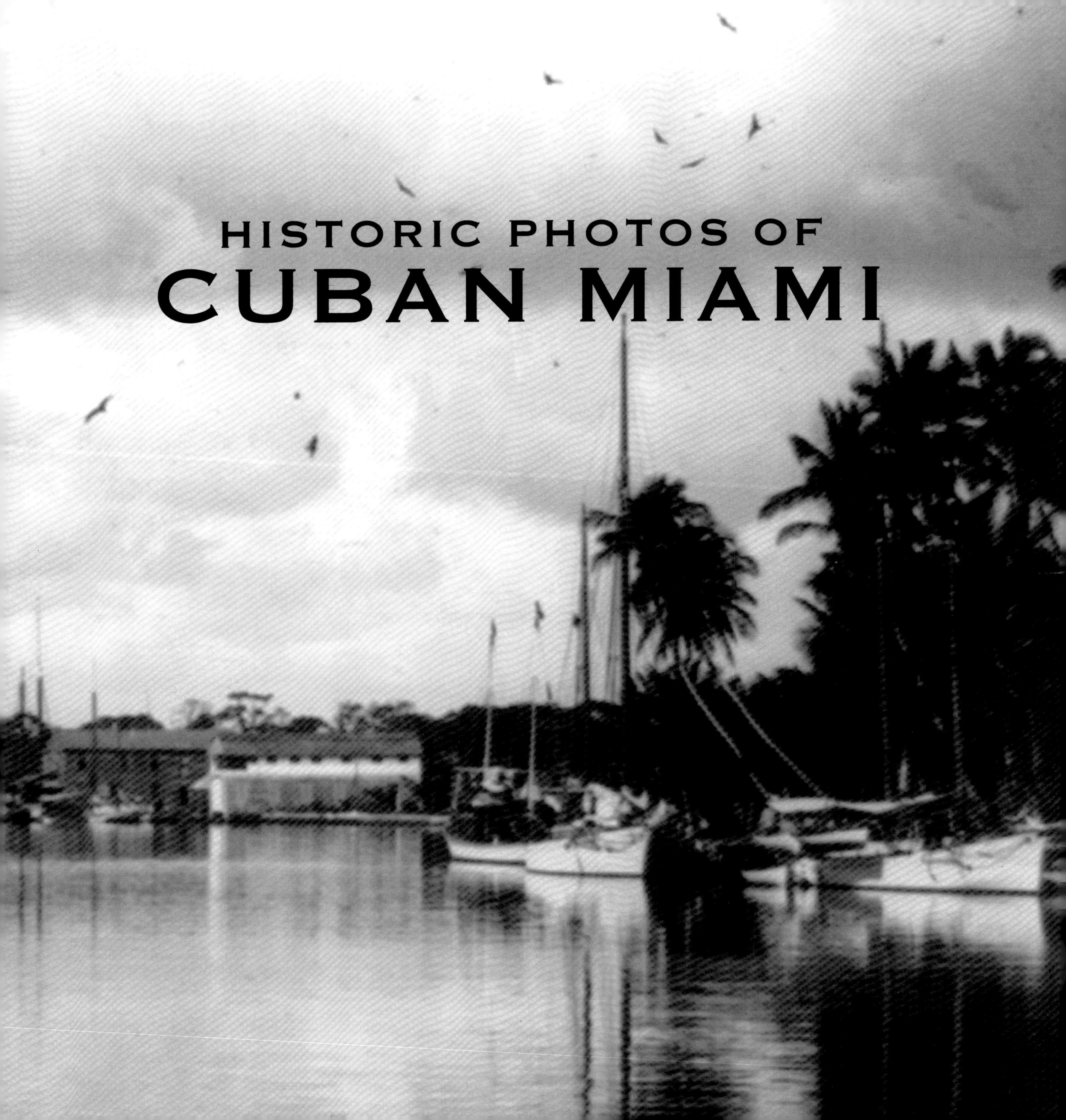

Turner Publishing Company
200 4th Avenue North • Suite 950
Nashville, Tennessee 37219
(615) 255-2665

www.turnerpublishing.com

Historic Photos of Cuban Miami

Library of Congress Control Number: 2009933010

ISBN: 978-1-59652-560-3

Printed in China

10 11 12 13 14 15 16 17—0 9 8 7 6 5 4 3 2 1

Contents

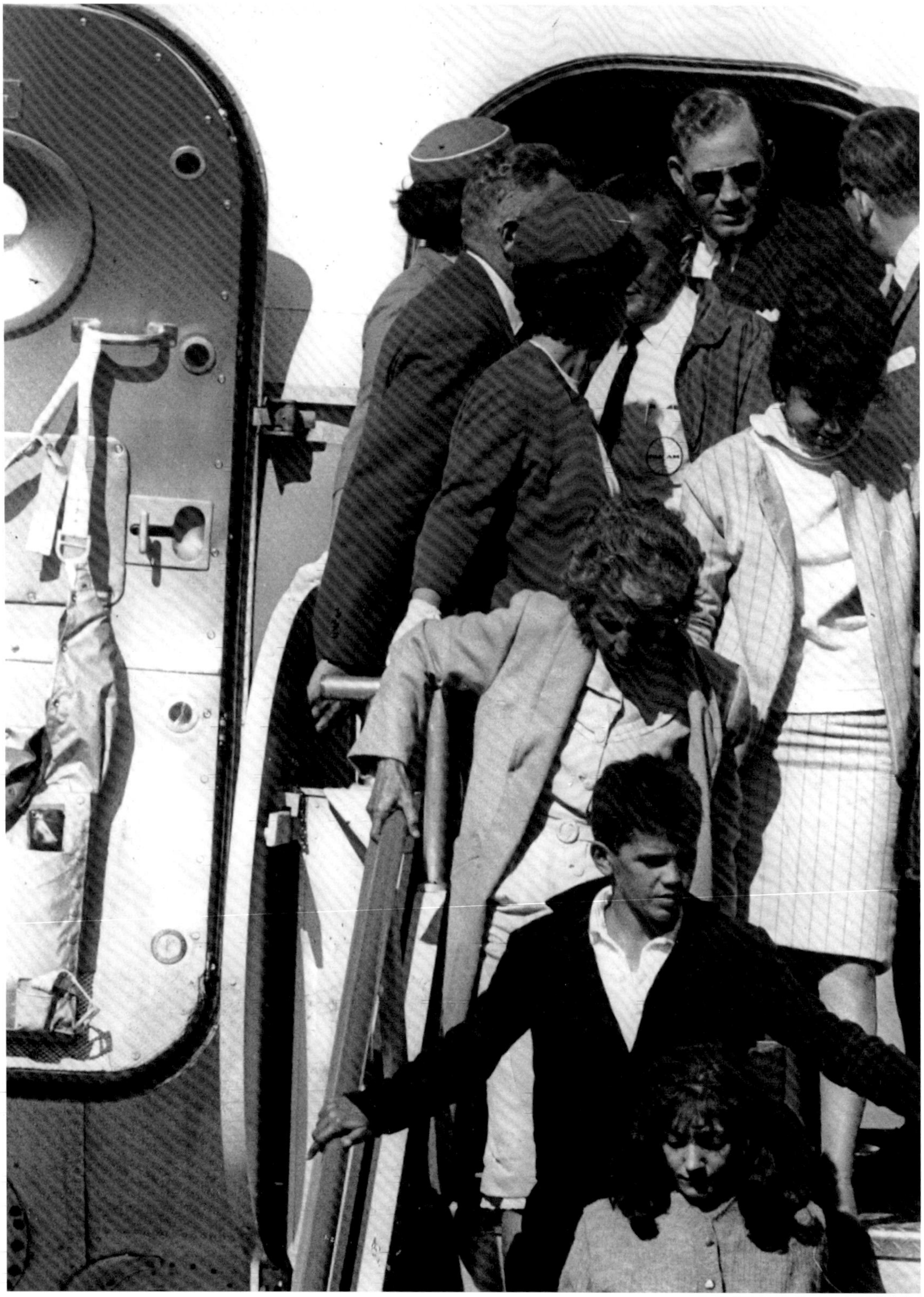

First wave Cuban exiles debark a Pan American plane at Miami International Airport. Given a new home, new life, and new culture, these Cubans brought their customs to Miami and transformed the city to what it is today.

Acknowledgments

This volume, *Historic Photos of Cuban Miami,* is the result of the cooperation and efforts of many individuals, organizations, and corporations. It is with great thanks that we acknowledge the valuable contribution of the following for their generous support:

Florida State Archives
Historical Museum of Southern Florida
Library of Congress

The writer would like to thank Dawn Hugh of the Historical Museum of Southern Florida, Ines Rojas-Lesinski and Eva Rosales for assisting in photo research. Gratitude is also owed to Teo Cuervo for generously allowing the use of his personal family photos. Gratitude is also expressed to members of the Pelaez and Ortiz families for the use of their personal photos. Thanks, also, to WPBT for the generous use of stills from *¿Qué Pasa, U.S.A?*

With the exception of touching up imperfections that have accrued with the passage of time and cropping where necessary, no changes have been made. The focus and clarity of many images is limited by the technology and the ability of the photographer at the time they were taken.

Preface

Miami and Cuba share a past that began before either was properly independent. The area now known as Miami was first settled by Spaniards, just as Cuba had been. In 1819, the Adams-Onis Treaty with Spain ceded Florida to the United States. For a very long time thereafter, Key West and Tampa enjoyed dominance as links in the relationship between the United States and Cuba. Not until Miami's incorporation as a city in 1896 and the Spanish-American War in 1898 did the relationship between Cuba and Miami begin to grow. As Henry Flagler's railroad in the 1890s and Miami real estate in the 1920s attracted growing numbers of Americans from other regions of the nation, the burgeoning city's links with Cuba also rose.

Nearly every president of Cuba went into exile in Miami, or at least visited and did business there while in exile in Florida, including Fulgencio Batista. Batista fundraised in Miami. When he returned to power, his rivals came to Miami to fundraise. The rise of Fidel Castro to power in Cuba in 1959 marked a turning point, as hundreds of thousands of Cuban refugees were welcomed by the United States to Miami over the ensuing three decades. The unusually large influx of exiles and a corresponding departure of Miami natives would turn Miami into a predominantly Hispanic city, with 65 percent of the population Hispanic by 2009, most of them from Cuba or of Cuban descent. Today, the city is known as an international gateway, a tropical playground, and a center for Latin culture.

This book is divided into four chapters marked by the major phases of the relationship between Cubans and Miami. The first chapter explores the years from the Spanish-American War to the rise of Castro. Chapter 2 takes a look at the First Wave of exiles and the Cuban airlifts in the 1960s. The turbulence and prosperity that followed this first wave occupy chapter 3, and chapter 4 concludes with the era marked by the controversial Mariel boatlift of the 1980s. This chronological approach parallels the growth and maturation of Miami along with the Cuban community.

Being a Cuban-American and having pursued the study of history and Latin American studies at university, I must say that working on *Historic Photos of Cuban Miami* was a privilege. This is the story of the culture that made me who I am today. I was born in Miami, to Cuban exile parents. I grew up visiting many of the places pictured in this book, places that formed the landscape of my childhood.

Well documented though the plight of the Cuban exiles in Miami has been, it was extremely challenging to find properly preserved photographs that demonstrate the historic significance that the Cuban community has had on the city in the last 50 years. This book is the result of countless hours of research and careful review of more than ten thousand photographs. While researching this book, I chatted with many exiles and listened to their personal histories. Each story shared gave me a new perspective. Some were heartbreaking, some comical, and others triumphant. Whether or not the conversation yielded a photograph (more often it did not), those stories shaped this project.

For this assistance, extreme gratitude is given to those who shared their stories, who carefully preserved the photographic history of Miami, and who helped in locating images for this book. I am proud to have worked on this book, and it has inspired me to see Miami with a different perspective. The hope is that you will gain new perspectives, too.

The goal of the Historic Photos series is to provide broader access to rare, historically informative, and sometimes extraordinary photographs. There is no limit to the age or ethnicity of those who can appreciate these books. Without *Historic Photos of Cuban Miami,* many would never have the privilege of seeing these images of the city or even know of their existence. For visitors and residents alike, it is hoped that these images will provide a new perspective on and historical knowledge of the Magic City.

—Jennifer Ortiz

Israel Diner, Gustav Tanenblatt, and Manuel Diner pose for a photograph on Michigan Avenue in Miami Beach after arriving from Cuba in 1956.

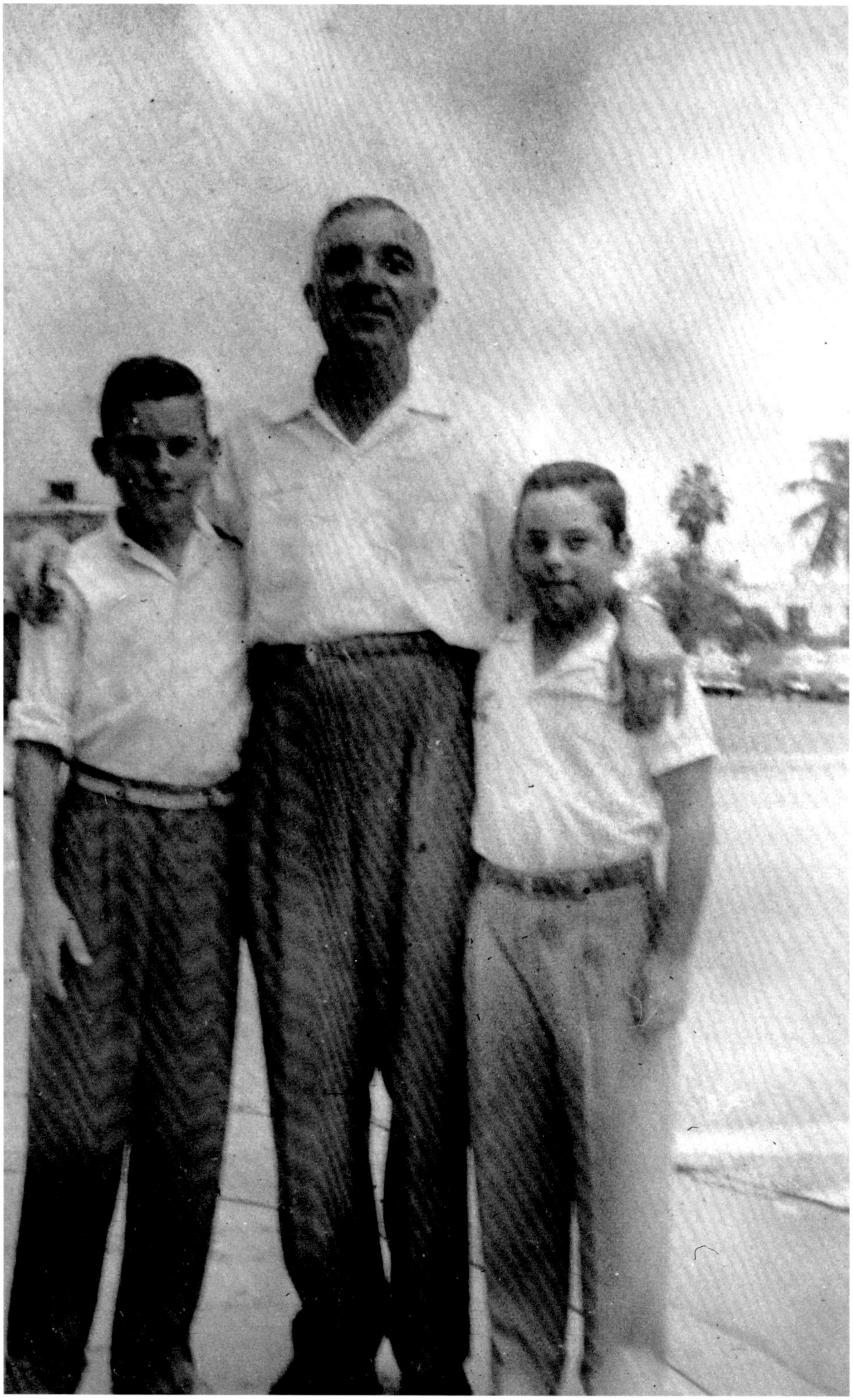

FROM THE SPANISH-AMERICAN WAR TO CASTRO (1880–1959)

Miami was named for the indigenous people who once inhabited the area surrounding Lake Okeechobee, the Mayaimis. The word *mayaimi* means "big water" in the language of the Mayaimi, Tequesta, and Calusa. Oddly enough, the Mayaimi tribe's territory did not extend into what is now Miami-Dade County, which was inhabited by the Tequestas, still less that of the Miami, a separate and unrelated tribe inhabiting parts of present-day Illinois, Indiana, Michigan, and Ohio.

Prior to being known as Miami, the area was called Biscayne Bay and Fort Dallas. Miami was founded through the efforts of Ohioans William Brickell and especially Julia Tuttle, earning it the distinction as the only city in the United States founded by a woman. Tuttle was a wealthy Cleveland transplant who saw the potential of Miami's no-freeze lands for growing citrus. She is credited with convincing Henry Flagler, whose early career had also begun in Ohio, to extend the East Coast Railway to Miami, offering part of her estate for a railroad station and hotel if he would do so. Following the great freeze of 1894-95, which destroyed citrus crops in the north and central part of the state, along with the promise of more acreage by the State of Florida, Flagler decided Tuttle's idea had merit and the city sprang to life in the summer of 1896.

With the outbreak of the Spanish-American War, Flagler would go on to tout Miami as an essential and strategic military location, but prior to the war, the city had little significance in Cuban-American relations. Key West and Tampa were the go-to cities for Cubans coming to America. After the Spanish-American War, Miami's relationship with Cuba began to grow, howsoever slowly. As Miami real estate boomed, imports from Cuba increased. Cuban building materials, like sandstone, tile, and antique woodwork, were frequently incorporated into new buildings in Miami, giving the buildings an instantly aged look. Miami, in turn, provided tires, gasoline, cattle, and other goods to Cuba. The opening of Pan American Airlines also boosted the relationship. By the 1920s, Miami and Havana were building reputations as exotic tourist destinations. Miami played up the exotic, Latin feel it borrowed from Cuba, and travel agents pushed the ease of accessibility to Cuba from Miami. Miami also became a common destination for Cuban presidents and other politicos who had fallen out of favor and needed a home in exile.

Originally, Miami was to be named after Henry Flagler, but he declined the offer. It was Flagler who insisted upon using the native word *maiyami.* His East Coast Railway provided means for bringing in settlers and supplies, and for exporting winter crops. Recognizing the opportunity for government investment, he promoted the strategic advantage Miami could provide in the impending Spanish-American War, through his newspaper the *Metropolis.*

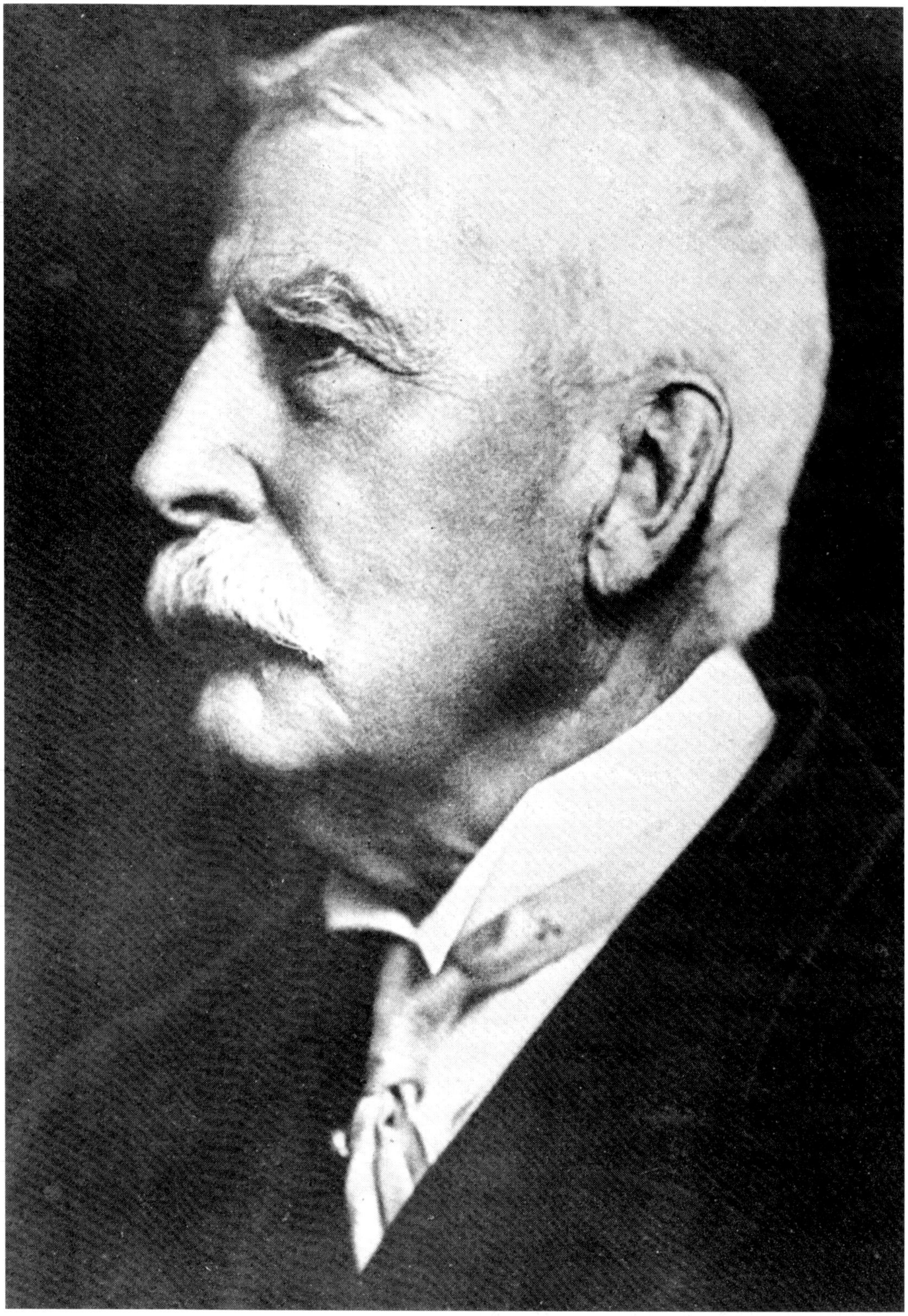

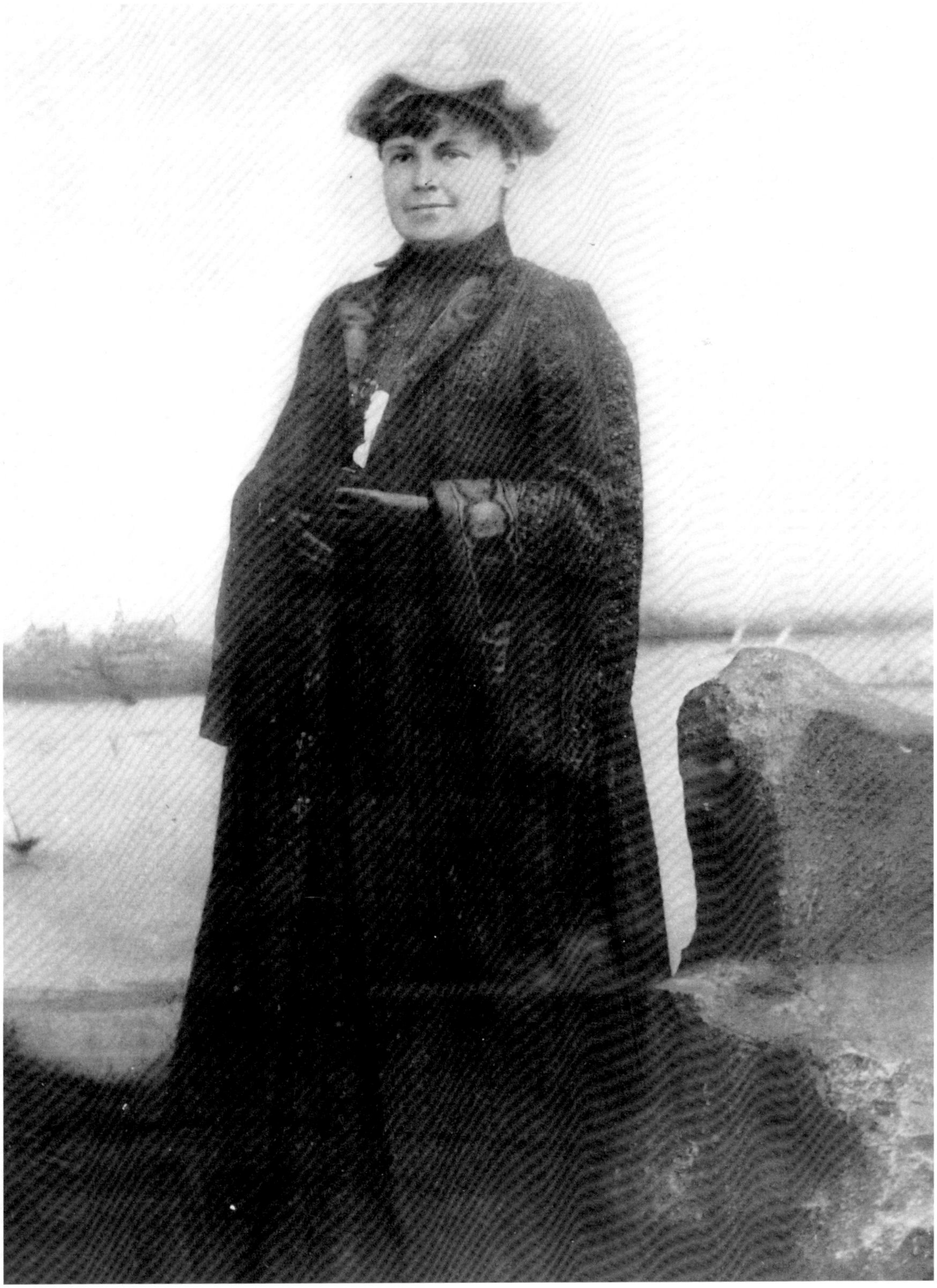

If Henry Flagler was the man of means behind Miami, then Julia Tuttle was the woman. She is credited with founding the city, by enticing Flagler to extend the East Coast Railway farther South. Tuttle struck a deal with Flagler, promising him tracts of land, which she awarded Flagler as he completed his end of the bargain. In April 1896, the East Coast Railway reached its destination and Flagler rode the first train to the new city.

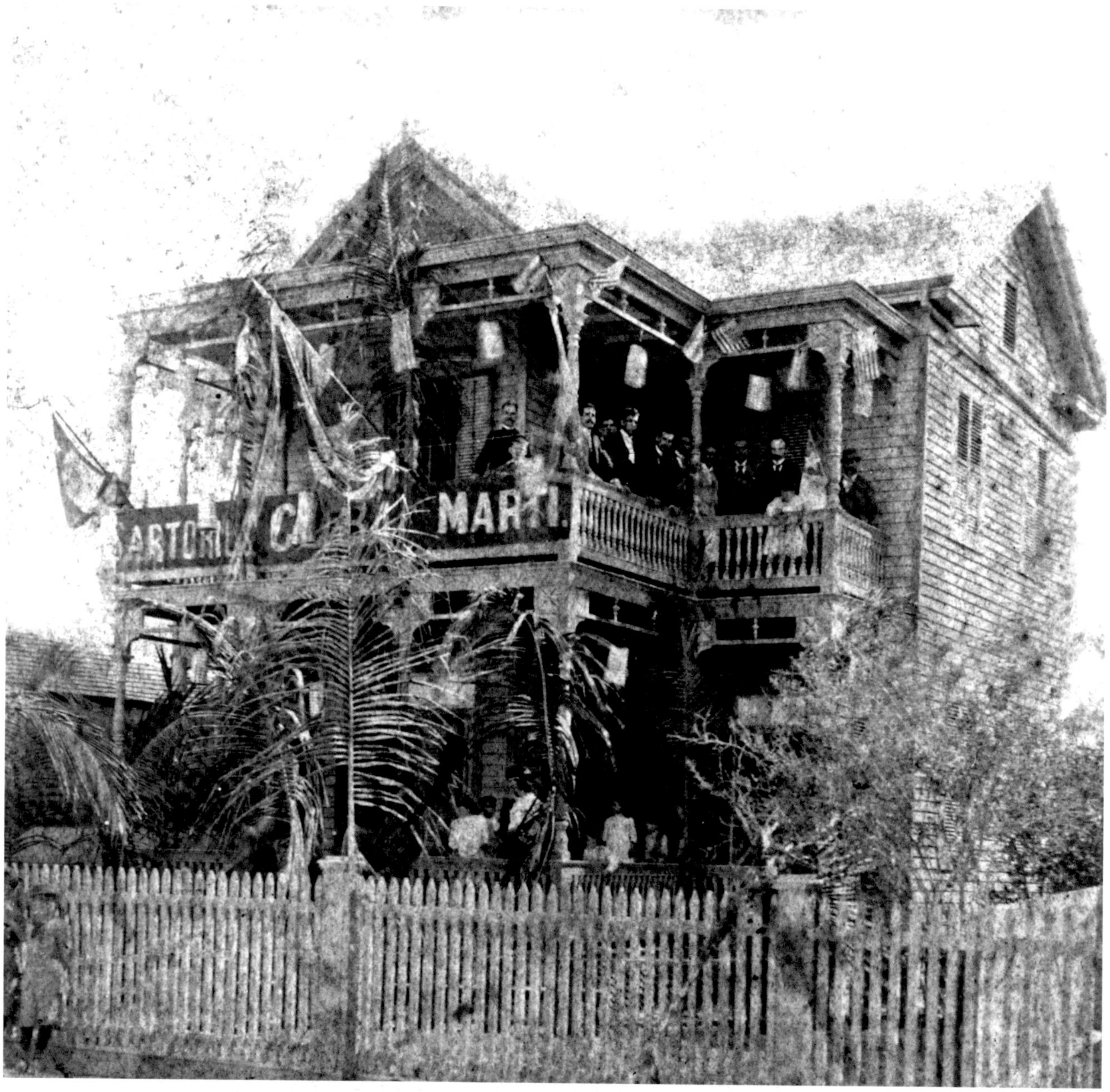

The famous Cuban poet and revolutionary Jose Martí (1853–1895) is seen here in 1891 visiting Key West, then part of Dade County. At the time, Dade County spanned an area as far north as Palm Beach. Miami was not yet a city. Strongly influenced by and admiring the freedoms, work ethic, and economic success of the United States, and angered at Spain for abuses that included falsifying elections, taxing Cubans heavily, and failing to abolish slavery, Martí is largely responsible for the movement toward Cuban independence from Spain, which led to the Spanish-American War. That war gave Cubans the independence they desired and marked the beginning of Cuba's relationship with Miami.

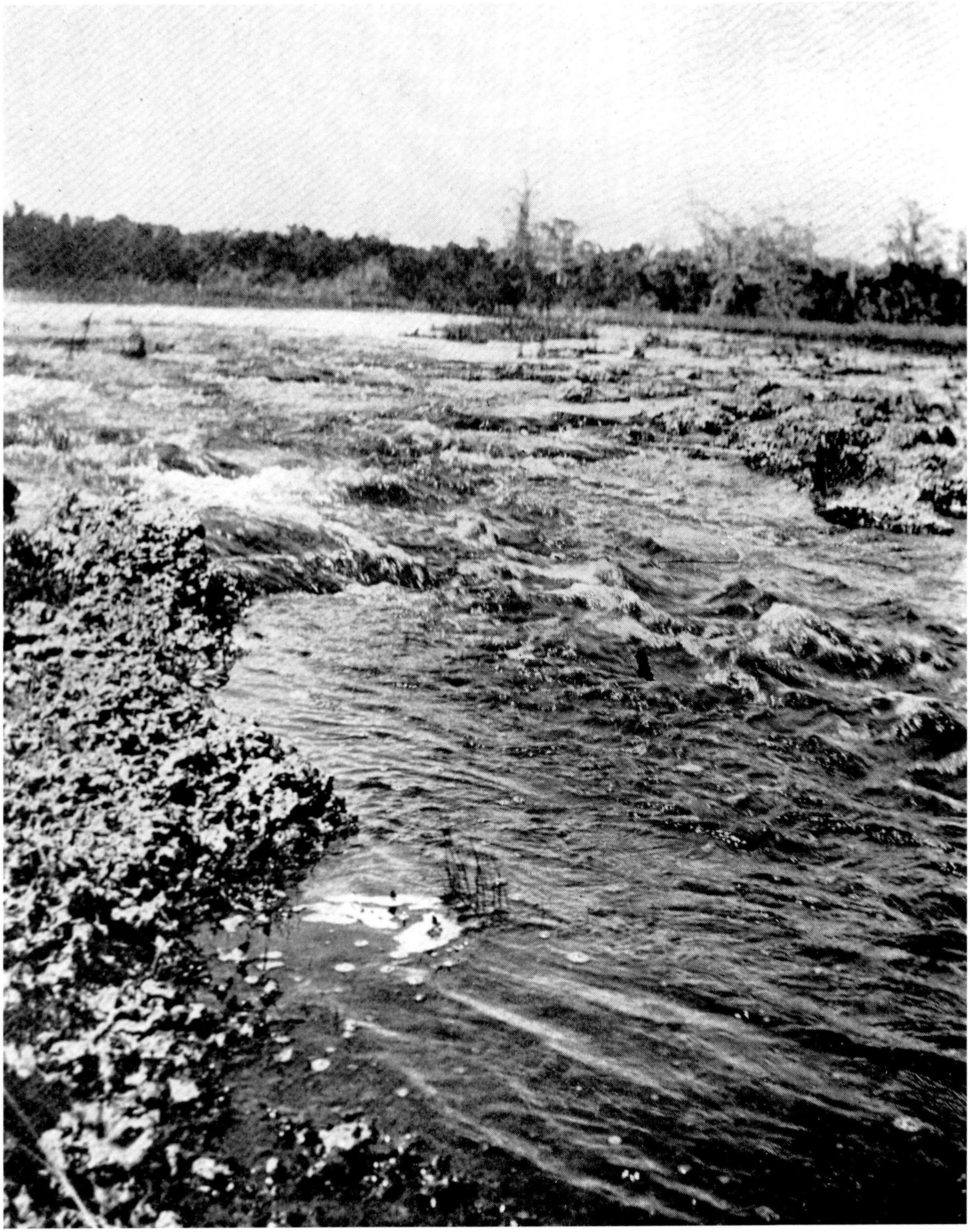

This photograph was taken in 1896, the year Miami was incorporated. Miami was as wild and untamed as the rapids on the Miami River. The rapids were soon tamed by dredging, ordered by Henry Flagler to make the waterway more accessible.

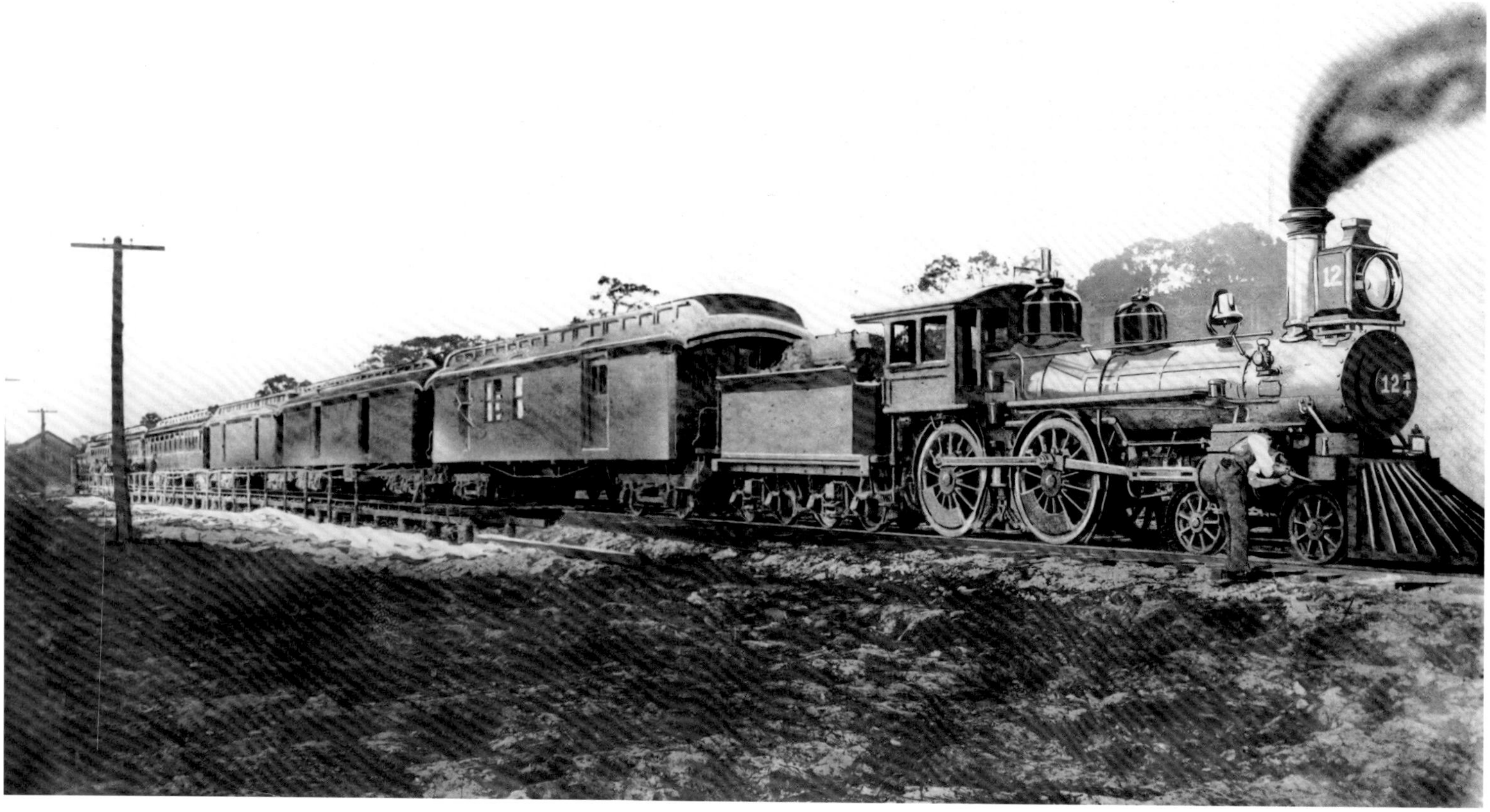

The first passenger train arrives in Miami in 1896. Henry Flagler was one of its passengers.

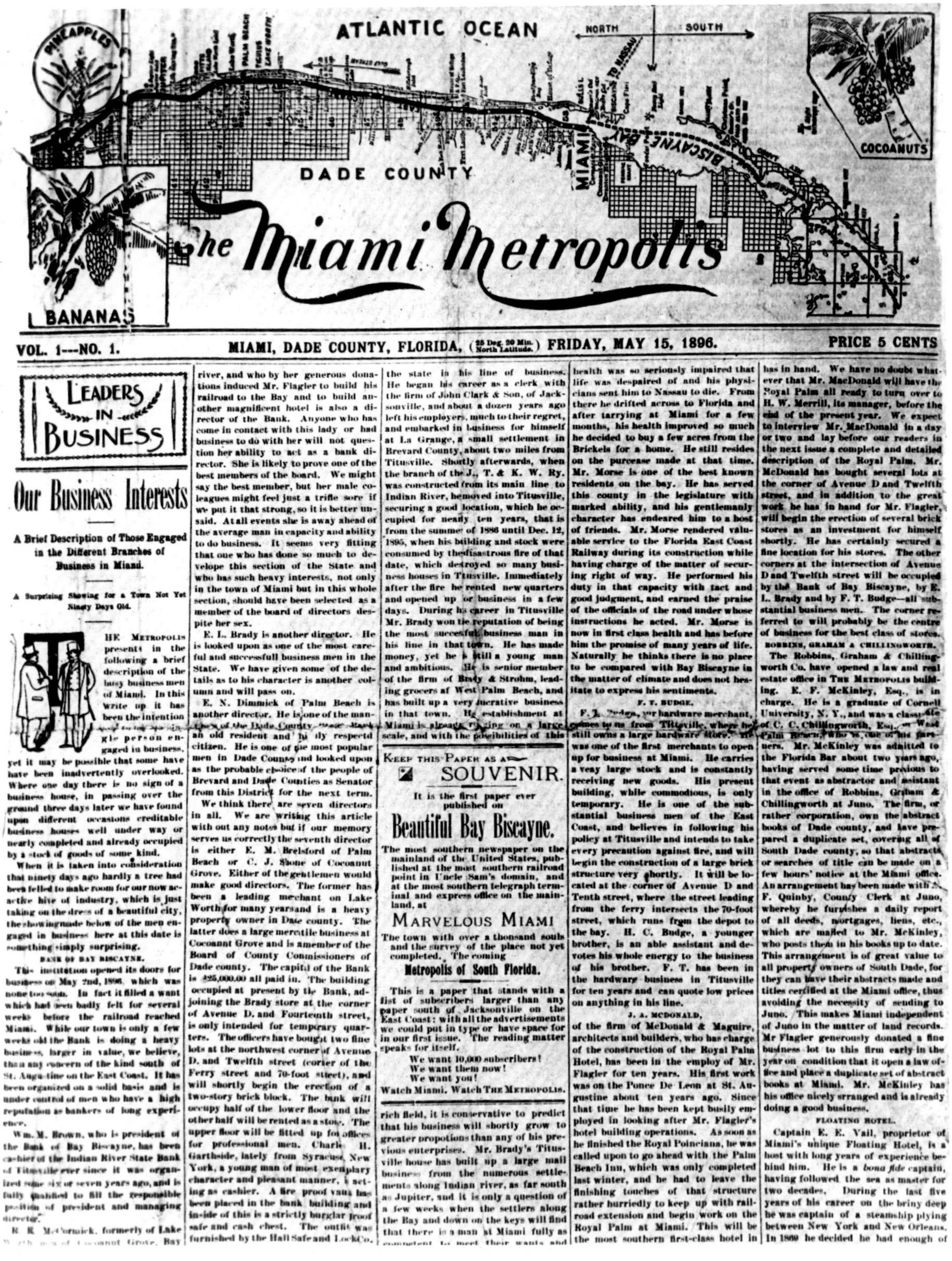

ATLANTIC OCEAN

NORTH SOUTH

PINEAPPLES

COCOANUTS

DADE COUNTY

MIAMI

BISCAYNE BAY

BANANAS

The Miami Metropolis

VOL. 1---NO. 1. MIAMI, DADE COUNTY, FLORIDA, (25 Deg. 20 Min. North Latitude.) FRIDAY, MAY 15, 1896. PRICE 5 CENTS

LEADERS IN BUSINESS

Our Business Interests

A Brief Description of Those Engaged in the Different Branches of Business in Miami.

A Surprising Showing for a Town Not Yet Ninety Days Old.

THE METROPOLIS presents in the following a brief description of the busy business men of Miami. In this write up it has been the intention [illegible] single person engaged in business, yet it may be possible that some have have been inadvertently overlooked. Where one day there is no sign of a business house, in passing over the ground three days later we have found upon different occasions creditable business houses well under way or nearly completed and already occupied by a stock of goods of some kind.

When it is taken into consideration that ninety days ago hardly a tree had been felled to make room for our now active hive of industry, which is just taking on the dress of a beautiful city, the showing made below of the men engaged in business here at this date is something simply surprising.

BANK OF BAY BISCAYNE.

This institution opened its doors for business on May 2nd, 1896, which was none too soon. In fact it filled a want which had been badly felt for several weeks before the railroad reached Miami. While our town is only a few weeks old the Bank is doing a heavy business, larger in value, we believe, than any concern of the kind south of St. Augustine on the East Coast. It has been organized on a solid basis and is under control of men who have a high reputation as bankers of long experience.

Wm. M. Brown, who is president of the Bank of Bay Biscayne, has been cashier of the Indian River State Bank of Titusville ever since it was organized some six or seven years ago, and is fully qualified to fill the responsible position of president and managing director.

R. R. McCormick, formerly of Lake Worth, now of Cocoanut Grove, Bay river, and who by her generous donations induced Mr. Flagler to build his railroad to the Bay and to build another magnificent hotel is also a director of the Bank. Anyone who has come in contact with this lady or had business to do with her will not question her ability to act as a bank director. She is likely to prove one of the best members of the board. We might say the best member, but her male coleagues might feel just a trifle sore if we put it that strong, so it is better unsaid. At all events she is away ahead of the average man in capacity and ability to do business. It seems very fitting that one who has done so much to develope this section of the State and who has such heavy interests, not only in the town of Miami but in this whole section, should have been selected as a member of the board of directors despite her sex.

E. L. Brady is another director. He is looked upon as one of the most careful and successfull business men in the State. We have given some of the details as to his character is another column and will pass on.

E. N. Dimmick of Palm Beach is another director. He is one of the man-[illegible] of the Dade County [illegible] an old resident and hi[illegible]ly respectd citizen. He is one of the most popular men in Dade County and looked upon as the probable choice of the people of Brevard and Dade Counties as Senator from this District for the next term.

We think there are seven directors in all. We are writing this article with out any notes but if our memory serves us correctly the seventh director is either E. M. Brelsford of Palm Beach or C. J. Shone of Cocoanut Grove. Either of the gentlemen would make good directors. The former has been a leading merchant on Lake Worth for many years and is a heavy property owner in Dade county. The latter does a large mercntile business at Cocoanut Grove and is a member of the Board of County Commissioners of Dade county. The capital of the Bank is $25,000.00 all paid in. The building occupied at present by the Bank, adjoining the Brady store at the corner of Avenue D. and Fourteenth street, is only intended for temporary quarters. The officers have bought two fine lots at the northwest corner of Avenue D. and Twelfth street (corner of the Ferry street and 70-foot street), and will shortly begin the erection of a two-story brick block. The bank will occupy half of the lower floor and the other half will be rented as a store. The upper floor will be fitted up for offices for professional men. Charles H. Garthside, lately from Syracuse, New York, a young man of most exemplary character and pleasant manner, is acting as cashier. A fire proof vault has been placed in the bank building and inside of this is a strictly burglar proof safe and cash chest. The outfit was furnished by the Hall Safe and Lock Co.

[illegible] the state in his line of business. He began his career as a clerk with the firm of John Clark & Son, of Jacksonville, and about a dozen years ago left his employers, much to their regret, and embarked in business for himself at La Grange, a small settlement in Brevard County, about two miles from Titusville. Shortly afterwards, when the branch of the J., T. & K. W. Ry. was constructed from its main line to Indian River, he moved into Titusville, securing a good location, which he occupied for nearly ten years, that is from the summer of 1886 until Dec. 12, 1895, when his building and stock were consumed by the disastrous fire of that date, which destroyed so many business houses in Titusville. Immediately after the fire he rented new quarters and opened up for business in a few days. During his career in Titusville Mr. Brady won the reputation of being the most successful business man in his line in that town. He has made money, yet he is still a young man and ambitious. He is senior member of the firm of Brady & Strohm, leading grocers at West Palm Beach, and has built up a very lucrative business in that town. His establishment at Miami is already r[illegible]ing on a large scale, and with the possibilities of this rich field, it is conservative to predict that his business will shortly grow to greater propotions than any of his previous enterprises. Mr. Brady's Titusville house has built up a large mail business from the numerous settlements along Indian river, as far south as Jupiter, and it is only a question of a few weeks when the settlers along the Bay and down on the keys will find that there is a man at Miami fully as competent to meet their wants and

KEEP THIS PAPER AS A

SOUVENIR.

It is the first paper ever published on

Beautiful Bay Biscayne.

The most southern newspaper on the mainland of the United States, published at the most southern railroad point in Uncle Sam's domain, and at the most southern telegraph terminal and express office on the mainland, at

MARVELOUS MIAMI

The town with over a thousand souls and the survey of the place not yet completed. The coming

Metropolis of South Florida.

This is a paper that stands with a list of subscribers larger than any paper south of Jacksonville on the East Coast: with all the advertisements we could put in type or have space for in our first issue. The reading matter speaks for itself.

We want 10,000 subscribers!
We want them now!
We want you!

Watch Miami. Watch THE METROPOLIS.

[illegible] health was so seriously impaired that life was despaired of and his physicians sent him to Nassau to die. From there he drifted across to Florida and after tarrying at Miami for a few months, his health improved so much he decided to buy a few acres from the Brickels for a home. He still resides on the purcease made at that time. Mr. Morse is one of the best known residents on the bay. He has served this county in the legislature with marked ability, and his gentlemanly character has endeared him to a host of friends. Mr. Morse rendered valuable service to the Florida East Coast Railway during its construction while having charge of the matter of securing right of way. He performed his duty in that capacity with tact and good judgment, and earned the praise of the officials of the road under whose instructions he acted. Mr. Morse is now in first class health and has before him the promise of many years of life. Naturally he thinks there is no place to be compared with Bay Biscayne in the matter of climate and does not hesitate to express his sentiments.

F. T. BUDGE.

F. T. Budge, our hardware merchant, comes to us from Titusville, where he still owns a large hardware store. He was one of the first merchants to open up for business at Miami. He carries a veay large stock and is constantly receiving new goods. His present building, while commodious, is only temporary. He is one of the substantial business men of the East Coast, and believes in following his policy at Titusville and intends to take every precaution against fire, and will begin the construction of a large brick structure very shortly. It will be located at the corner of Avenue D and Tenth street, where the street leading from the ferry intersects the 70-foot street, which runs from the depot to the bay. H. C. Budge, a younger brother, is an able assistant and devotes his whole energy to the business of his brother. F. T. has been in the hardware business in Titusville for ten years and can quote low prices on anything in his line.

J. A. MCDONALD,

of the firm of McDonald & Maguire, architects and builders, who has charge of the construction of the Royal Palm Hotel, has been in the employ of Mr. Flagler for ten years. His first work was on the Ponce De Leon at St. Augustine about ten years ago. Since that time he has been kept busily employed in looking after Mr. Flagler's hotel building operations. As soon as he finished the Royal Poinciana, he was called upon to go ahead with the Palm Beach Inn, which was only completed last winter, and he had to leave the finishing touches of that structure rather hurriedly to keep up with railroad extension and begin work on the Royal Palm at Miami. This will be the most southern first-class hotel in [illegible] has in hand. We have no doubt whatever that Mr. MacDonald will have the Royal Palm all ready to turn over to H. W. Merrill, its manager, before the end of the present year. We expect to interview Mr. MacDonald in a day or two and lay before our readers in the next issue a complete and detailed description of the Royal Palm. Mr. McDonald has bought several lots at the corner of Avenue D and Twelfth street, and in addition to the great work he has in hand for Mr. Flagler, will begin the erection of several brick stores as an investment for himself shortly. He has certainly secured a fine location for his stores. The other corners at the intersection of Avenue D and Twelfth street will be occupied by the Bank of Bay Biscayne, by E. L. Brady and by F. T. Budge—all substantial business men. The corner referred to will probably be the centre of business for the best class of stores.

ROBBINS, GRAHAM & CHILLINGWORTH.

The Robbins, Graham & Chillingworth Co. have opened a law and real estate office in THE METROPOLIS building. E. F. McKinley, Esq., is in charge. He is a graduate of Cornell University, N. Y., and was a class[illegible] of C. C. Chillingworth, Esq., [illegible] West Palm Beach, who is one of his partners. Mr. McKinley was admitted to the Florida Bar about two years ago, having served some time previous to that event as abstractor and assistant in the office of Robbins, Graham & Chillingworth at Juno. The firm, or rather corporation, own the abstract books of Dade county, and have prepared a duplicate set, covering all of South Dade county, so that abstracts or searches of title can be made on a few hours' notice at the Miami office. An arrangement has been made with A. F. Quinby, County Clerk at Juno, whereby he furnishes a daily report of all deeds, mortgages, liens, etc., which are mailed to Mr. McKinley, who posts them in his books up to date. This arrangement is of great value to all property owners of South Dade, for they can have their abstracts made and titles certified at the Miami office, thus avoiding the necessity of sending to Juno. This makes Miami independent of Juno in the matter of land records. Mr Flagler generously donated a fine business lot to this firm early in the year on condition that it open a law office and place a duplicate set of abstract books at Miami. Mr. McKinley has his office nicely srranged and is already doing a good business.

FLOATING HOTEL.

Captain E. E. Vail, proprietor of Miami's unique Floating Hotel, is a host with long years of experience behind him. He is a *bona fide* captain, having followed the sea as master for two decades. During the last five years of his career on the briny deep he was captain of a steamship plying between New York and New Orleans. In 1869 he decided he had enough of

Front page for the *Miami Metropolis,* vol. 1 no. 1, published on May 15, 1896. "Keep this Paper as a souvenir," it says. "The most southern newspaper on the mainland of the United States, published at the most southern railroad point in Uncle Sam's domain, and at the most southern telegraph terminal and express office on the mainland, at Marvelous Miami. The town with over a thousand souls and the survey of the place not yet completed."

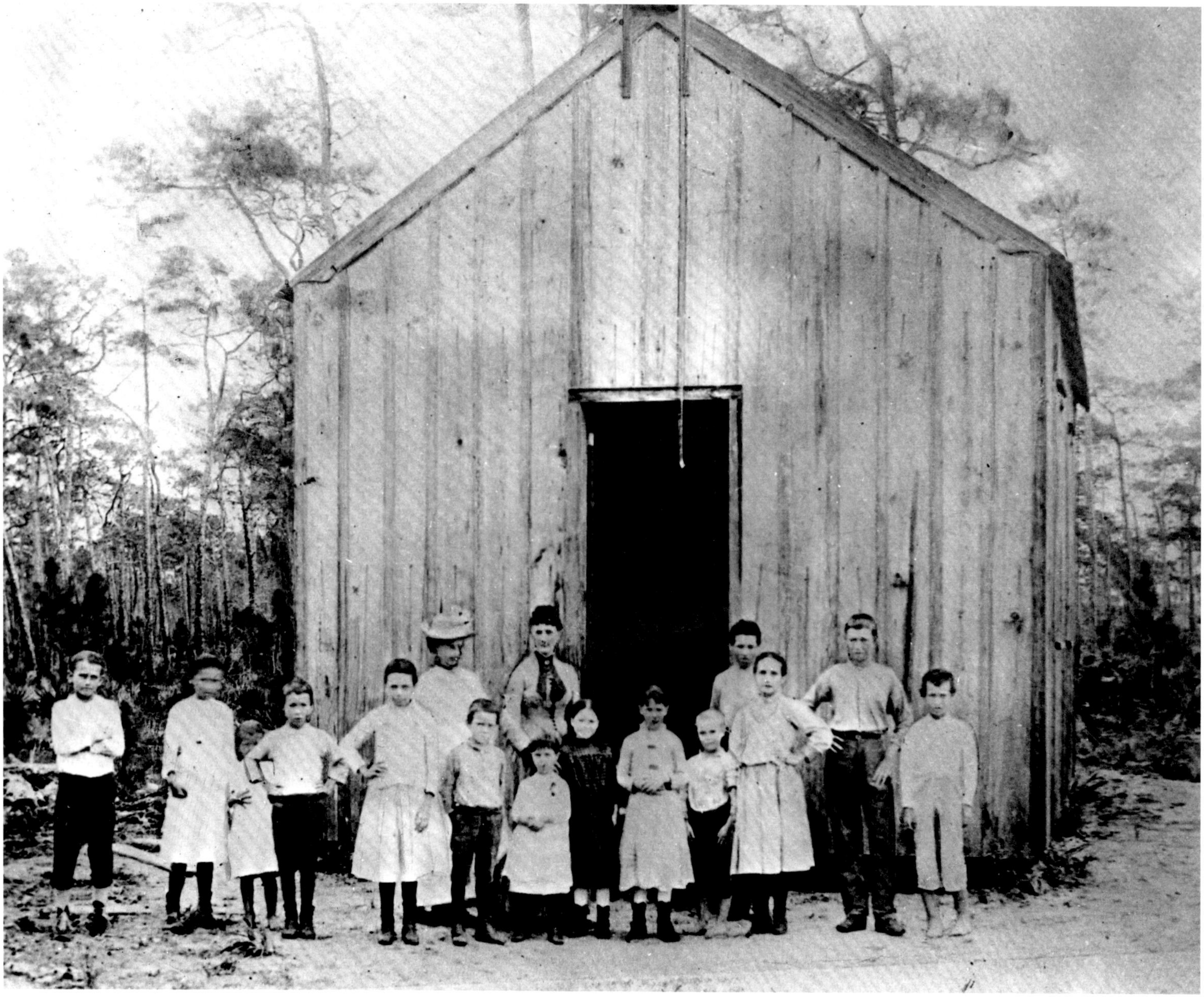

Dade County's first school was located in Lake Worth in current day Palm Beach County. The school pictured here in 1889 was first a Sunday school and later became the first school to open in Miami. Today, Miami-Dade schools have more than 350,000 students. The school system helped push bilingual education programs, which led to the Bilingual Education Act of 1968.

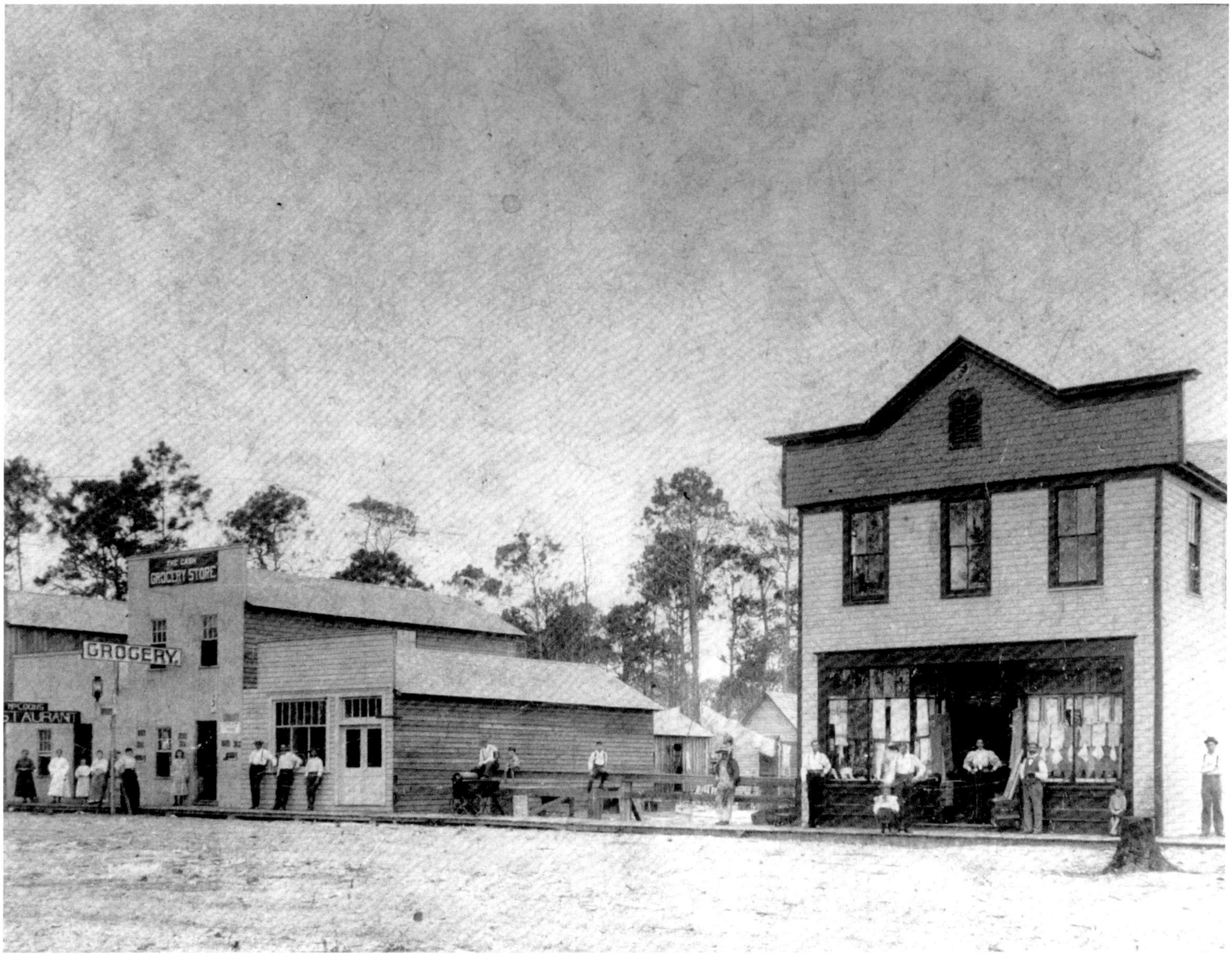

An 1896 view of office buildings near what is now NW 1st Street and Miami Avenue in downtown Miami. Miami showed financial promise early on with rail access, no-freeze farmland, and a coastal location ideal for shipping. Miami's proximity to Cuba set it apart as a natural hub for Latin American trade. Within a century, the city would become headquarters for the Latin American operations of more than 1,000 multinational corporations.

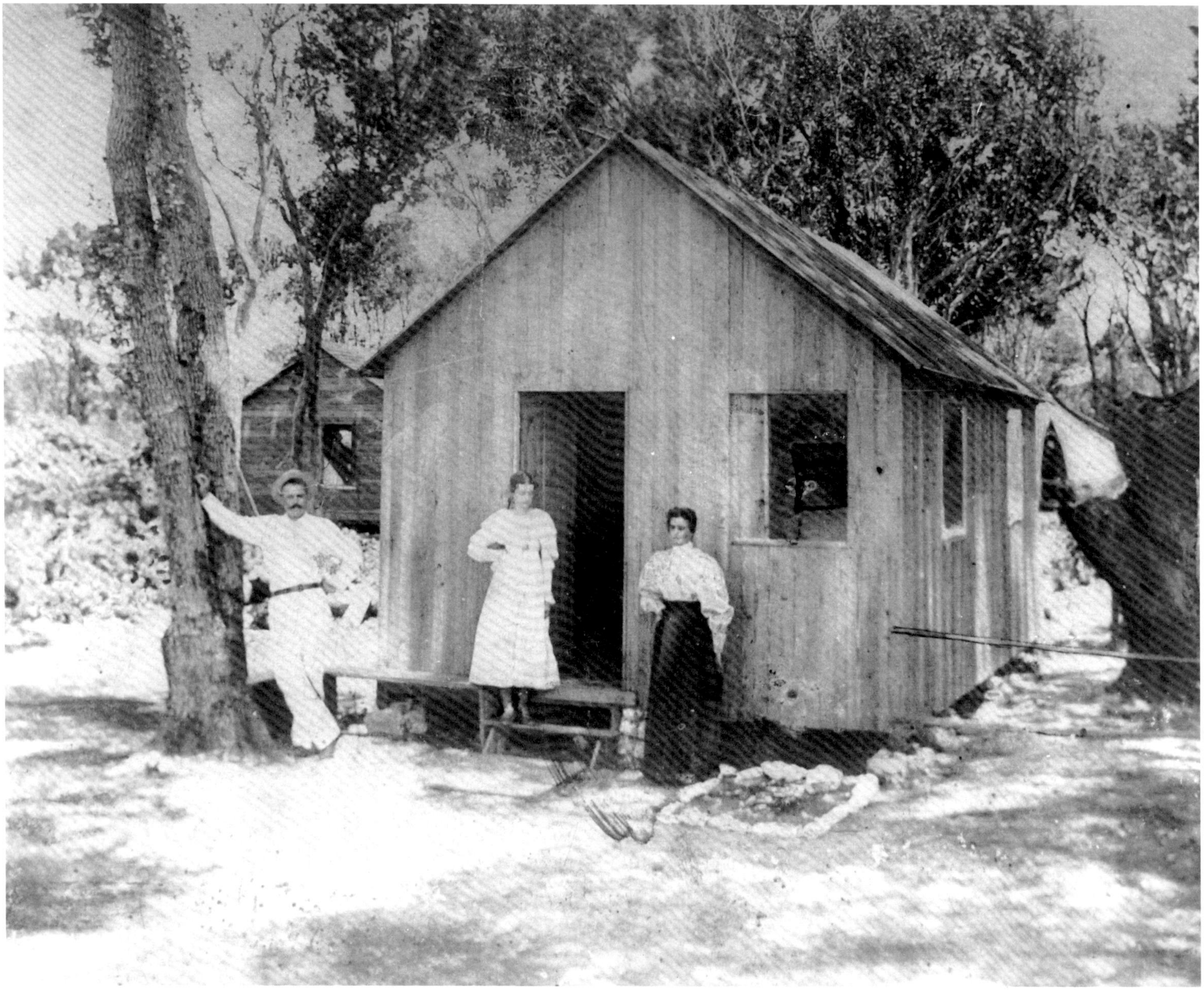

A family outside their home near present-day downtown Miami in 1896. At the time, the population of the new city was around 300 residents, mostly from other regions of the United States. In the next 100 years, Miami's population would boom, largely owing to the city's relationship with Cuba and U.S. asylum policies for political refugees, eventually reaching a Hispanic population of more than 60 percent.

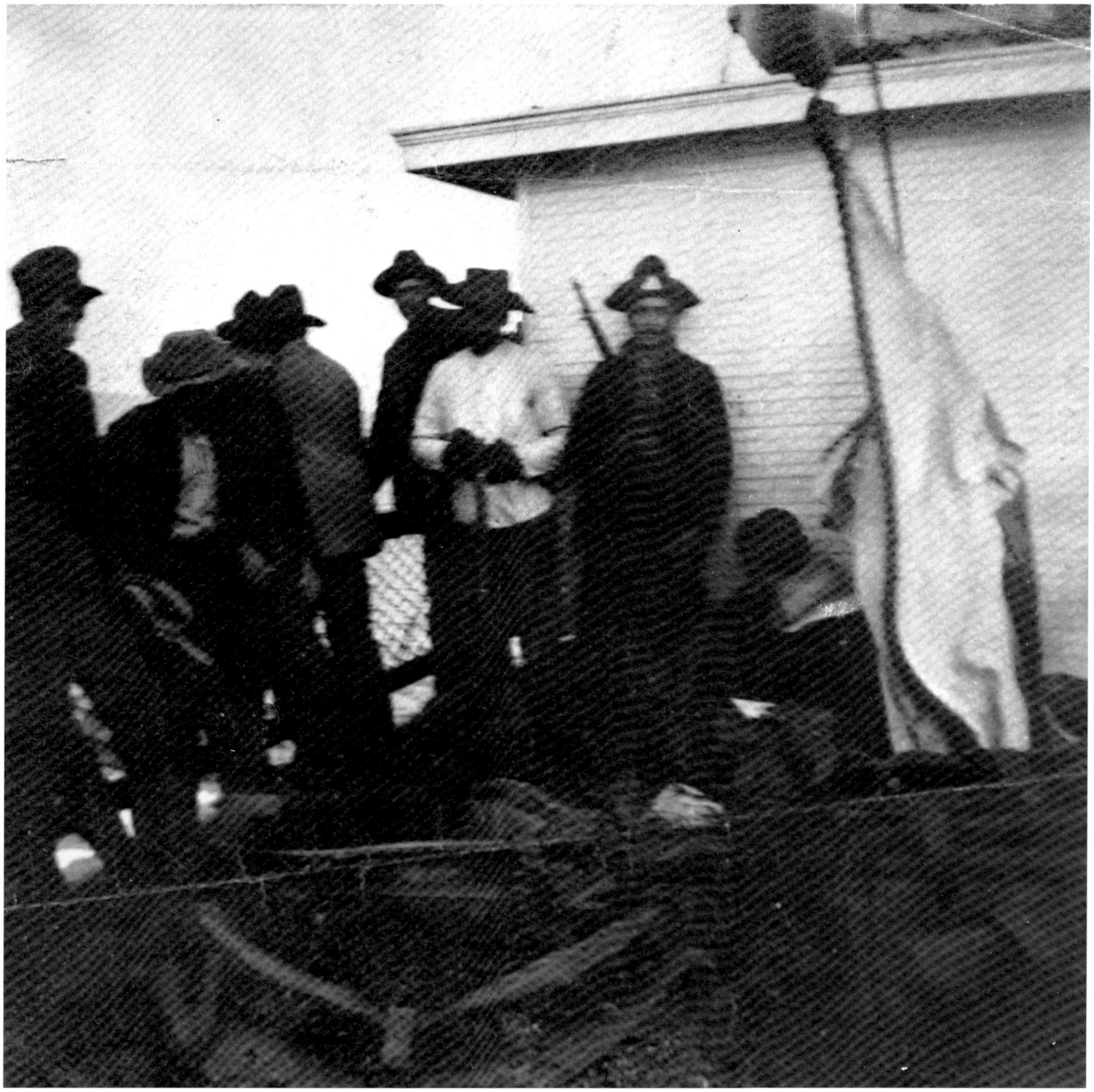

The *Three Friends,* a steamboat run by future governor Broward, was used to filibuster, or smuggle arms, to Cuba in the build-up toward the Spanish-American War. Broward eluded capture by loading munitions at night and traveling down the coast and on rivers.

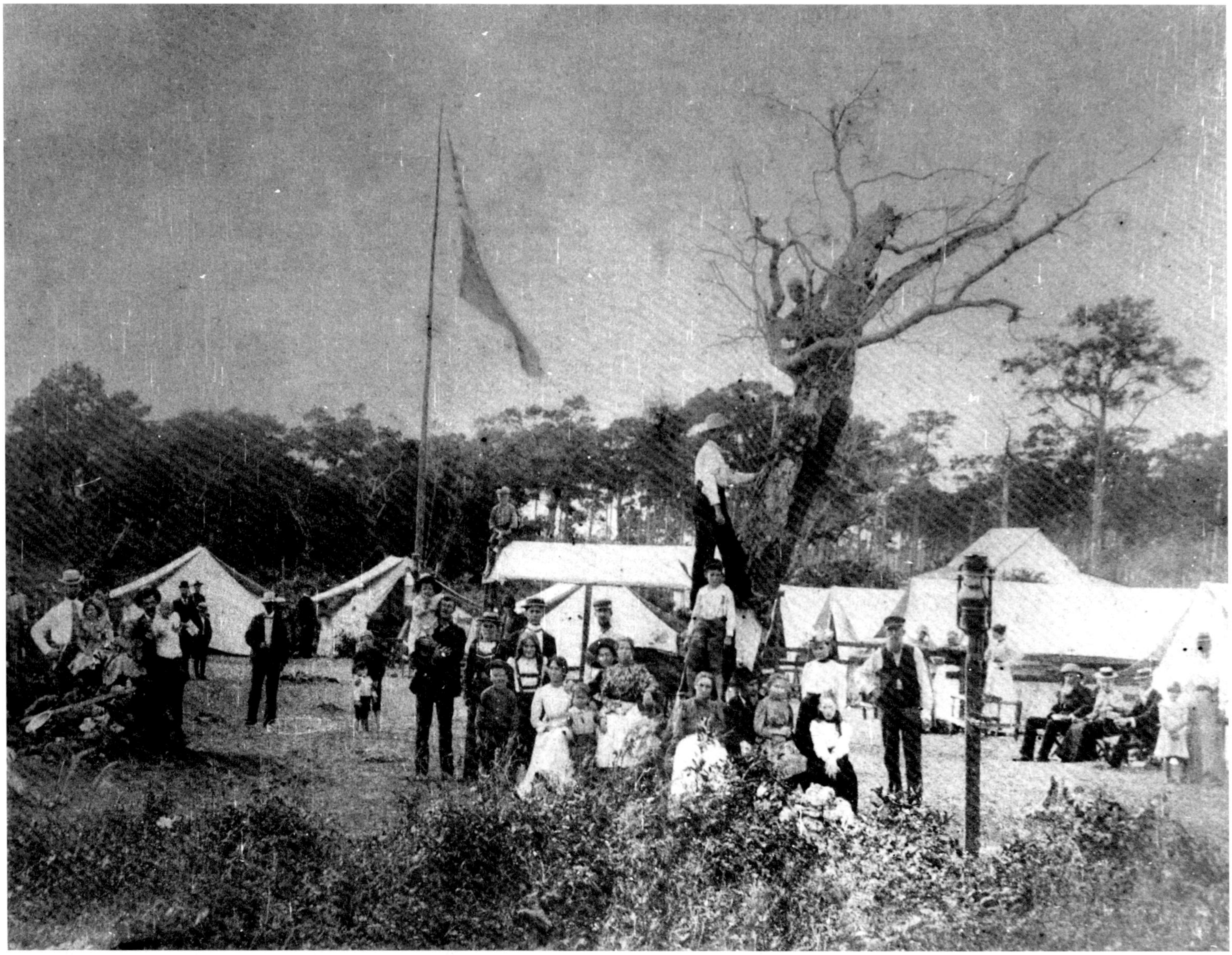

Prior to the Spanish-American War, Miami had no standing in Cuban-American relations. That status would change in 1898, when troops were stationed there in a tent camp. After the destruction of the *Maine* off the coast of Cuba in Havana harbor, more than 7,000 troops arrived, ready to fight. The camp was known as "Camp Hell," because of the heat, illness, and mosquitoes.

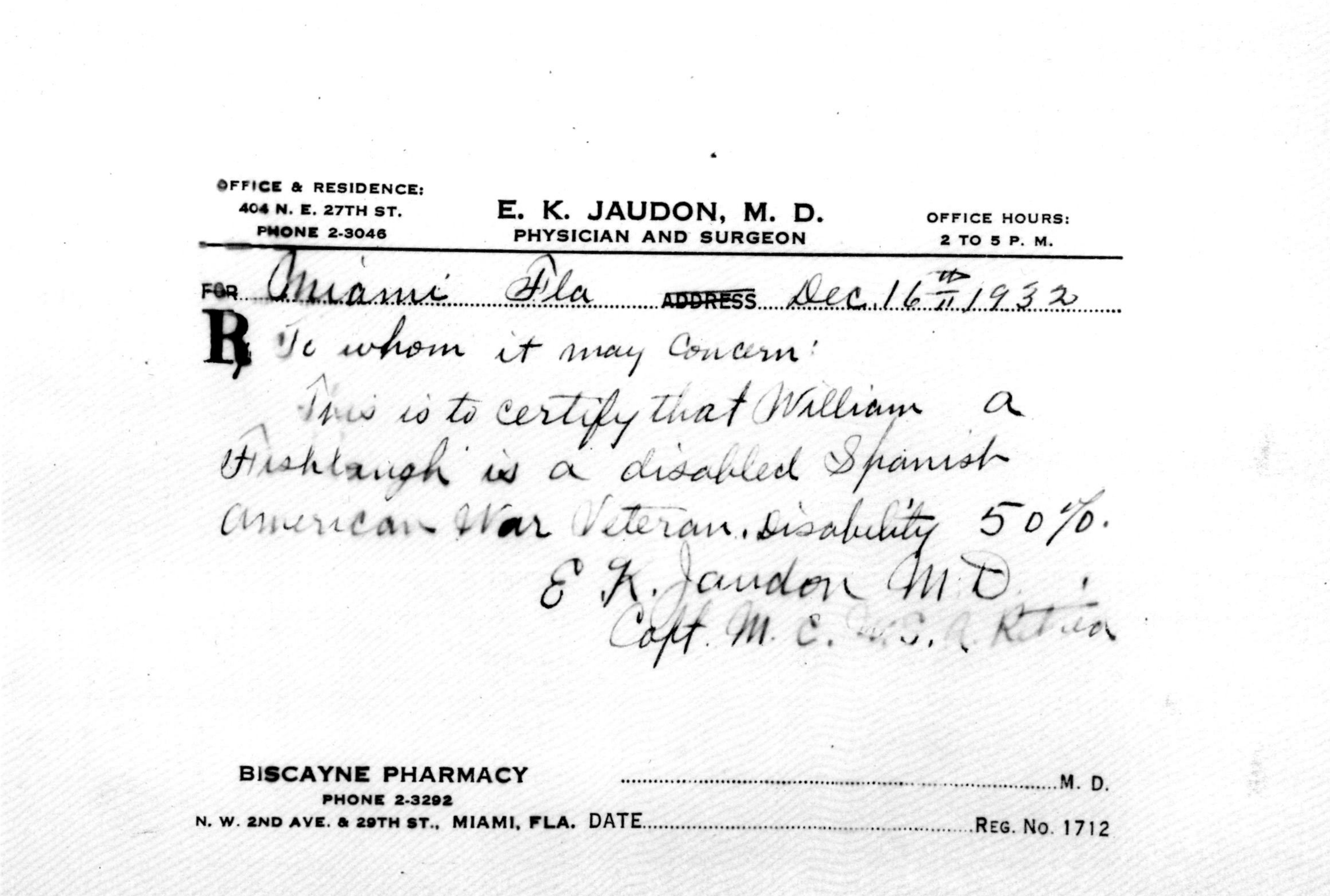

OFFICE & RESIDENCE:
404 N. E. 27TH ST.
PHONE 2-3046

E. K. JAUDON, M. D.
PHYSICIAN AND SURGEON

OFFICE HOURS:
2 TO 5 P. M.

FOR Miami Fla ~~ADDRESS~~ Dec 16th 1932

℞ To whom it may Concern:

This is to certify that William A Fishbaugh is a disabled Spanish American War Veteran. Disability 50%.

E. K. Jaudon M.D.
Capt. M. C. U.S.A. Retired

BISCAYNE PHARMACY
PHONE 2-3292
N. W. 2ND AVE. & 29TH ST., MIAMI, FLA. DATE .... M. D.
REG. NO. 1712

Certificate written by Dr. E. K. Jaudon identifying W. A. Fishbaugh as a disabled veteran of the Spanish-American War.

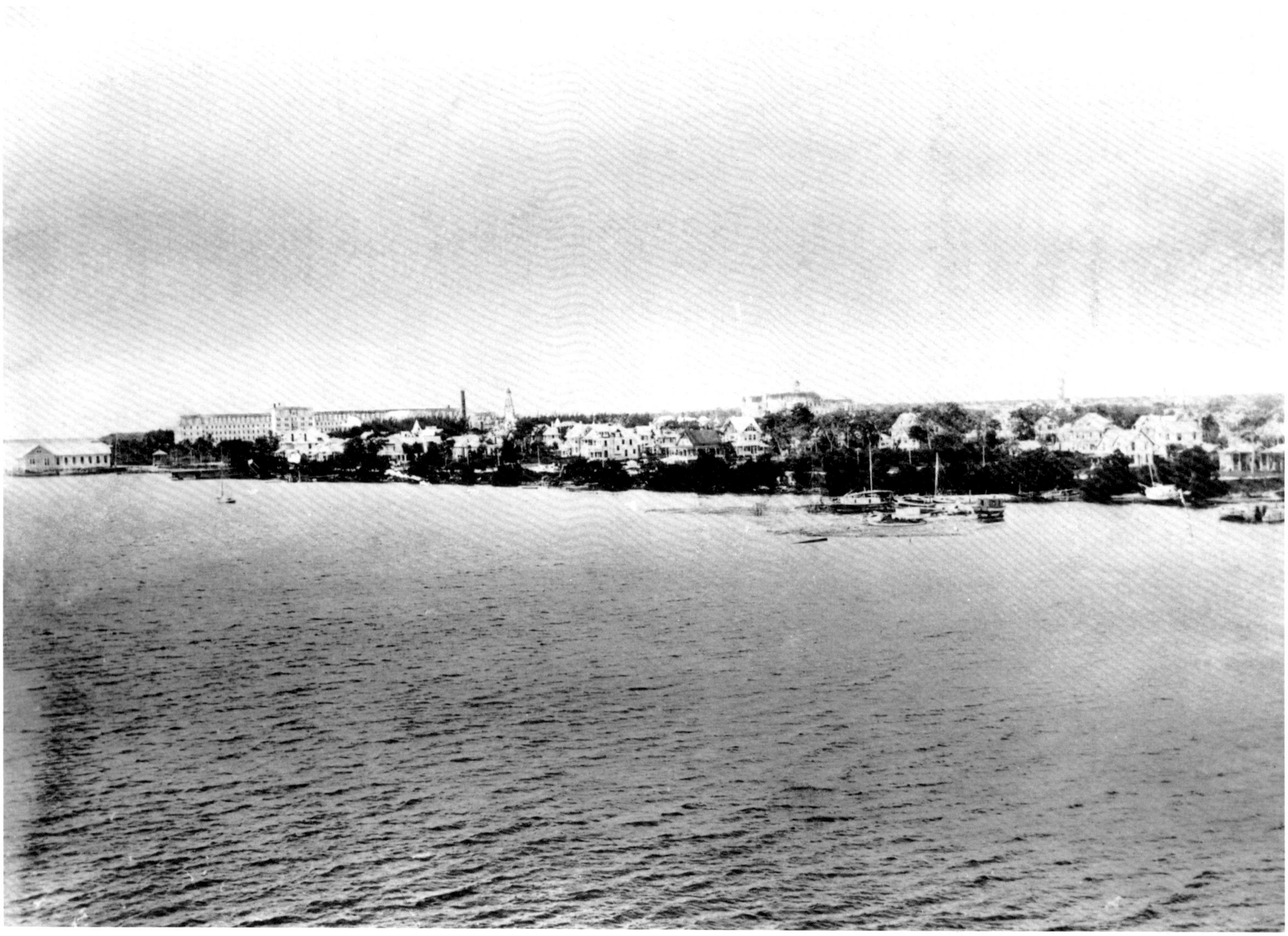

A view of the young Miami skyline in 1910. This skyline would change dramatically, especially in the late twentieth century, when skyscrapers became dominant. For Cubans fleeing their homeland, a view of the Miami skyline meant that the freedom they hoped for was at last within grasp.

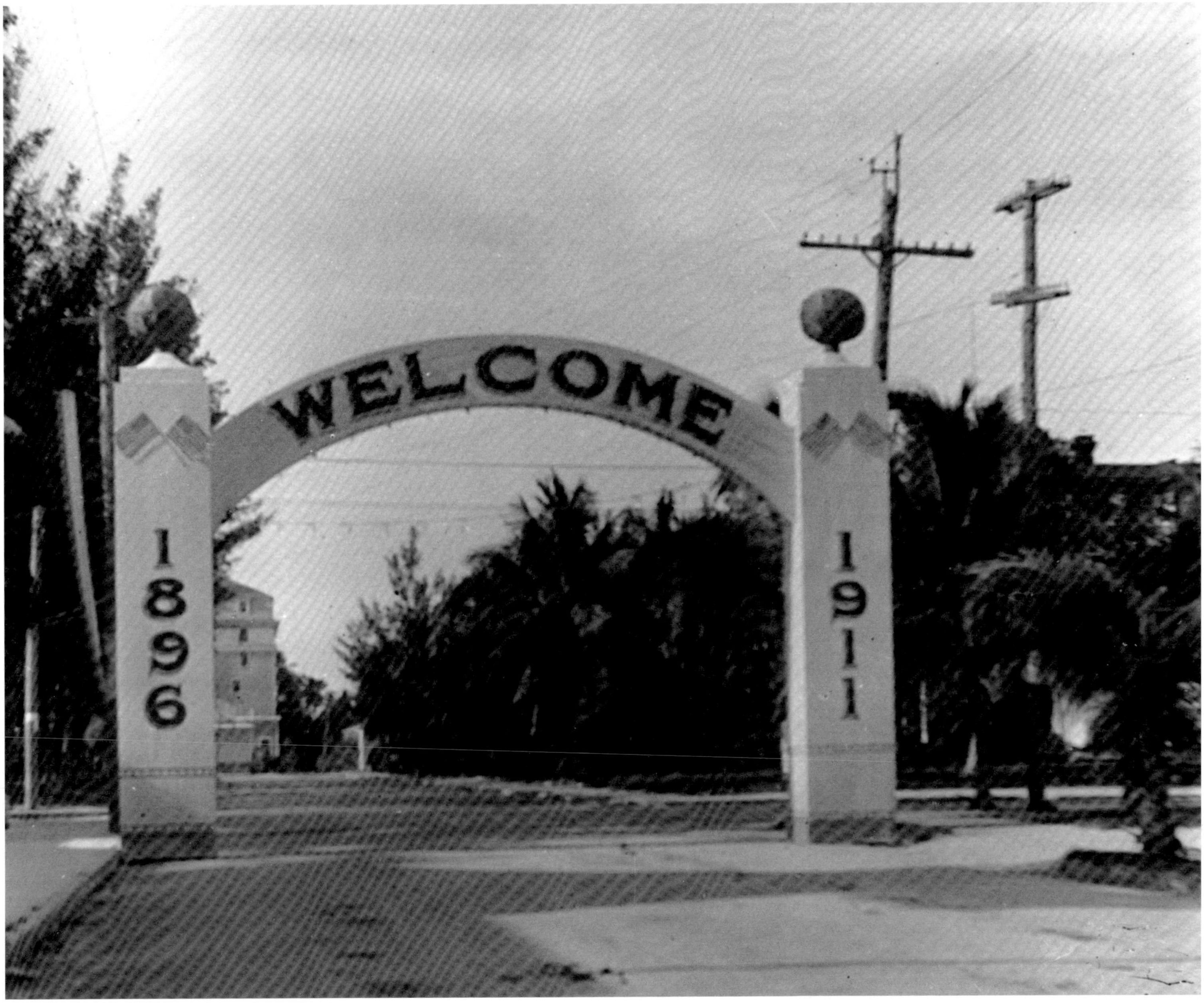

The entrance to the city of Miami in 1911.

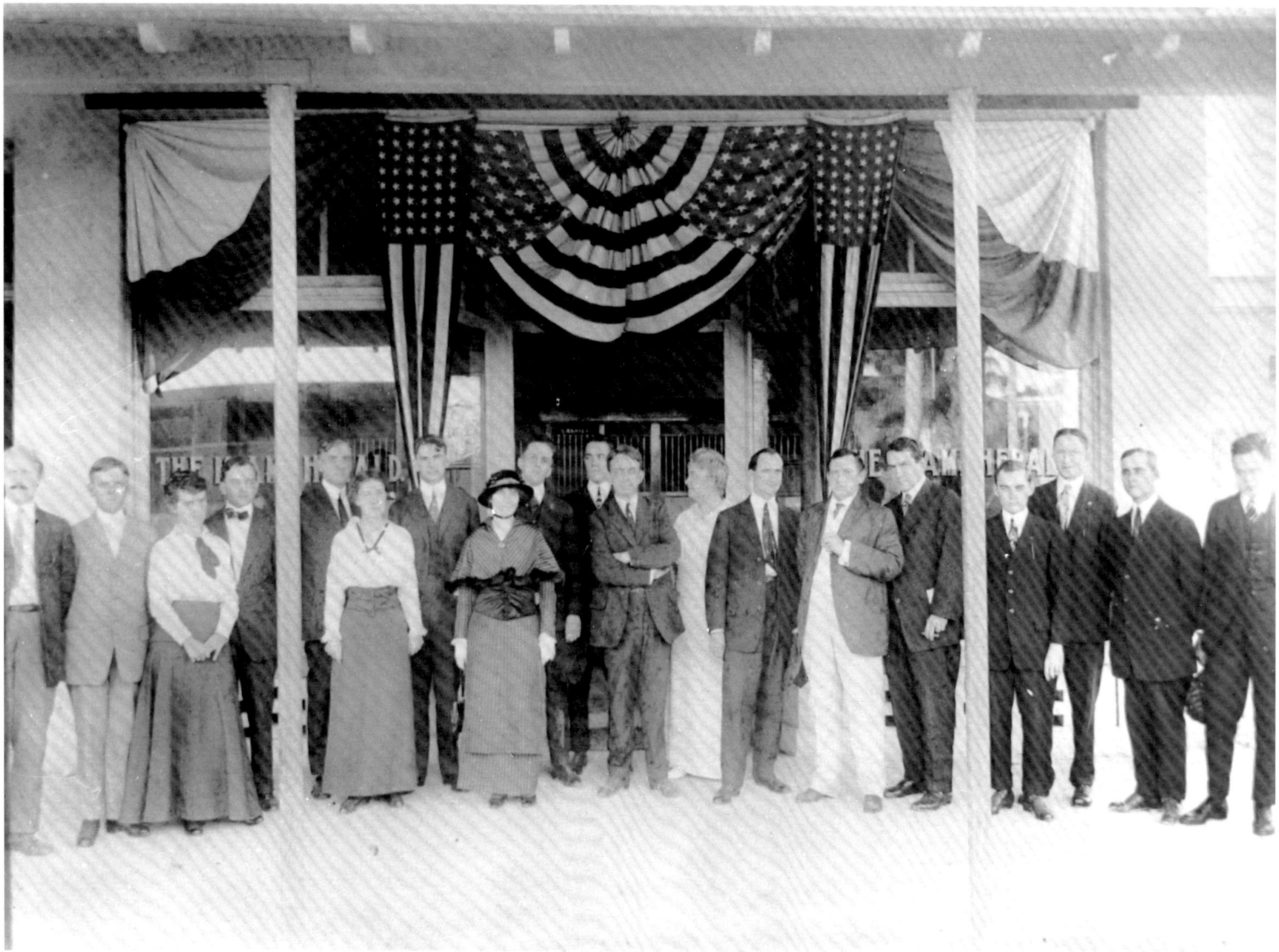

Miami Herald newspaper employees in 1914. The *Herald* became another leading newspaper in Miami and eventually shared operations with the *Miami News.* The *Miami News* ceased production in the 1980s. The *Herald* is still in operation today and now publishes a Spanish language daily paper called *El Nuevo Herald.*

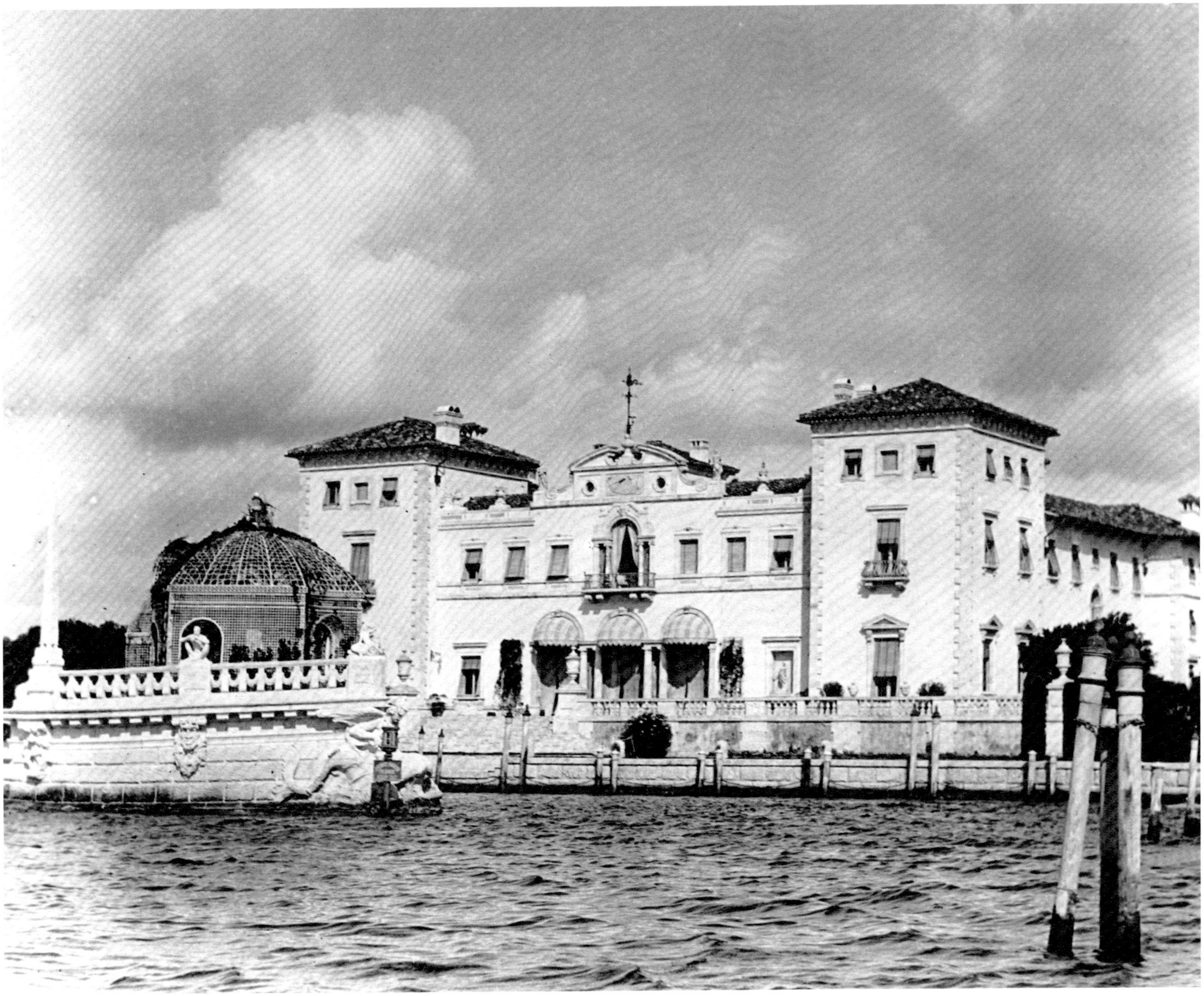

Vizcaya, also known as the Deering Estate, was photographed from the water in 1919. Like many buildings in Miami, the estate features materials imported from Cuba, particularly Cuban sandstone. Since its conversion to a public museum and gardens, Vizcaya has been popular with the Cuban-American community. It is a favorite location for wedding and quince photography.

Later dubbed "Mr. Miami Beach," Carl Fisher was responsible for bringing to Florida a highway for tourists, and the game of polo for the well-heeled. Fisher arranged for the first polo game to be played at the fields in Miami Beach, which attracted glamorous spectators, including a Russian princess—exactly the image of Miami Beach he wished to convey. Fisher arranged for the first polo game against Cuba in March 1920.

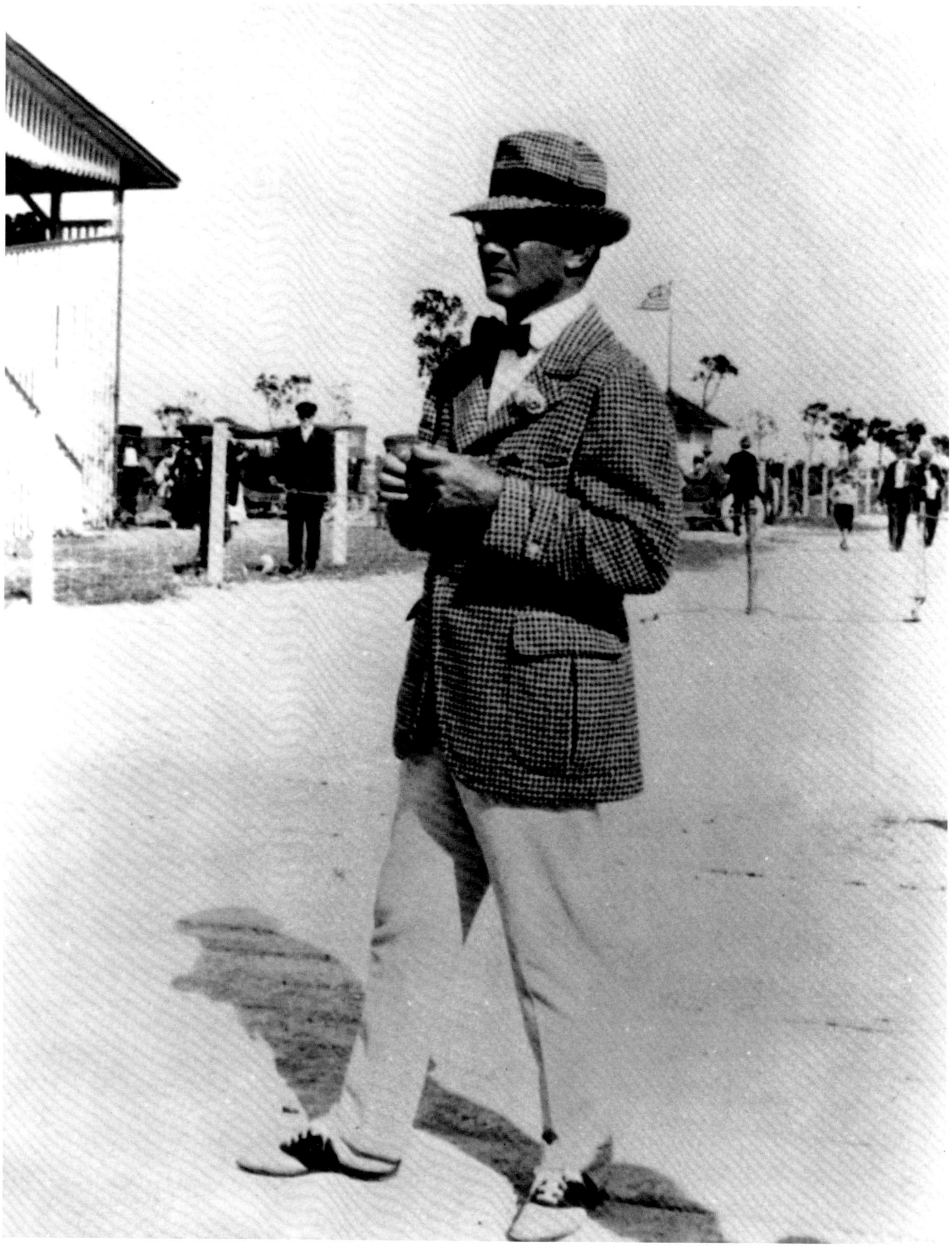

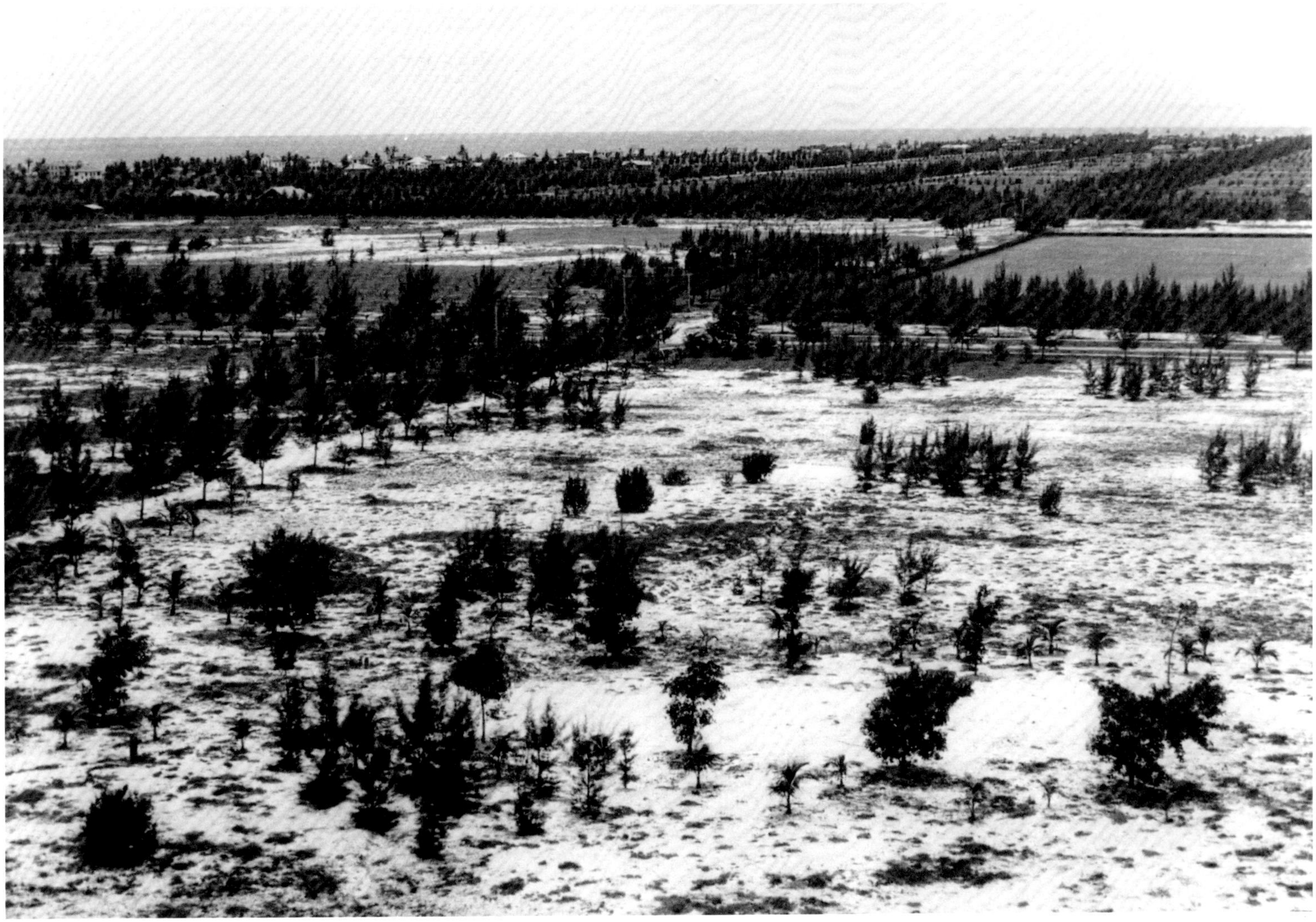

An aerial view of the polo fields in Miami Beach.

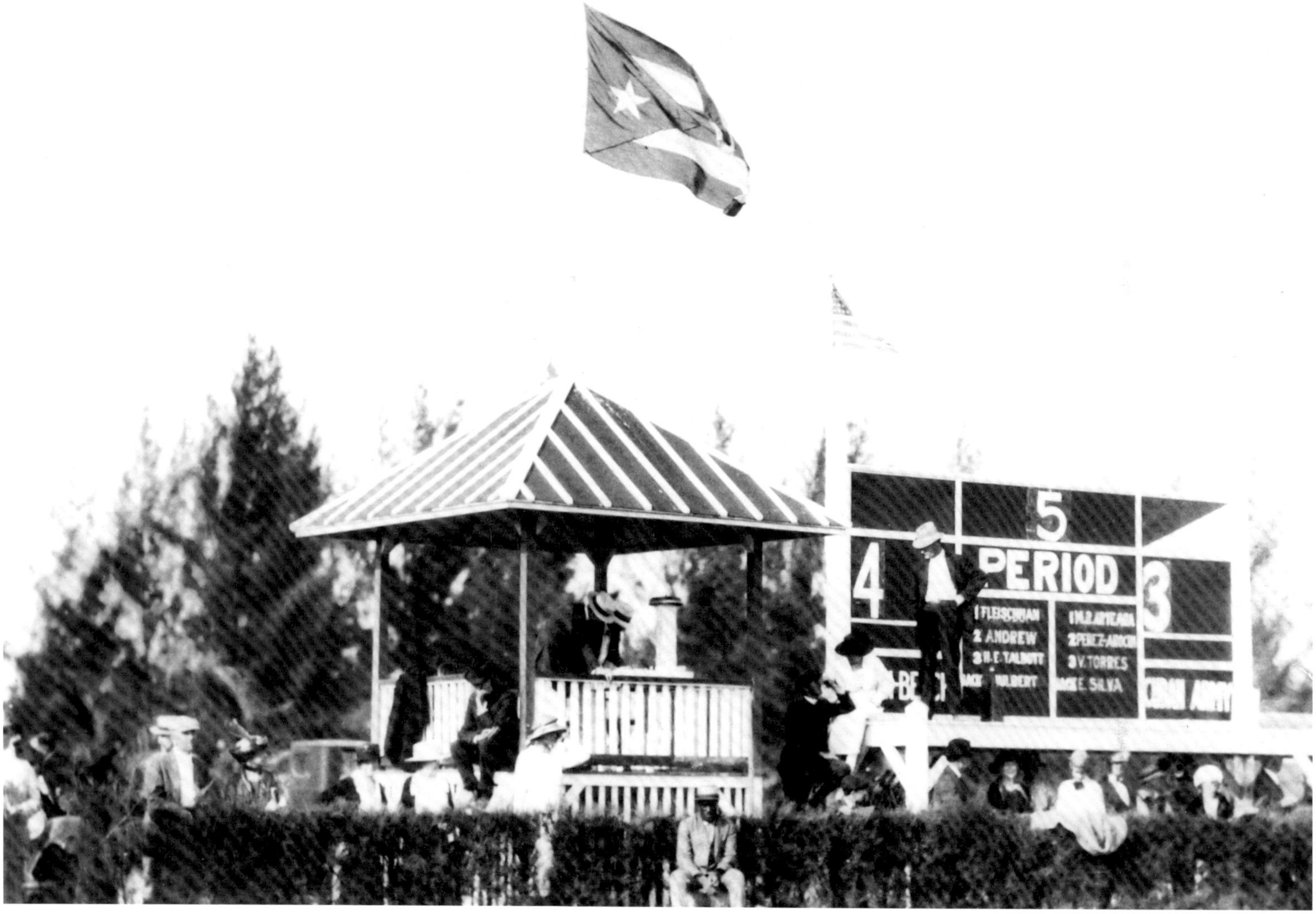

The first polo match between a U.S. team and a Cuban team took place on March 11, 1920, at the fields on Miami Beach. The U.S. team won, 6–5.

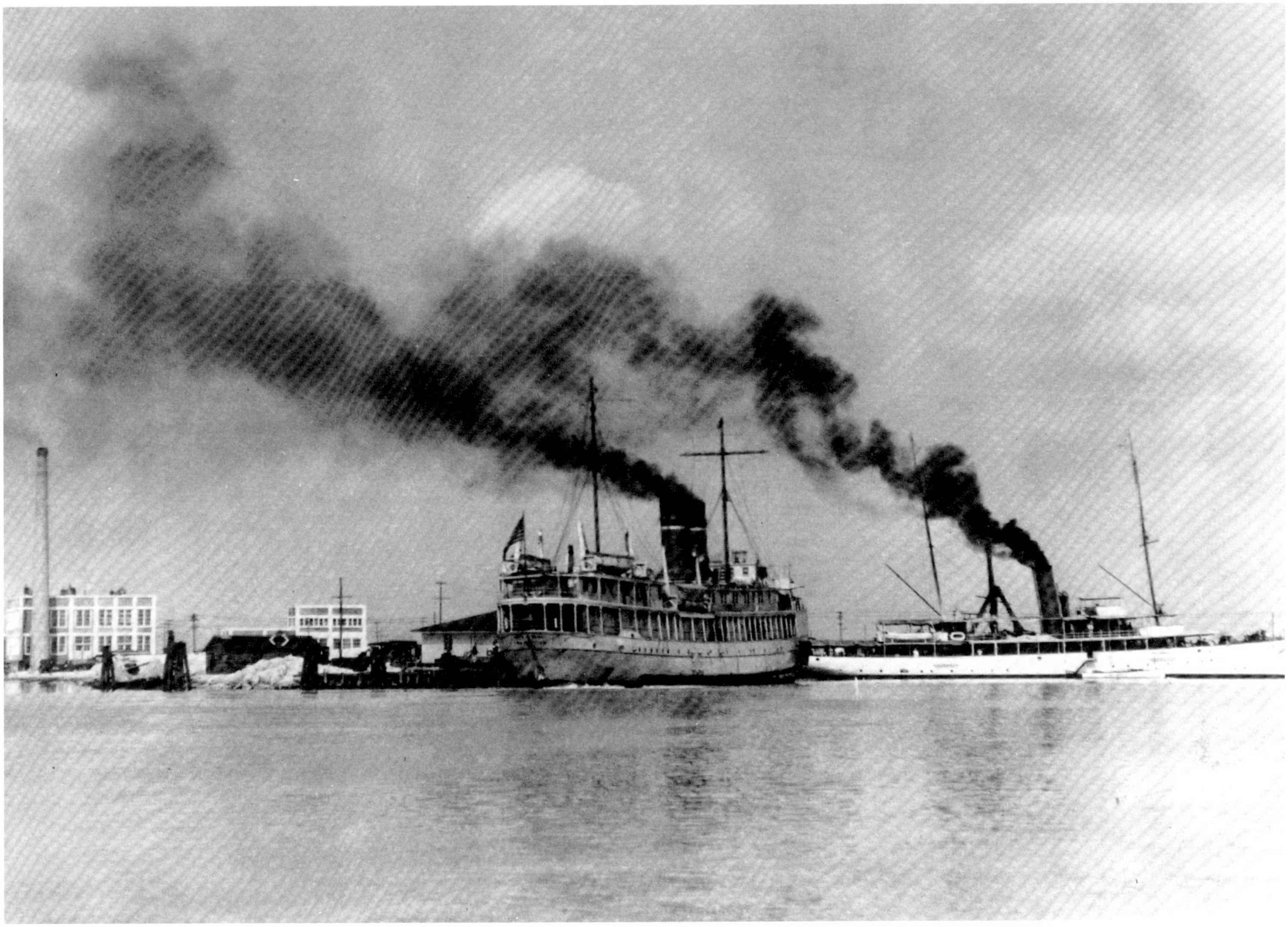

The Cuban steamship *Hauley* lands in 1921 carrying a Cuban polo team for a second year of U.S.-Cuba polo tournaments.

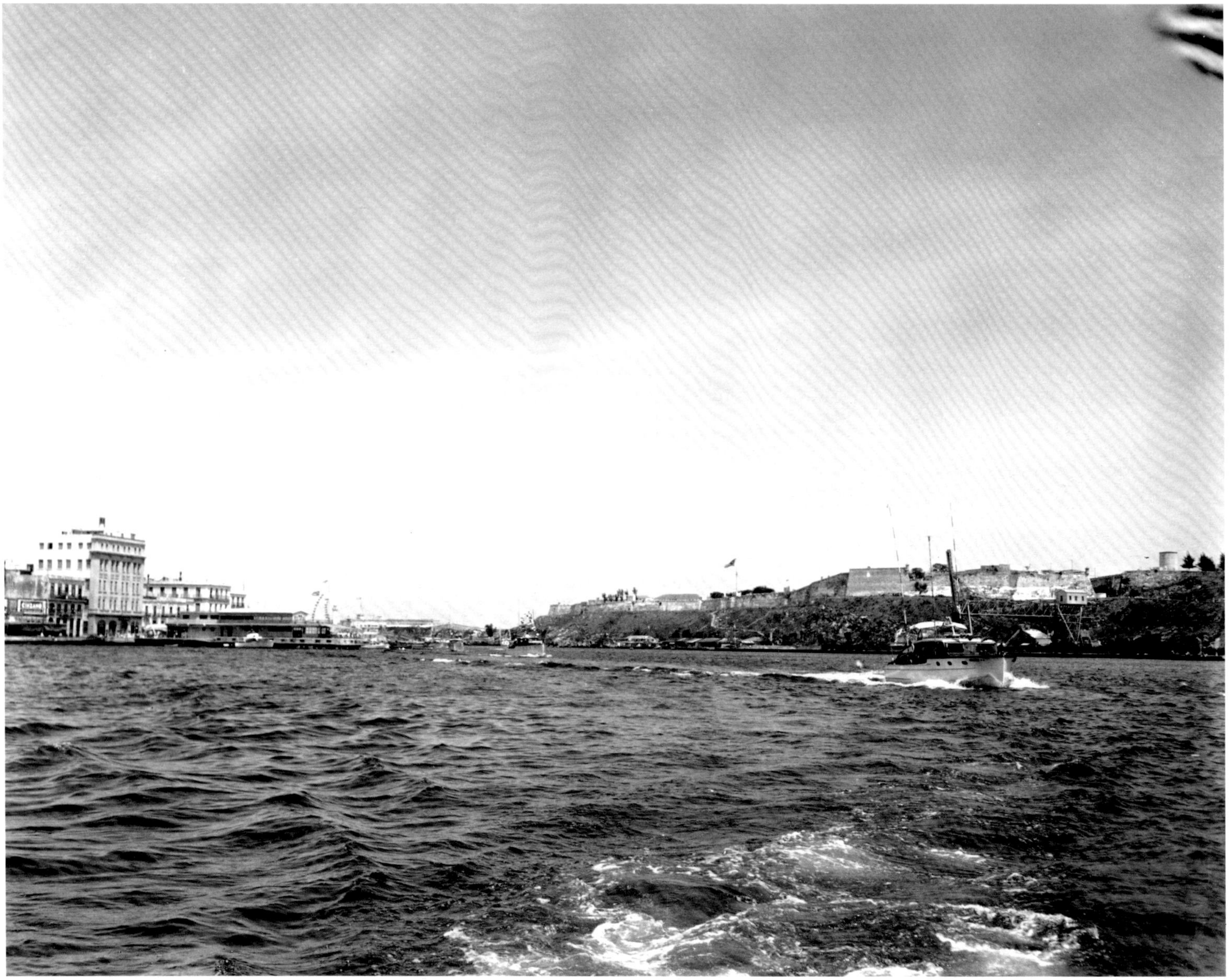

Boating cruises from Miami to Havana were popular until Castro's communist revolution. Havana is less than 90 miles from Key West. Because of the embargo imposed against the Castro regime after President Kennedy's foiled invasion and the Cuban Missile Crisis of the early 1960s, Americans are not permitted to travel to Cuba, except under special circumstances.

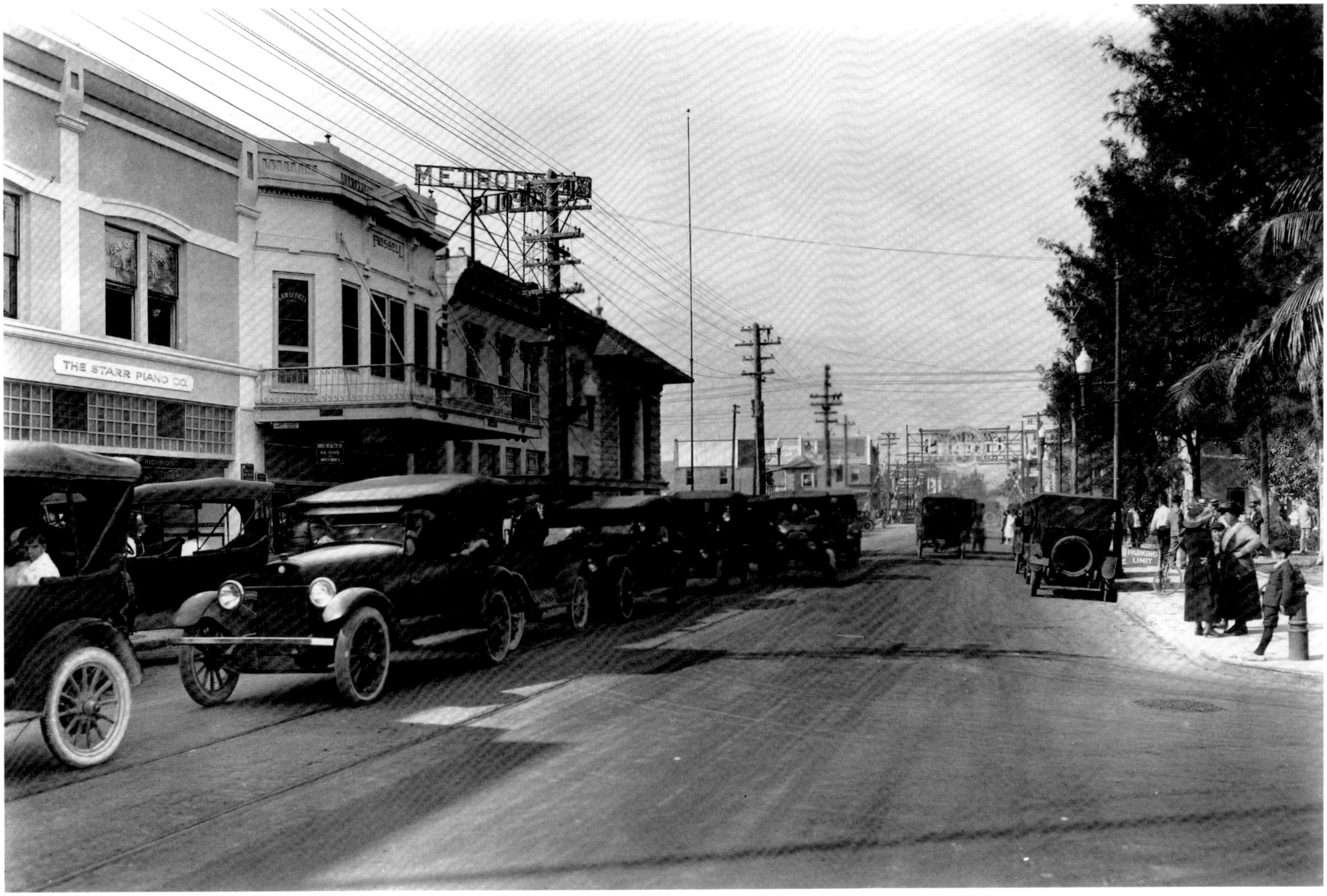

Looking down West Flagler Street in the year 1921. West Flagler would someday become part of Little Havana.

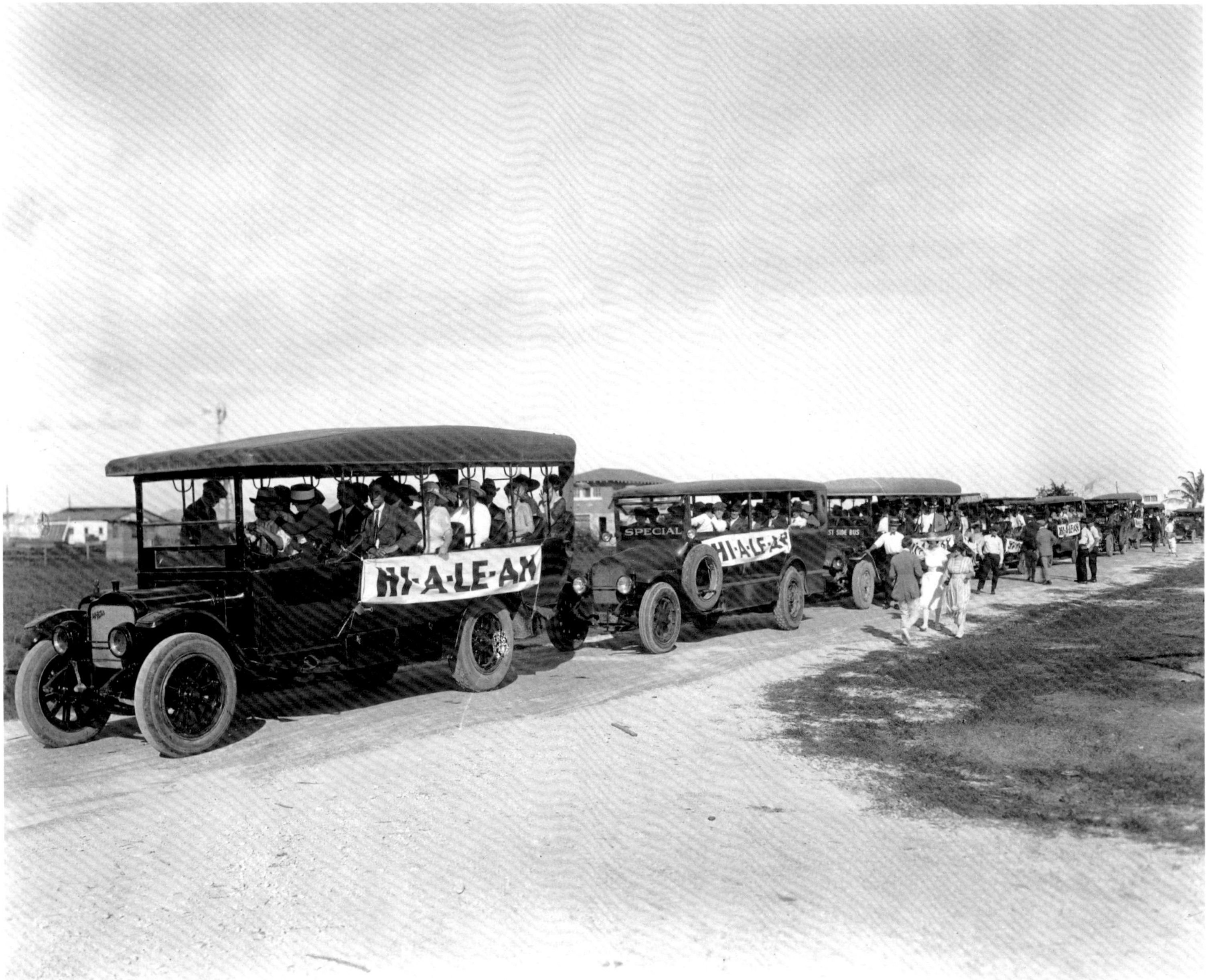

During the Florida real estate boom of the 1920s, land developers brought tour buses filled with groups interested in owning a piece of paradise. Hialeah was originally imagined as a leisurely city full of wealthy residents, closer to the image Boca Raton or Miami Beach now portrays. World War II and Cuban exiles altered that vision, as Hialeah became an industrial, working-class community.

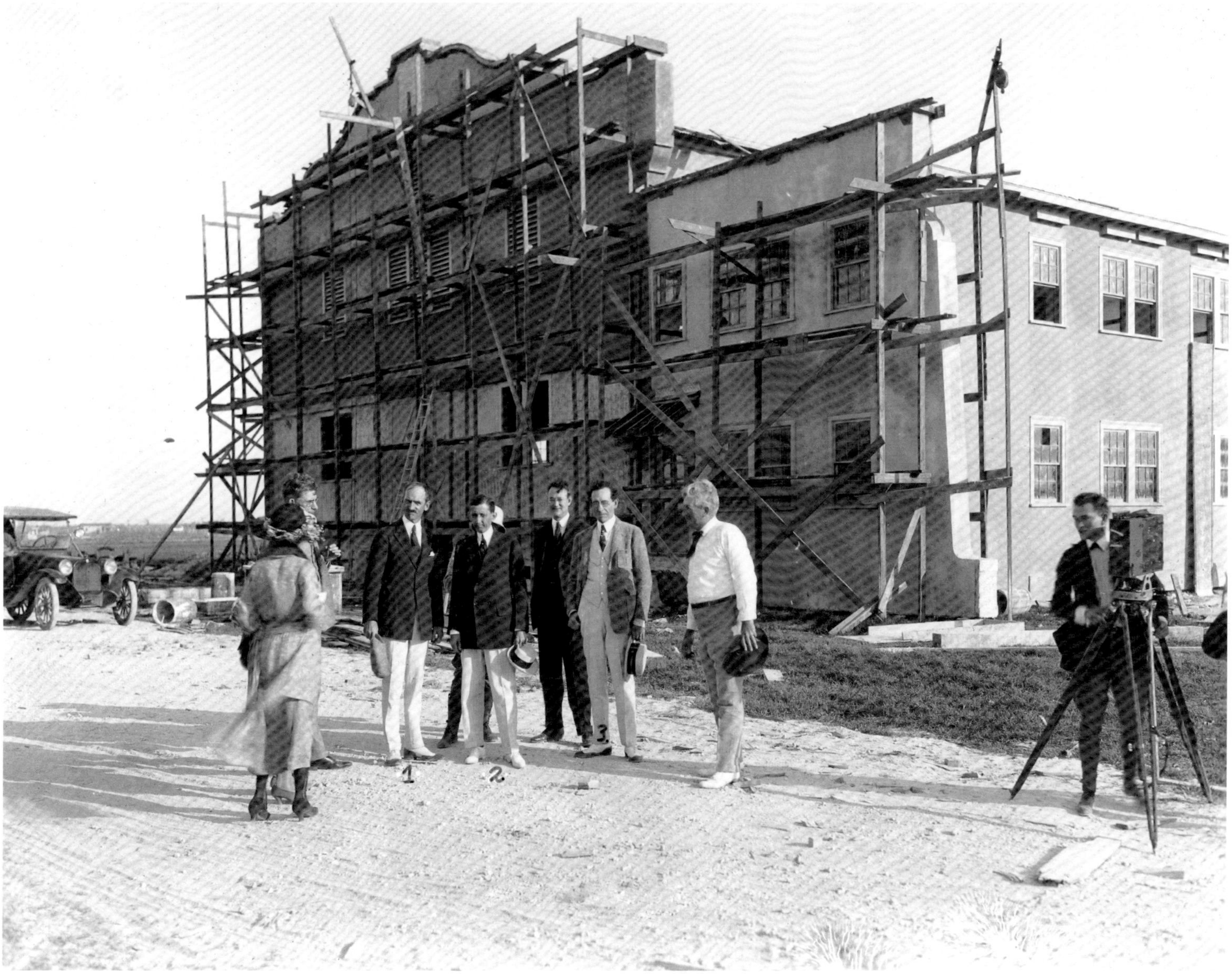

Miami Studios, seen here in 1922, is under construction in Hialeah. More evidence that Hialeah was once imagined as a glamorous center of the South, akin to Miami Beach, Hollywood, or Boca Raton.

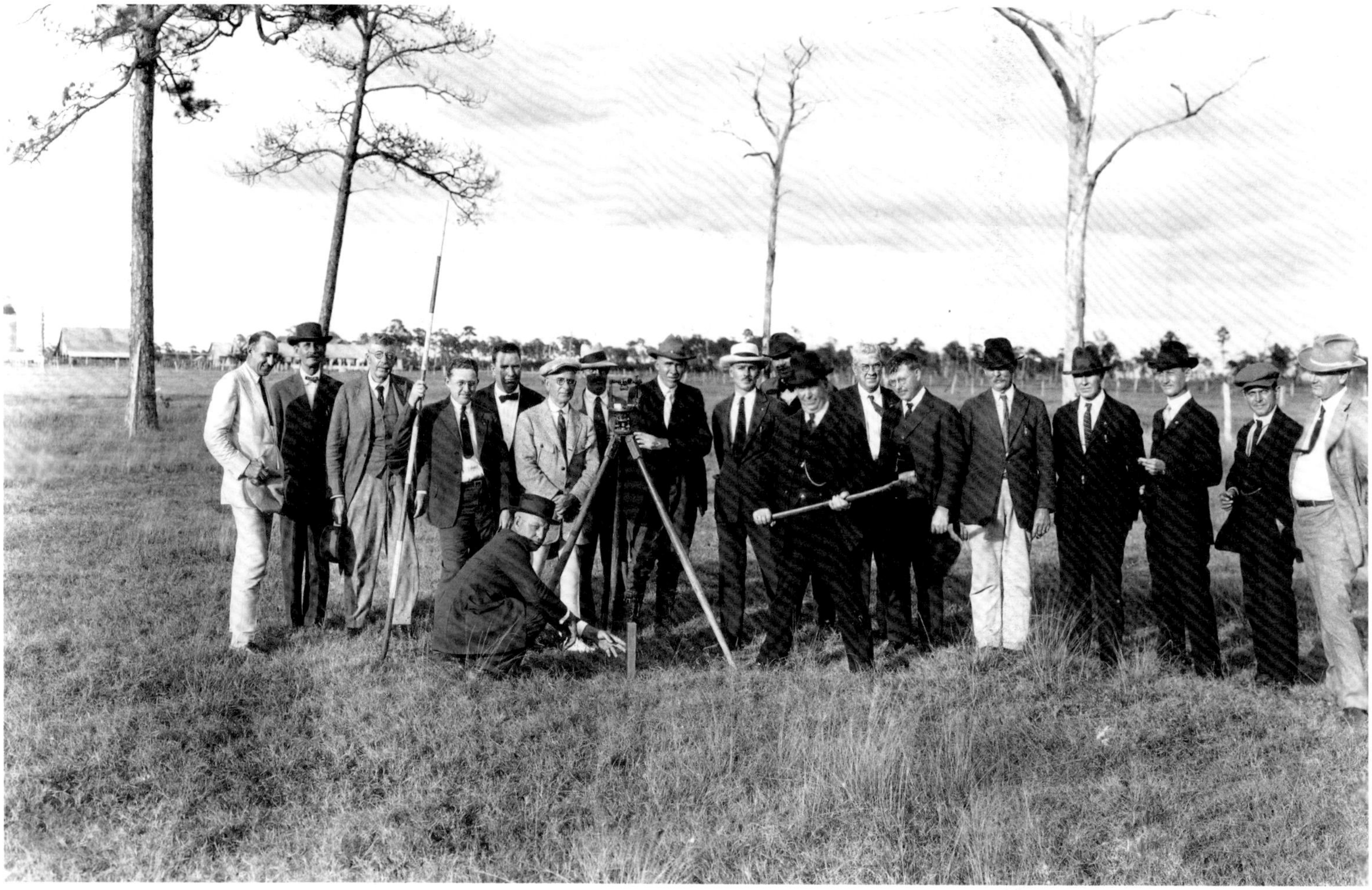

Henry Flagler amassed a fortune as a partner with John D. Rockefeller in Standard Oil Company, which enabled Flagler to pursue his interest in developing the eastern coast of Florida. The men shown here stand at the site of an oil well in 1922. Petroleum was one of the main exports to Cuba in the early twentieth century.

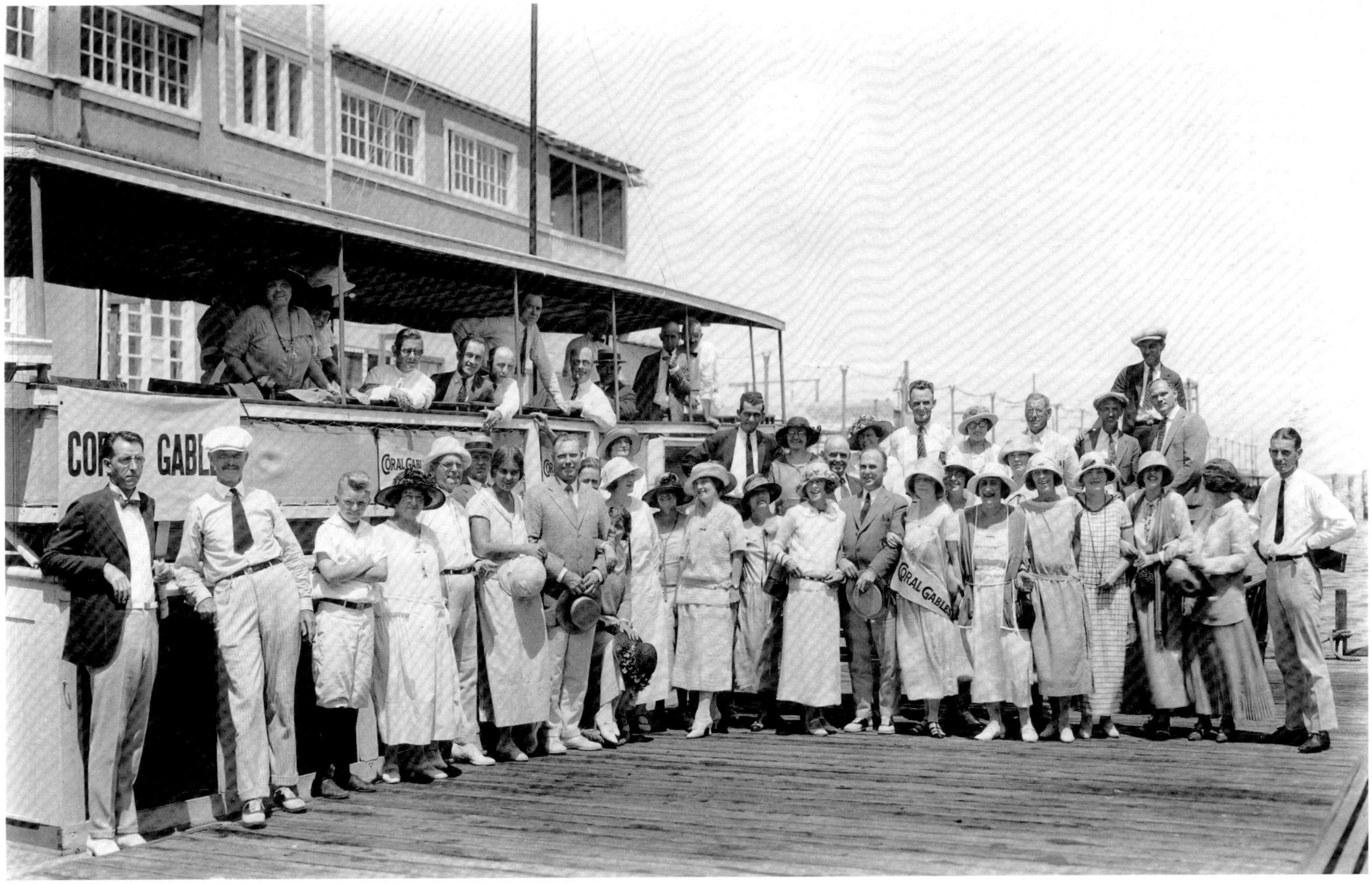

Shown here in 1923, George E. Merrick (at center holding a straw hat), was responsible for the development of Coral Gables. A fan of Cuban architecture, he went so far as to name streets after Cuban surnames and use building materials imported from Cuba.

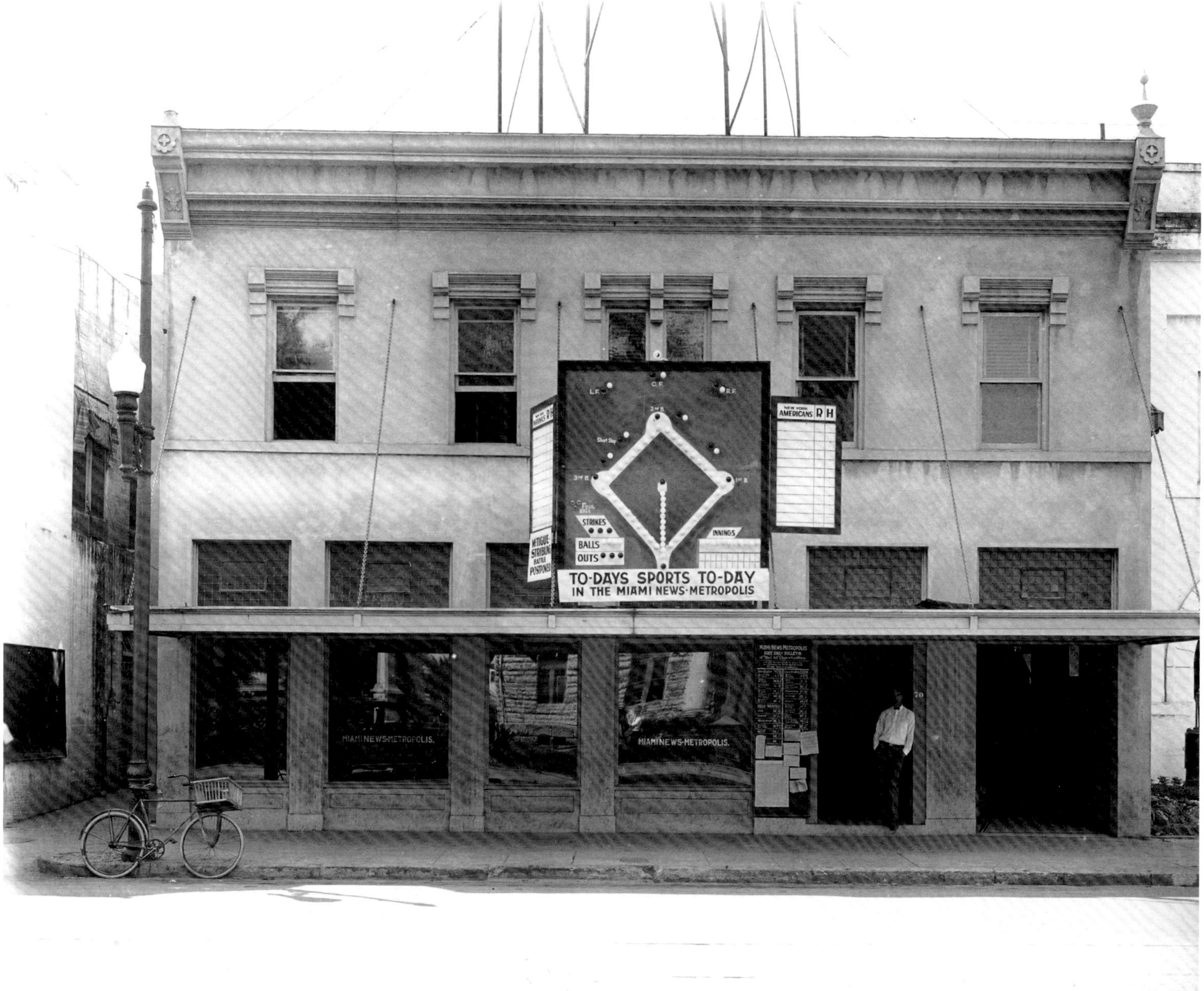

The *Miami News,* originally published as the *Miami Metropolis,* was the second newspaper in the area, preceded only by the *Tropical Sun.* In view here is the front of the Miami News–Metropolis Building in 1923. The building featured roof tiles imported from Cuba, and an electric scoreboard mounted on the front of the building, "To-days Sports To-day" offered baseball fans play-by-play updates of games in progress.

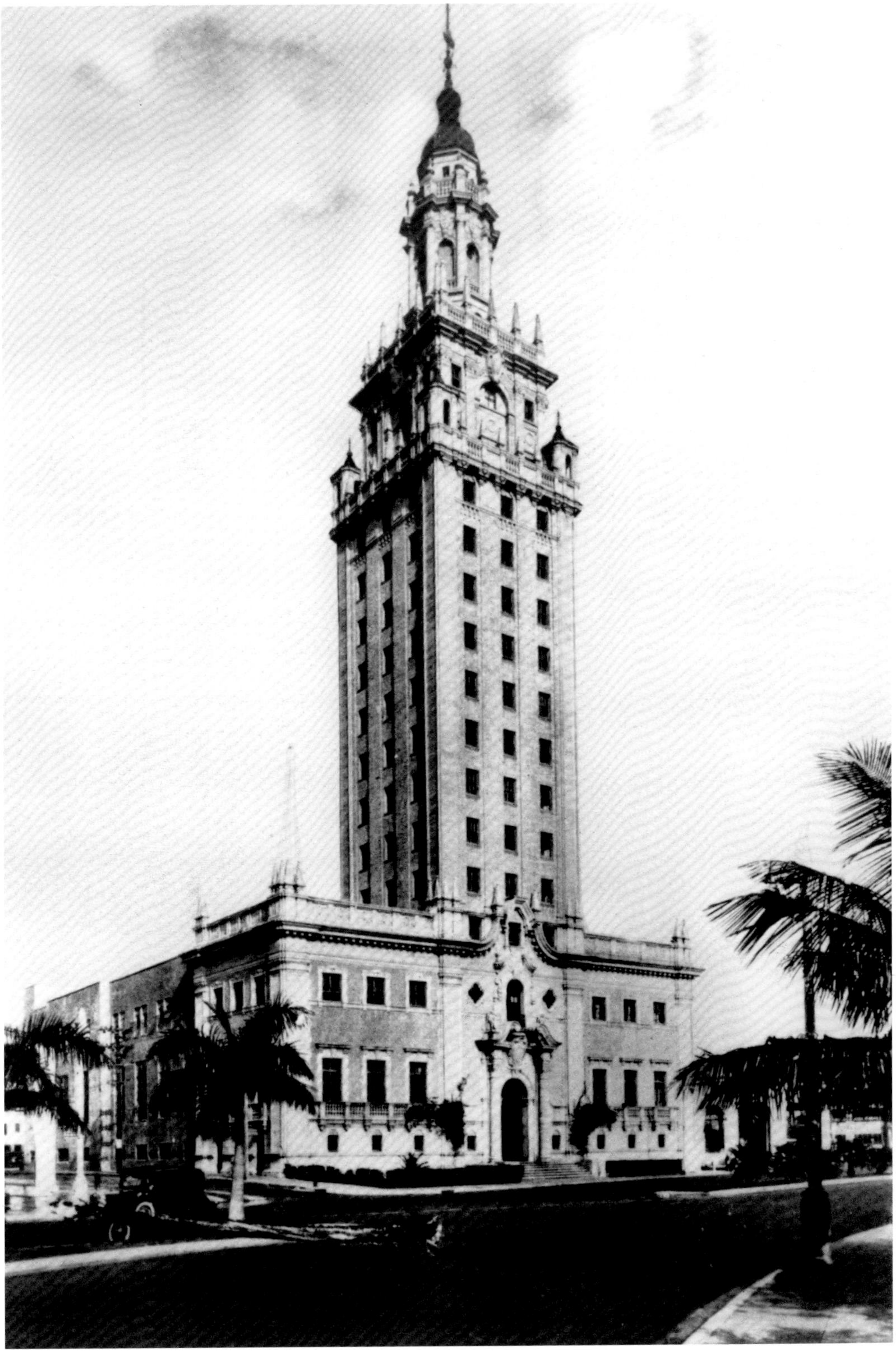

The Miami News Tower opened in 1925. In 1957, the newspaper moved to a new building and the News Tower shut its doors. It was not long before the tower was utilized by the federal government to process and provide medical services to incoming Cuban refugees. For this reason, the tower became known as the Freedom Tower and was called the "Ellis Island of the South." In 2006, the tower was donated to Miami Dade College.

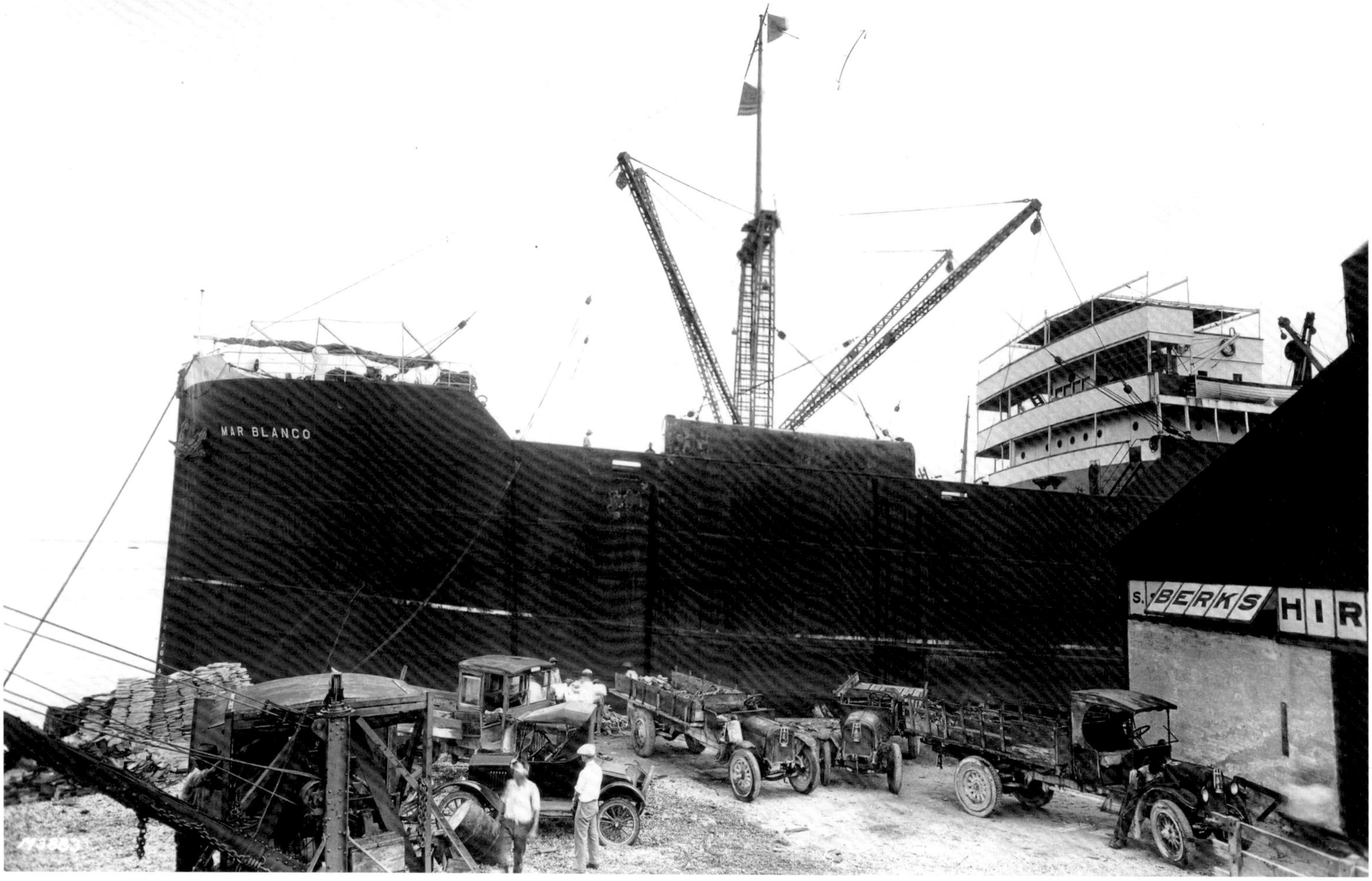

In this photograph, Cuban roof tiles are being unloaded in Miami. From 1925 to 1926, more than two million roof tiles were imported. Doors, sandstone, and windows were also imported from Cuba, sold from functional or abandoned structures for reuse in Miami construction.

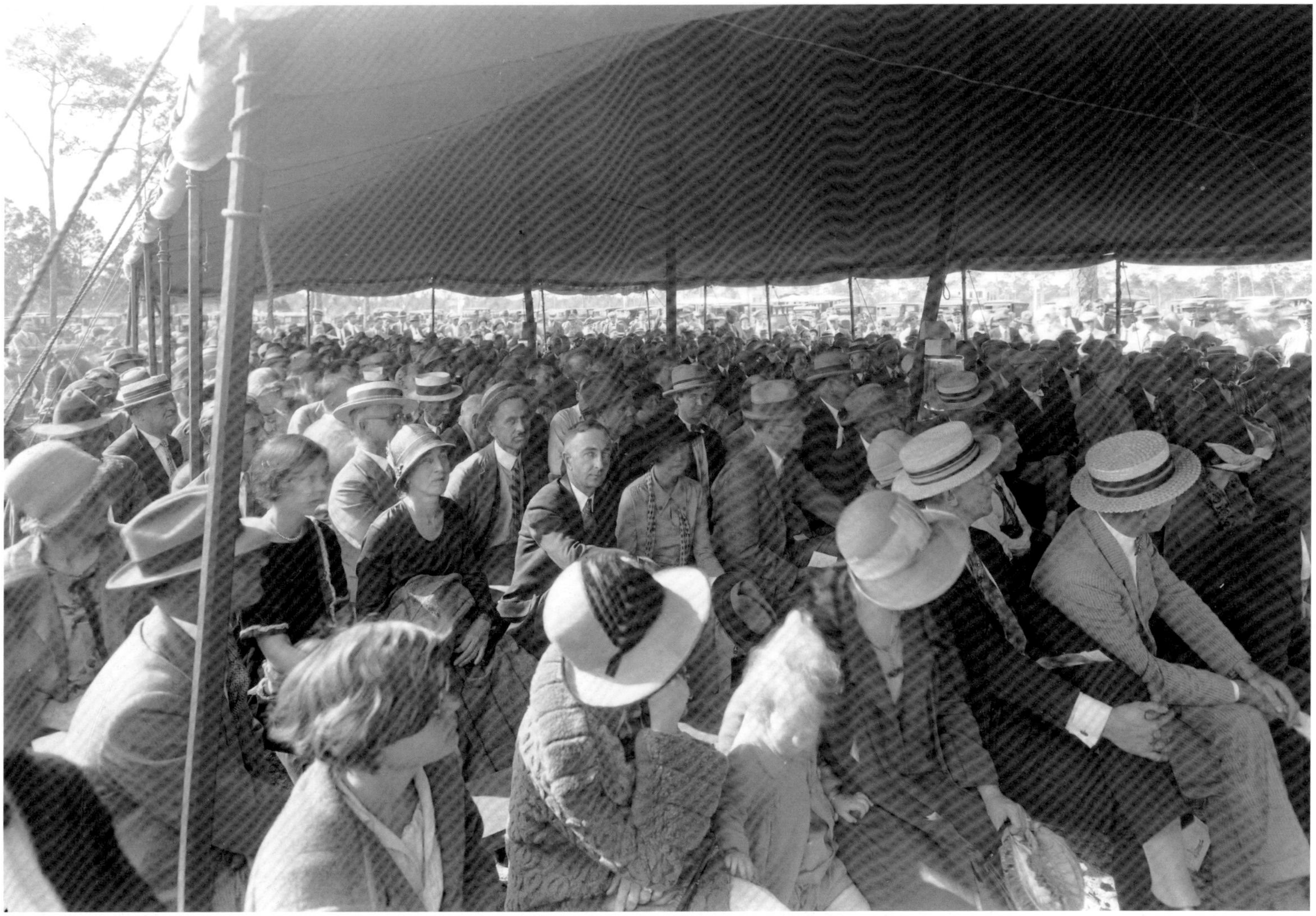

A crowd gathers for an auction of the Almendares subdivision in Miami, named after a river in Cuba, during the real estate boom of the 1920s.

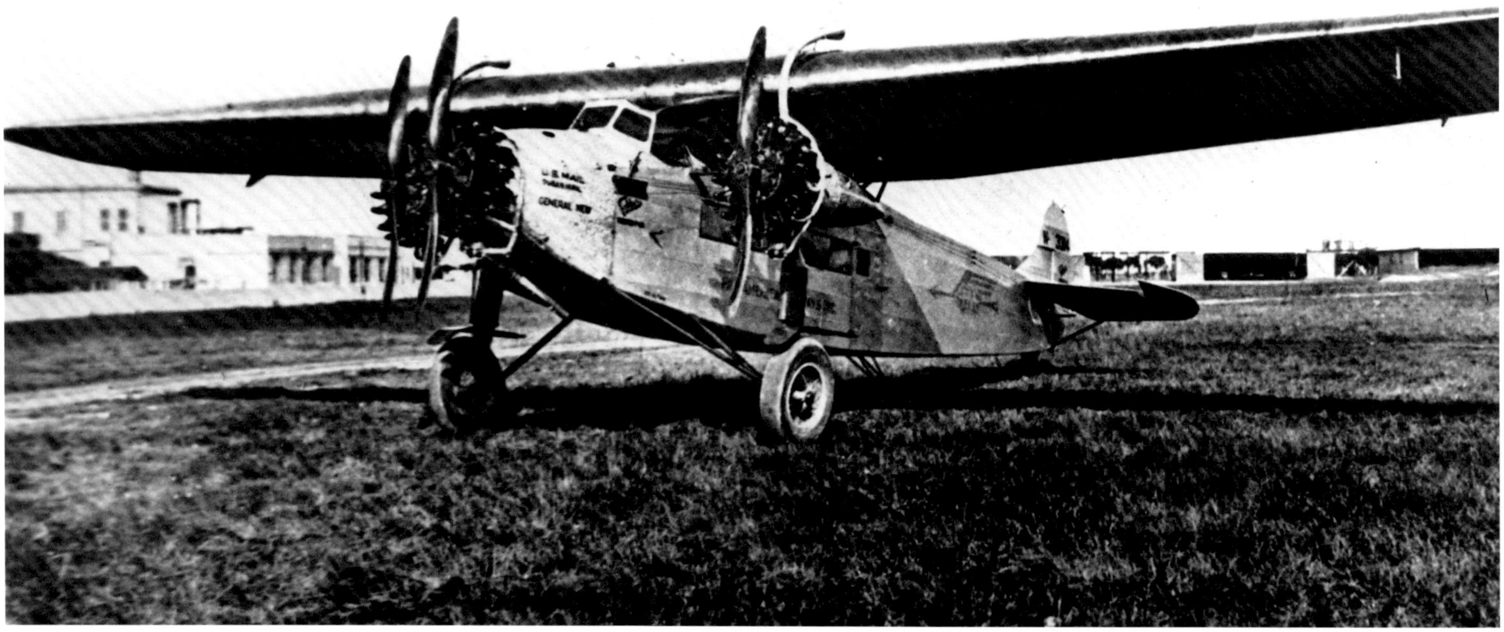

This C-2 Tri-motor Fokker airplane, on the strip at Pan American Field (later known as Miami International Airport), was the first type of plane used when Pan American World Airways (Pan Am) launched service in 1927. Pan Am's first route took air mail and passengers between Key West and Havana. Soon after, Pan Am began service between Miami and Havana.

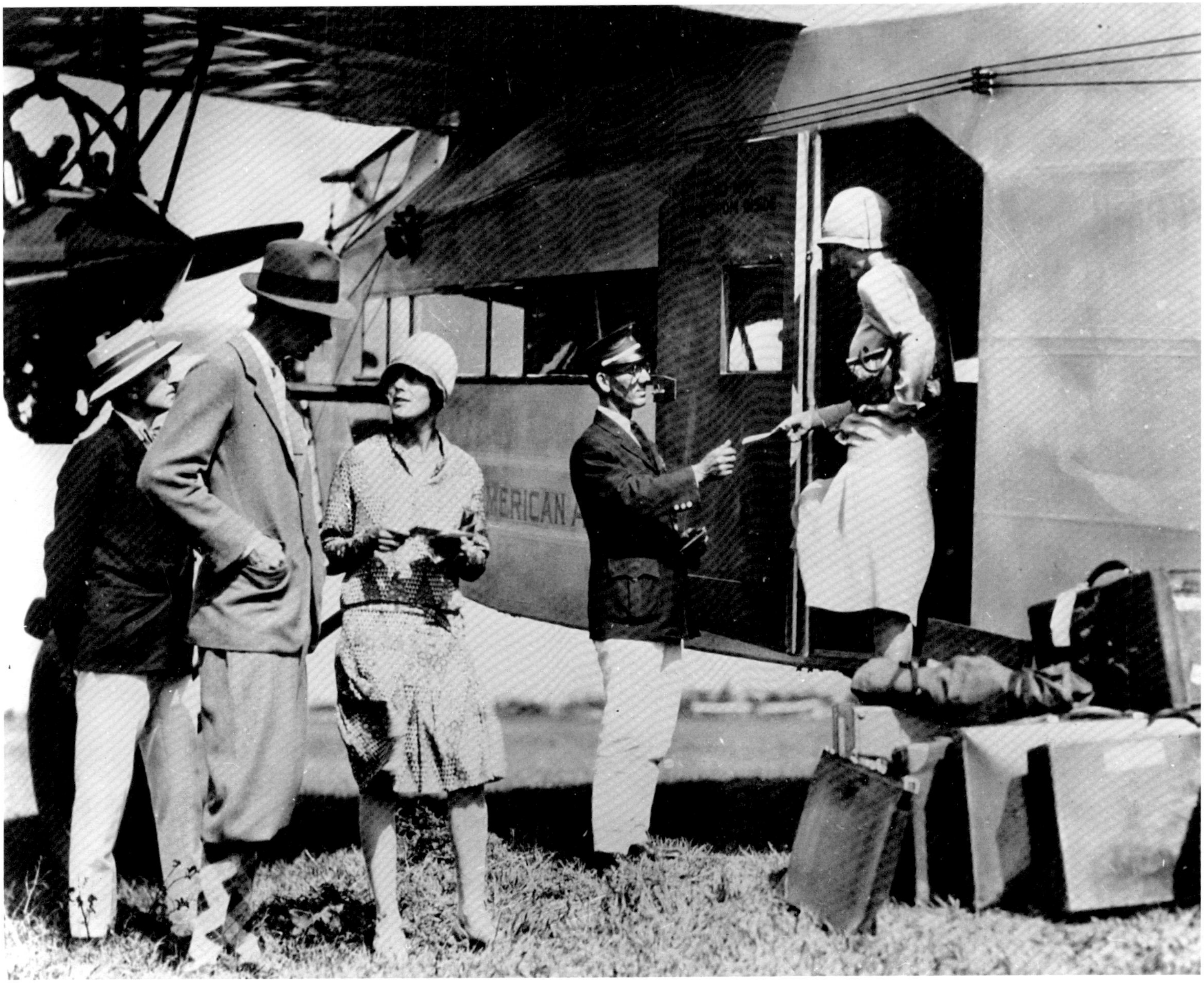

A group leaves for Havana on a Pan American F-7 flight from Miami.

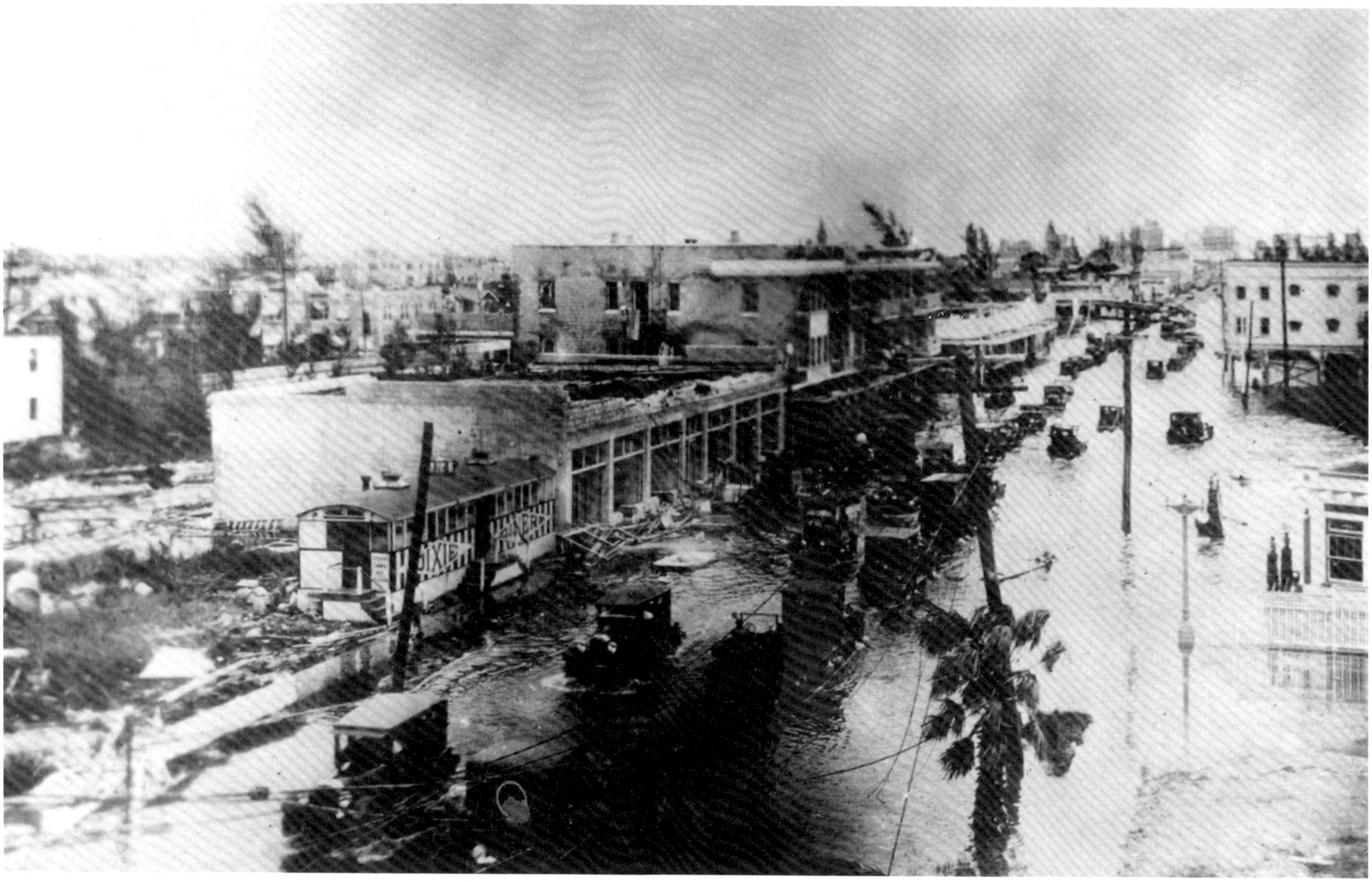

On September 16, 1926, a category 4 hurricane made landfall in Miami. With only hours of warning prior to landfall, residents of young Miami were not evacuated. Little knowledge of what damage a hurricane could do to the area left the city vulnerable and unprepared. This is a view of West Flagler Street after the 1926 hurricane.

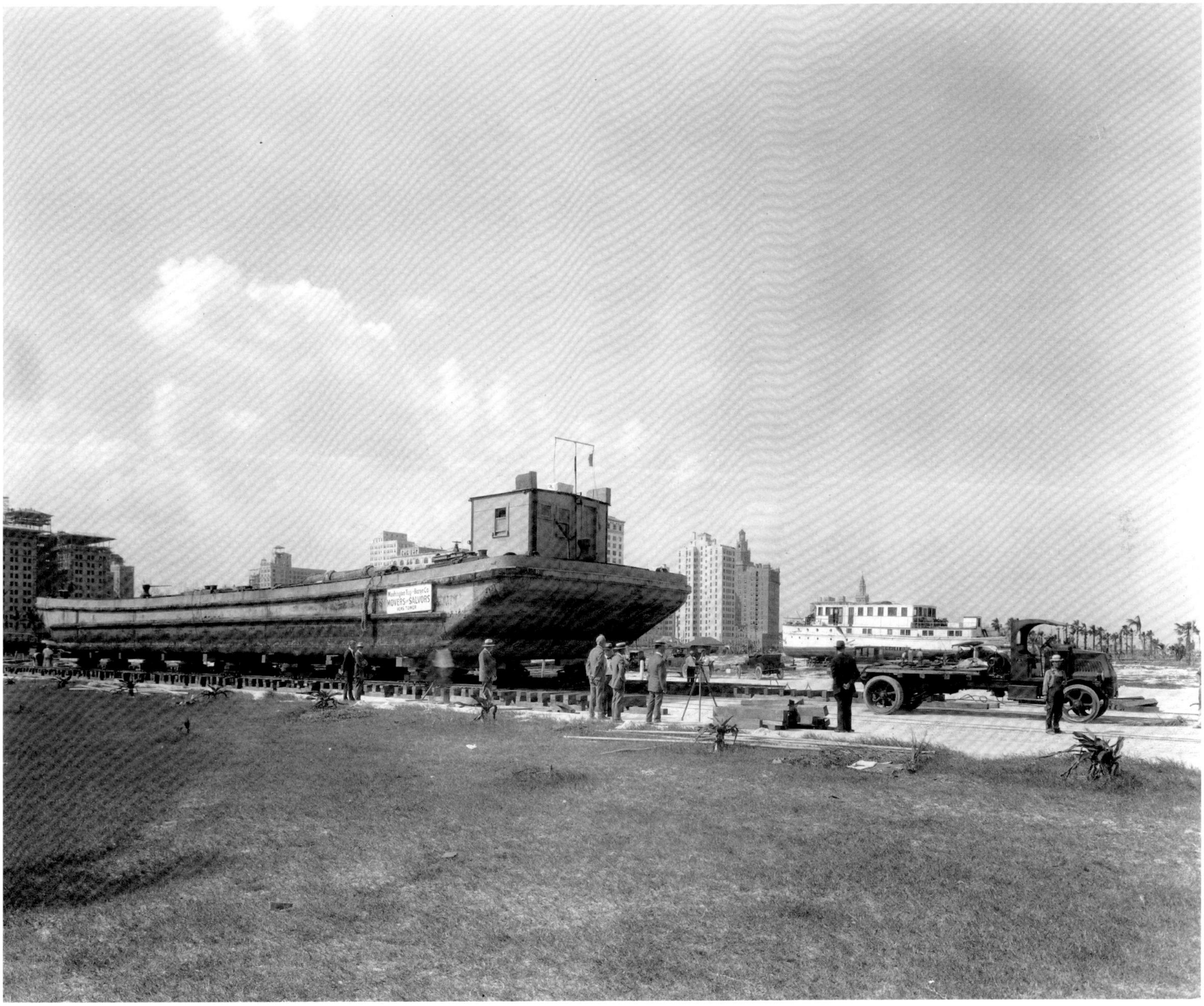

Accompanied by the crash of the Florida real estate market and the onset of the Great Depression just a few years later, the 1926 hurricane marked the beginning of hard times in Miami. Evident in this photograph, the hurricane caused disruptions in the crucial shipping industry of the city.

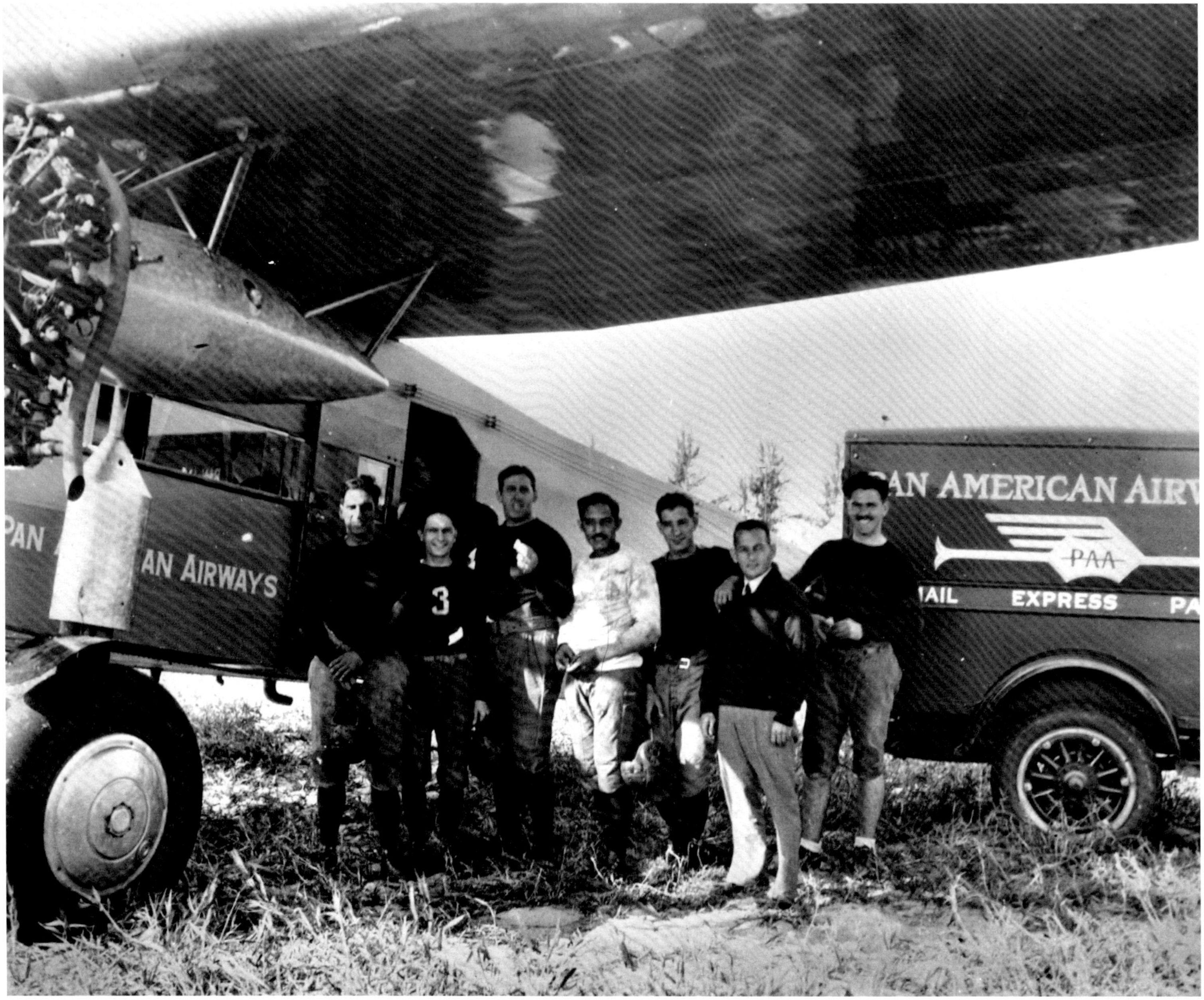

The Cuban Athletic Club, a Cuban football team, on a visit to Miami. The team is pictured next to a Pan American Airways clipper and passenger vehicle. As strange as it may seem to think of an American-style football team in a Latin American country, Cuba played in and hosted many games, including the Bacardí Bowl series. In 1928, the team even played against the University of Miami Hurricanes!

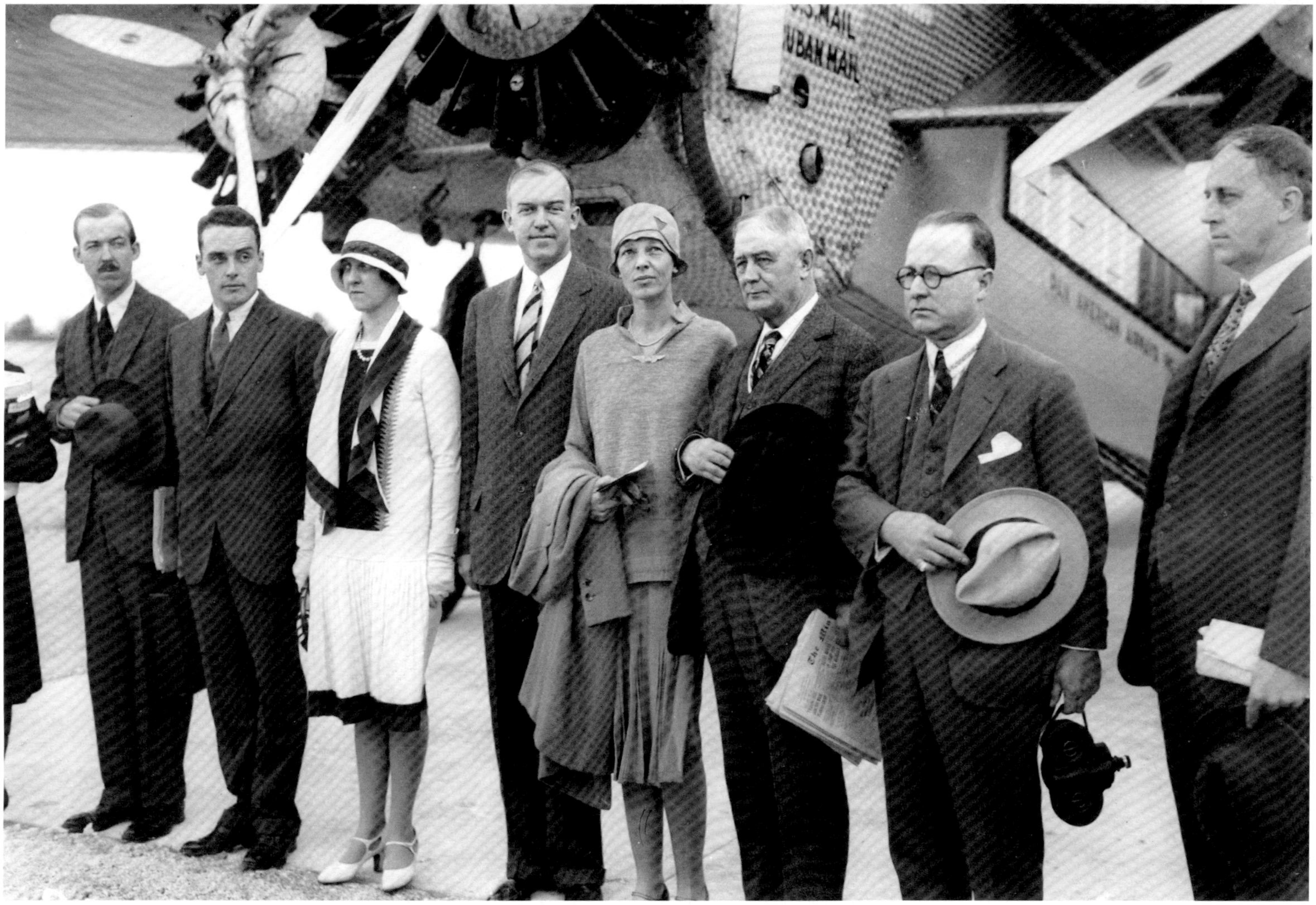

On January 9, 1929, Pan Am held an official inauguration for its new terminal at Miami. Left to right are Bruce Gould of the *New York Evening Post;* Colonel John A. Hambleton, vice-president; Ruth Elder, aviatrix; William MacCracken; Amelia Earheart, aviatrix; Harry S. New, postmaster general; and Irving Glover, assistant to the postmaster general.

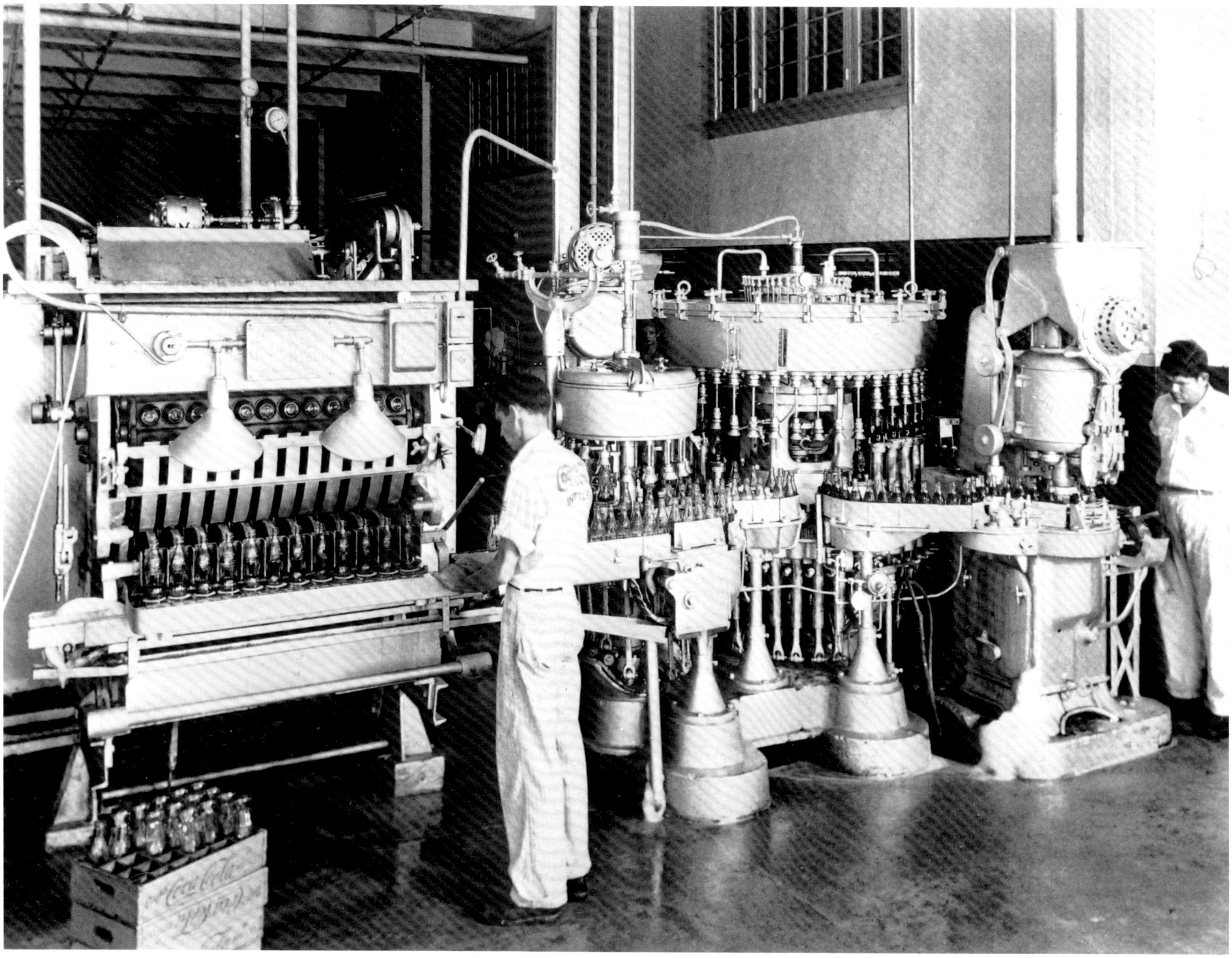

The Coca-Cola bottling works in Miami during the 1920s. Years later, a Cuban exile would become Coca-Cola's CEO. Coca-Cola was invented by John Pemberton in Atlanta, Georgia, in 1886, and first bottled in Chattanooga, Tennessee.

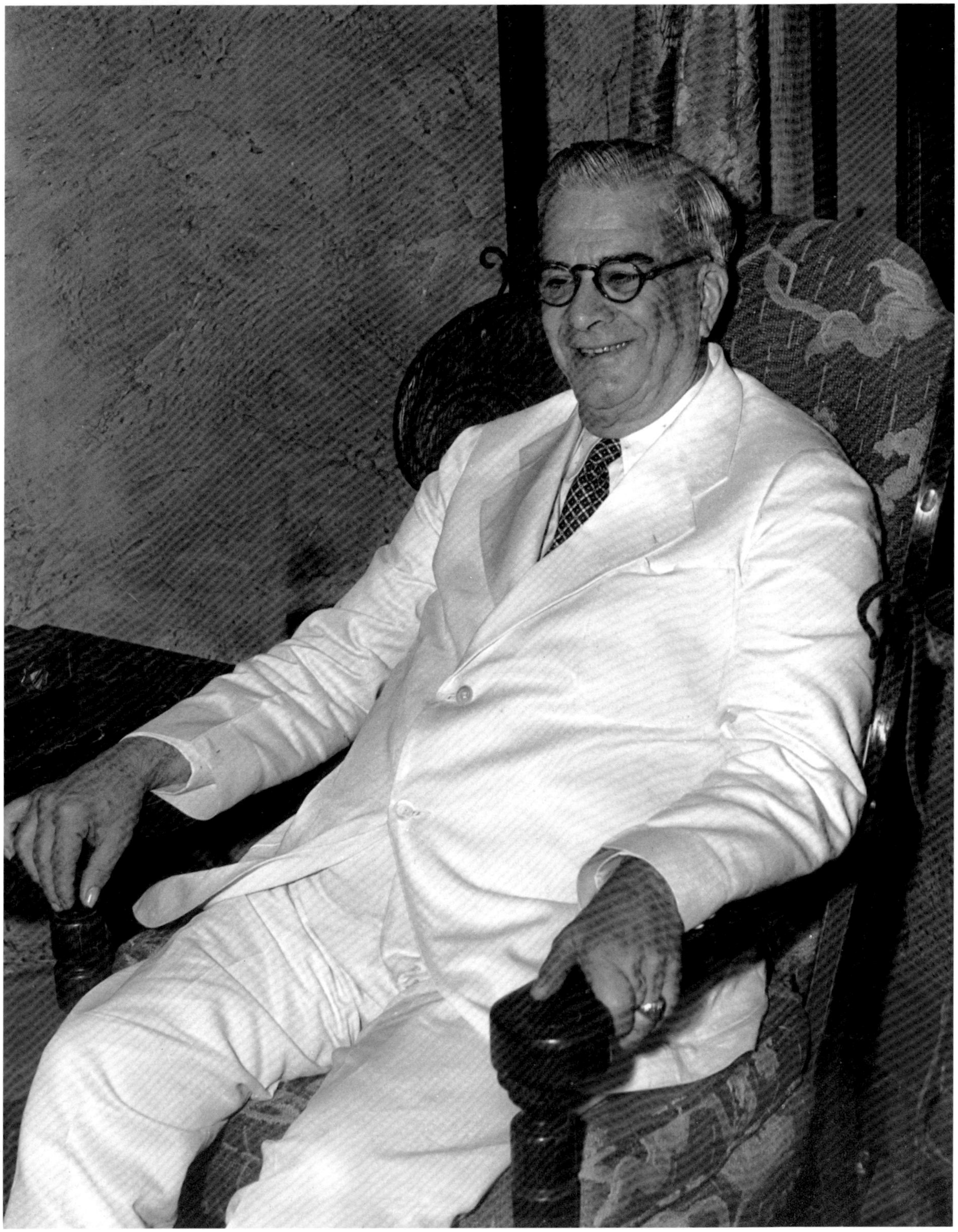

Before the advent of Fidel Castro, most of Cuba's presidents either visited or lived in exile in Miami. Gerardo Machado, pictured here around 1935, was president of Cuba from 1925 to 1933. He died in exile in Miami Beach.

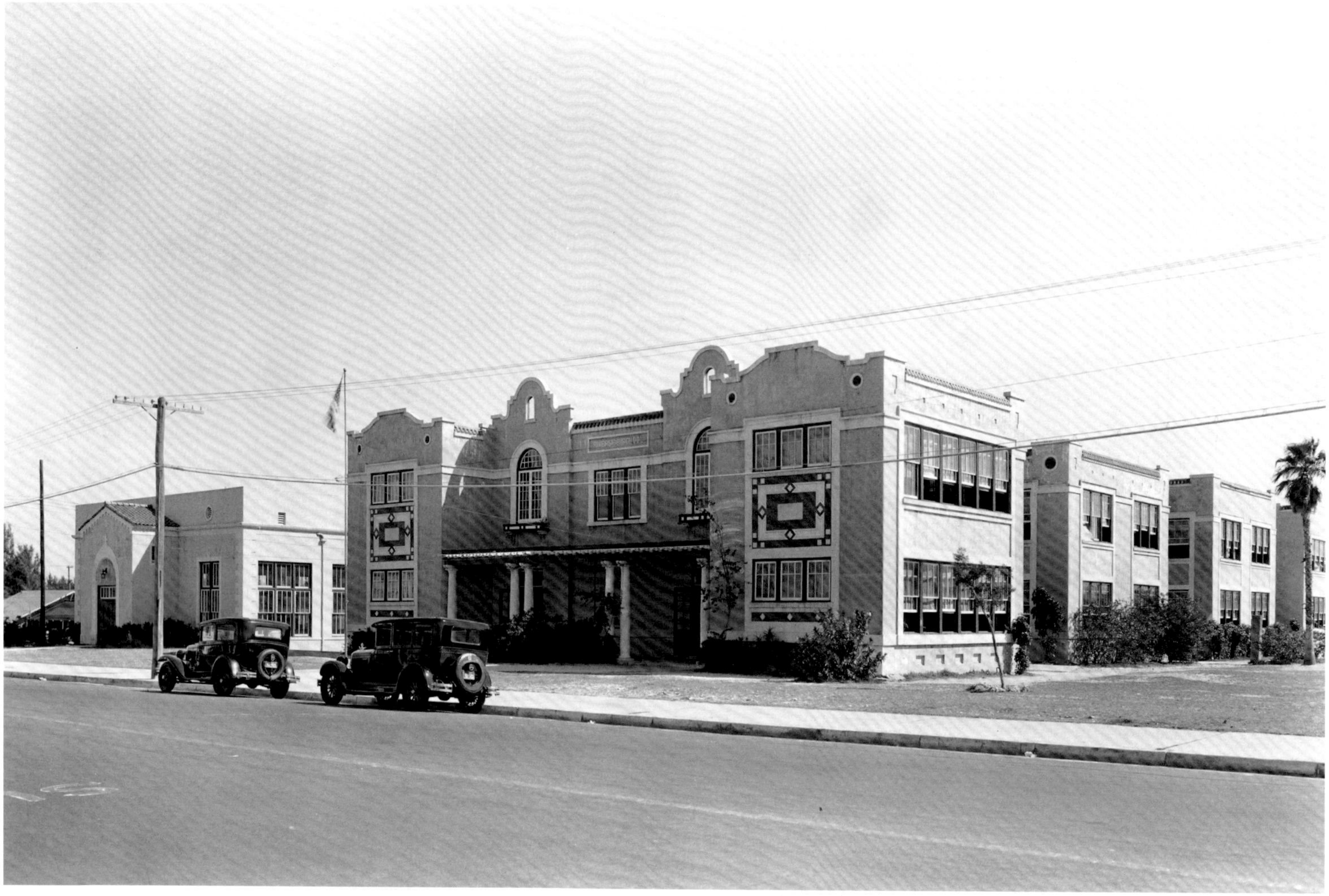

In the early 1900s, Riverside was a quaint suburb of Miami. This is Riverside Elementary School as it appeared in the 1930s. By the 1960s, when the first wave of exiles arrived, Riverside had become rundown. It would become part of eastern Little Havana as Cubans moved in and breathed life into the area.

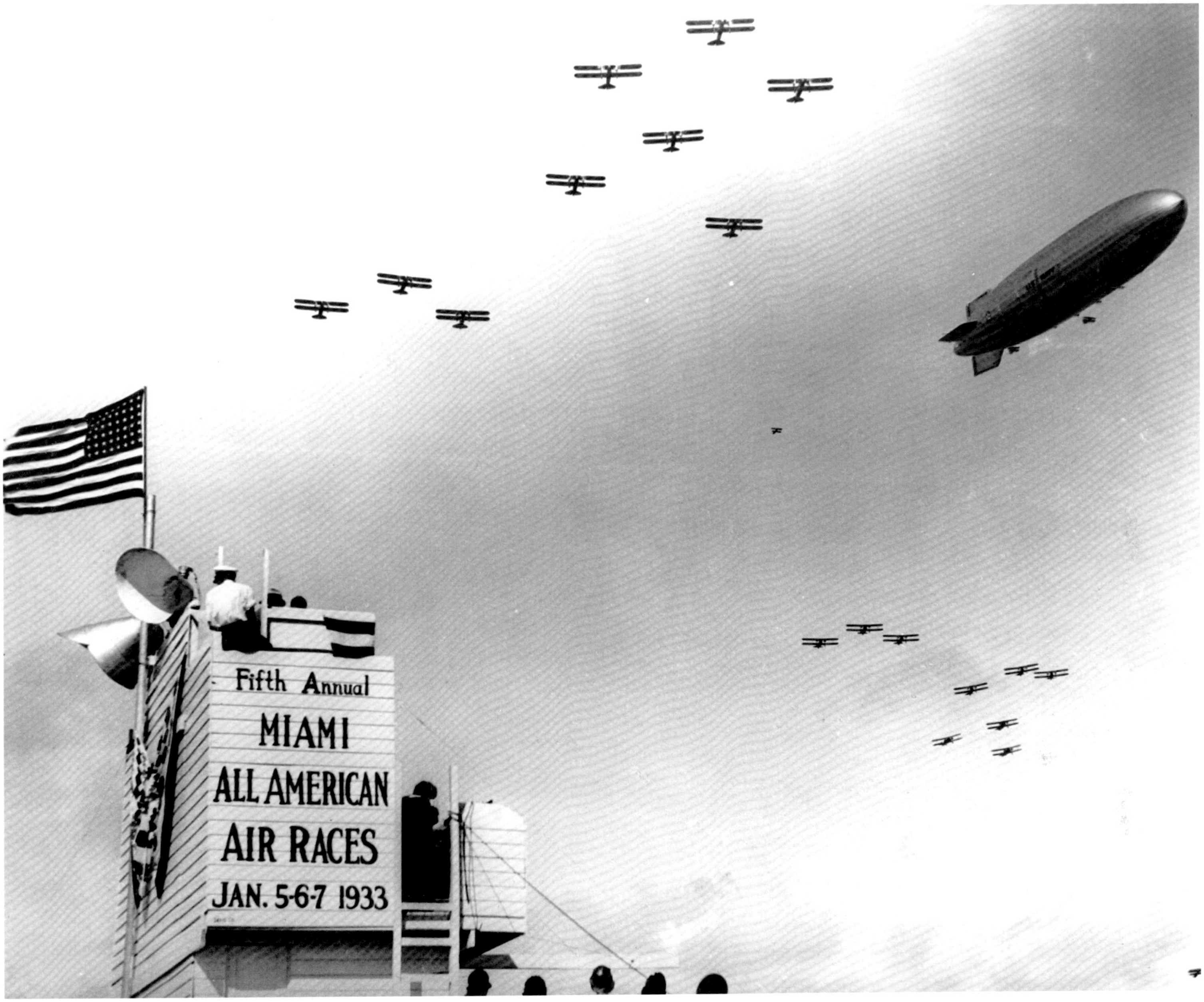

The airship *Akron* leaves for Cuba with a bomber escort during the Fifth Annual Miami All American Air Races in January 1933. The *Akron* was on its way to view operations in Guantanamo. A few months later, the airship would crash off the coast of New Jersey.

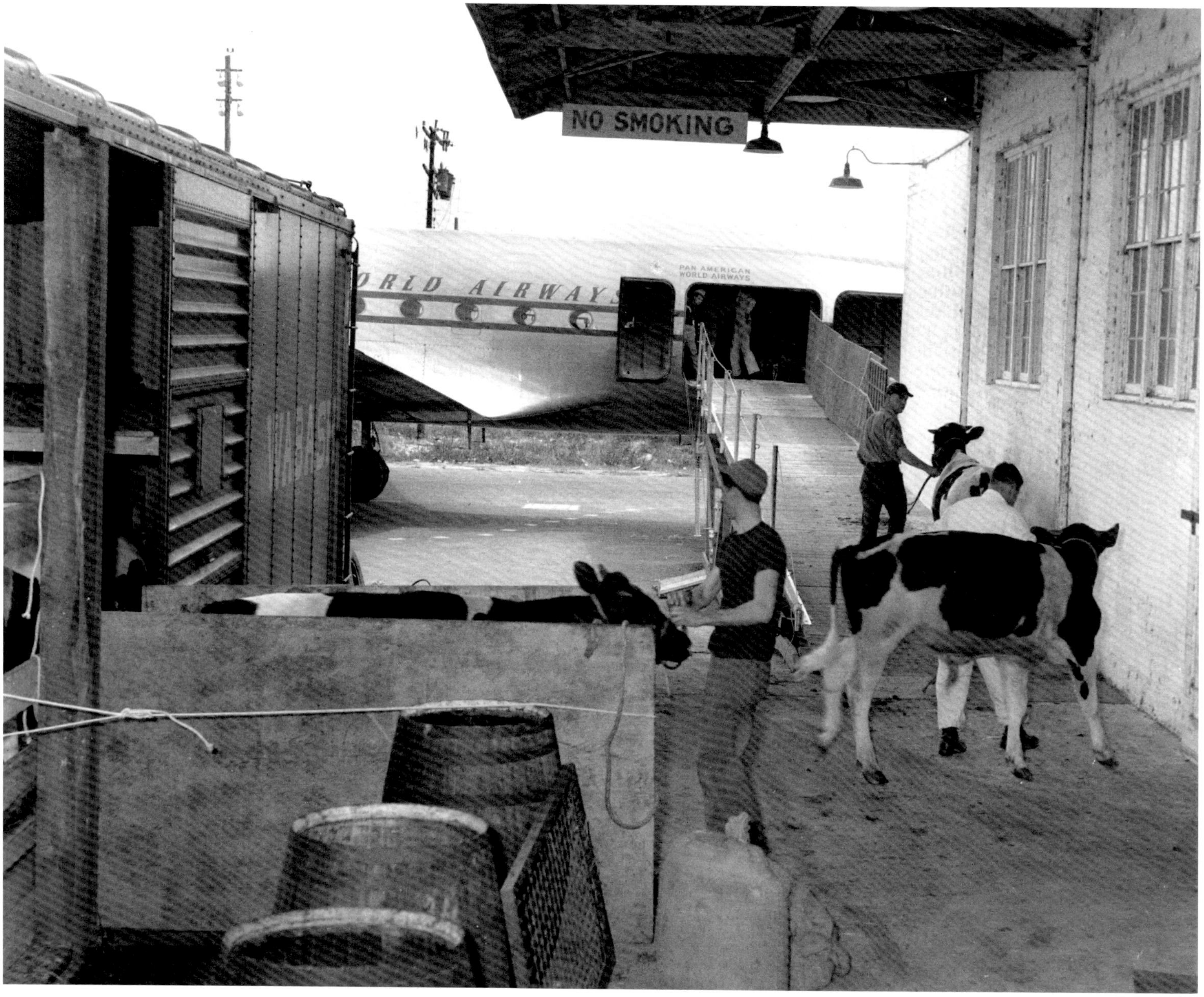

Cattle en route from Canada to Cuba on Pan Am Airlines are being transferred at the Miami depot here in 1934. Pan Am had devised this system for transferring livestock directly from railroad cars through the depot and onto the waiting cargo clipper.

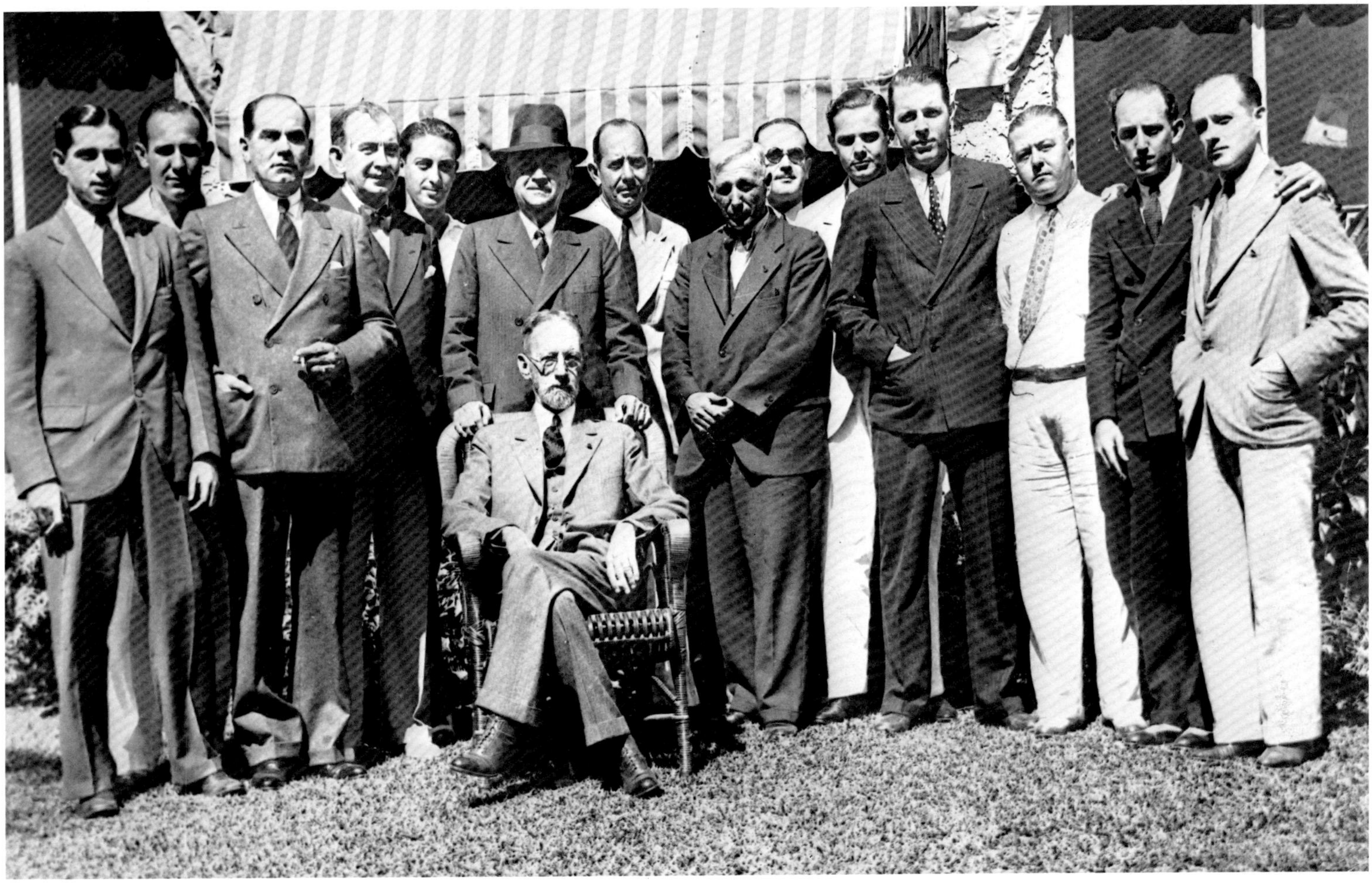

Major General Mario G. Menocal, former president of Cuba and leader of the Miami exiles, is shown here seated. Standing with him are Martin G. Menocal, Santiago Cerdeja, German S. Lopez, Julio Rabel, J. M. Lasa, Elicio Arguelles, Luis Hernandez, Pedro M. Fraga, E. Arguelles, Jr., Raoul Menocal, M. Llaneras, E. A. Rueda Martinez, Arturo Mora, and one unidentified individual.

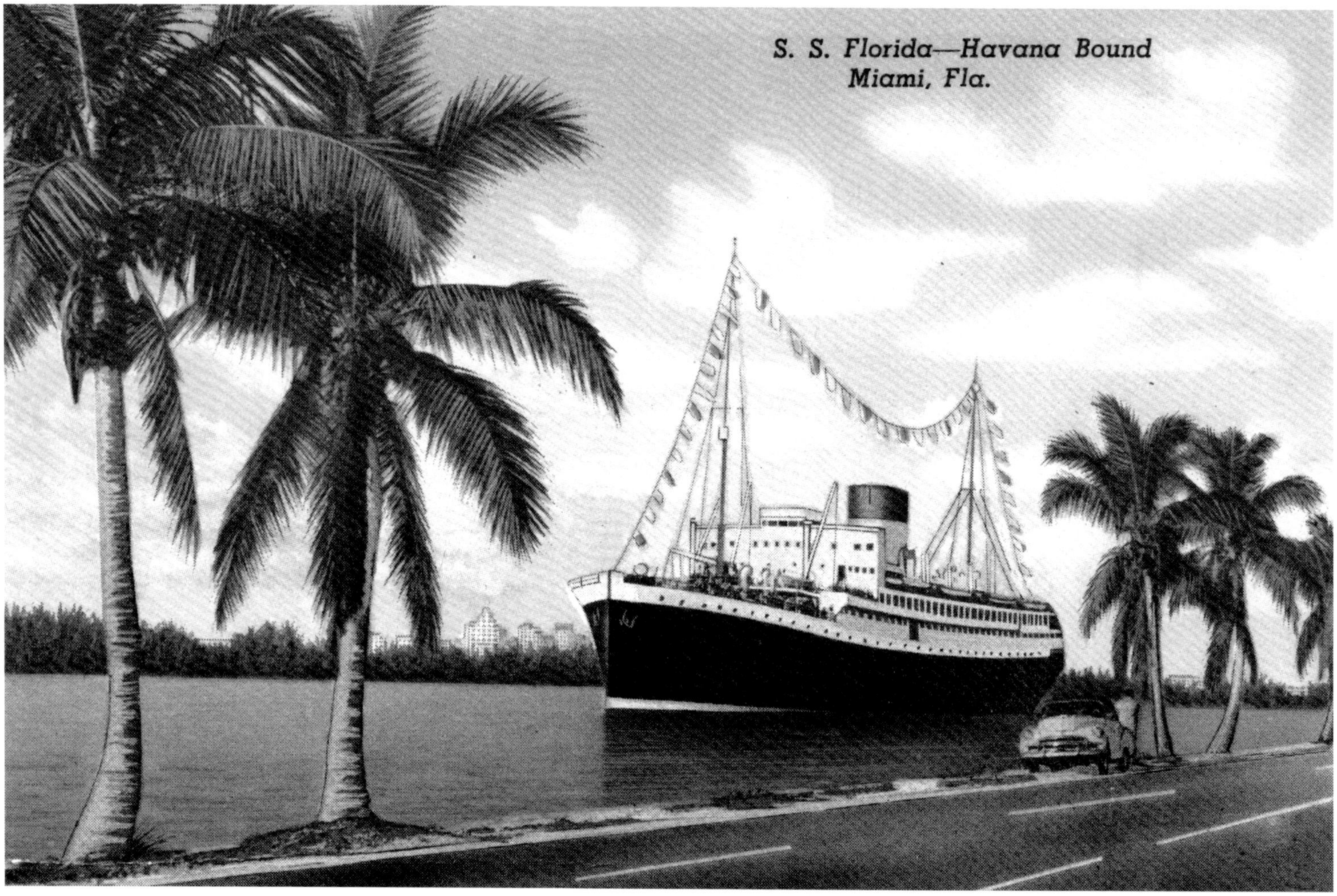

The SS *Florida* is bound for Havana in this photograph from a souvenir viewbook published around 1934.

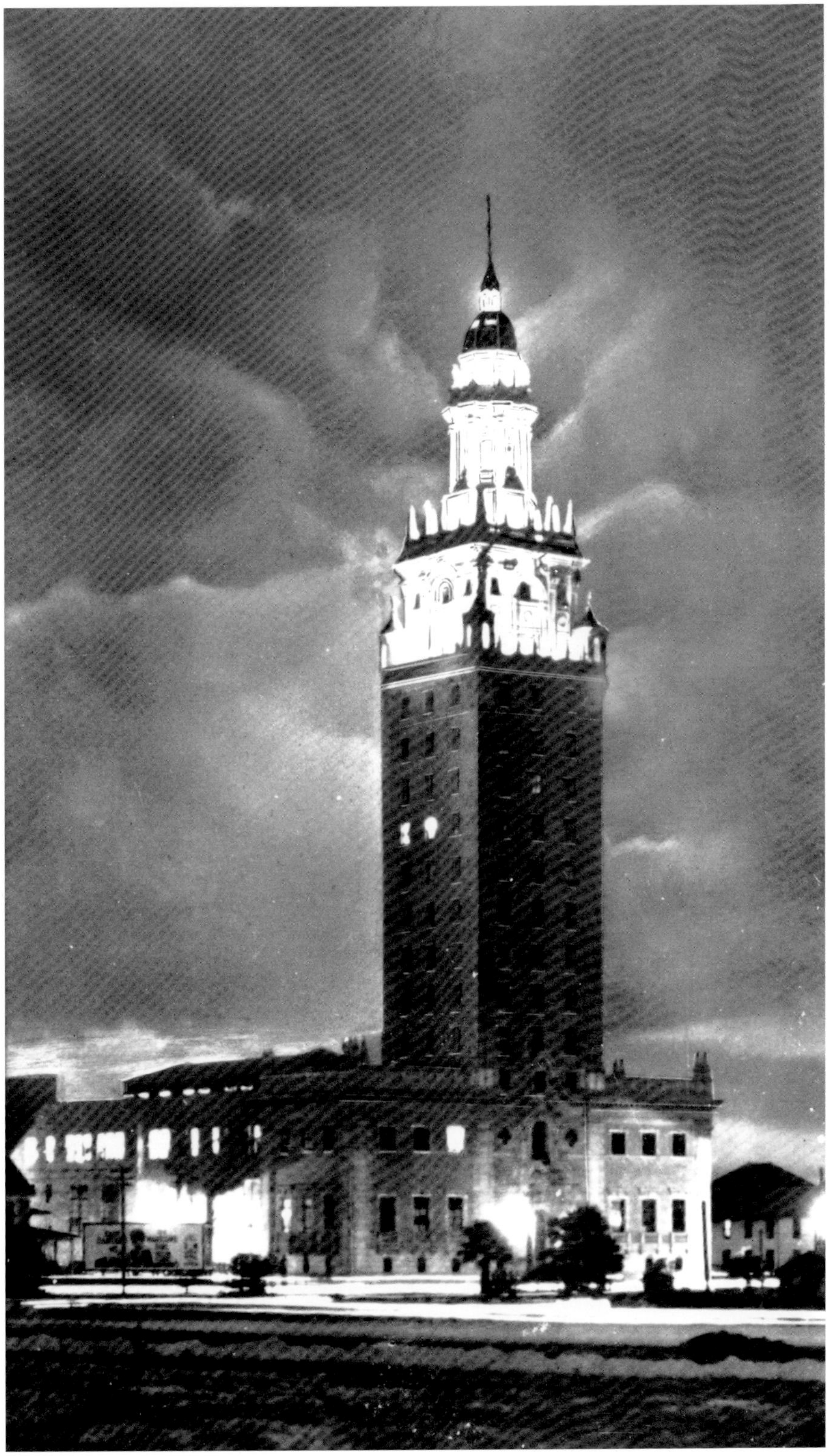

The Miami Daily News Tower at night.

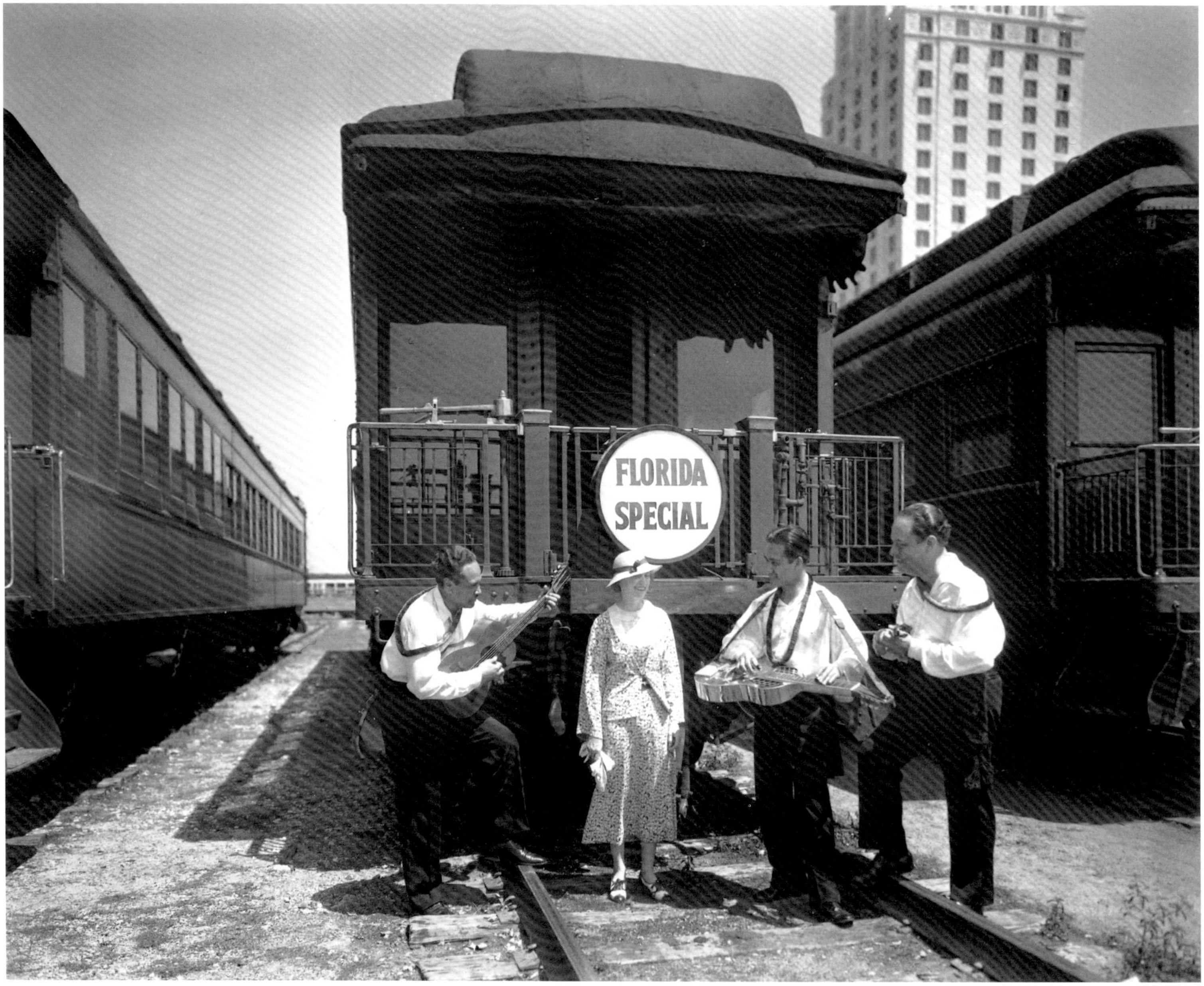

A visitor gets a taste of Miami's early Cuban flavor in 1936. Miami became a popular tourist destination by emphasizing its tropical and Havana-like exoticism in everything from music to architecture. Many hotels featured Cuban orchestras and rumba clubs, and Cuban workmanship could be seen throughout structures in Miami. Most Cubans living in Miami prior to 1959 were either musicians, craftsmen, or political exiles who had fallen out of favor.

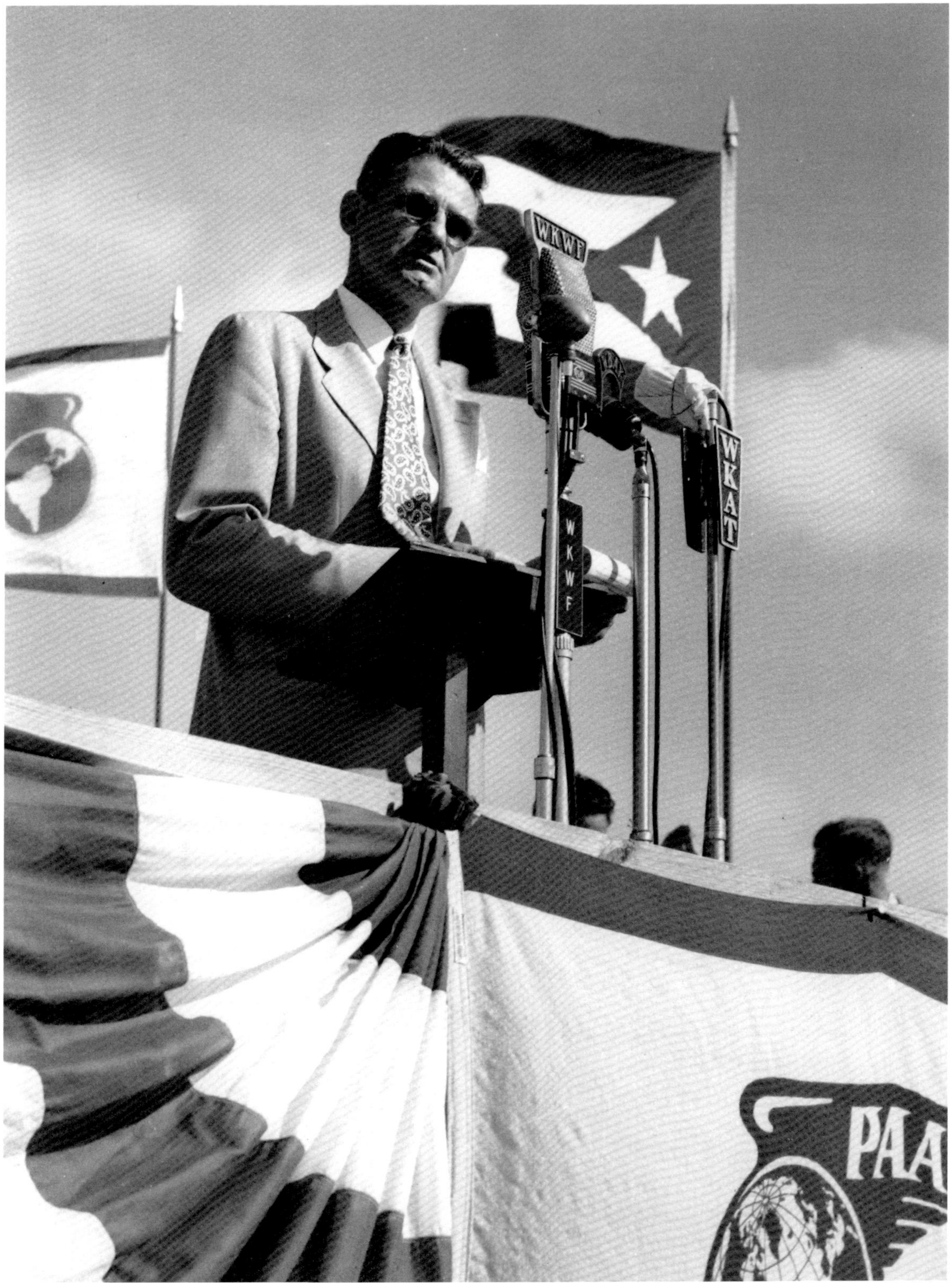

Governor Caldwell speaks at a commemoration marking Pan American World Airways air mail service to Cuba and the subsequent success of international transport.

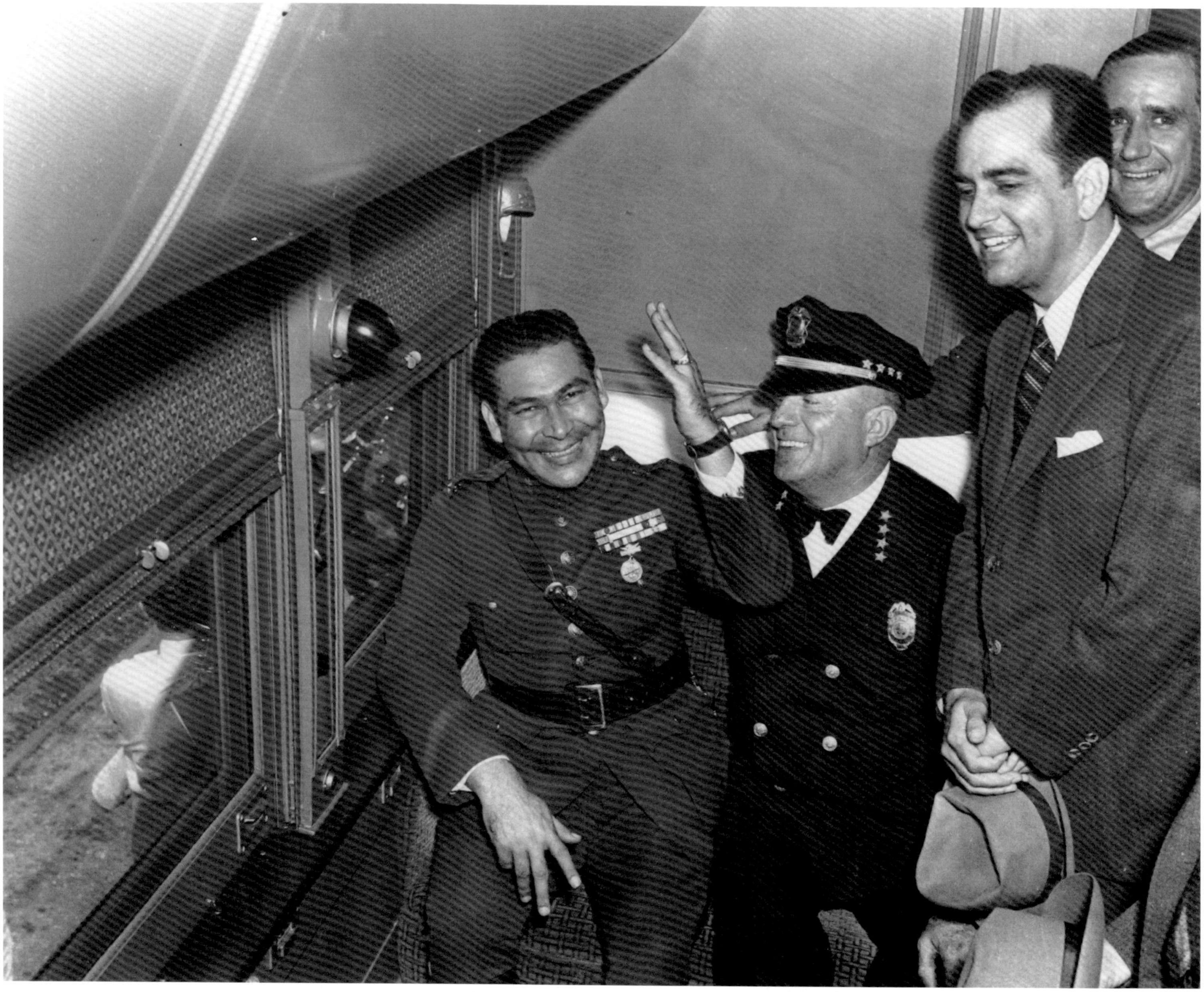

At the Miami depot in 1938, Cuban army chief of staff, Fulgencio Batista, sits in a train en route to Washington with Miami chief of police Leslie Quigg. Batista, nicknamed "strongman" by the press, was leader of Cuba at the time. Batista controlled the puppet presidency from 1934 until he was elected in 1940. In 1944, Batista's chosen successor would lose to Ramon San Grau. Batista was given asylum in the United States and lived a self-imposed exile in Florida until 1952.

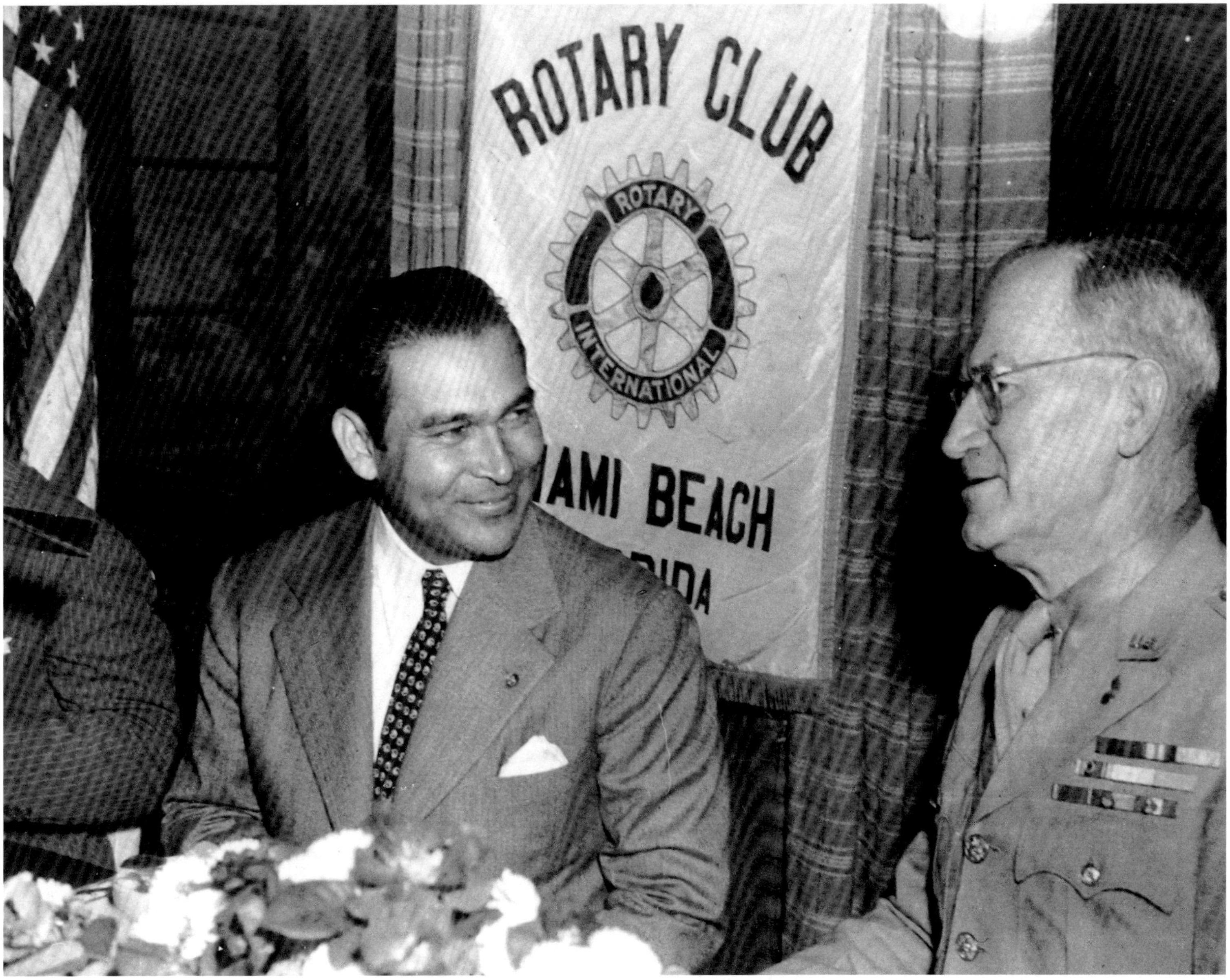

Batista and Colonel Charles Metzler at a Miami Beach Rotary Club meeting during the 1940s. During his exile, Batista lived a plush life in Daytona Beach, with frequent visits to South Florida. Batista was elected to the Cuban senate *in absentia* in 1948, returning to Cuba for another presidential run in 1952. Instead, he led another coup and canceled elections, installing himself as president. He would be unseated by Castro in 1959.

Following Spread: An aerial view of the Hialeah racetrack in 1947. Famous for its flamingos and architecture, the racetrack was a huge success in the first half of the twentieth century. The track closed in 2001 but has been granted permits for racing and a restoration project is under way. Racing returned to the tracks in November 2009.

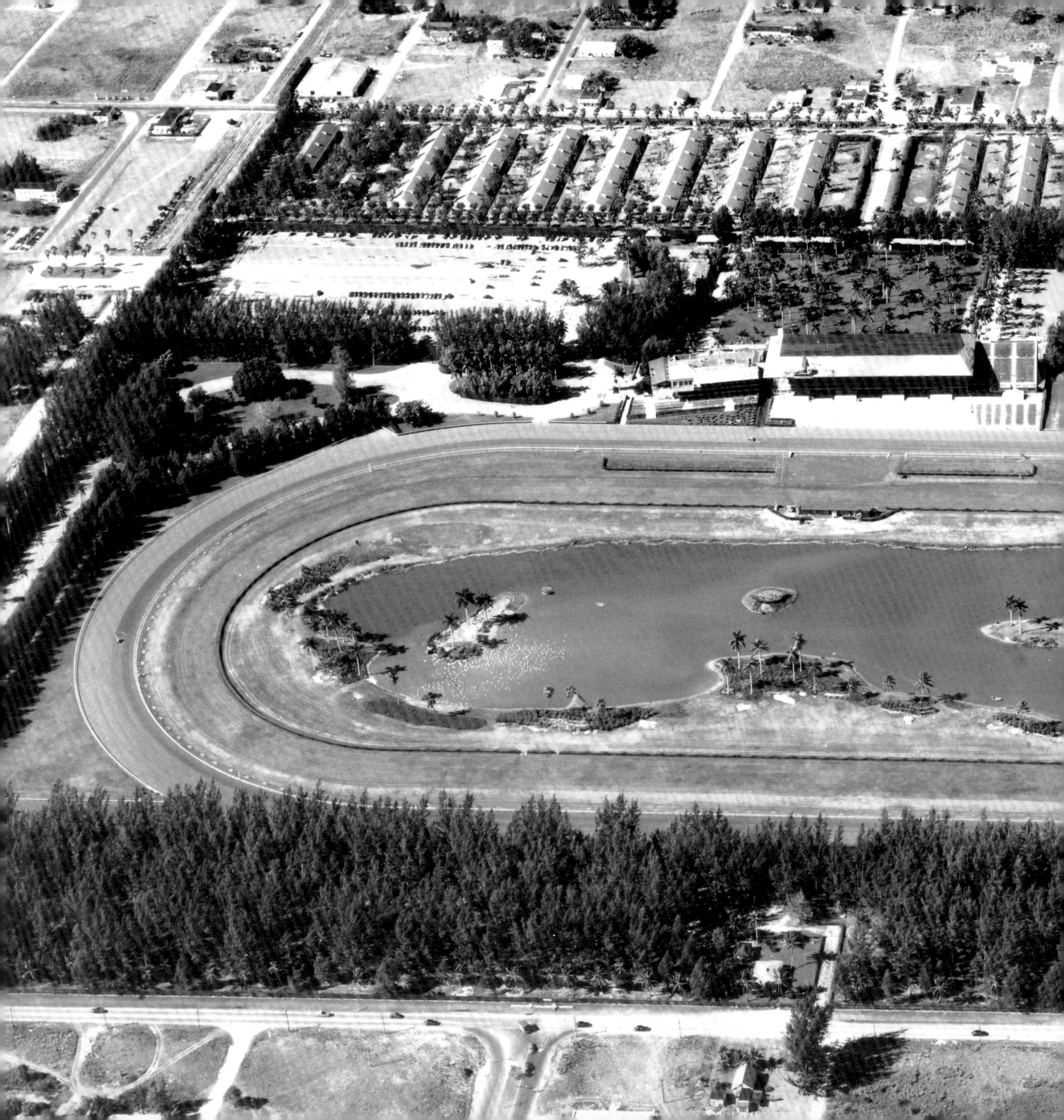

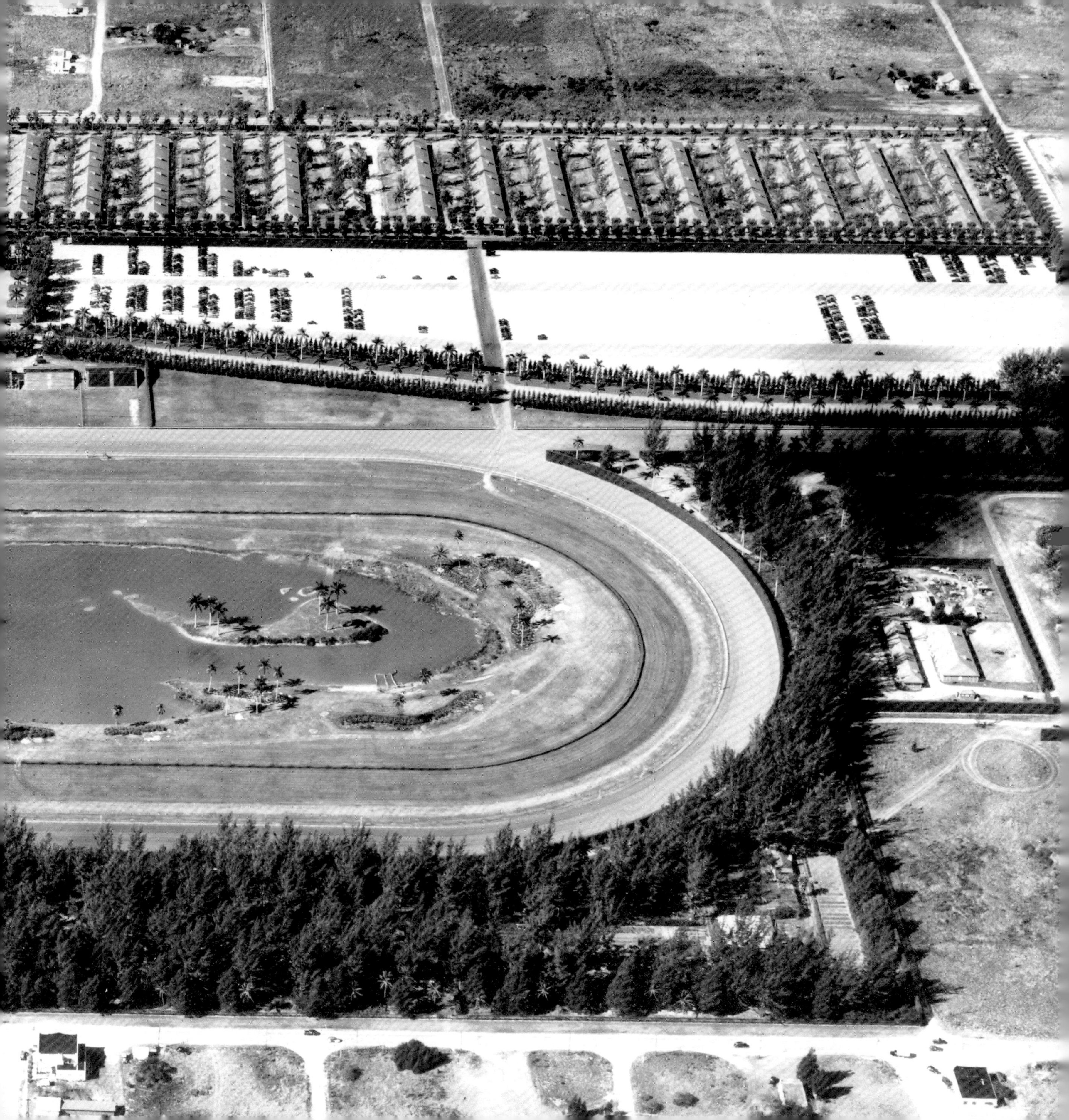

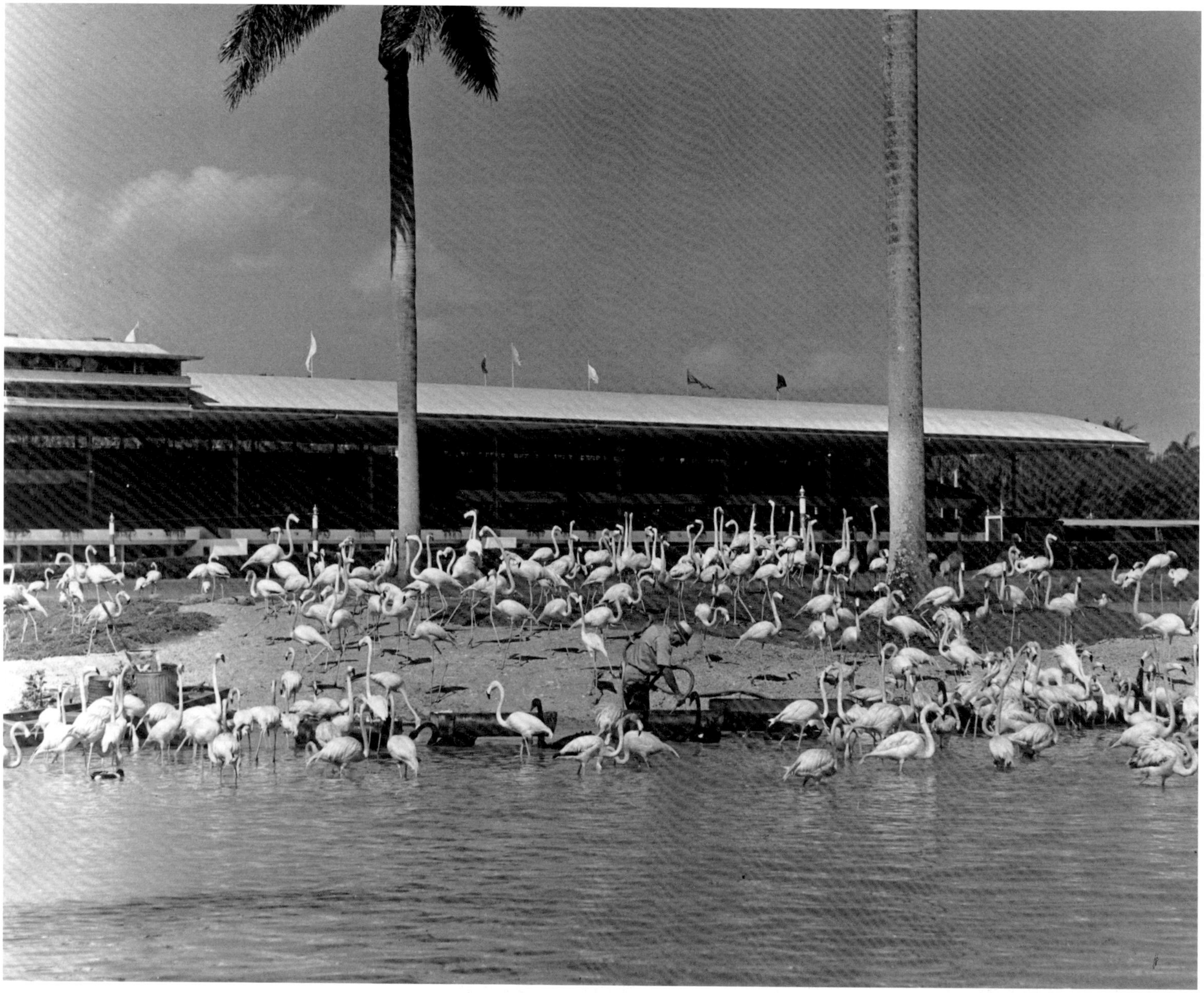

The famous flamingos of the Hialeah Park racetrack were originally imported from Cuba. The first group of imports flew straight back to Cuba upon release. The wings of the second group were clipped, and like other Cuban imports, have become part of Miami history. The colony eventually multiplied to hundreds. Most flamingos in Florida descend from the Hialeah Park racetrack colony.

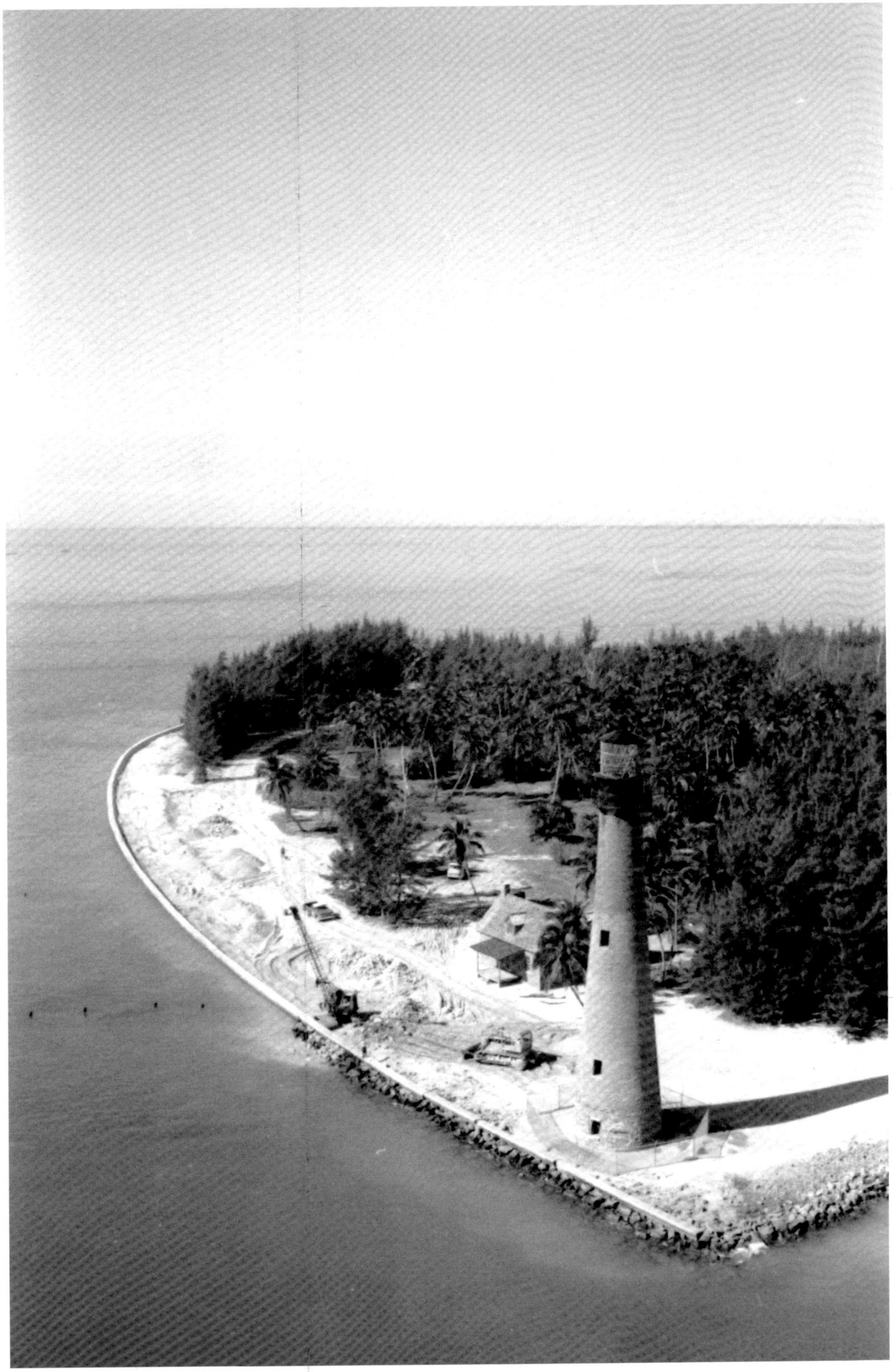

Following accusations of embezzlement while serving as minister of education in Cuba, José Áleman, Sr., fled to Miami. In 1948, he bought the Cape Florida property in Key Biscayne from the Deering Estate, including the Cape Florida lighthouse, the oldest structure still standing in the county. He tried to donate a portion of land and the lighthouse to the National Park Service, but was rejected. Years after his death, the area would be turned into Bill Baggs Cape Florida State Park.

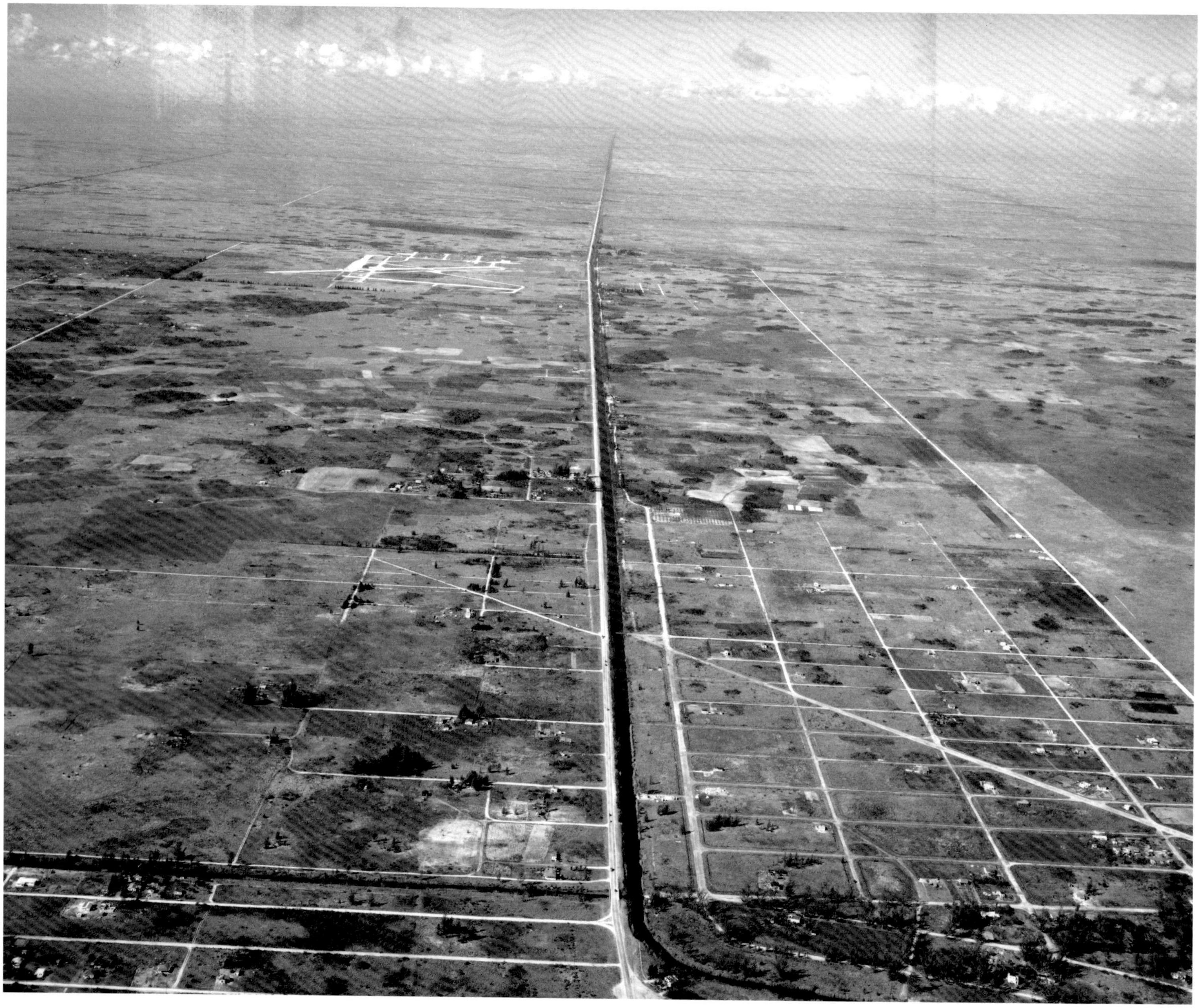

An aerial view of the Tamiami Trail at Miami around 1947. The Miami part of the trail is also known as SW 8th Street, the most famous street in Little Havana.

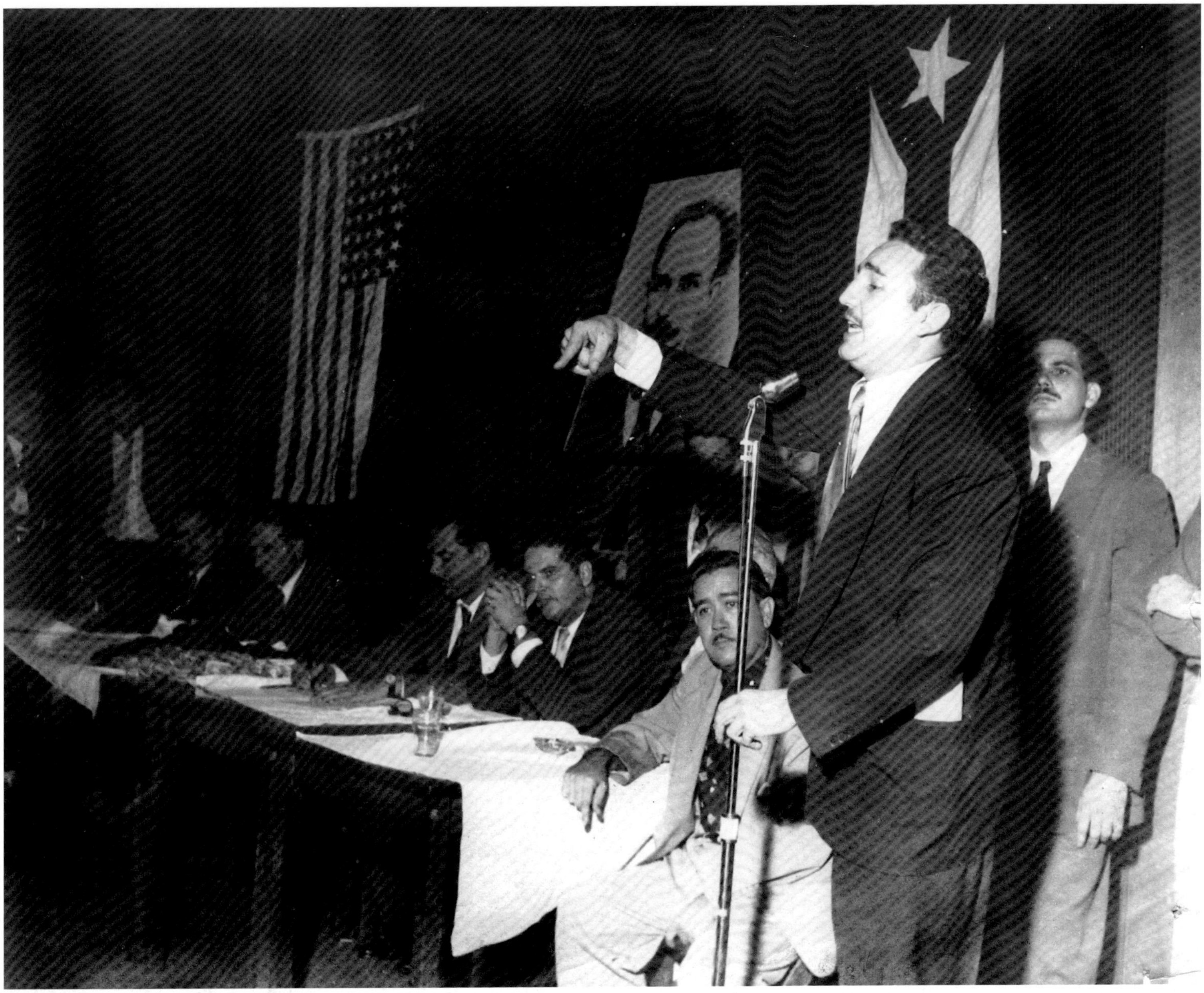

As an exile visiting Miami, Fidel Castro pontificates at the Flagler Theater in November 1955. In 1959, his ongoing guerrilla war against the forces of Batista would overcome the government, causing Batista to flee Cuba and giving Castro dictatorial control of the nation. Castro's band of Marxist revolutionaries included Argentinian Che Guevara, who would rise to prominence as one of Castro's lieutenants.

A south-facing view of Palm Avenue in 1959 Hialeah. This view would soon change dramatically, as Cubans fleeing Castro were granted asylum and poured into Miami and the surrounding areas. These days, Cuban-Americans may encourage visitors to Miami to see "El Pal Avenue."

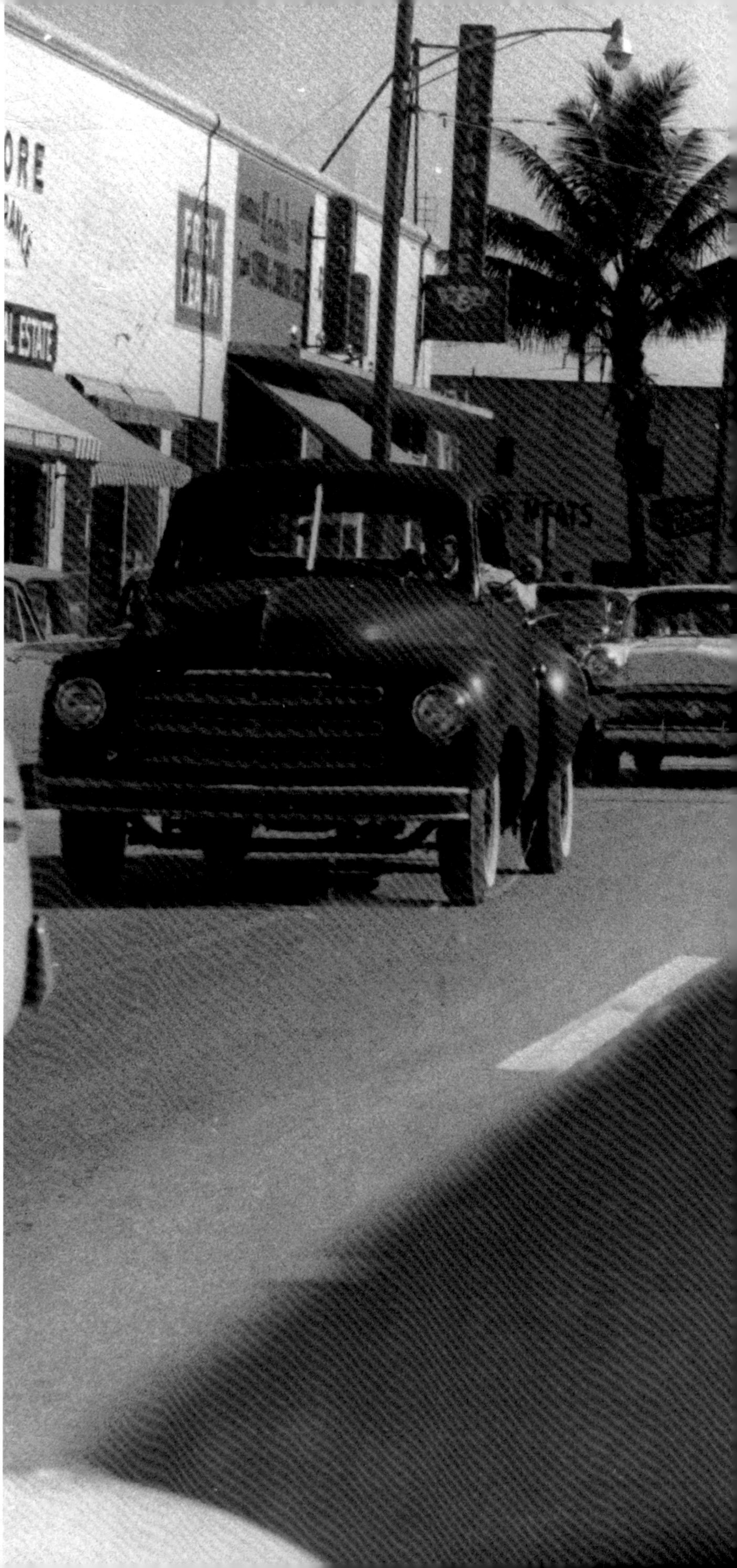

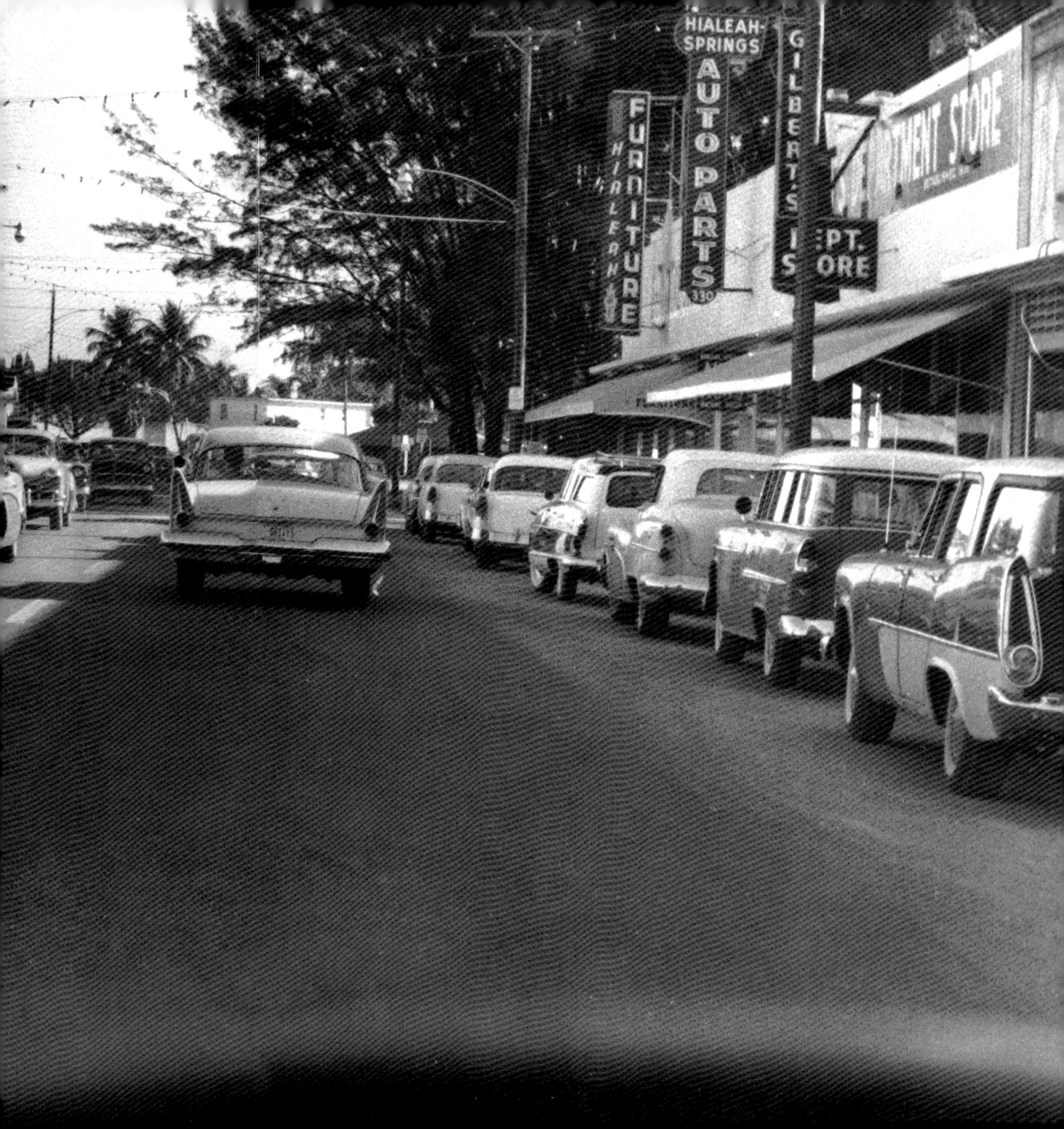
HIALEAH-SPRINGS
AUTO PARTS
330
HIALEAH
FURNITURE
GILBERT'S

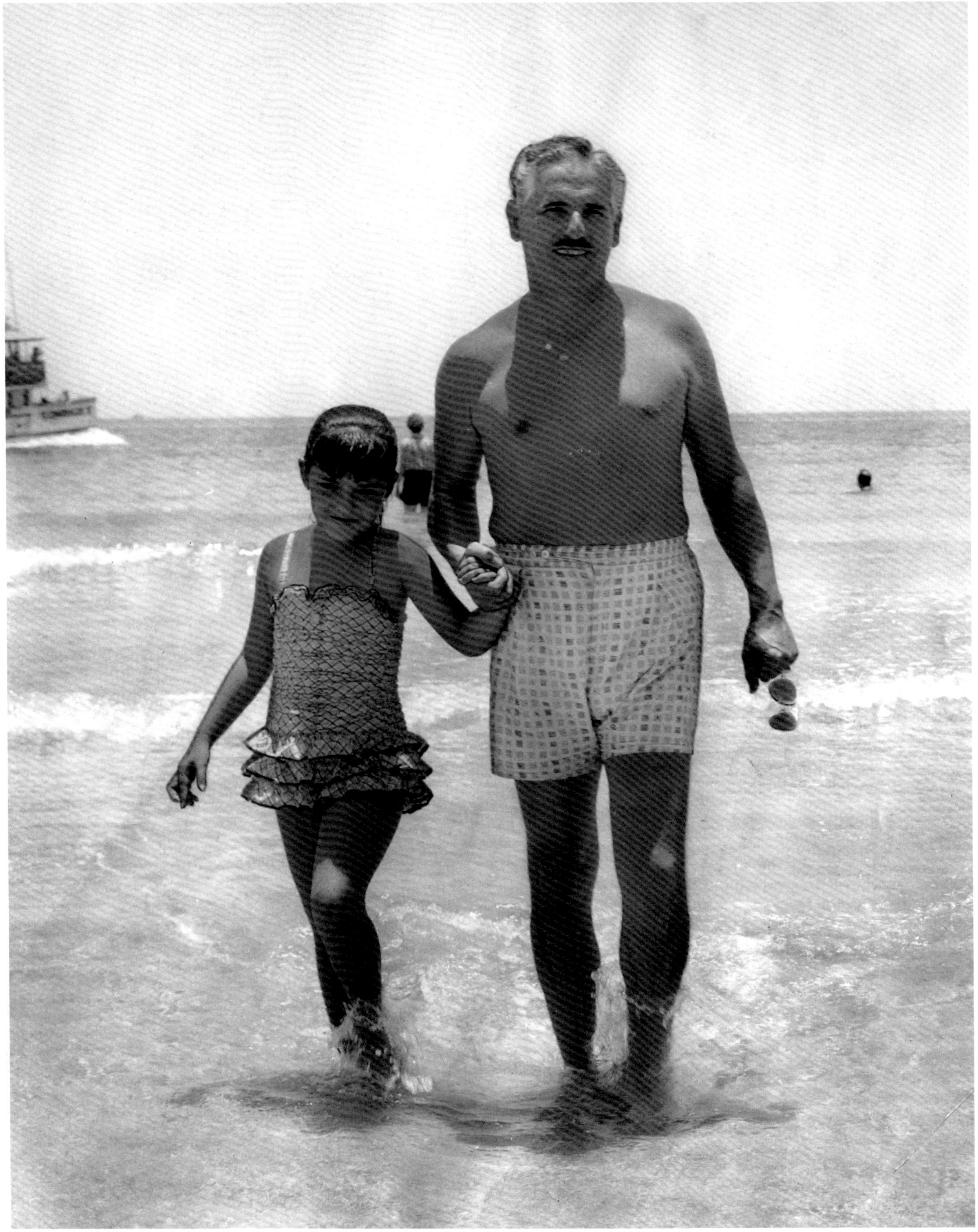

Former Cuban president Dr. Carlos Prio Socarrás and daughter pose for the camera on the beach in 1956. Prio Socarrás was known as "the cordial president," a name he took pride in. He was the last constitutionally elected president of Cuba to date. Ousted by Fulgencio Batista, he was given asylum in Miami, having refused to mount any defense against Batista's coup. Prio Socarrás later financed Castro's coup, helping in this way to oust Batista, but eventually he denounced Castro's communist policies.

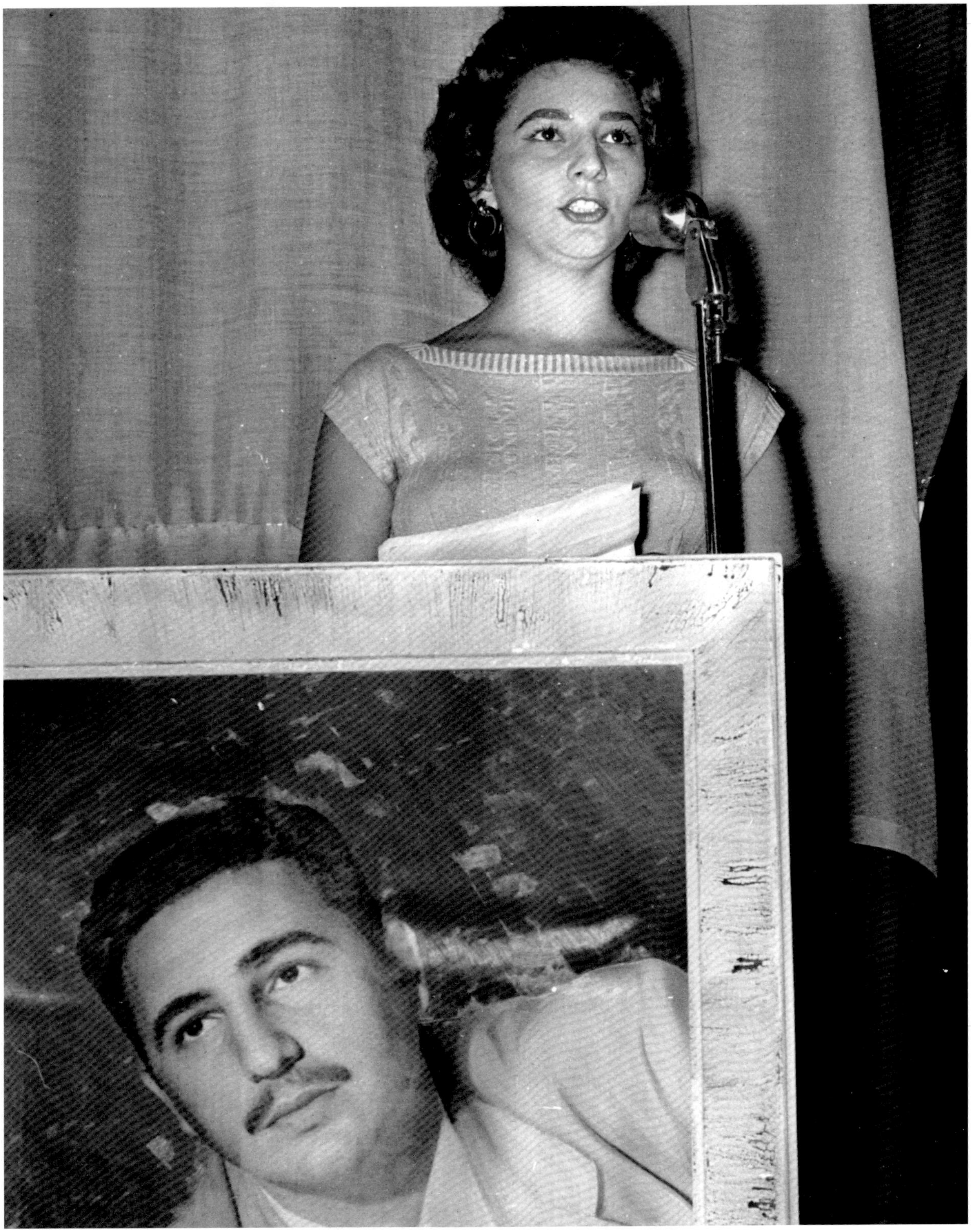

Emma Castro gives a speech at a 1957 anti-Batista rally in Miami next to a large portrait of her brother Fidel. Most exiles living in the United States at the time were pro-Castro and anti-Batista. Many of the exiles returned to Cuba during the Castro revolution, later fleeing to Miami again, disillusioned.

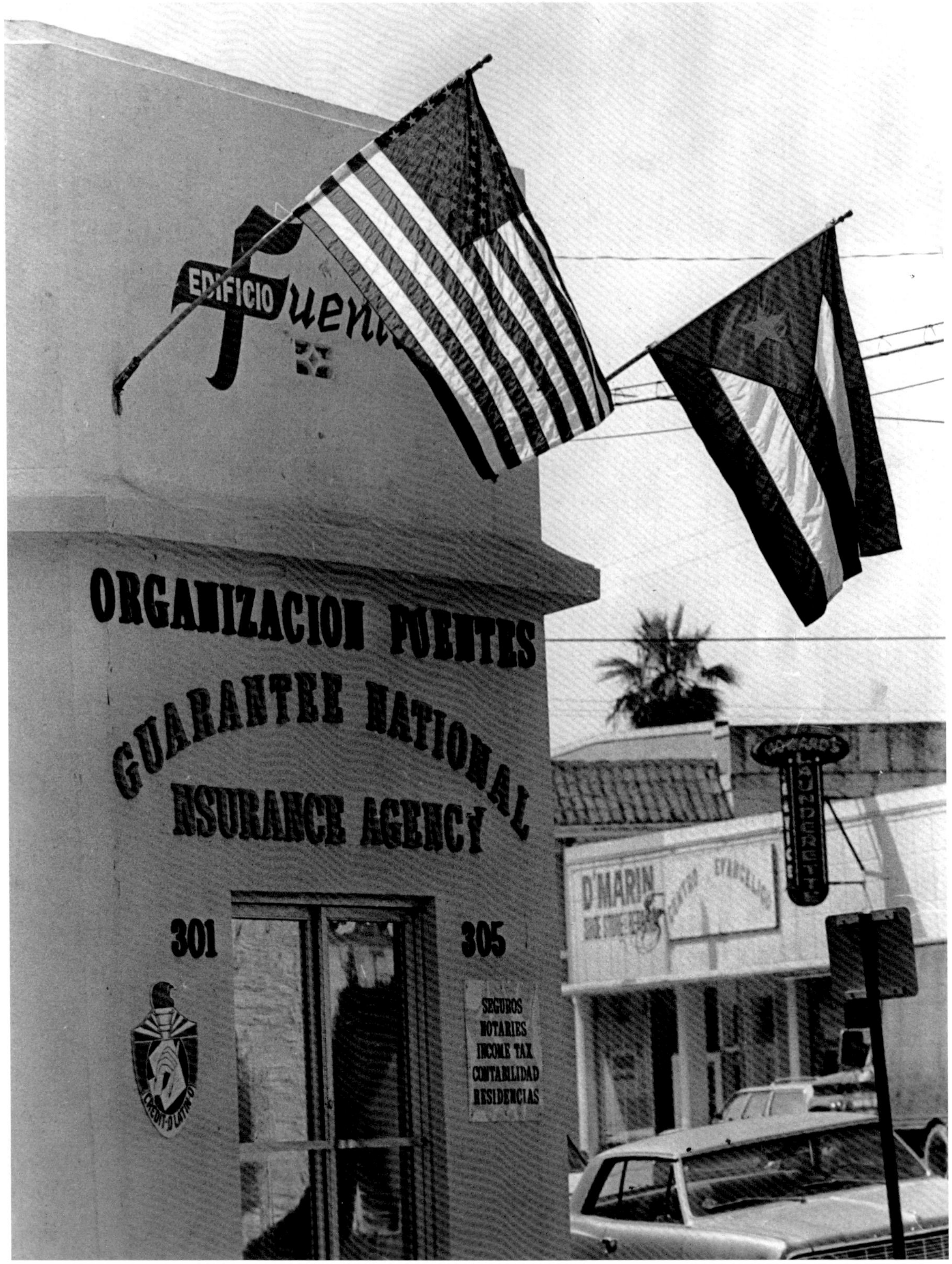

From the Cuban and American flags displayed next to each other to the mixing of Spanish and English in signage, Organización Fuentes Guarantee National Insurance Agency is an example of Cuban exile business in Miami.

The First Wave and Cuban Airlifts (1960–1973)

The rise of Fidel Castro changed Cuba forever and altered the landscape of Miami dramatically. Despite Cuba's rocky political history and frequently exiled leaders, no Cuban coup ever led to a mass exodus from the island as did that of Fidel Castro's revolution. At first, many of the exiles who had been living in New York or Miami prior to 1959 made their way back to Cuba with grand hopes for the new revolution. As Castro's brand of change became evident however, disillusionment set in, and those who could return to the United States did so. Others had to wait until the first airlifts or even later.

The very first Castro exiles were those who immediately recognized his communist ambitions or those who had been persecuted by members of the Revolution. Most of these refugees were well educated. They had been successful in Cuba, and knew how to make money. Many of them—educators, doctors, lawyers, bankers, and entrepreneurs—made their way to Miami. Upon arrival, they got to work at any job they could find. Being ambitious and having enjoyed previous success, most of these exiles moved on to more-rewarding professions. It is because of these Cubans that the old area known as Riverside, which had recently declined, was reincarnated as Little Havana. It is also because of these Cubans that Hialeah, a suburb of Miami, grew to have one of the largest Cuban exile populations in the United States. As their wealth grew, the emigrants moved to areas like Coral Gables, Miami Beach, and Biscayne.

These Cubans, who arrived between 1960 and 1973, are part of what is known as "the First Wave" of Cubans given refuge by the United States as political exiles. They came mainly through the air, on Pan American Airlines. Others made their way by boat, being picked up by the U.S. Coast Guard. Thousands poured into Miami during these years, changing the city and its suburbs.

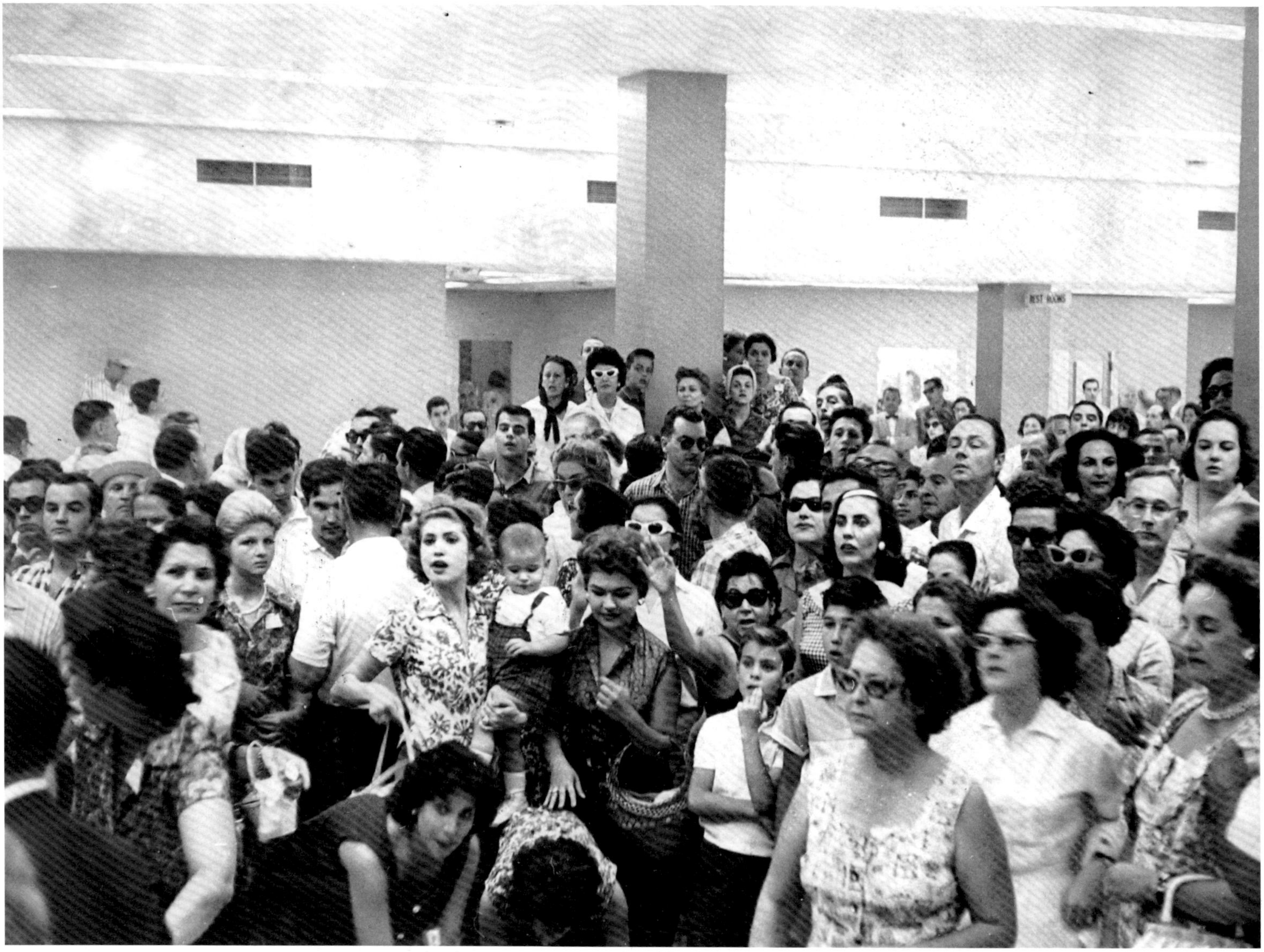

Cuban refugees enter Miami International Airport after an airlift in 1961. In April, President Kennedy would launch a CIA-sponsored covert military operation in a bid to rid Cuba of its new communist regime. Kennedy's perceived indecisiveness and the failure of the operation, known commonly as the Bay of Pigs invasion, would embolden the Soviet Union to arm the island with nuclear warheads a year later, giving rise to the Cuban Missile Crisis in October 1962.

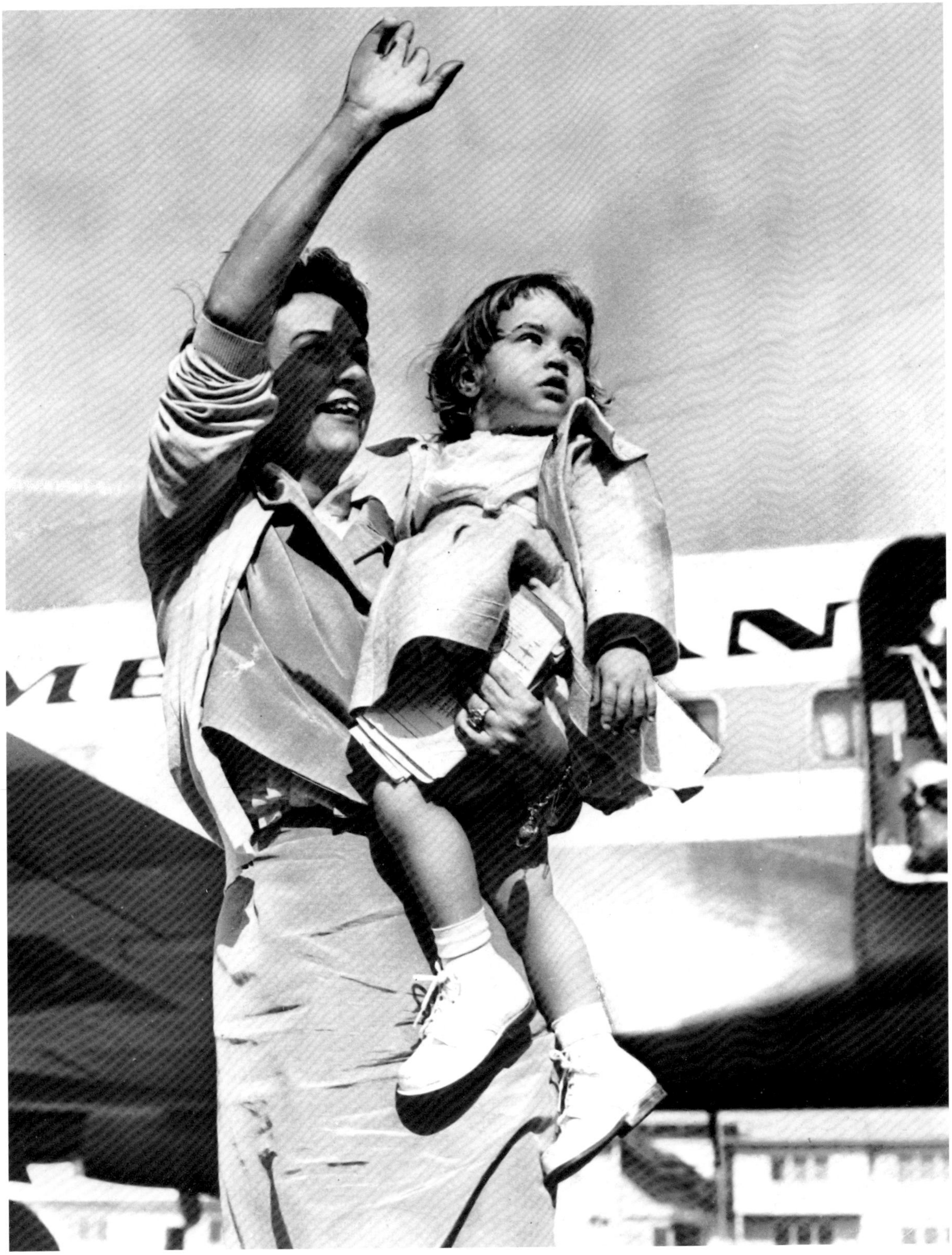

A mother with child waves in recognition after a Pan American flight in 1961. Between 1960 and 1962, more than 14,000 children were sent from Cuba to Miami in a program called Operation Pedro Pan. Pedro Pan was coordinated by the CIA and the Archdiocese of Miami. Eventually, the program allowed parents to come with their children, but many children were sent alone by parents who feared their children would be taken from them by the Cuban government.

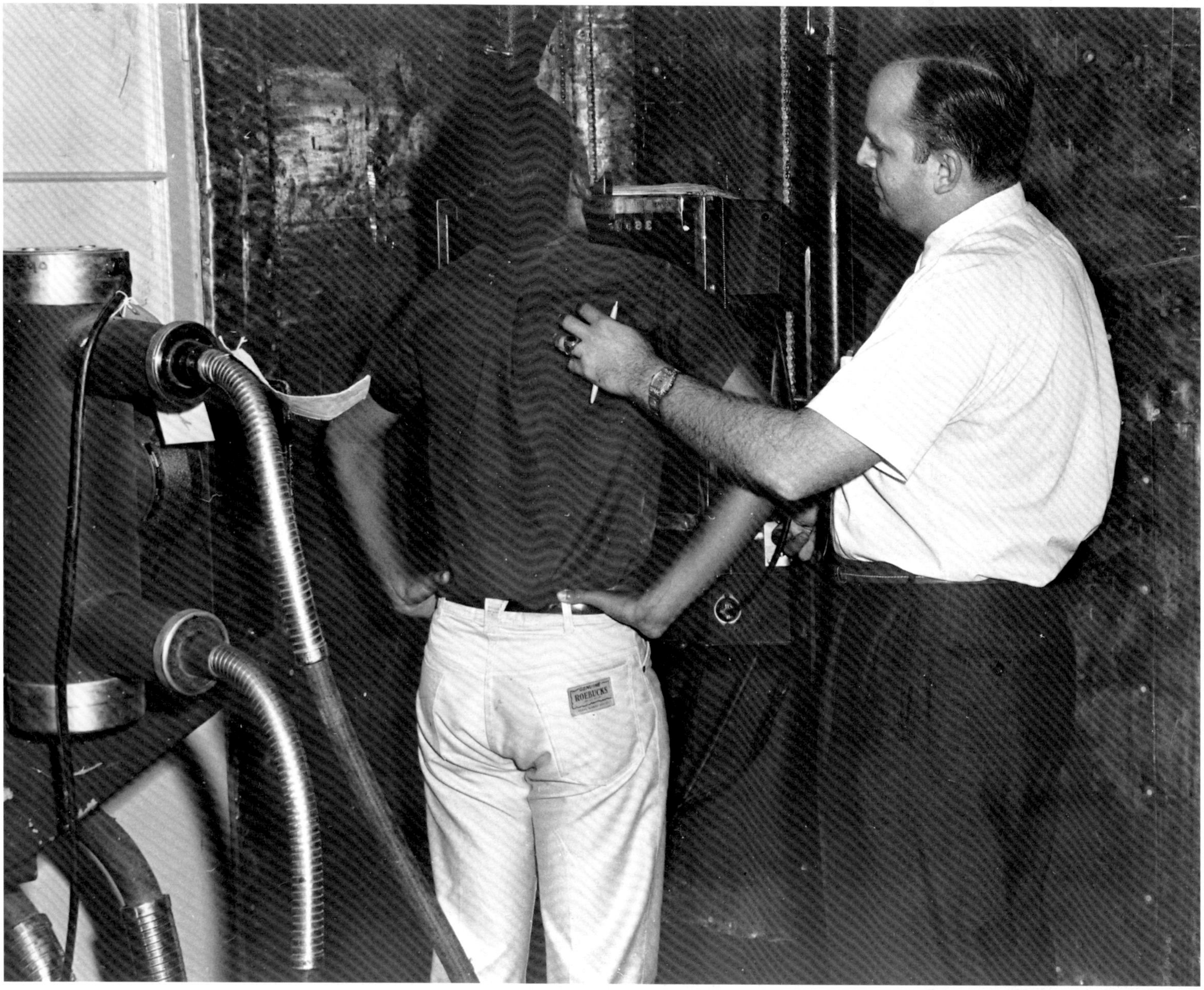

X-rays were standard procedure for processing Cuban refugees accepted into the United States.

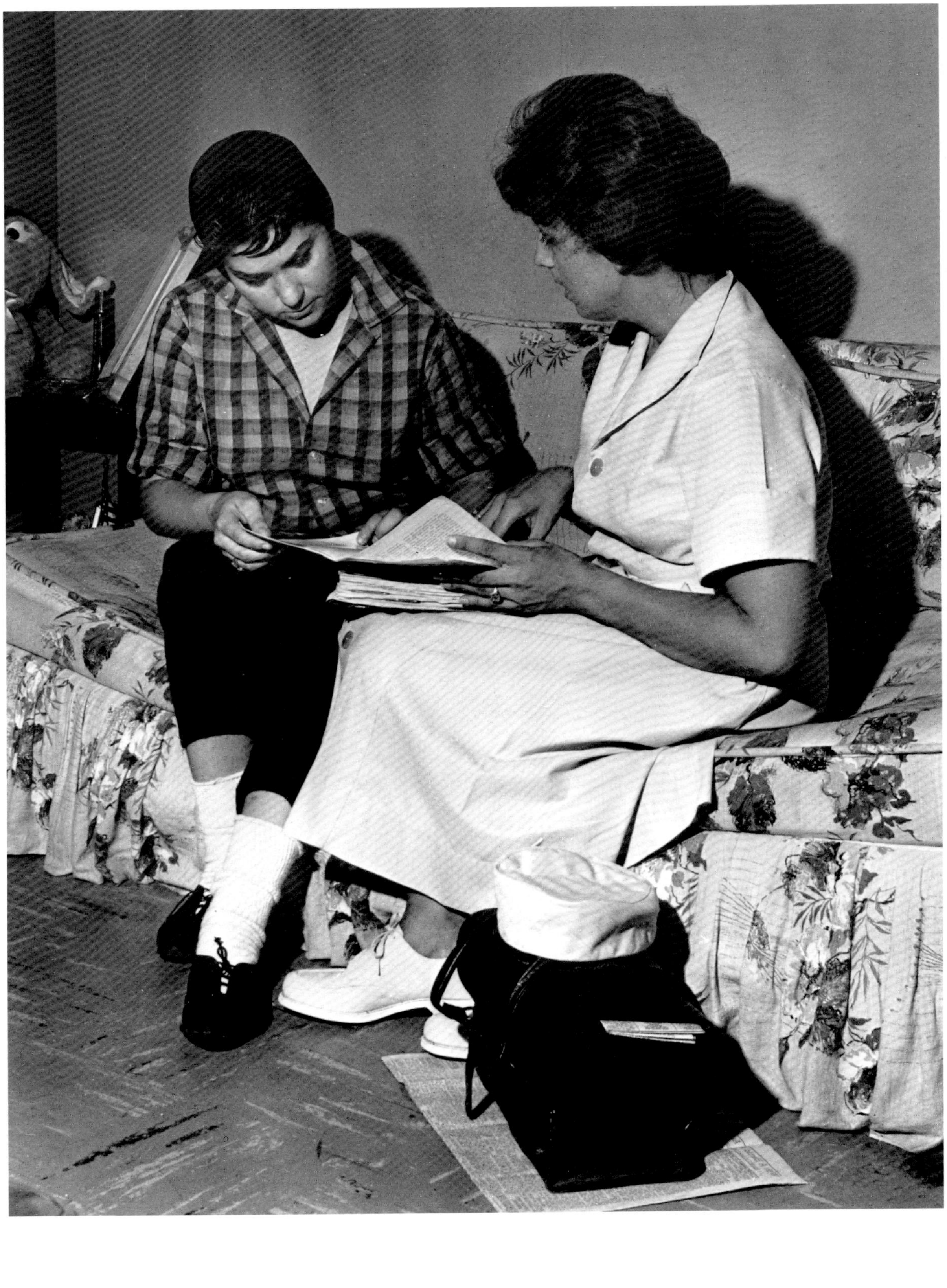

With the sudden influx of Spanish-speaking Cubans in Miami, Spanish-speaking medical professionals were increasingly called upon. In this image, a young Cuban woman is visited at home by a Spanish-speaking nurse around 1960.

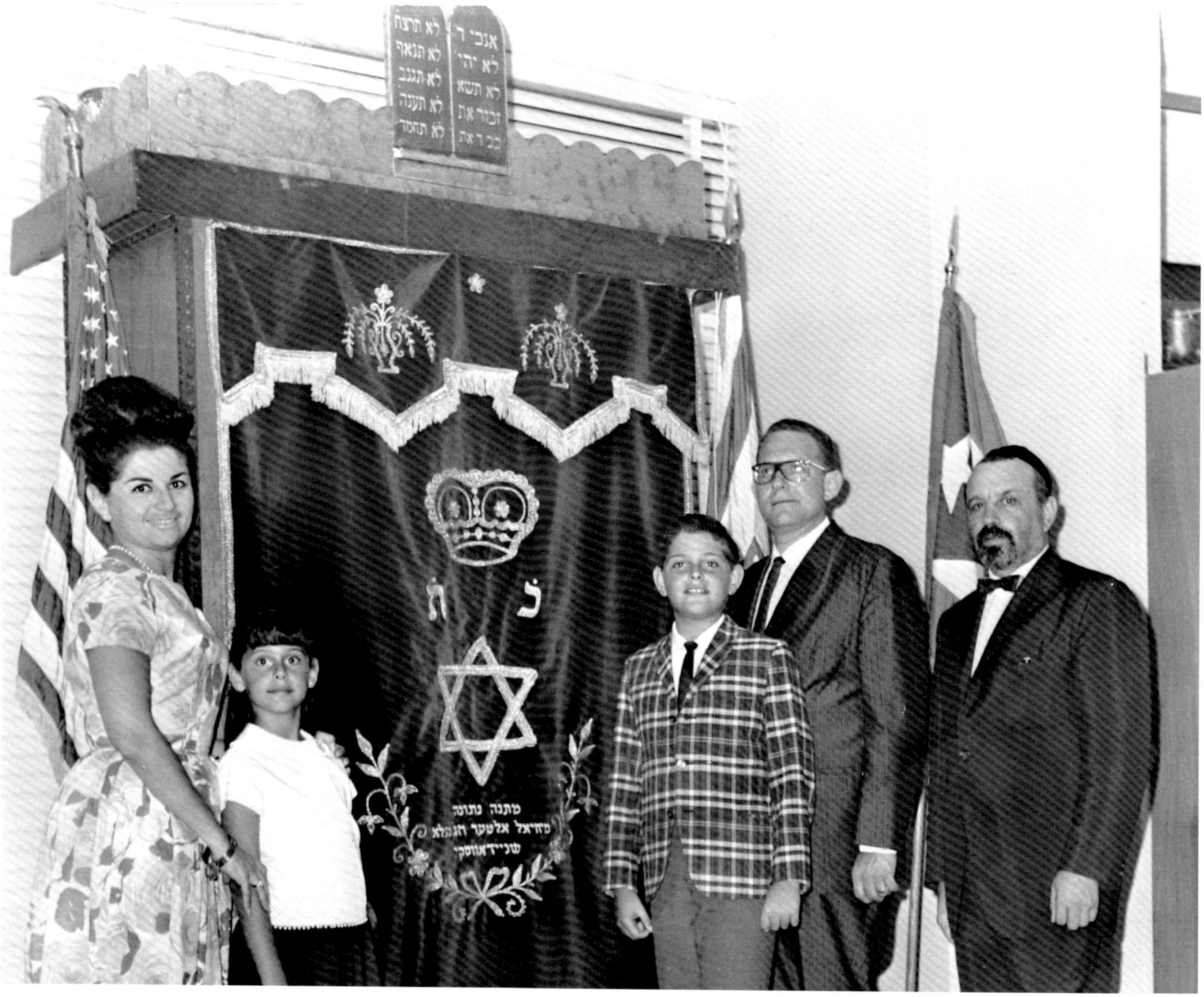

The Schiadoski family and Rabbi Dow Rozencwaig pose for the camera at the Temple Beth Shmuel Cuban Hebrew Congregation of Miami's dedication of the ark curtain.

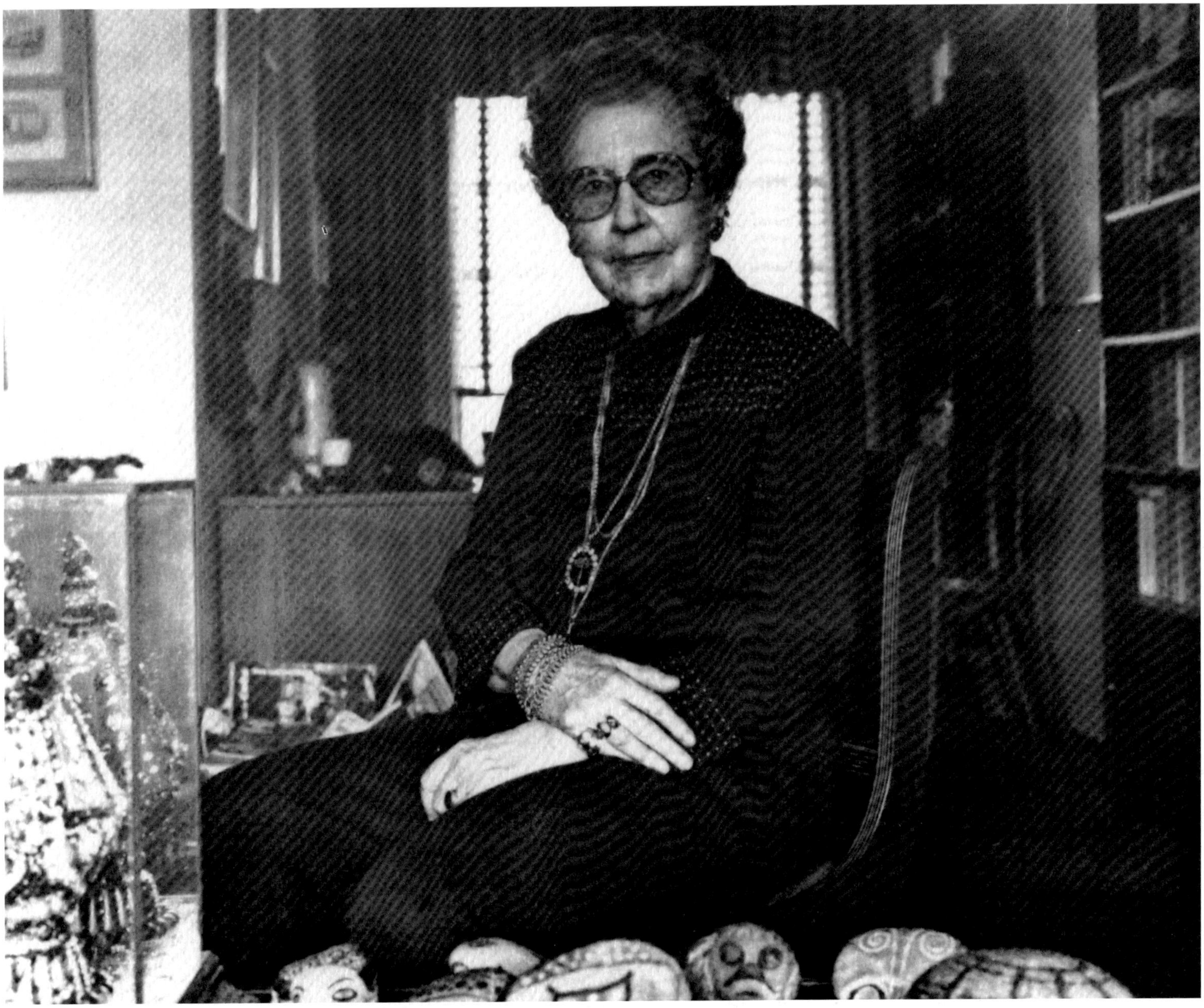

Lydia Cabrera, poet and author of hundreds of books, poses for a portrait around 1960 in Miami. Cabrera was a famous ethnologist and anthropologist and considered a leading authority on Afro-Cuban culture and religion, especially Santeria.

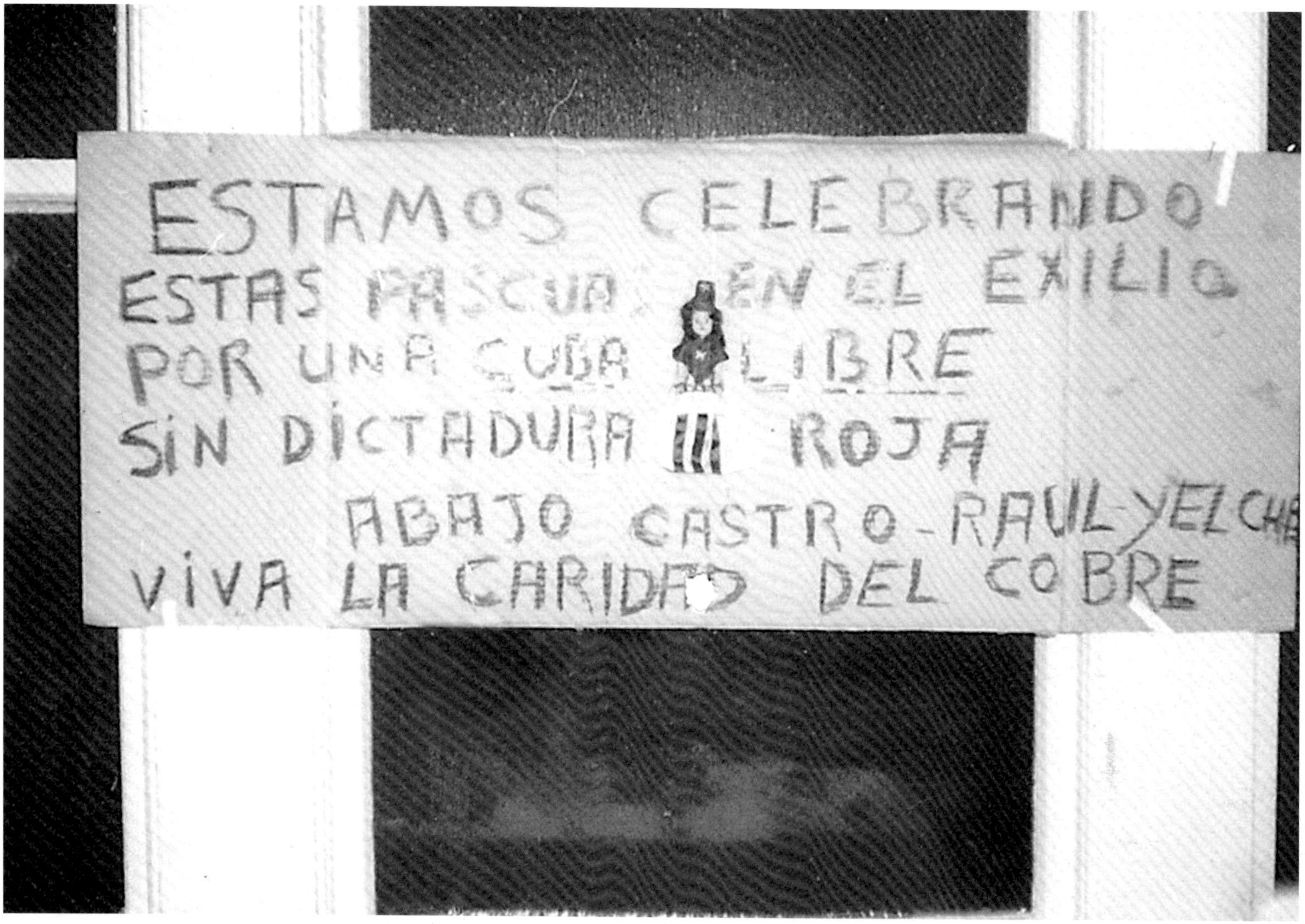

Translation: "We are celebrating this Christmas in exile. To a free Cuba, without a red dictator. Down with Castro, Raul, and Che. Long live La Caridad del Cobre." (Caridad del Cobre is the patron saint of Cuba.)

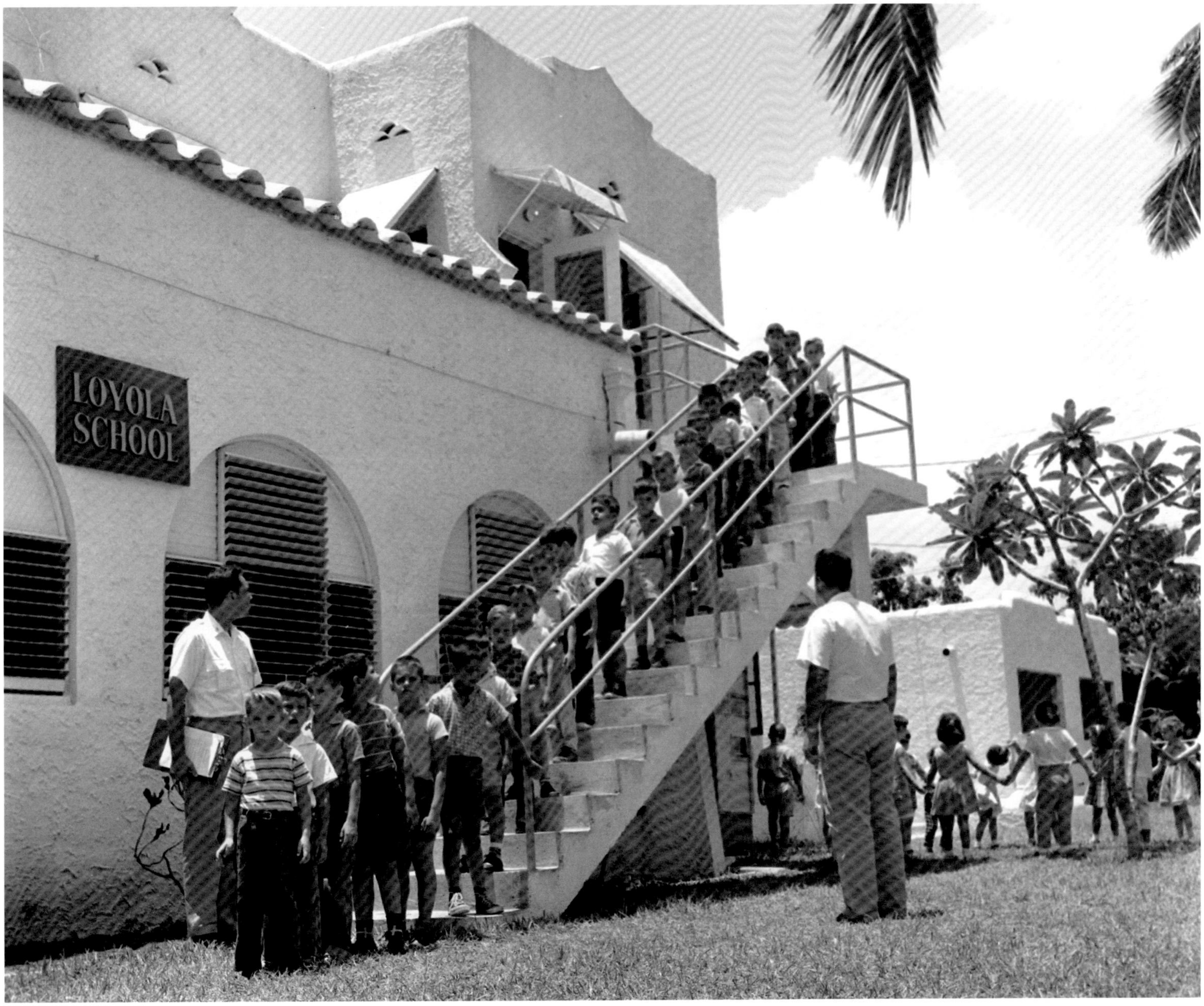

The Loyola School for Refugees, located at 904 SW 23rd Avenue in 1961, is now one of the Lincoln-Martí schools.

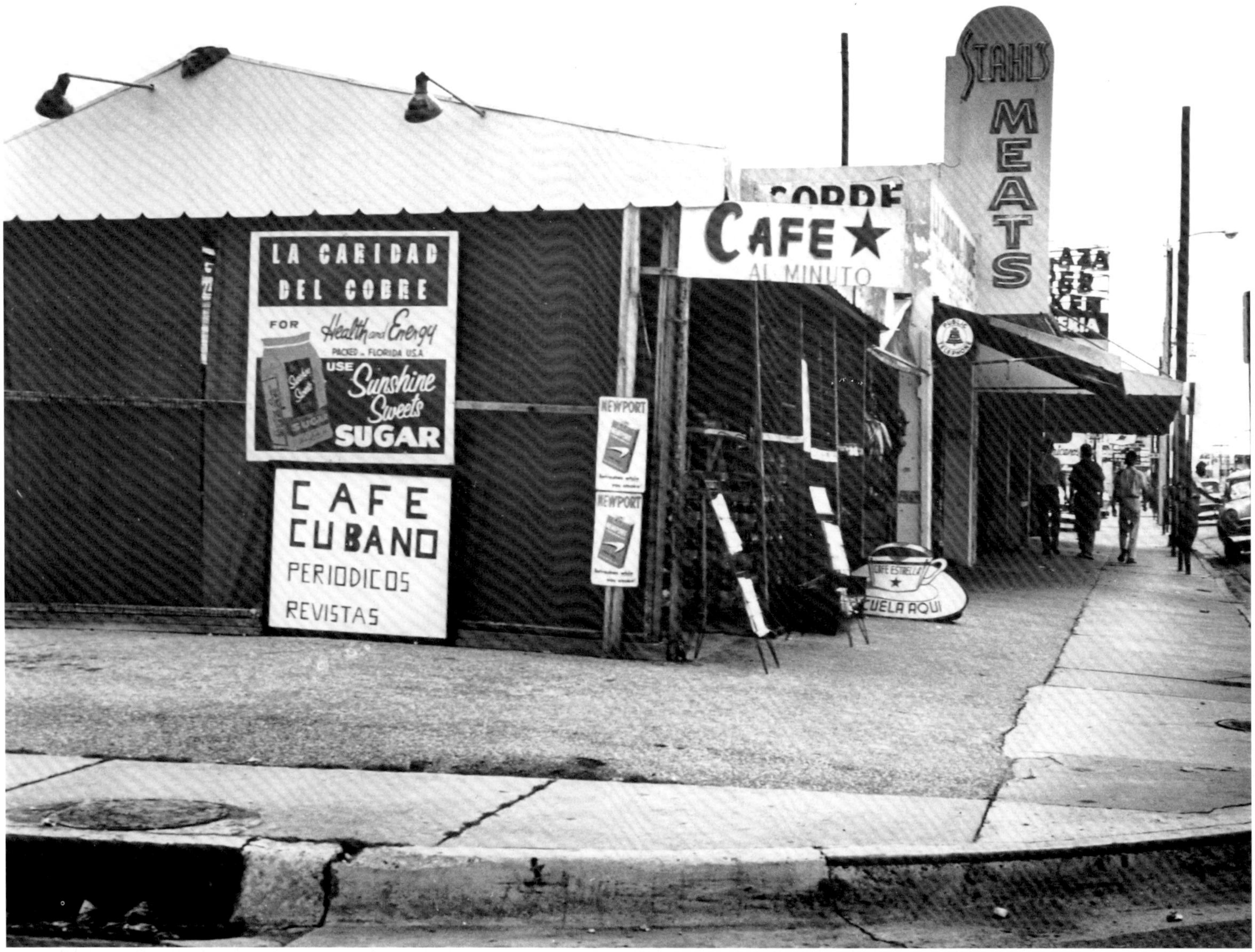

Cafe al Minuto, a tiny corner cafe and shop in Little Havana. This photograph was taken in 1961, before the first freedom flights and only two years after Castro's takeover. It is clear that the Cuban community was already hard at work in Little Havana.

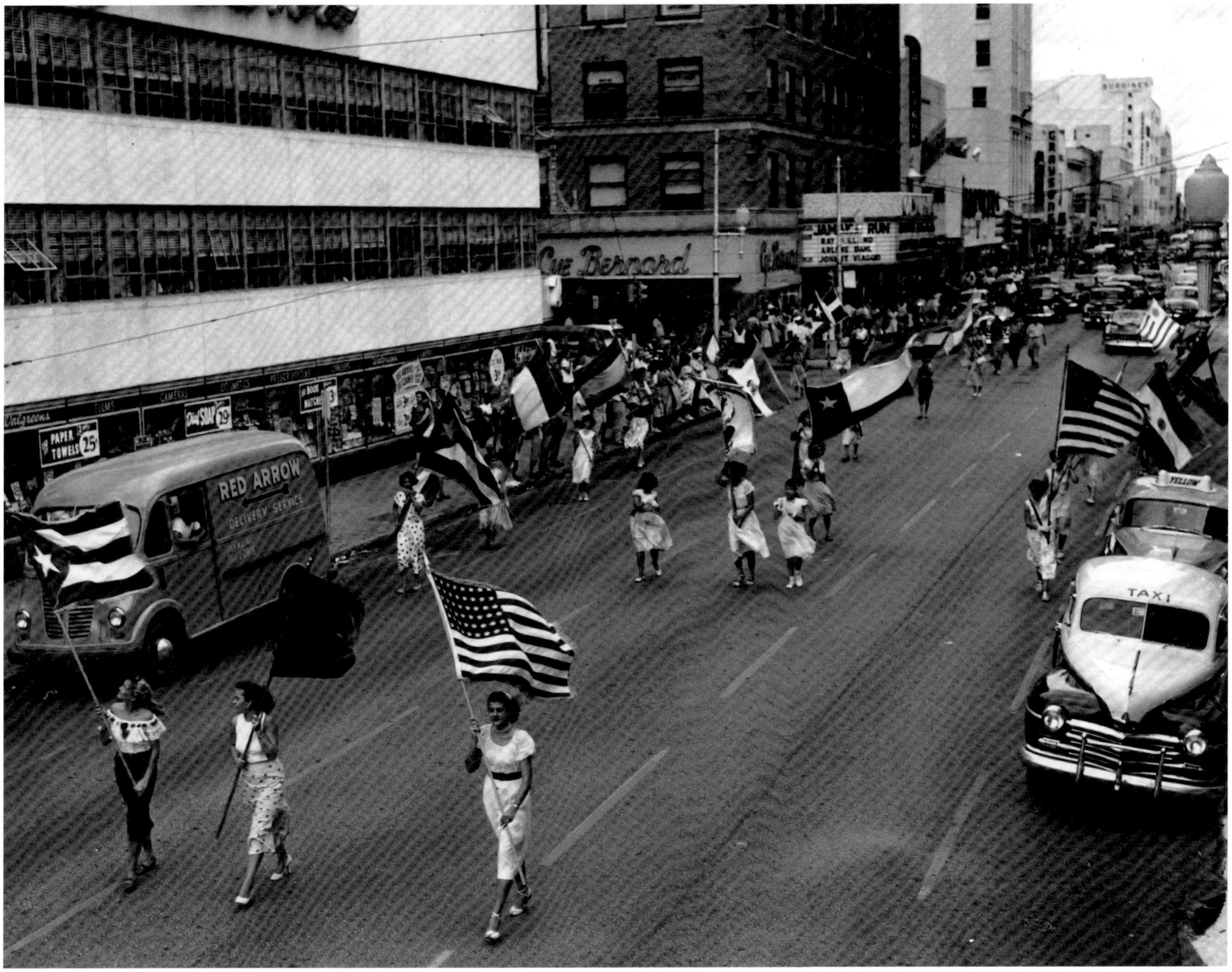

Cuban women bearing the Cuban and American flags lead a parade down Flagler Street that includes the flags of various Latin American nations, carried by other women and children.

Abel Holtz has been an active member of the community in Miami but has seen trouble as well. Holtz founded Capital Bank and enjoyed a successful career serving on its board before being convicted of misleading a grand jury and bribing a government official.

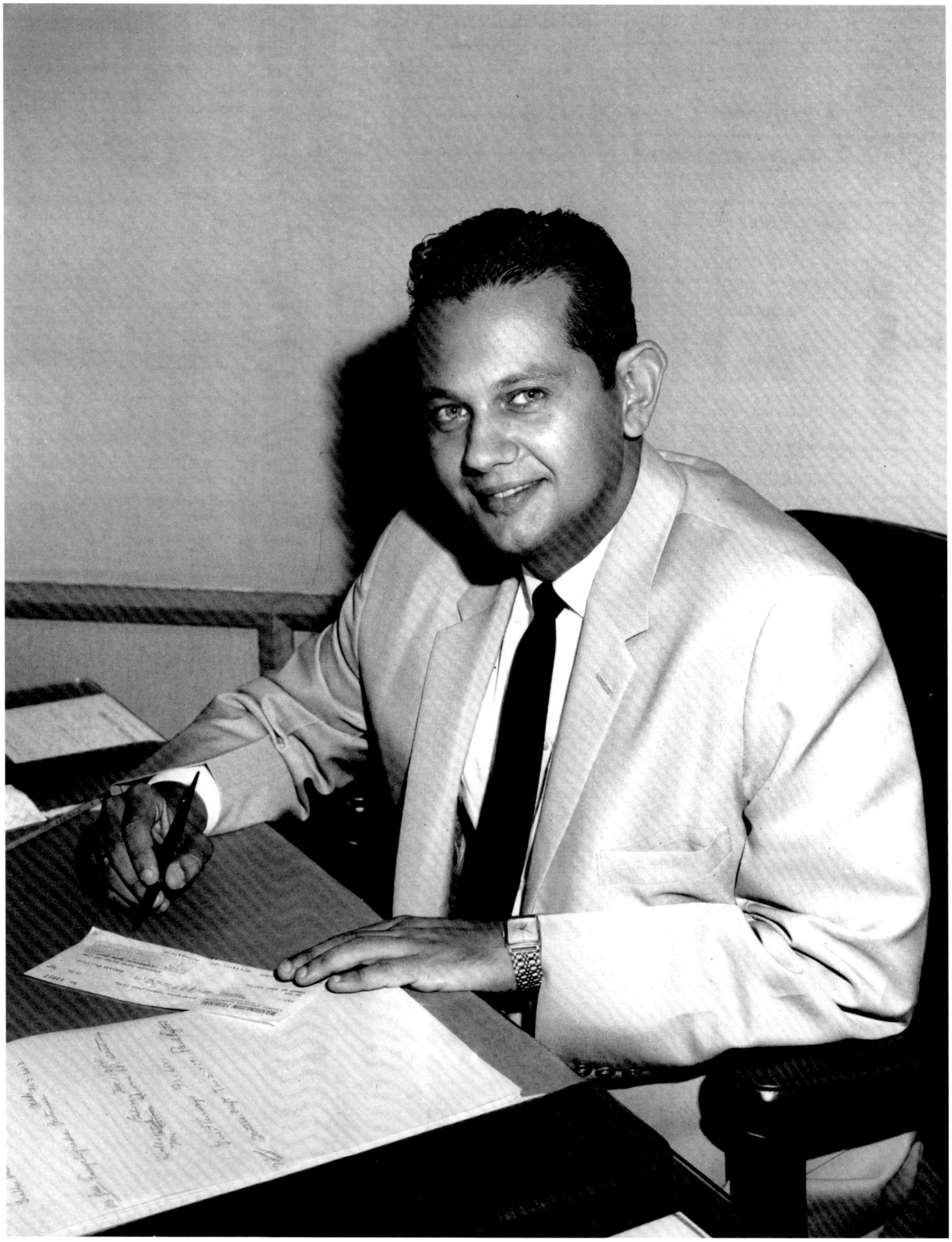

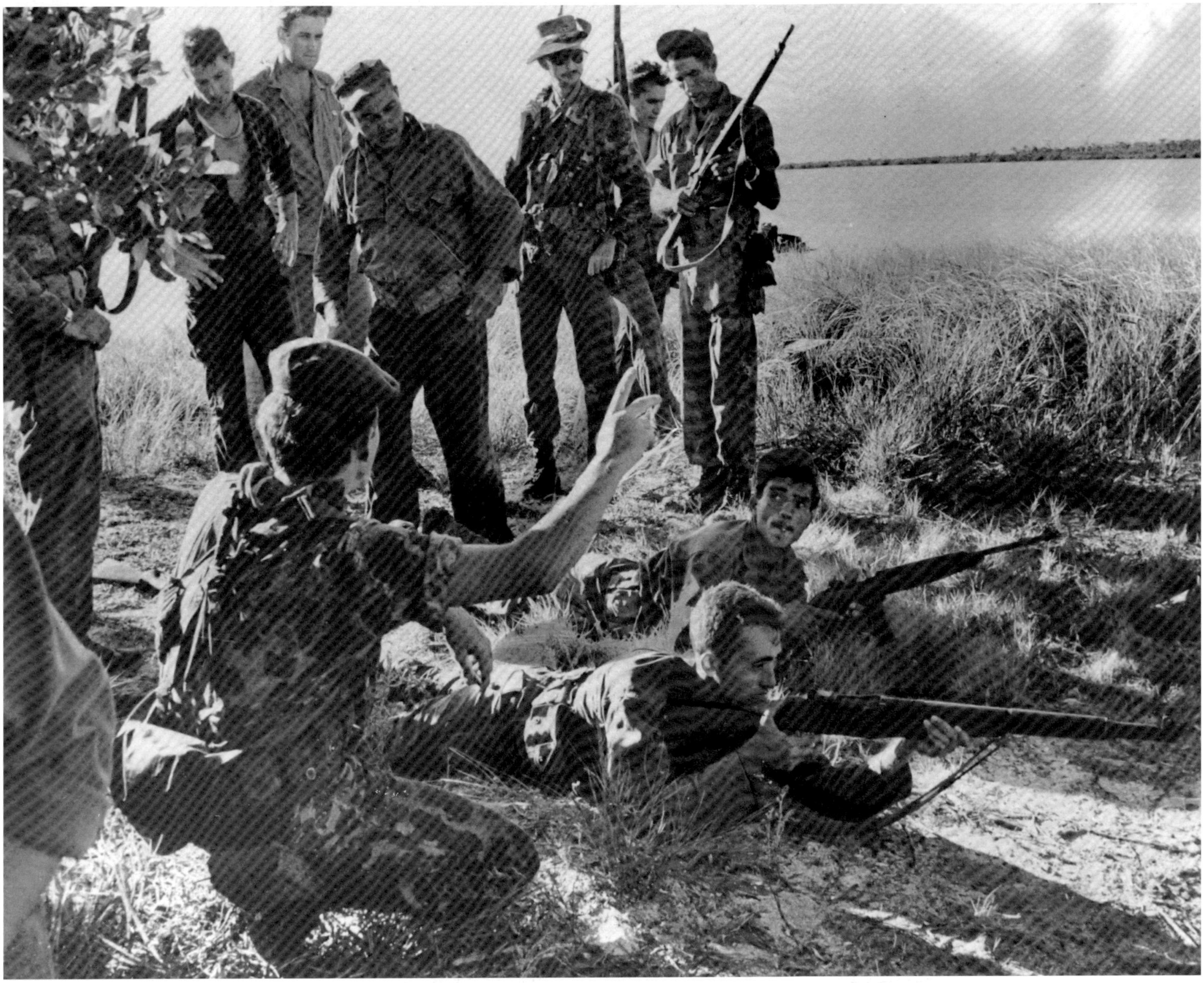

Alpha 66 trains in the Everglades in the 1960s. The paramilitary group was originally formed by 66 exiles in Puerto Rico, with the goal of armed invasion against communist Cuba. With the debacle at the Bay of Pigs, no invasion ultimately took place. Trainees work with rifles in this exercise.

The Centro Vasco Restaurant, located on SW 8th Street, serves a fusion of Cuban-Basque cuisine. Vasco was relocated from Havana to South Florida in 1962, just like its patrons.

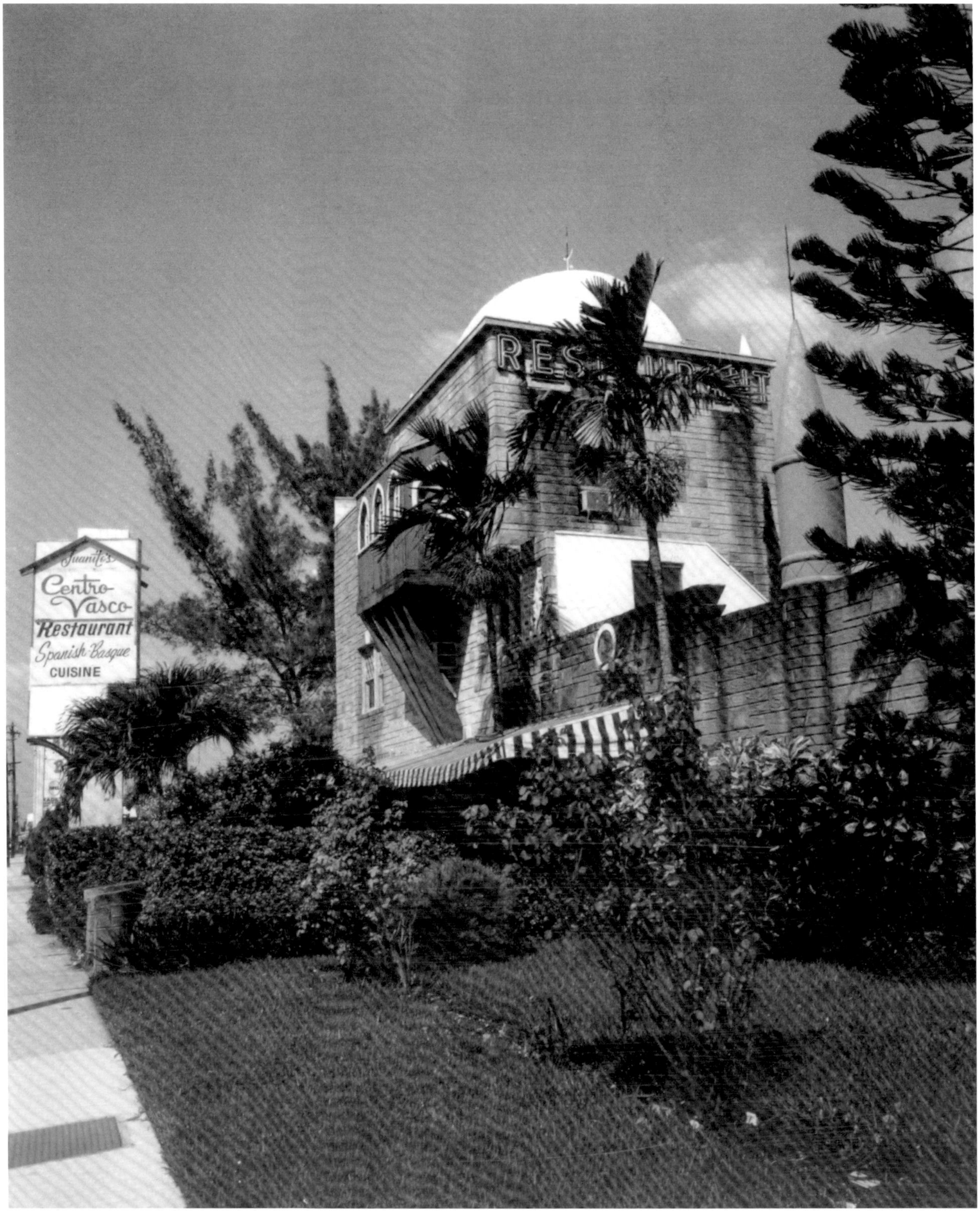

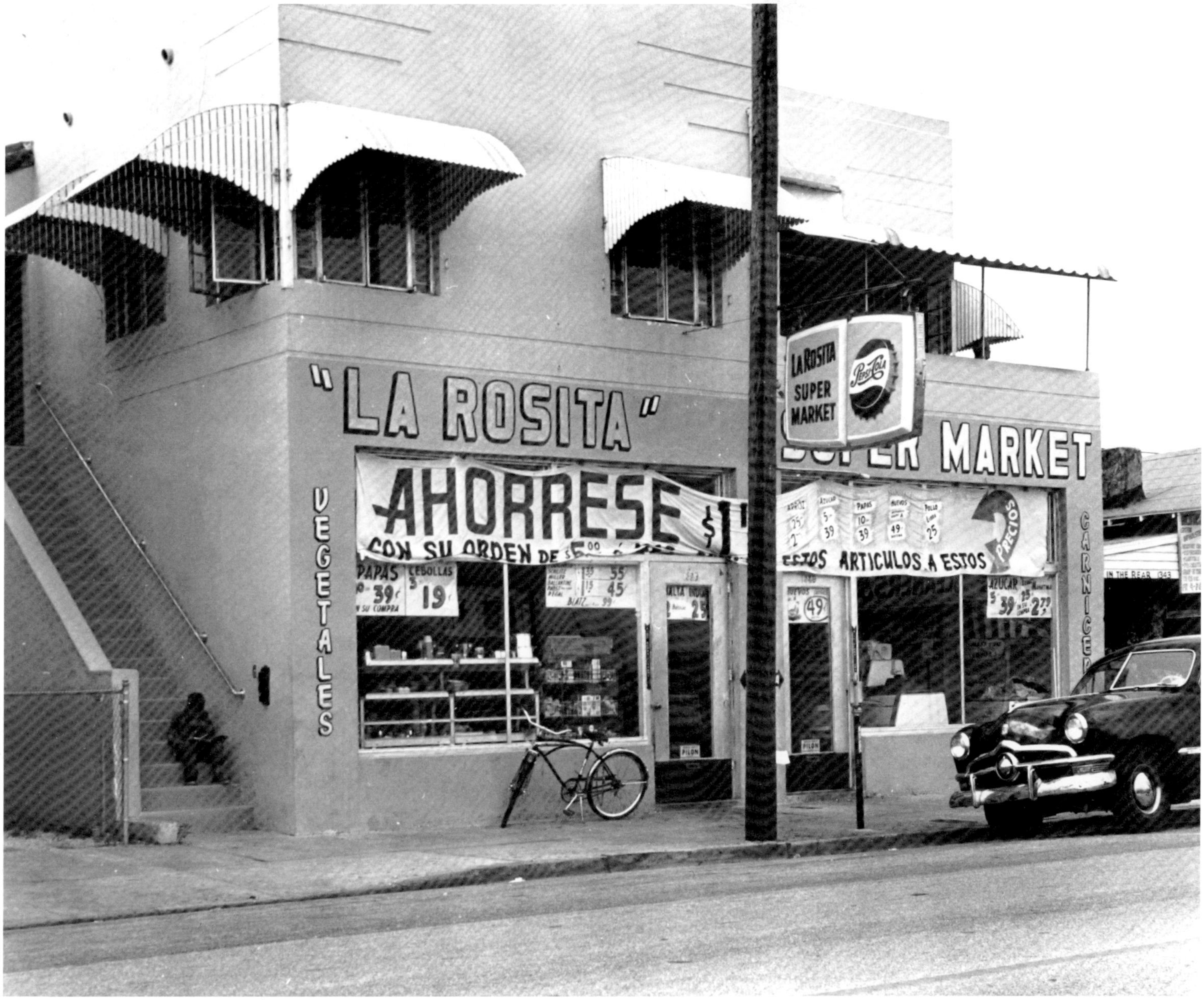

Many small Cuban "supermarkets" opened up throughout Little Havana and Miami's surrounding areas serving the tastes and needs of the Cuban population. The typical Cuban diet is very different from that of most Americans, creating a need for stores familiar with Cuban tastes. The most successful Cuban supermarket is Sedanos, which opened first in Little Havana and spread throughout the rest of what is now Miami-Dade County in the next 50 years.

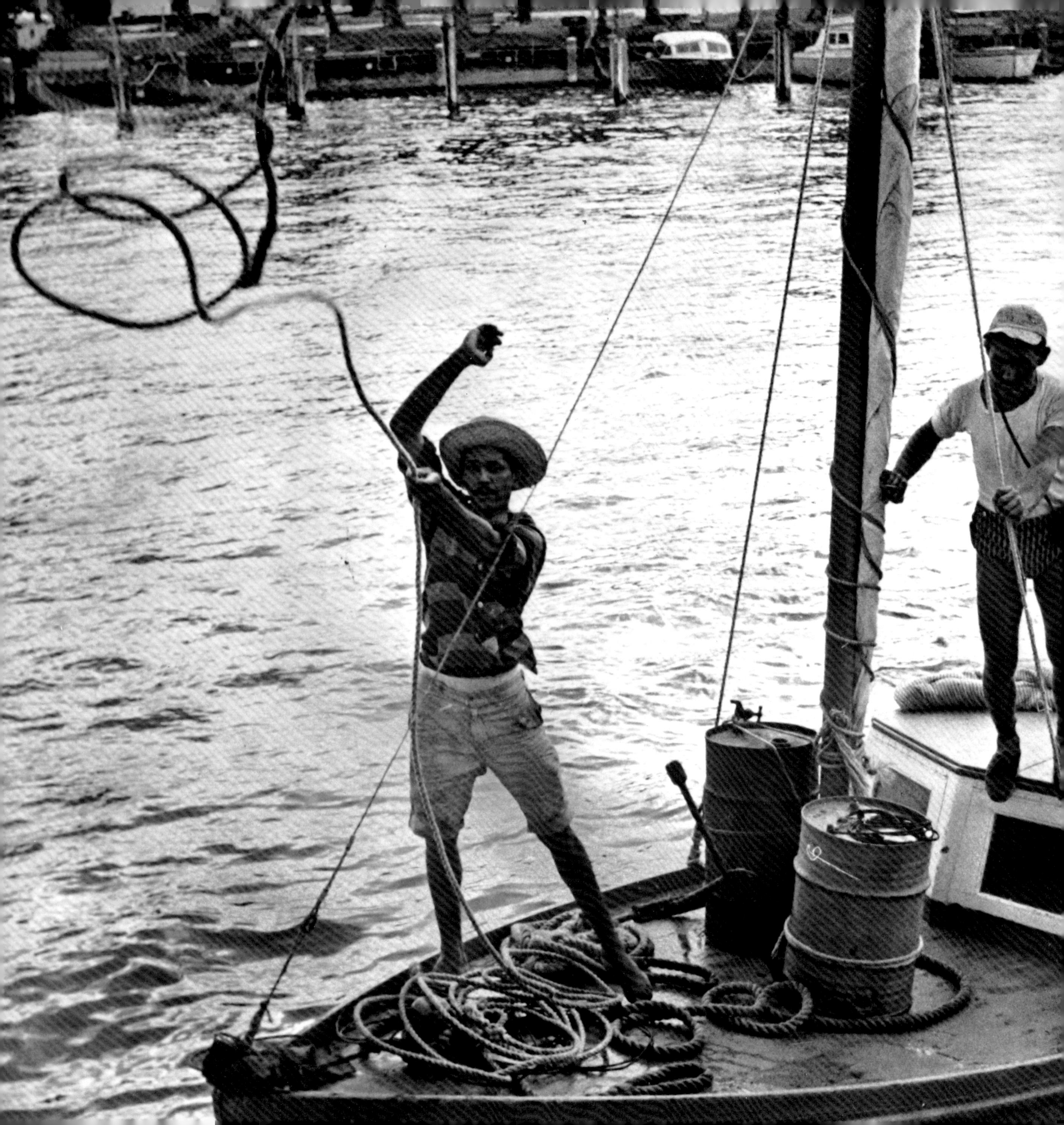

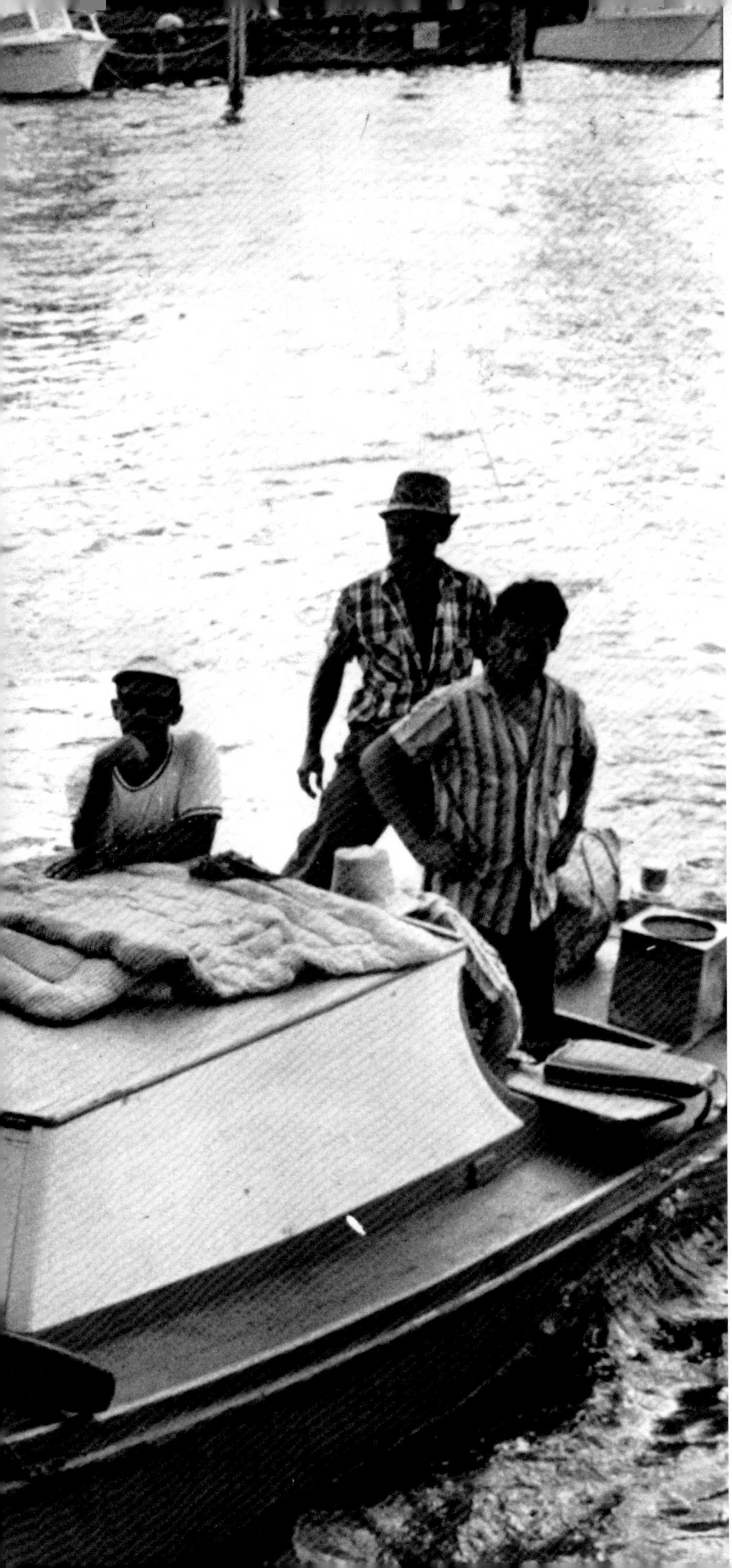

Five Cuban refugees arrive in Miami by boat in 1962.

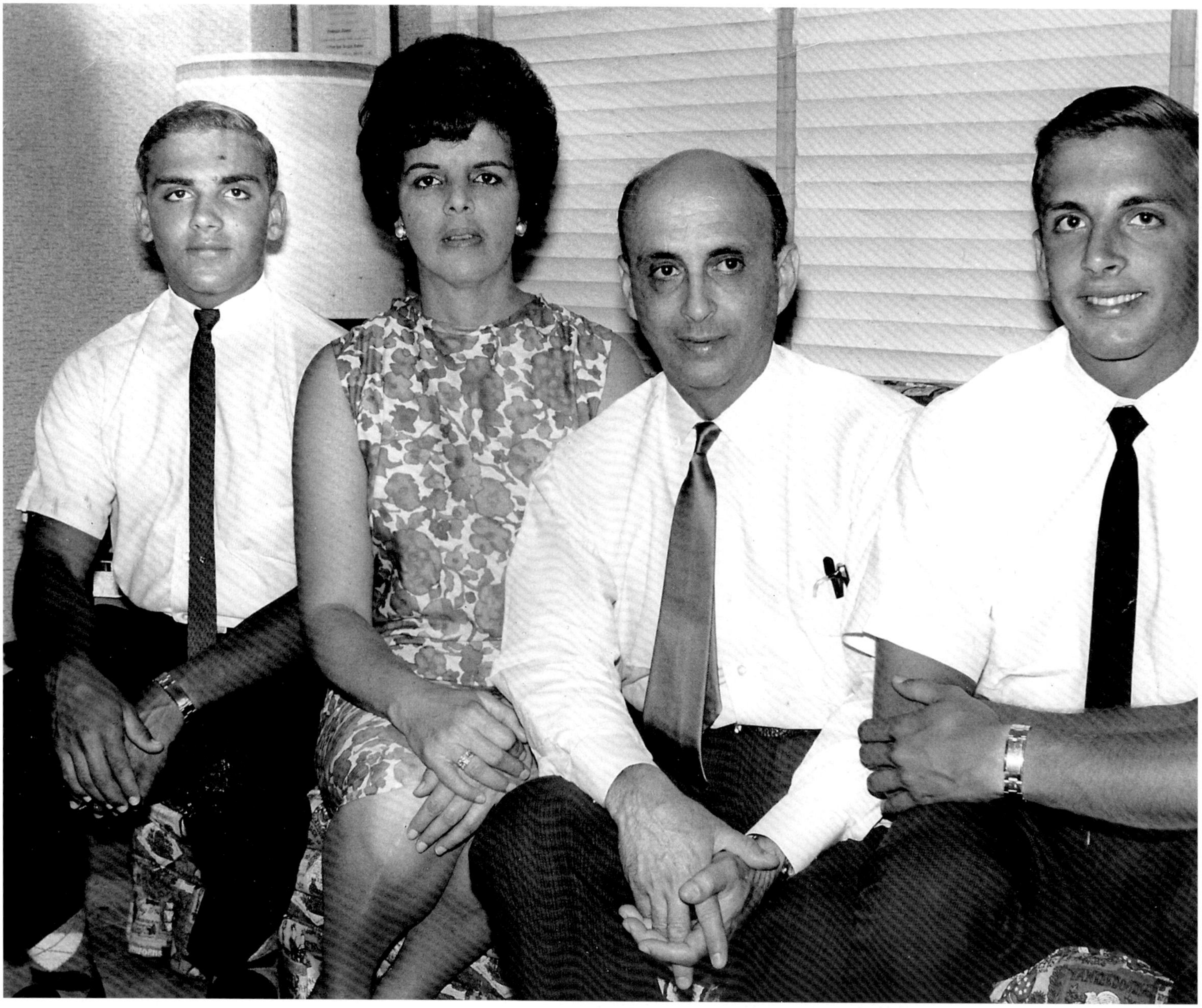

Dr. Cuervo Castillo and family are interviewed in Little Havana in 1964. Cuervo Sr. had served as chief of military medical services in Cuba. Having prior knowledge of the Bay of Pigs Invasion, Cuervo Sr. removed his son from Cuba's naval academy. Failing to leave Cuba, Cuervo Sr. and his two sons were considered deserters and went into hiding separately. Cuervo Sr. was smuggled into the German and Dutch embassies before receiving asylum by the Panamanian embassy.

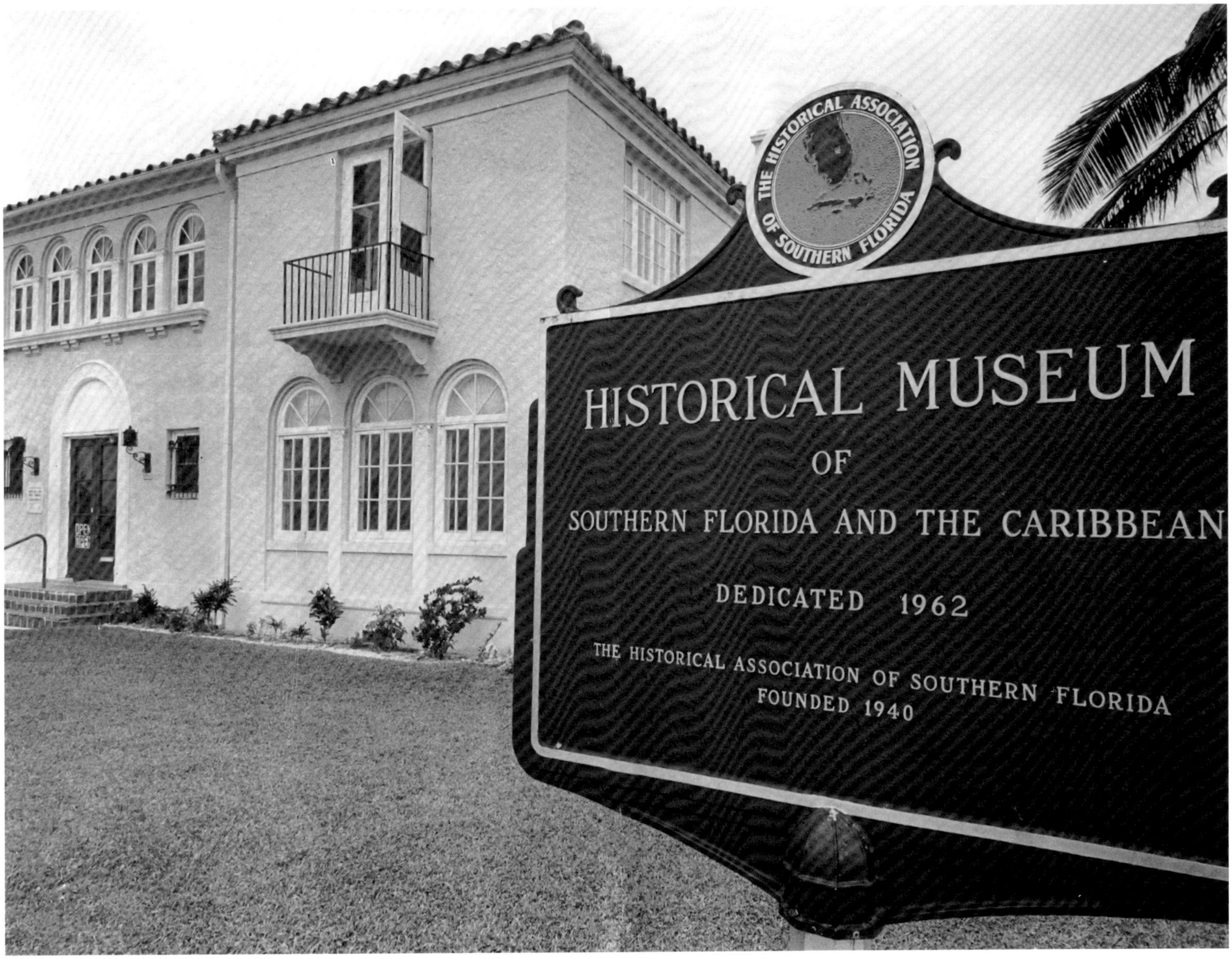

The Historical Museum of Southern Florida was dedicated in 1962. It houses one of the largest photographic archives containing photos of Cuban-Americans in Miami. The museum is currently located in downtown Miami off of Flagler.

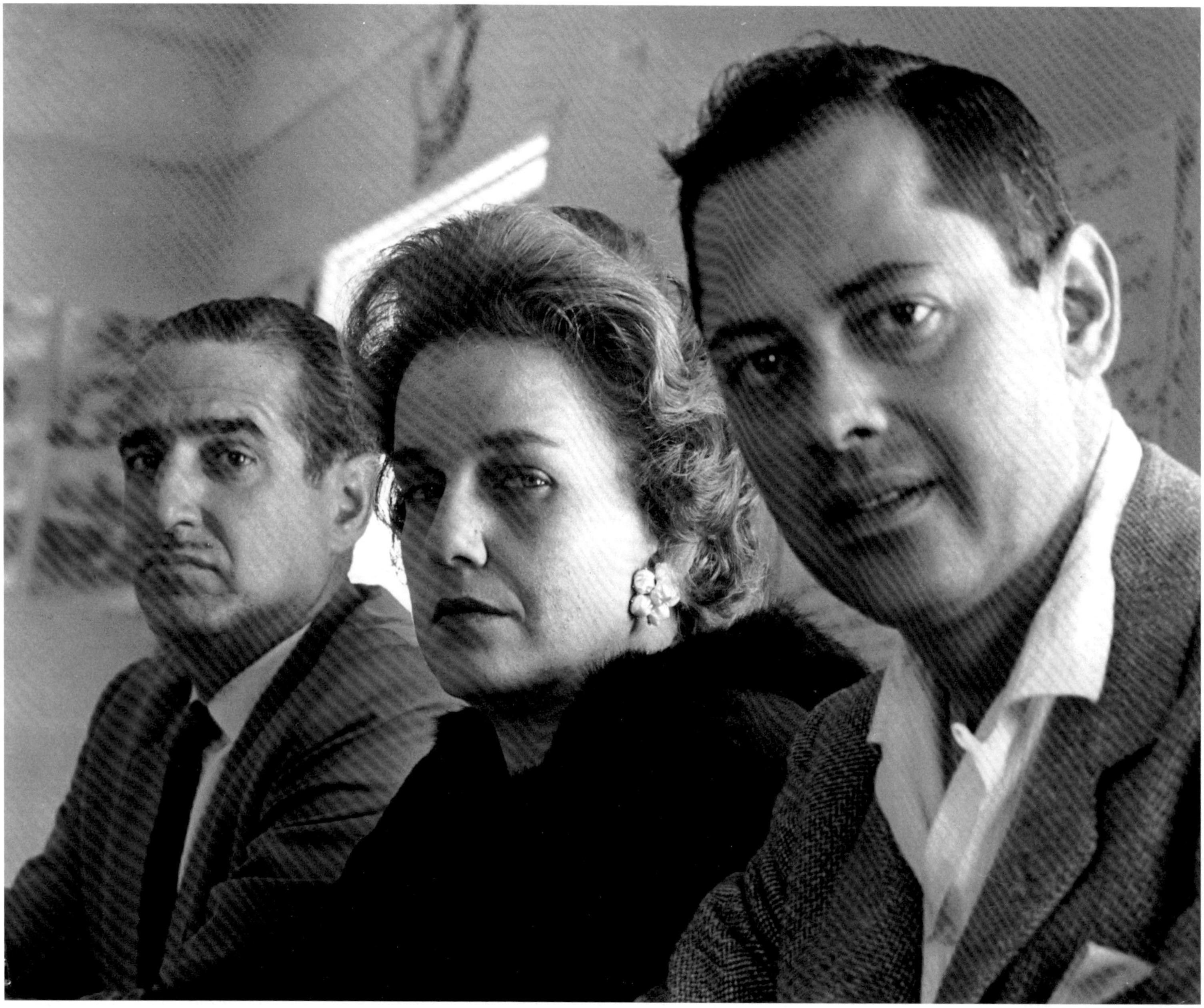

Gerardo Abascal, Isabil Beguer De Leon, and Justavo Garcia Montes graduate from democracy training to educate exiles. To many exiles, the democratic process was foreign and intimidating. These trainees were meant to help those confused and to teach the children, who had little knowledge of democracy.

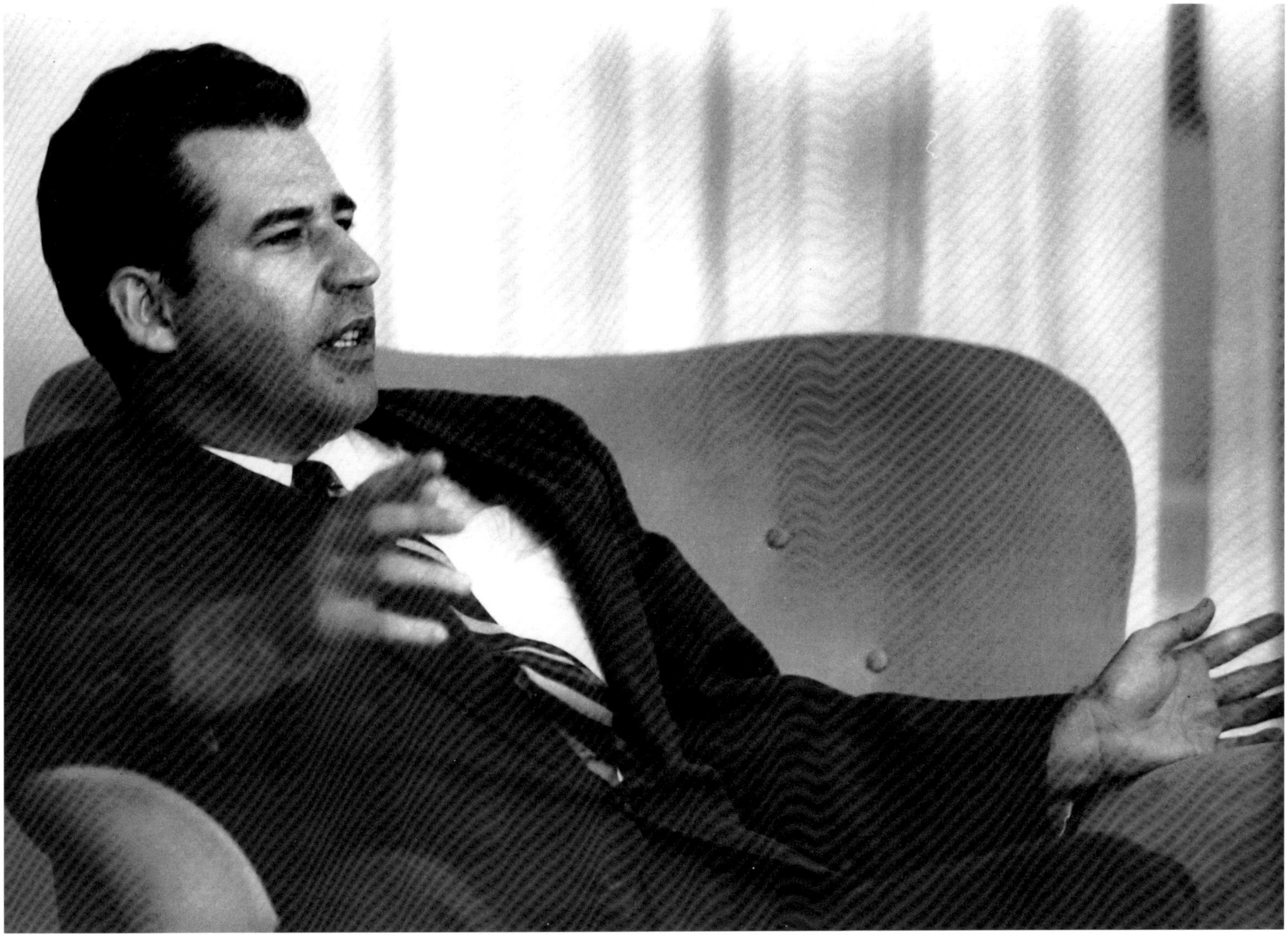

Jose Aleman, Jr., owner of the Miami Stadium, engages in conversation in 1962. Aleman's family fled to the United States after it was discovered that Aleman's father sponsored an army to take over the Dominican Republic. That army included Fidel Castro. Aleman Jr. backed the attack on Cuba's presidential palace against Batista, but Castro later confiscated Aleman's assets. Aleman took his own life and that of several relatives in 1983. The stadium bequeathed to him by his dying father in 1949 was razed in 2001.

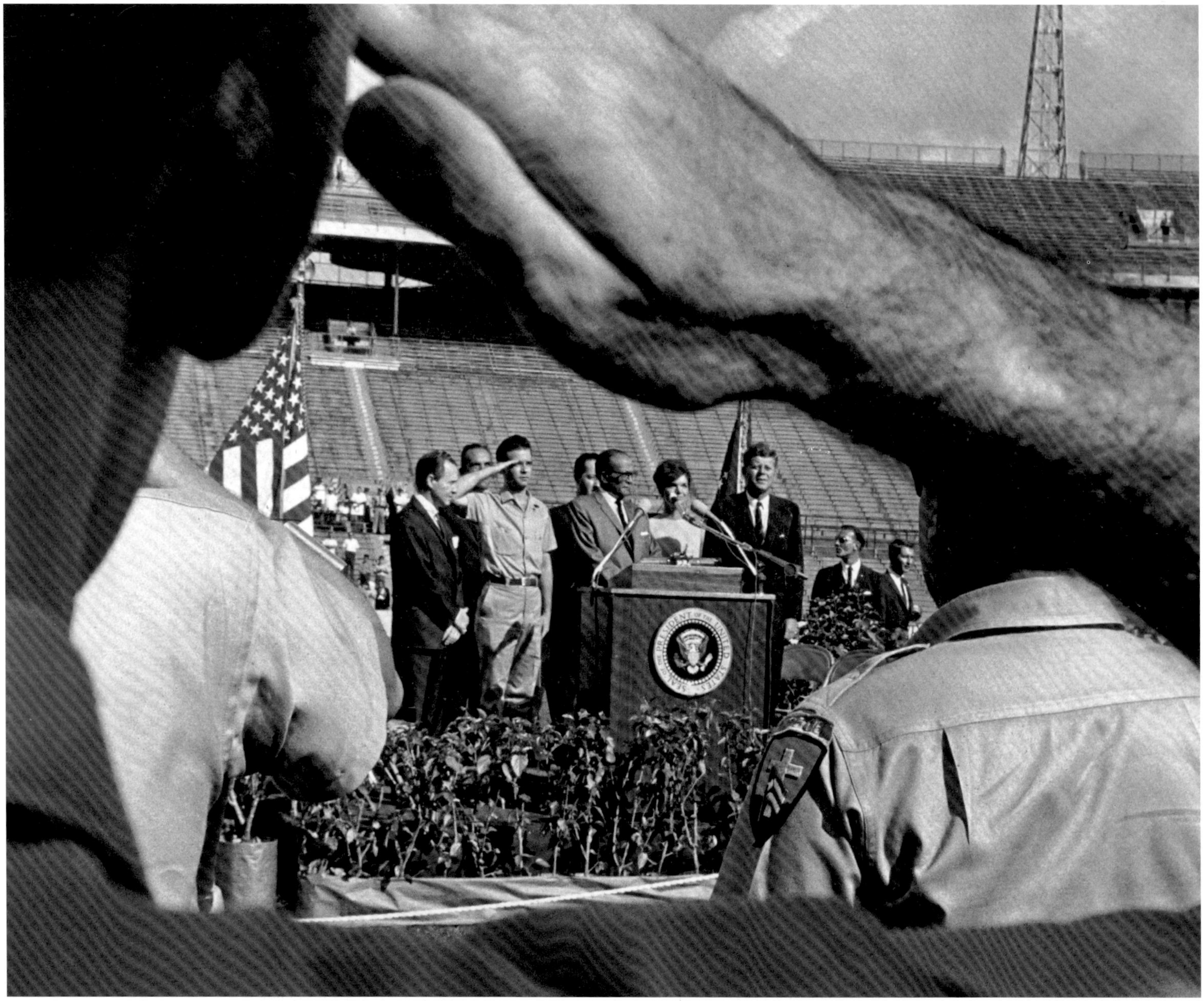

President John F. Kennedy with First Lady Jackie at the Orange Bowl on December 29, 1962, officiates at a ceremony honoring those returning from the Bay of Pigs mission.

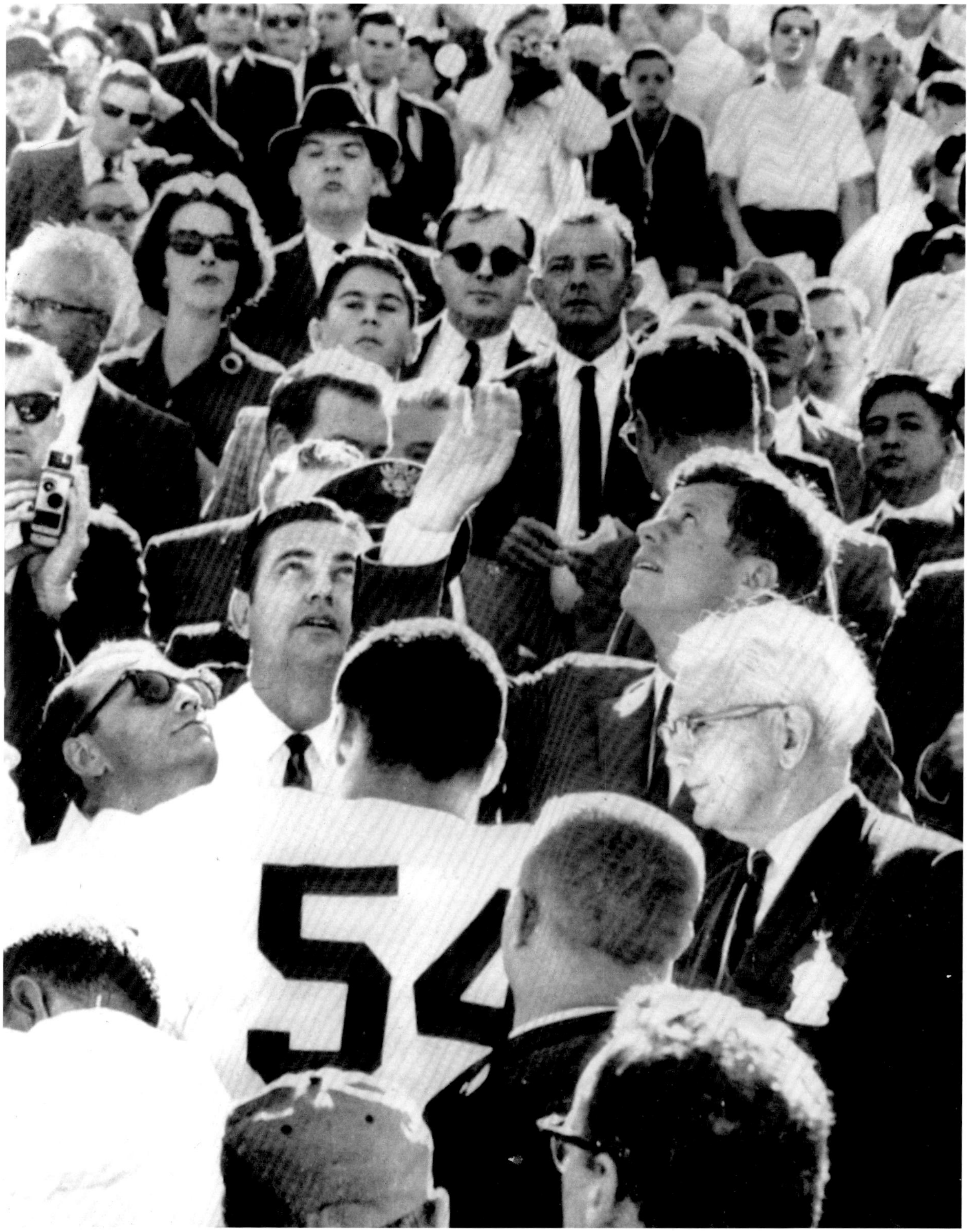

President Kennedy tosses a coin to start the Orange Bowl on January 1, 1963, only months after the Cuban Missile Crisis and days after honoring the returning heroes of the failed Bay of Pigs mission in the very same stadium.

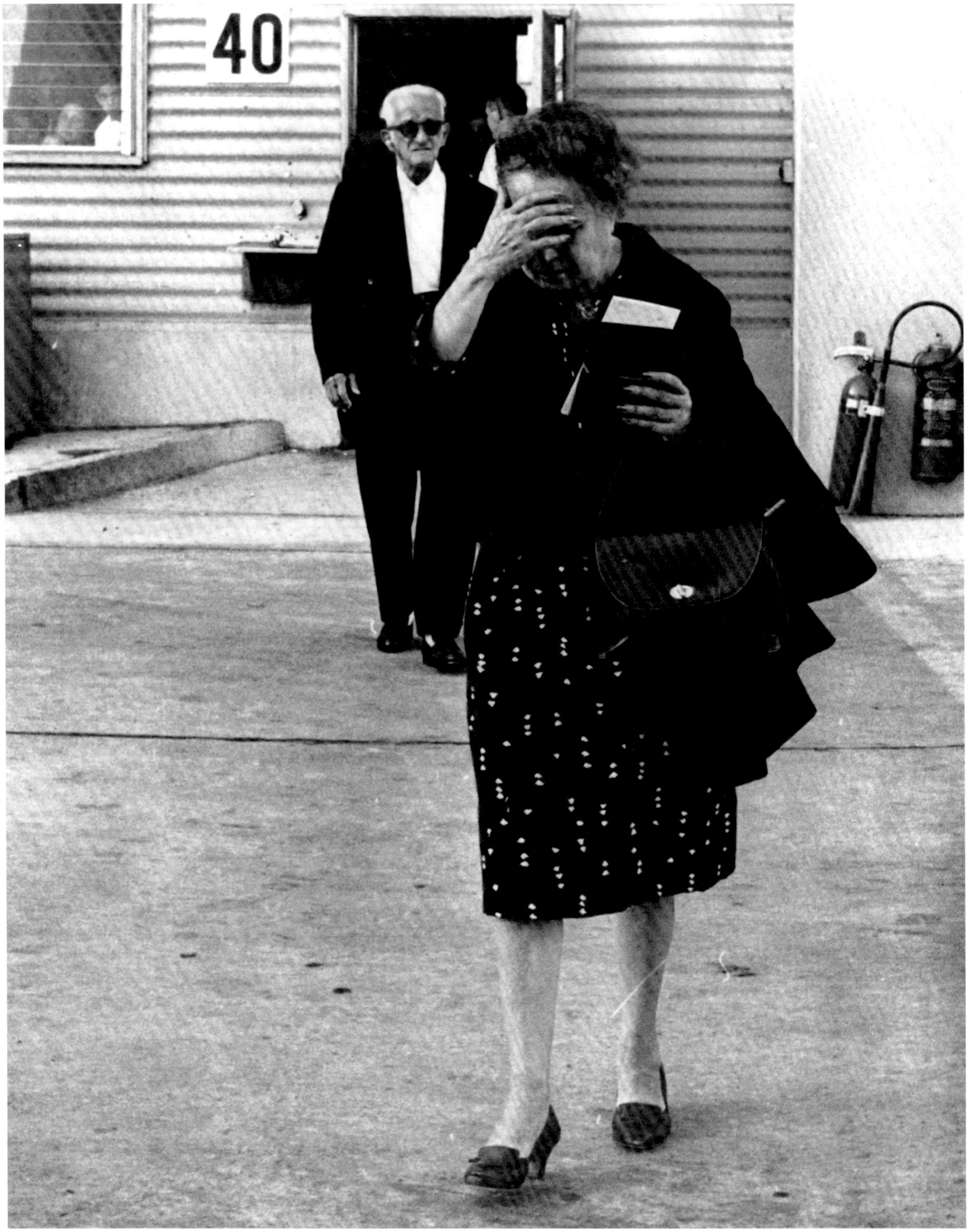

Despite years of political turmoil and violence, leaving their beloved Cuba was a heartbreaking moment for many exiles, even those fleeing for their lives.

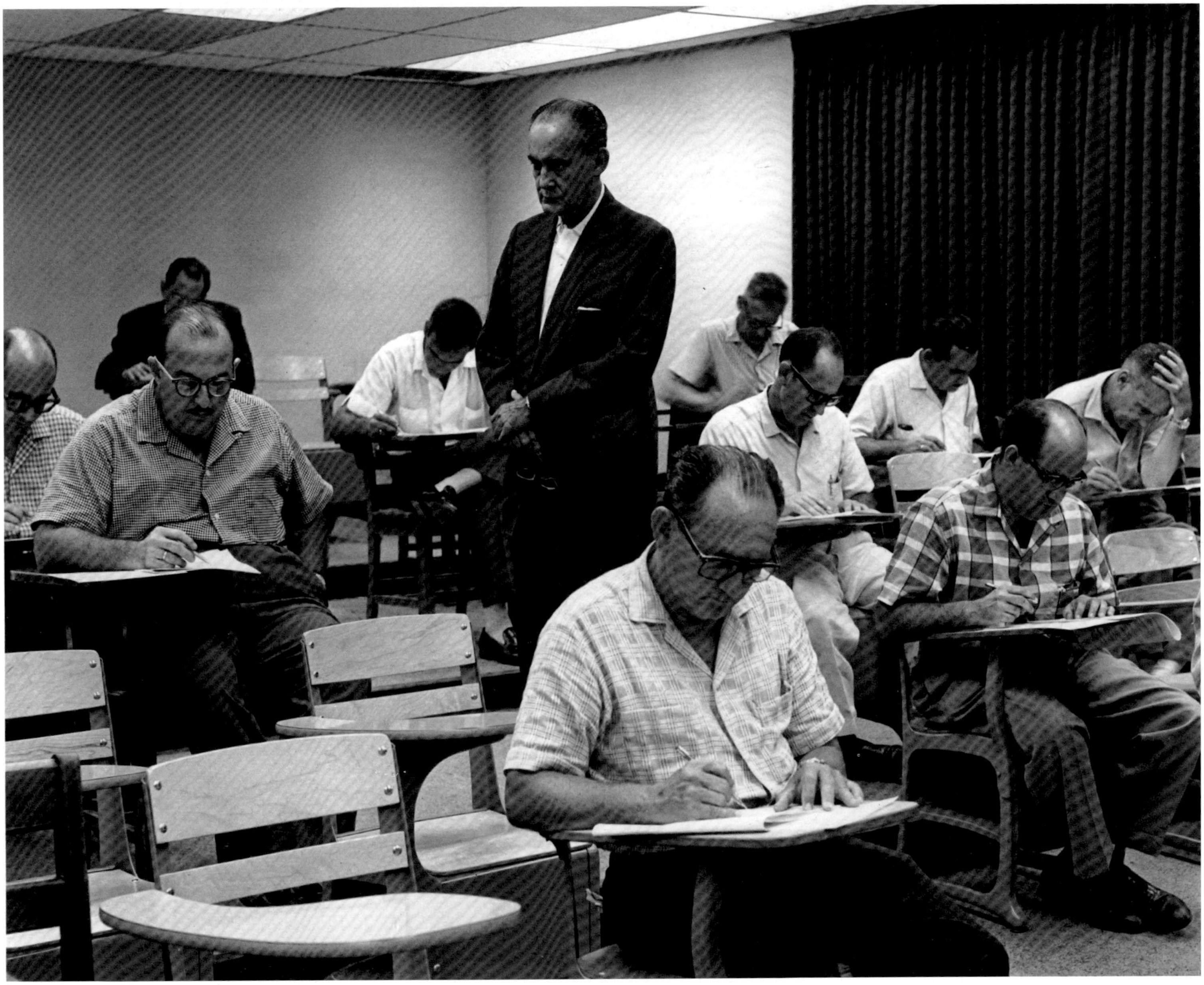

Most first-wave Cuban exiles came from professional backgrounds. They included lawyers, doctors, dentists, professors, and business owners. After 1959, this group contributed immensely to Miami's new wealth and industry, but success never comes easily. In the early days, it was not uncommon to find a lawyer waiting tables. Those in medical fields were able to retrain, intern, and take exams, like this person, to become doctors.

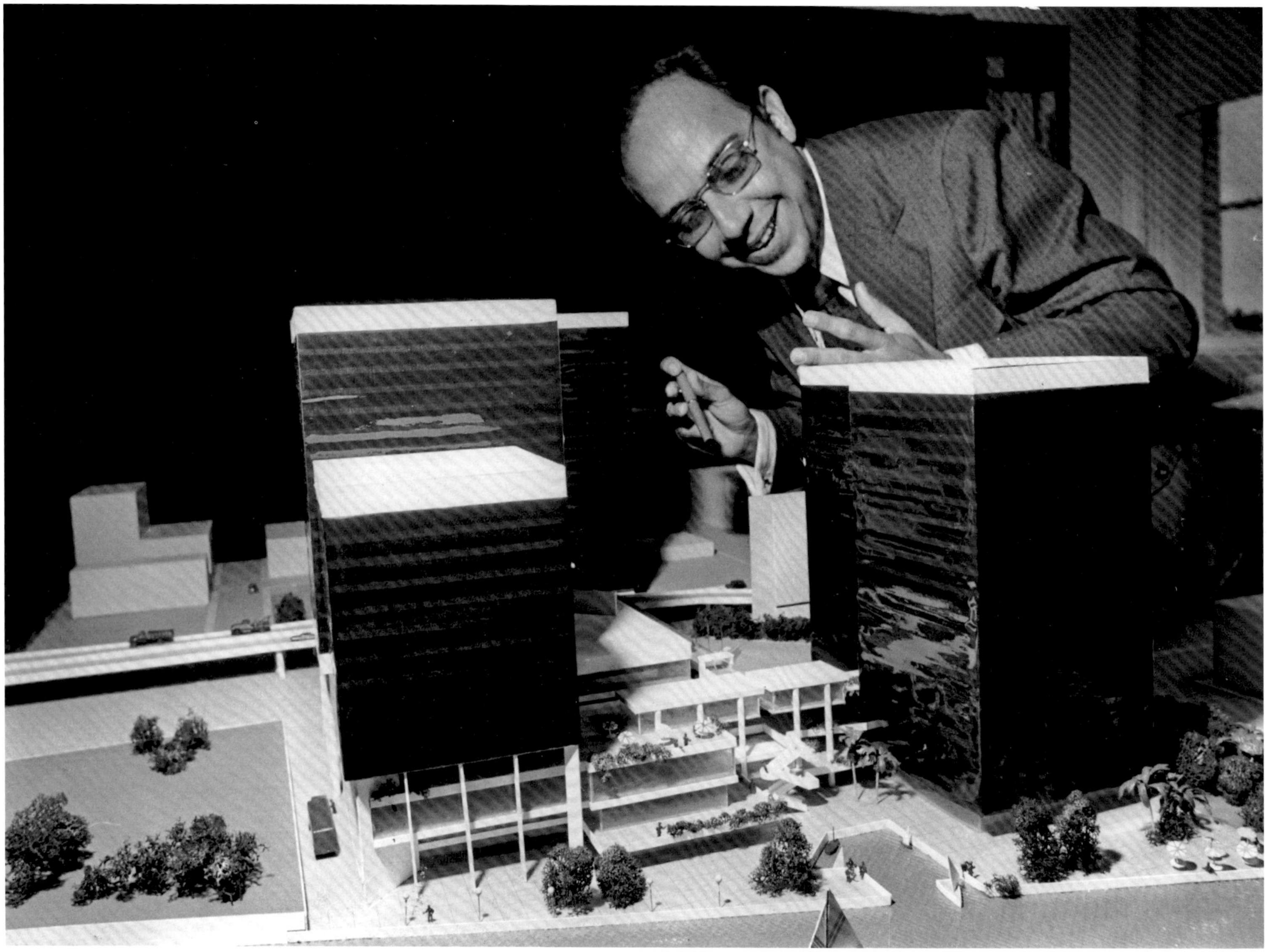

Famed architect Hilario Candela with models of buildings. Candela is the principle of what he claims is the largest Hispanic-owned architectural firm in the United States. His firm designed the Miami Marine Stadium, which is currently listed as one of America's 11 most endangered historic places.

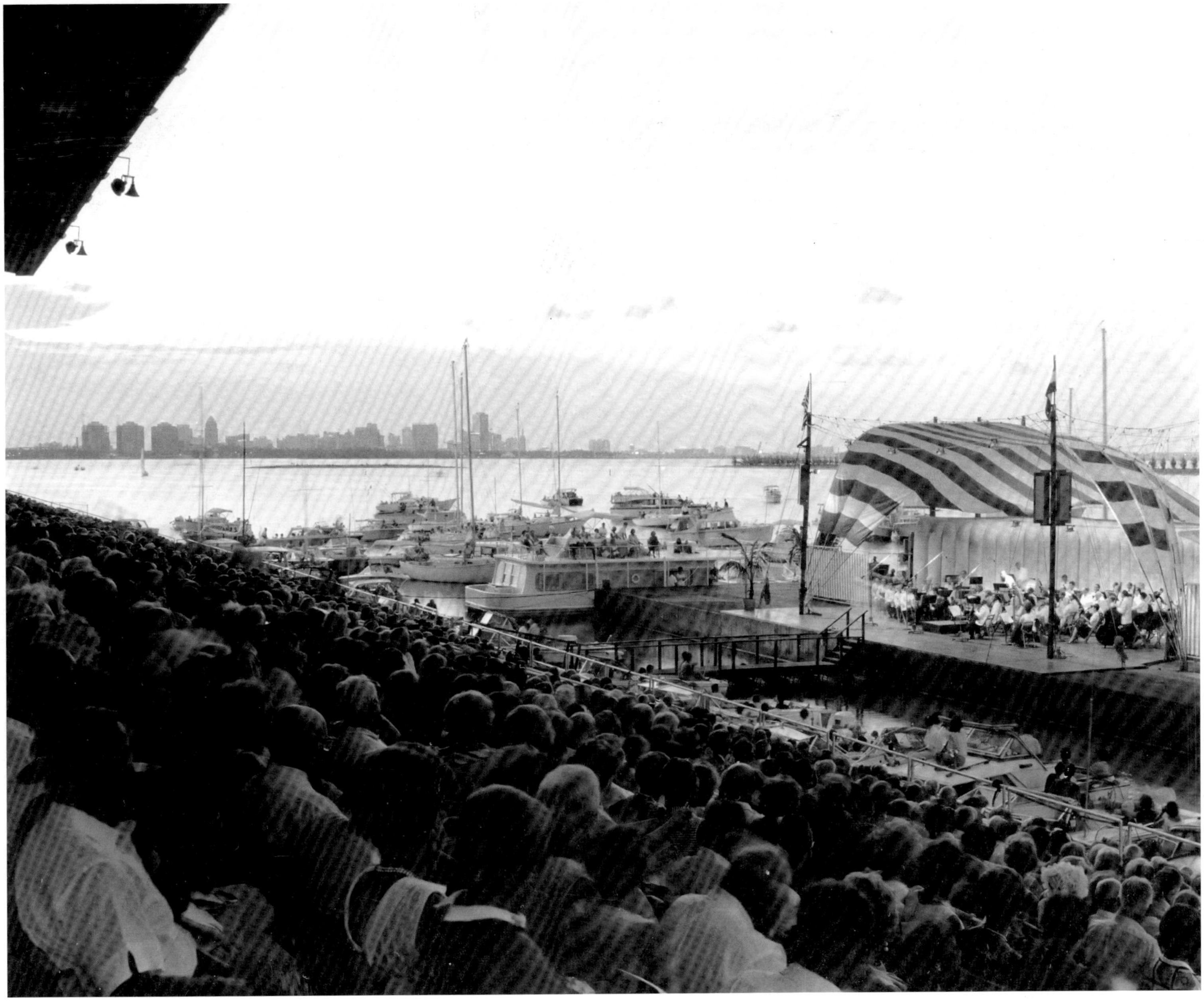

A concert is under way at Miami Marine Stadium in the 1960s. The stadium was built by well-known Cuban architect Hilario Candela in 1963, then recently ashore from Cuba, and currently stands abandoned, the victim of stiff competition from other venues and Hurricane Andrew in 1992. There has been a movement to restore the structure, on its merits as a leading example of modernist design. City officials have made promises, but no progress has been made.

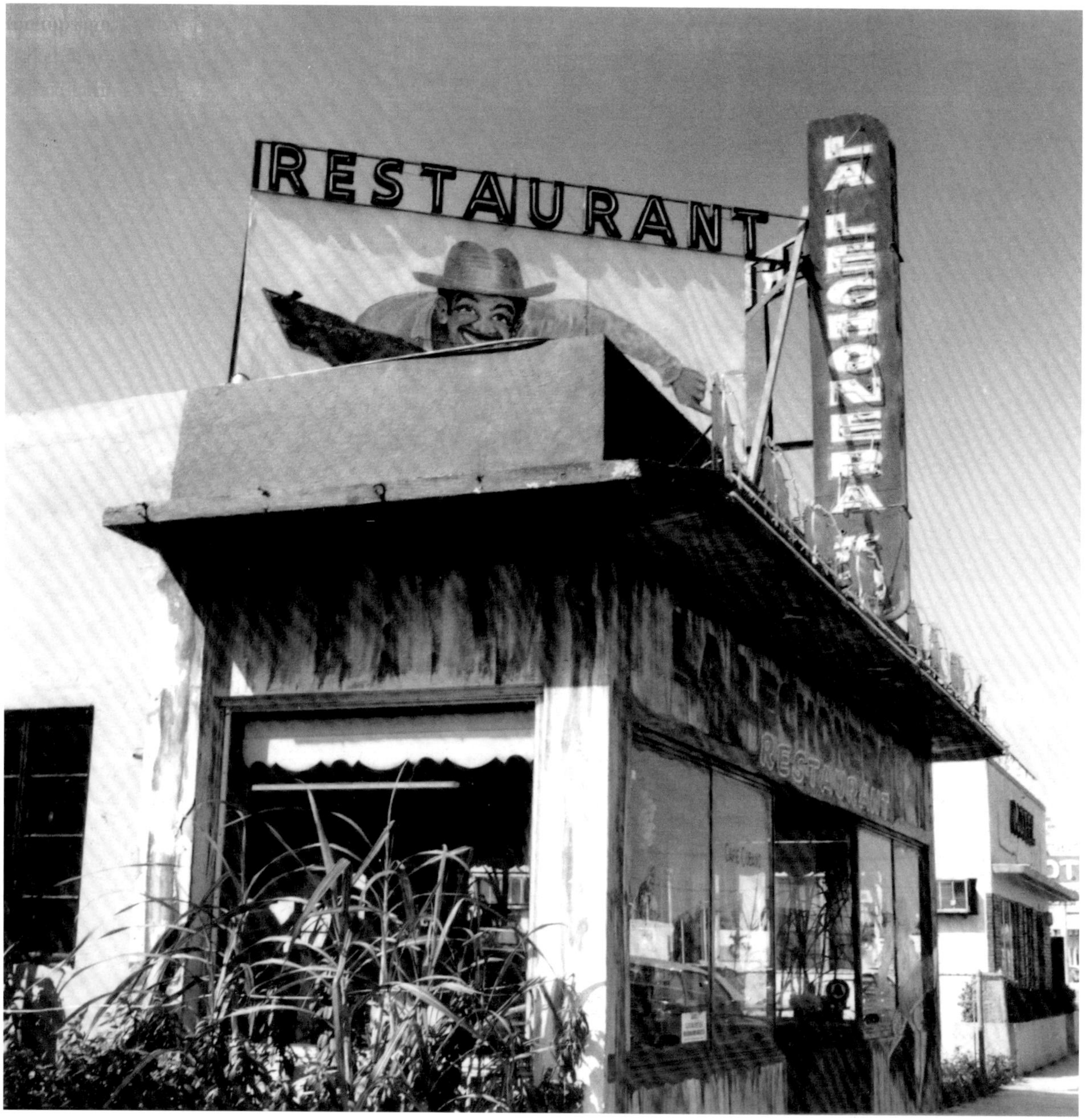

La Lechonera Restaurant, established in the 1960s, later grew to La Lechonera Products. They now bottle and sell "mojo," a mix of spices and flavorings, used to marinate a variety of Cuban dishes.

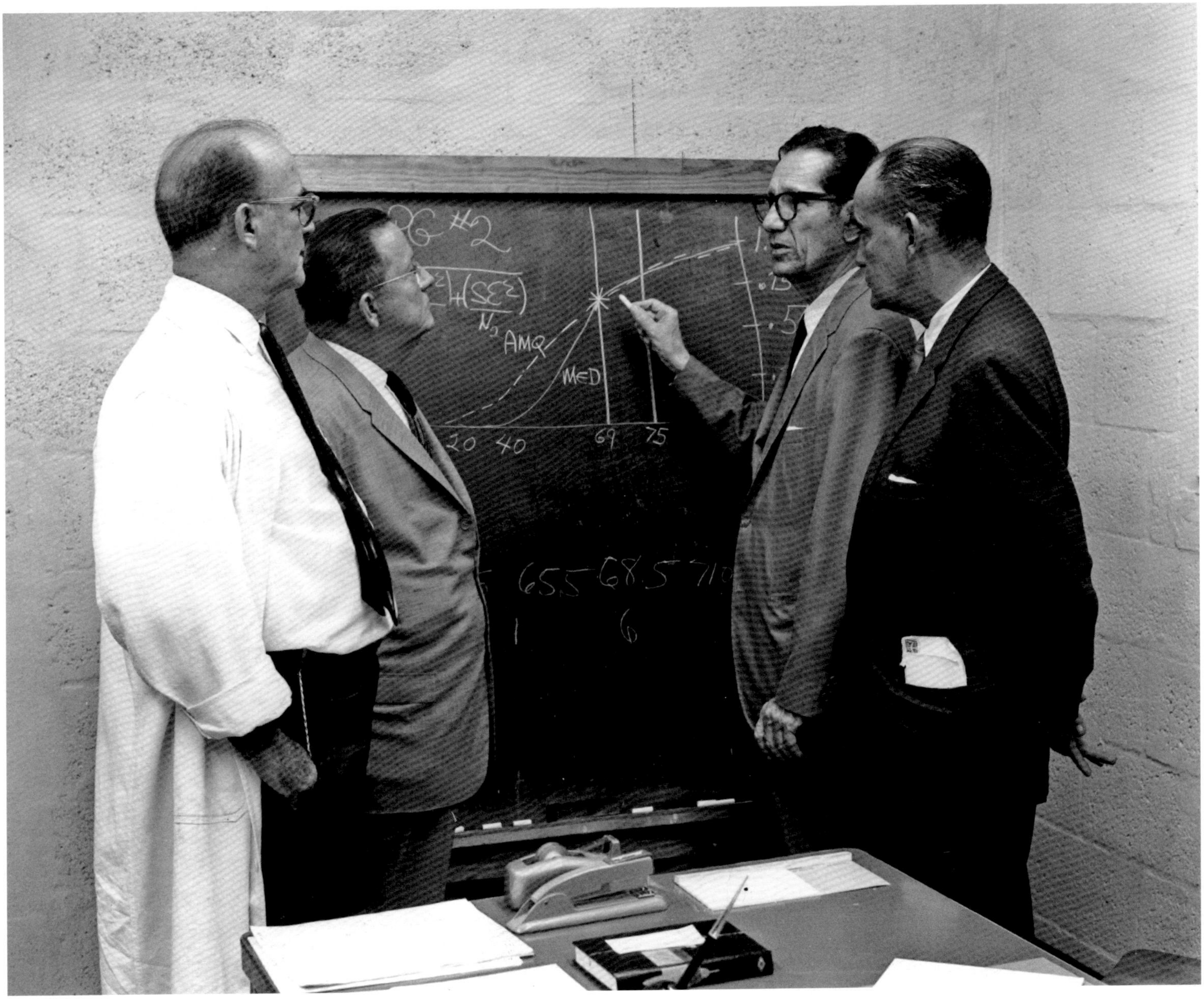

Cuban professionals are shown here at work in the early 1960s.

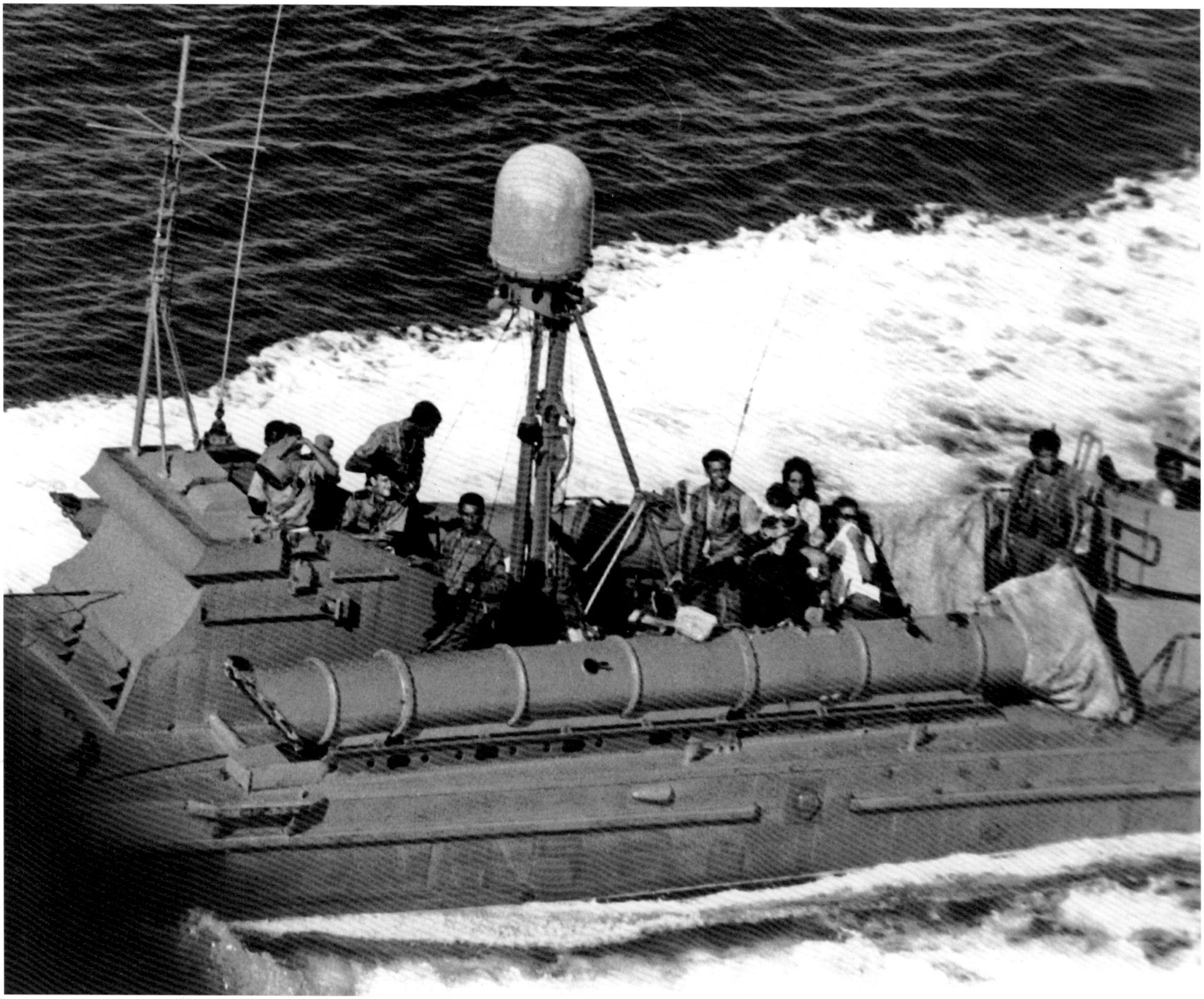

This boatload of Cubans were picked up by the U.S. Coast Guard on August 13, 1963.

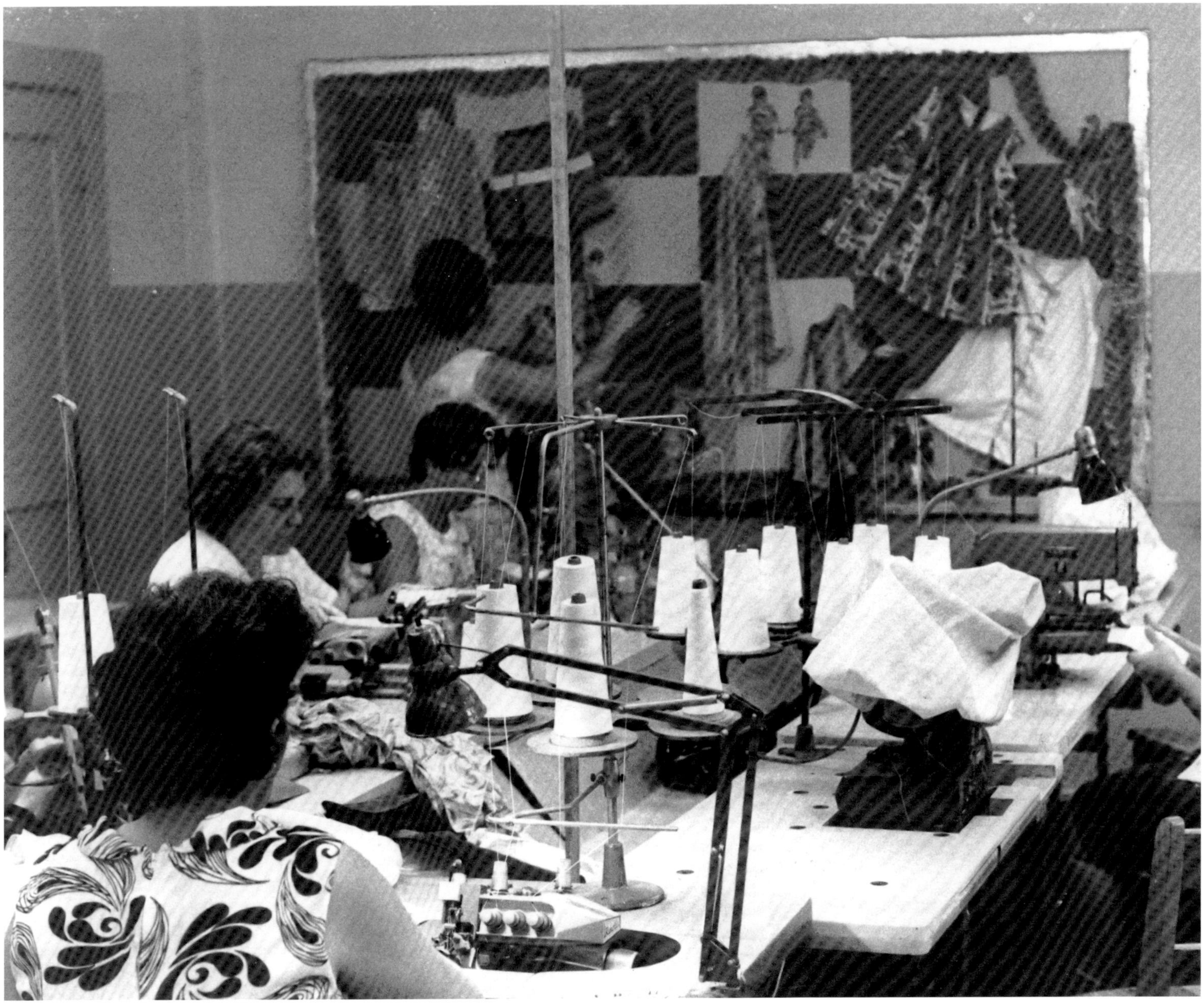

The Cuban Refugee Assistance Program was initiated in the 1960s as the first federally funded program for domestic assistance to refugees. It remained in effect until 1981. The program provided for a variety of services, including medical clinics, which were mostly staffed by Cuban exiles.

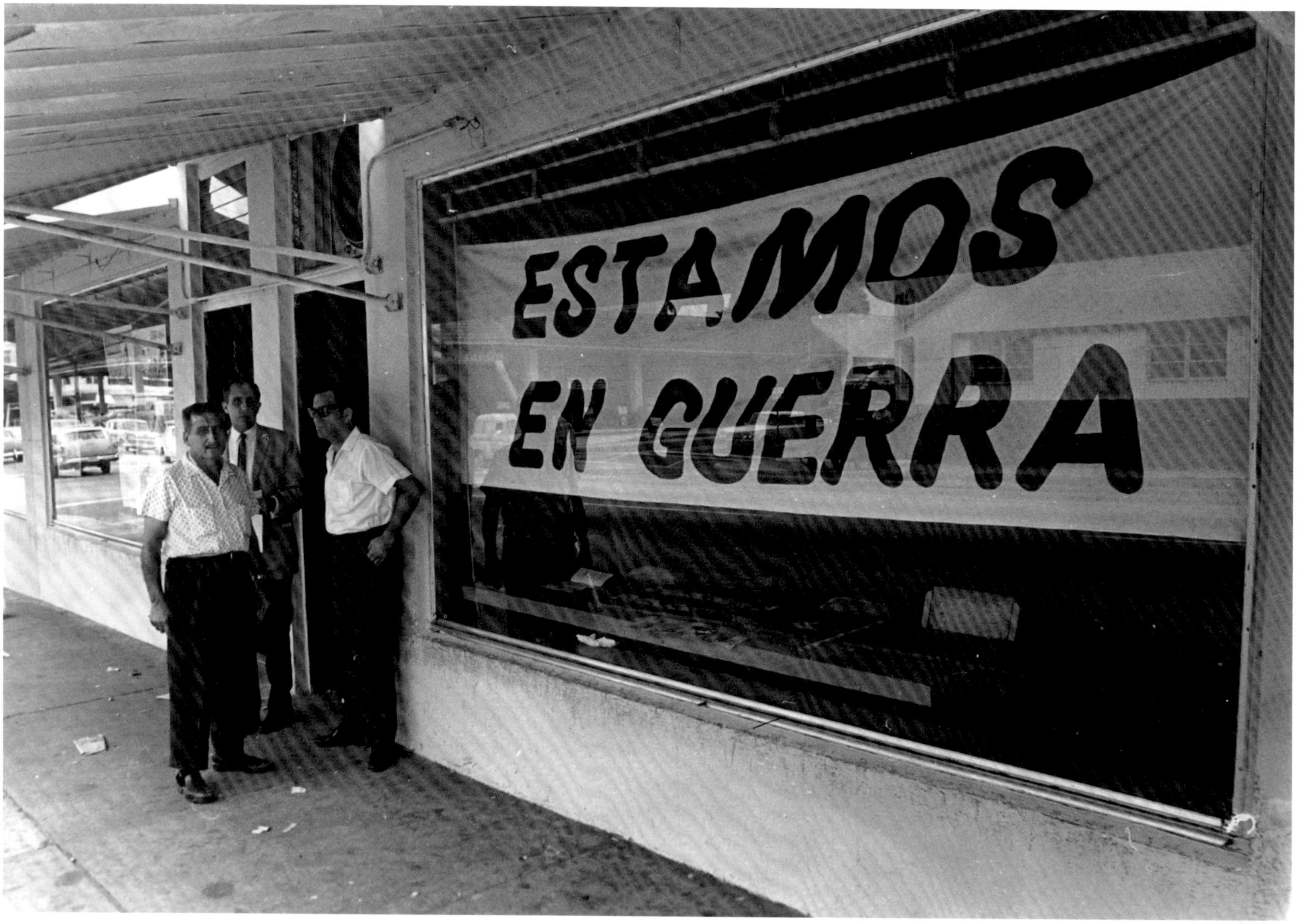

Anti-Castro Miami Headquarters in 1964. The sign on the window reads, "We are at war!" Many hardline Cubans felt this way in the 1960s and continue to feel that way today.

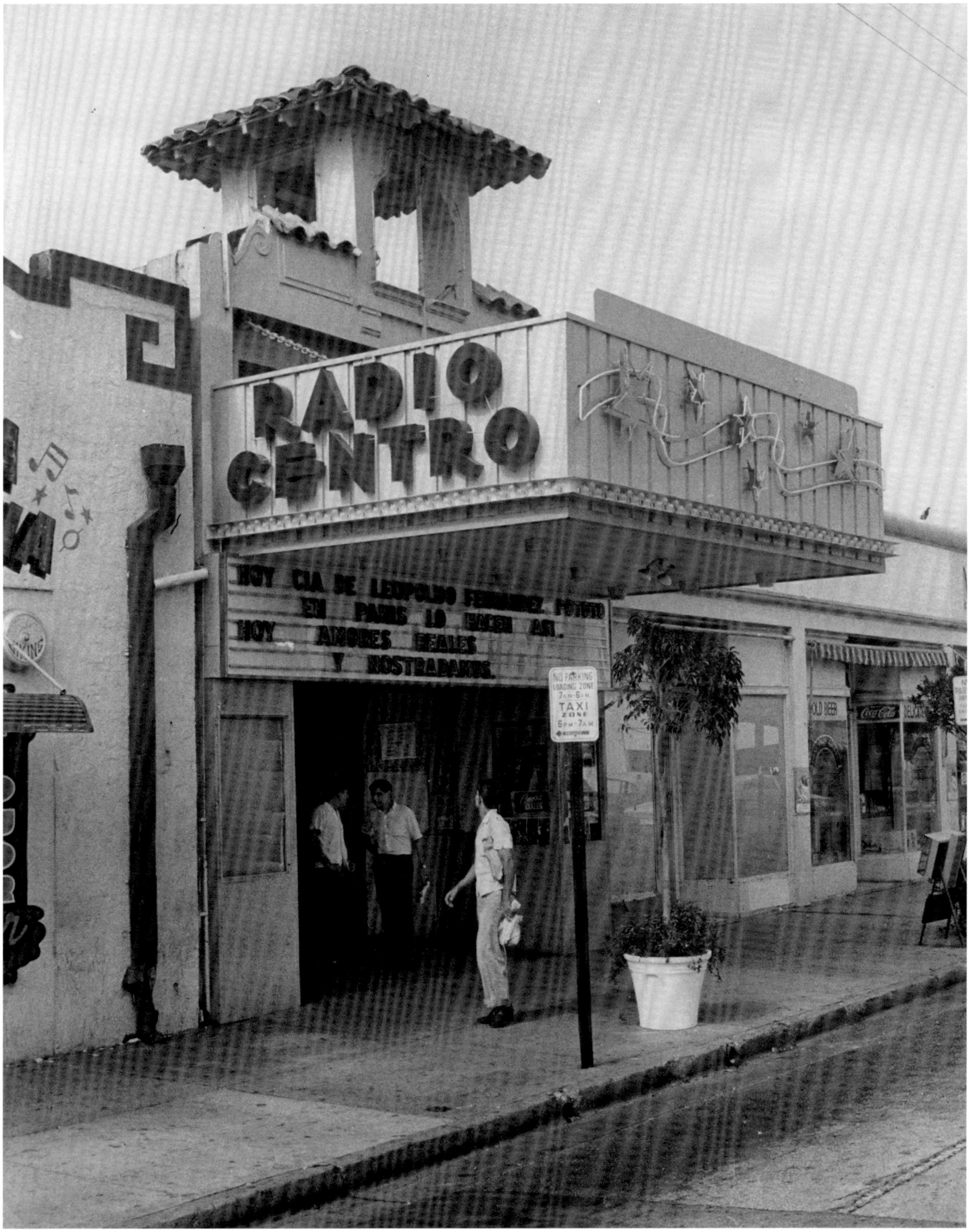

Previously known as the Flagler Theater, where Fidel Castro spoke and fundraised prior to his 1959 coup, Radio Centro Theater became one of the first Spanish-language theaters in Miami. The theater would be razed for construction of I-95.

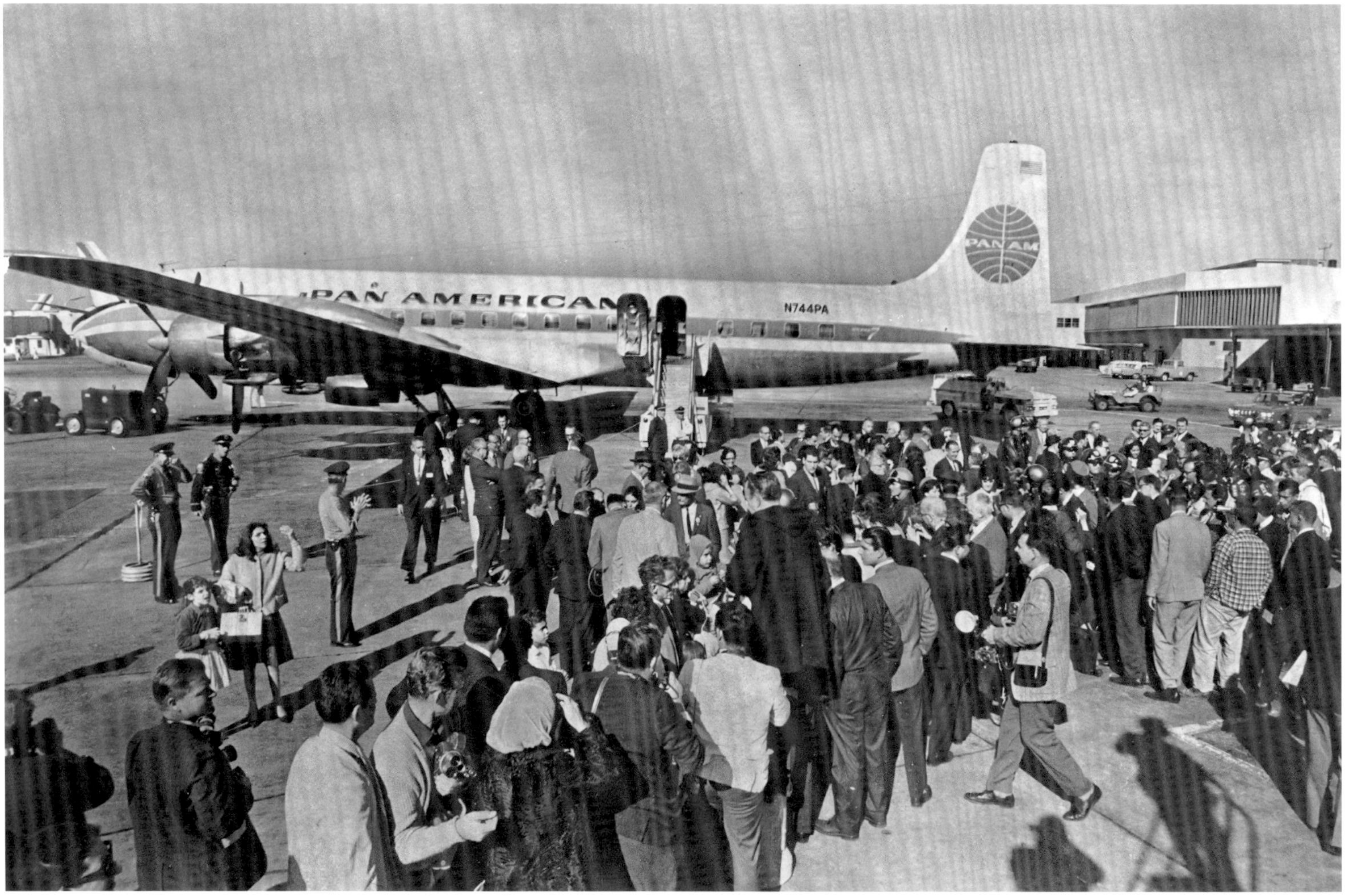

On September 28, 1965, Castro opened Cuba to freedom flights. This image depicts one of the first airlifts on Pan American Airlines. The freedom flights would run until 1973.

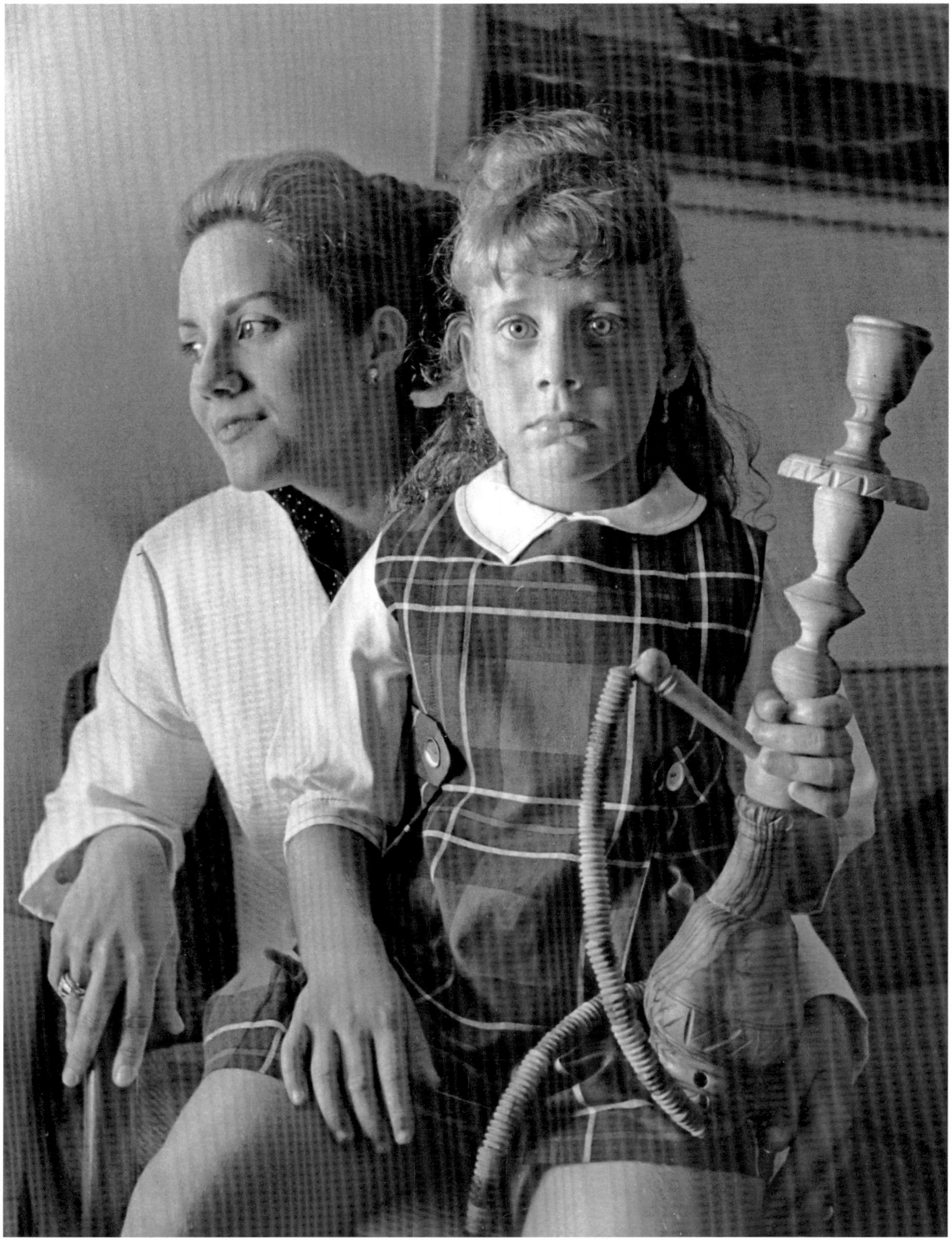

Miriam Alonso and her daughter pose for the camera. Alonso became City Commissioner and was later accused of misappropriating donations and other forms of corruption.

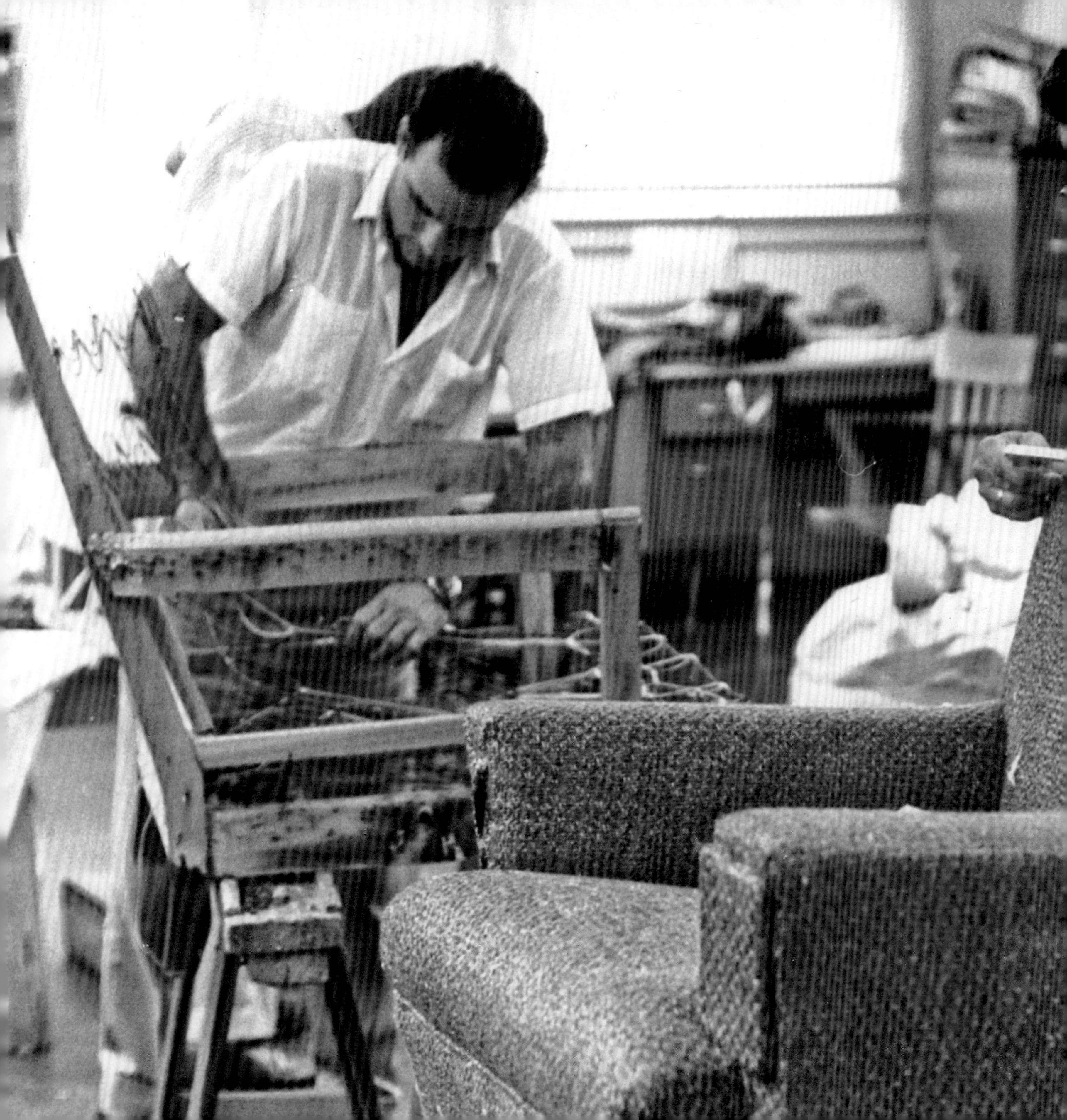

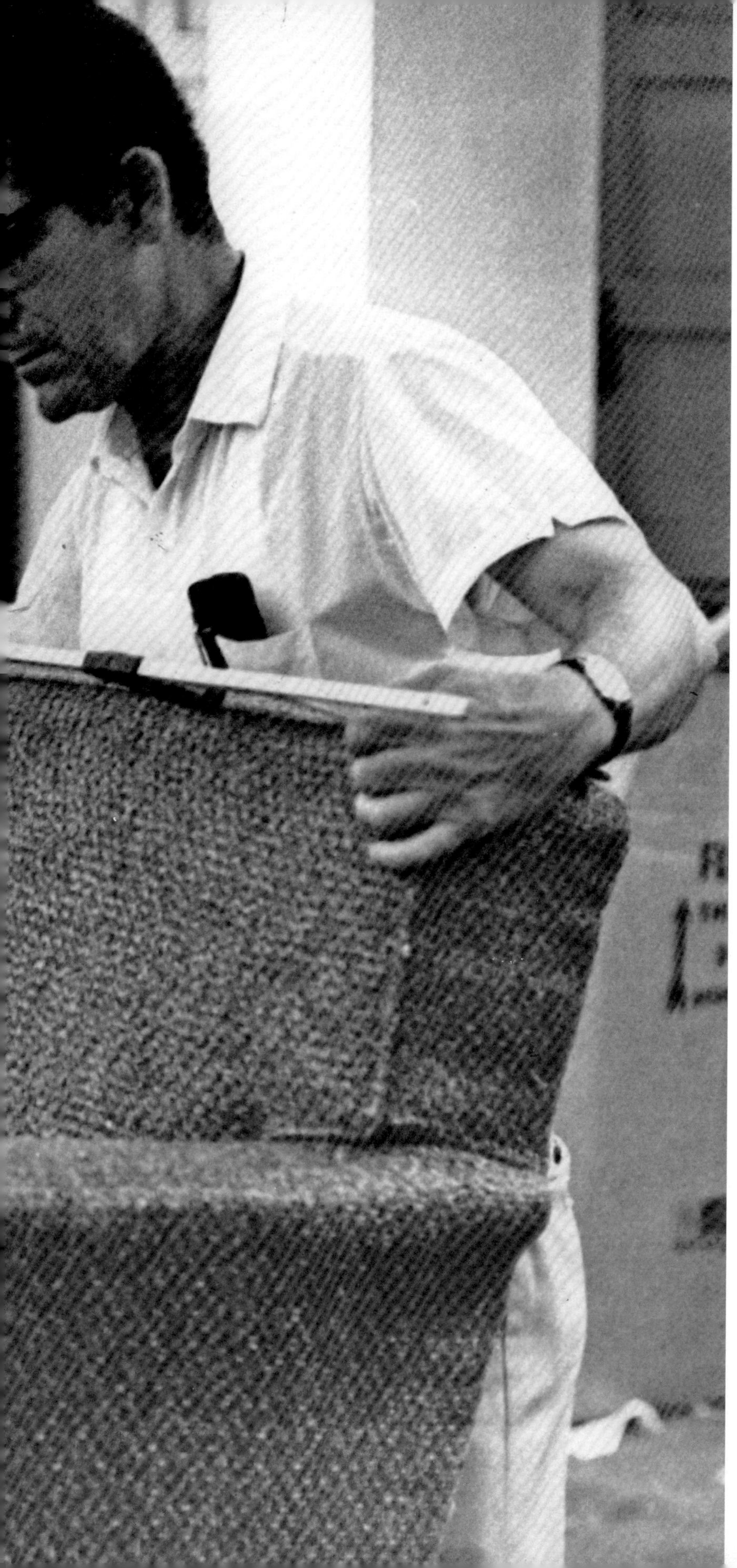

Two men work on furniture at the Cuban Refugee Center, located in the Freedom Tower (formerly the Miami News Tower) in 1968.

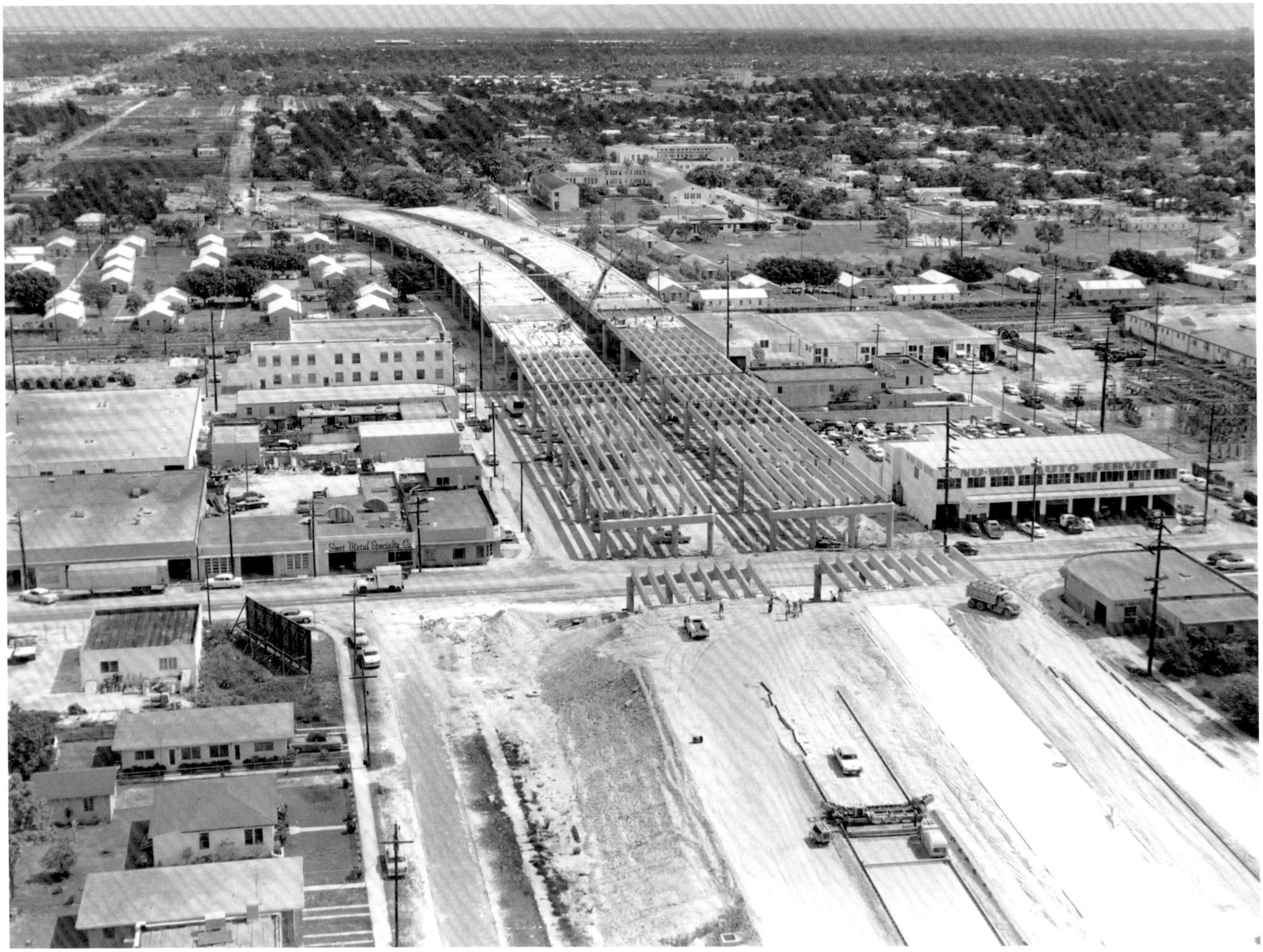

An aerial view of Interstate 95, under construction. I-95 would eventually provide the eastern border of Little Havana and claim the Flagler Theater as a casualty. In the 1980s, Tent City, temporary housing for the Mariel Boatlift, would be set up under I-95.

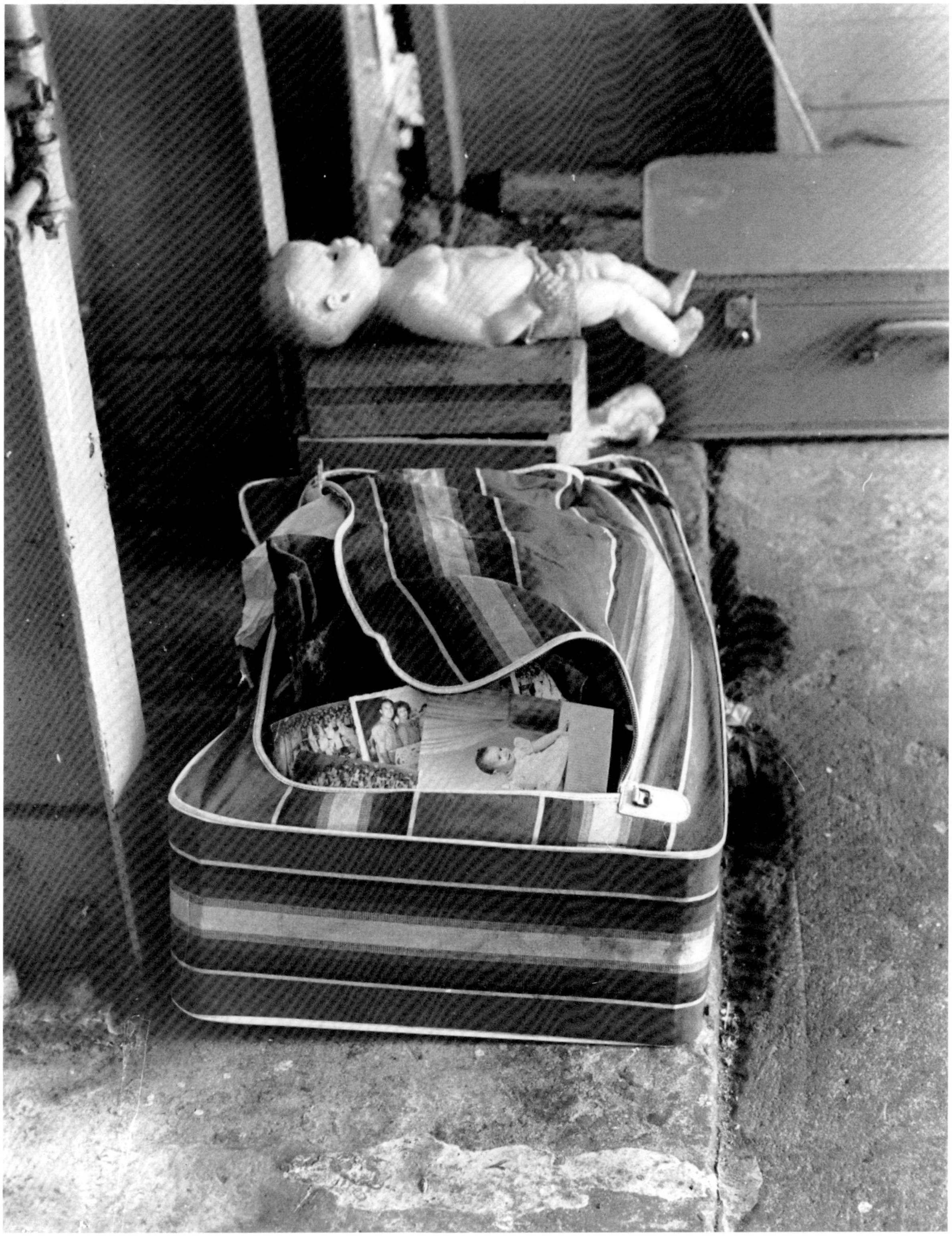

A suitcase filled with family photos and a child's doll. Many Cubans were not lucky enough to escape Cuba with any possession whatsoever.

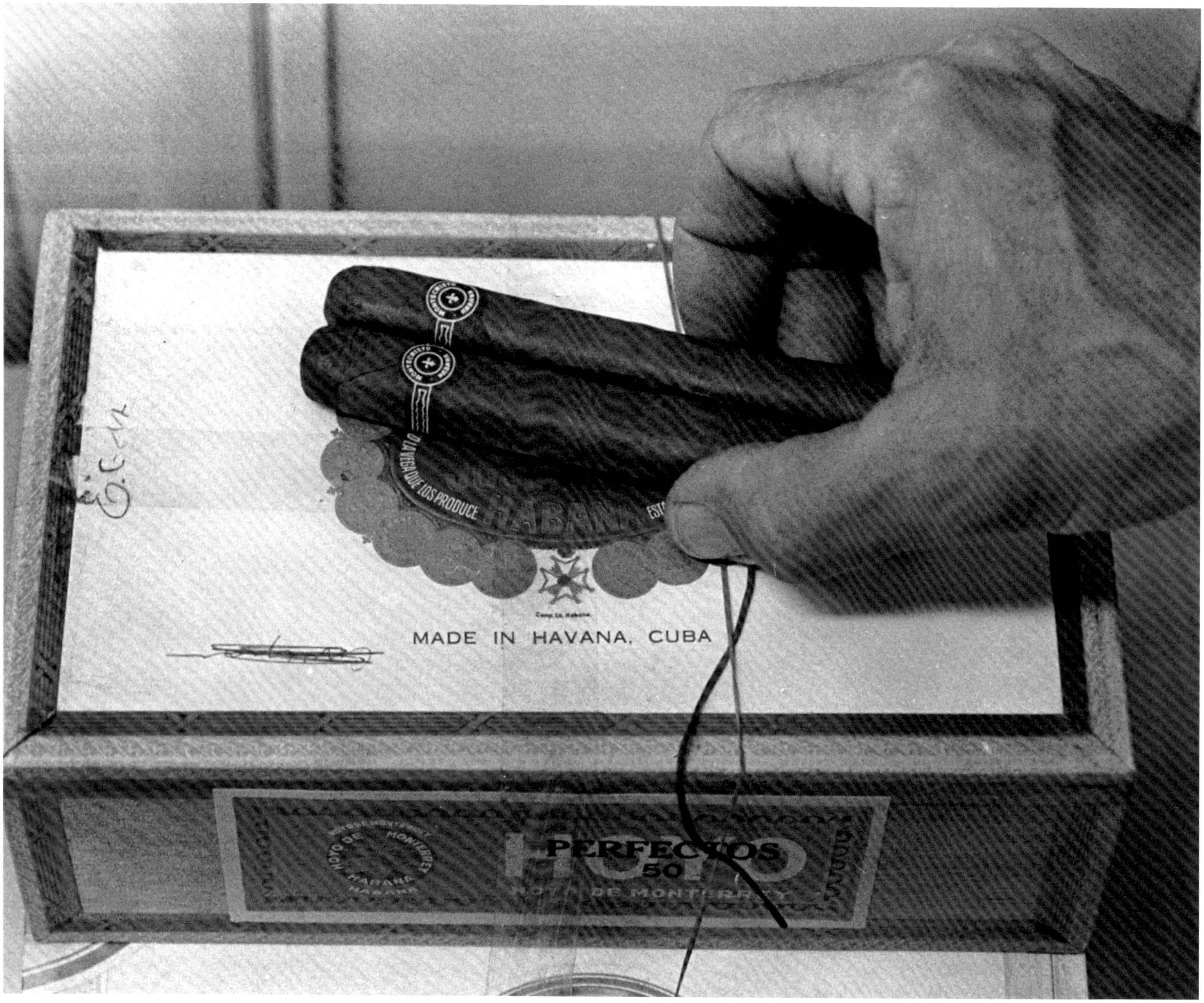

Cuban cigars caught at U.S. customs being smuggled. The Kennedy administration embargo banned the import and export of goods with Cuba, an embargo that continues today. This included Cuban tobacco, which the Florida cigar industry had relied on. Cigar makers had to adapt by importing Dominican tobacco. The overall quality of cigars has never been quite the same, making the best Cuban cigars even more desirable simply for being forbidden.

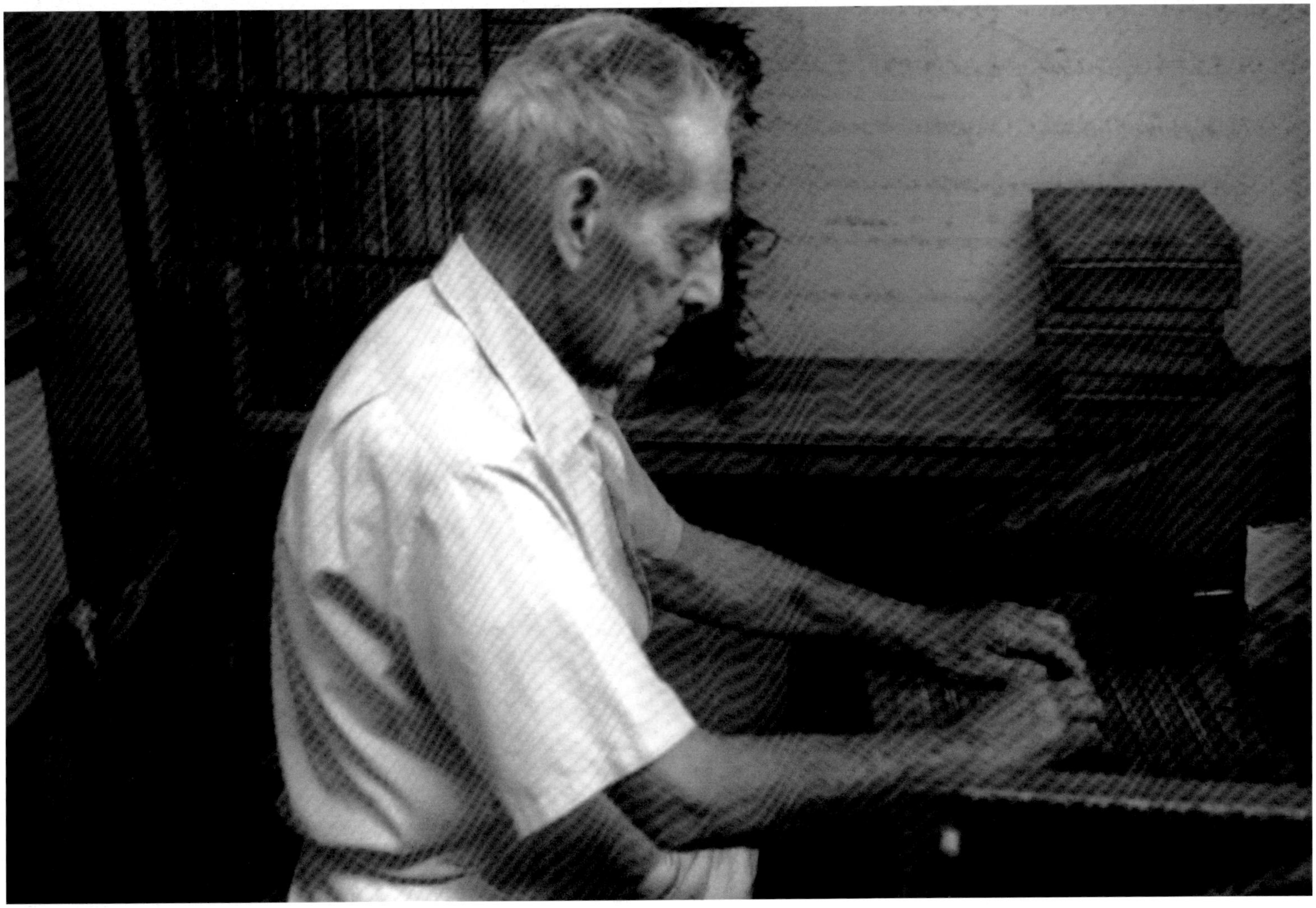

A craftsman rolls cigars at Ramar Cigars in Little Havana.

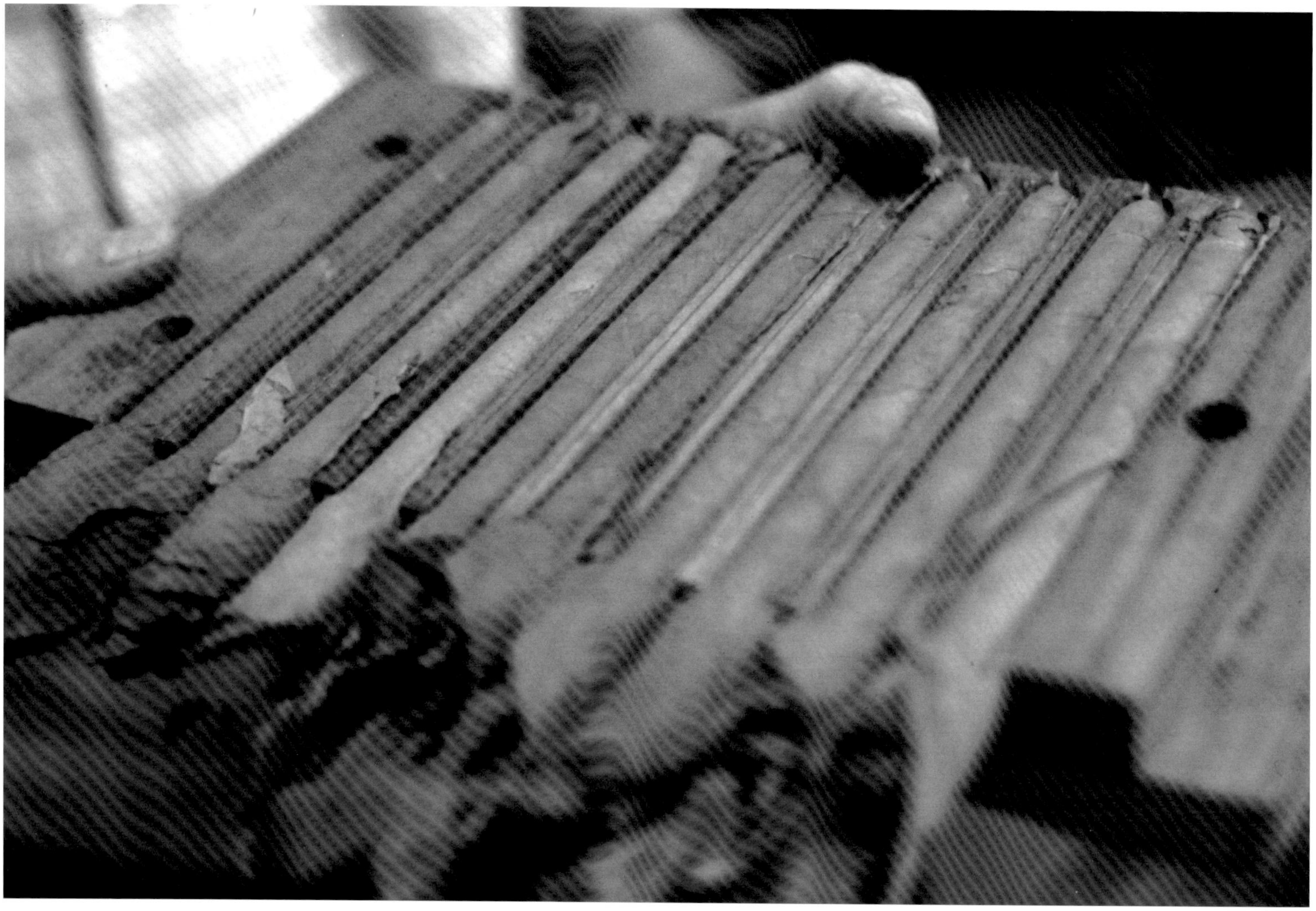

Cigars in a mold are ready to be pressed in a facility in Miami. The Florida cigar industry dates back to before the Spanish-American War and the existence of Miami. Tampa's Ybor City and the Cuban community in Key West were both built around the Cuban cigar industry. Later, some cigars began to be manufactured in Miami, but never on a scale approaching that of Tampa or Key West.

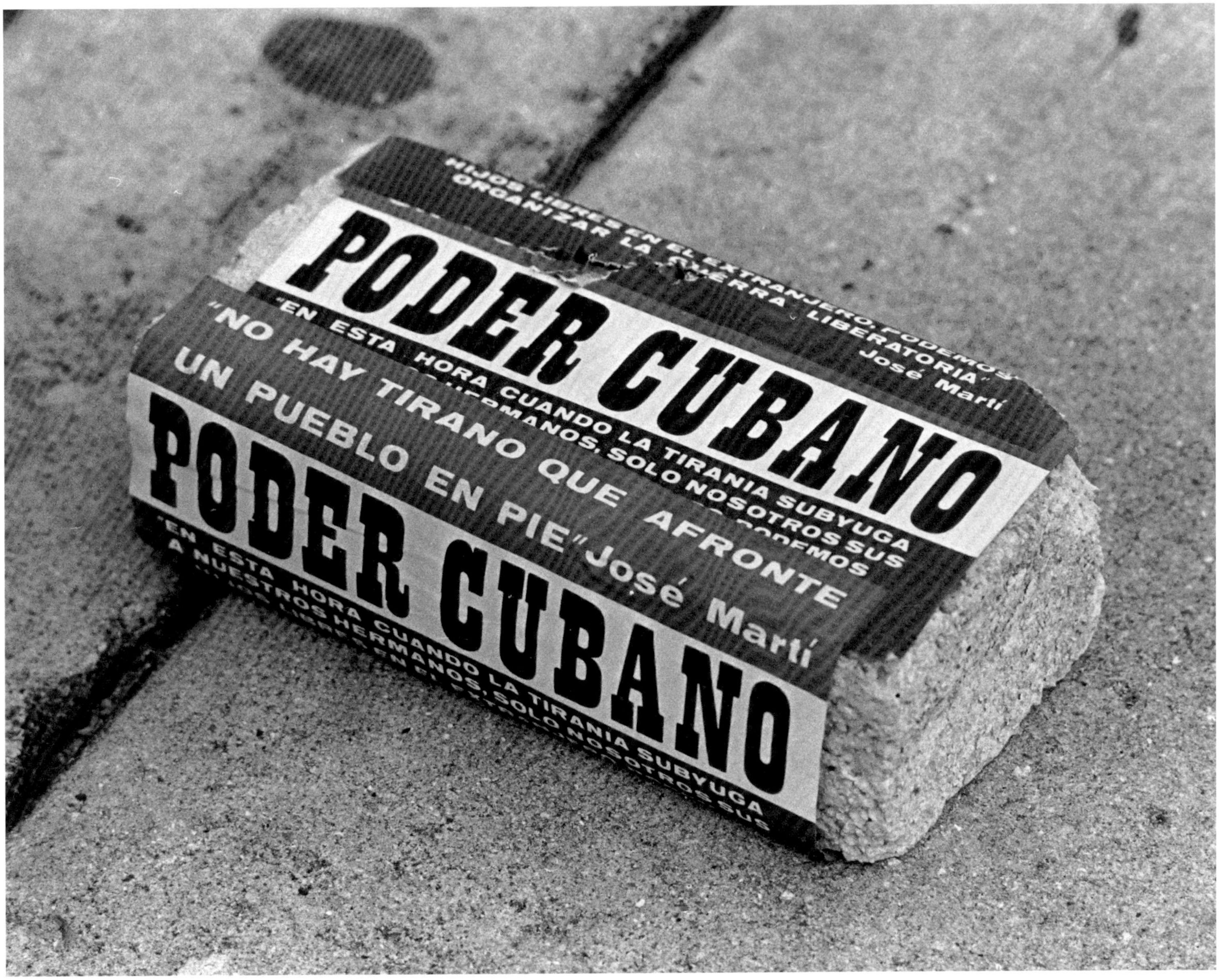

A brick wrapped in "Poder Cubano" paraphernalia. Poder Cubano was a Cuban exile terrorist group led by Orlando Bosch, responsible for setting off countless bombs and extreme violent acts. Bosch was responsible for the bombing of Cubana Airlines, which resulted in 73 deaths. The group fell apart when several members were arrested in 1968. The quotation on the brick says, "There is no tyrant that can resist the uprising of the people."

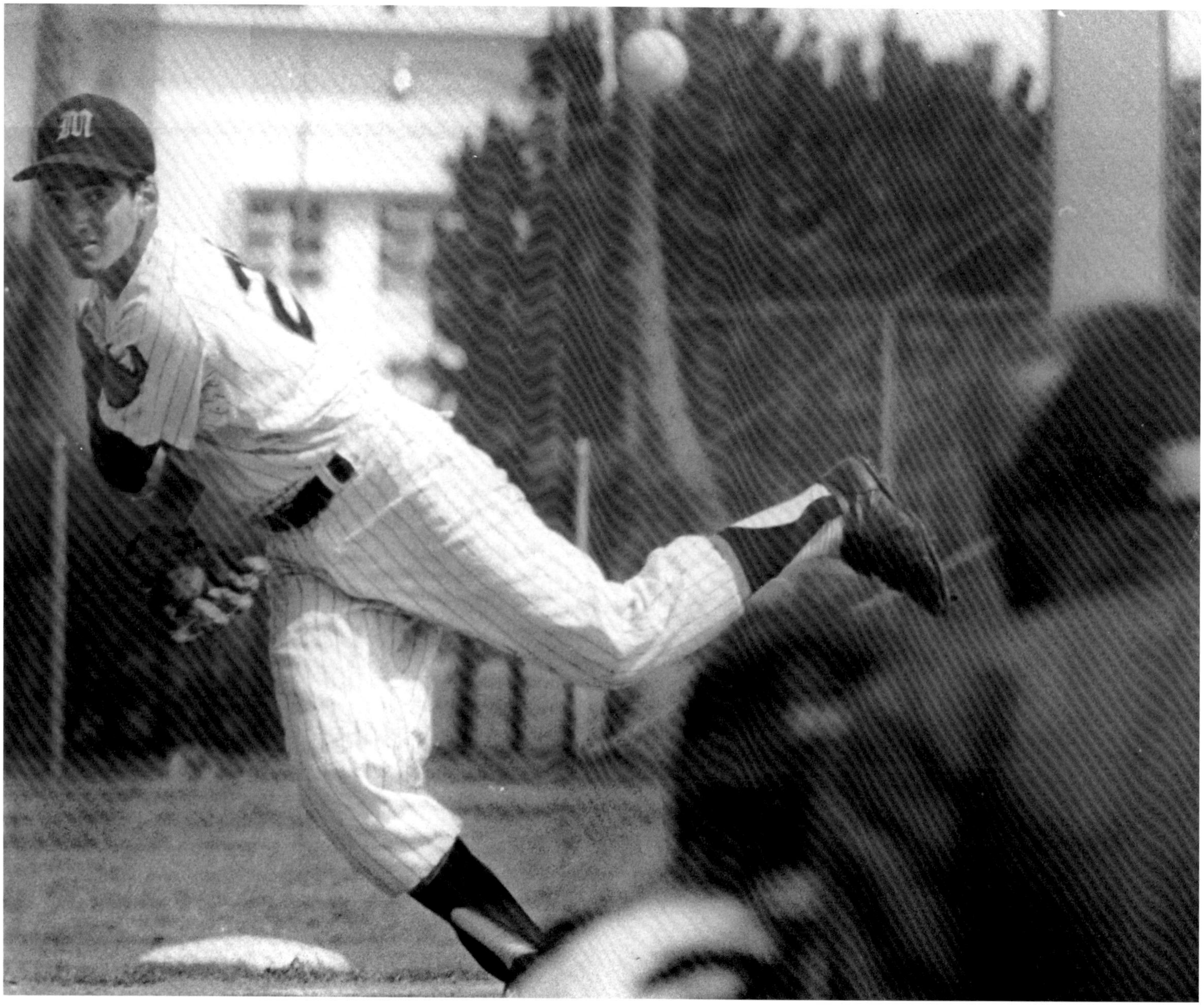

Joe Zabala pitches for the Miami Stingers. For Americans, baseball is still one of the most popular sports, and for Cubans, it remains the most popular sport.

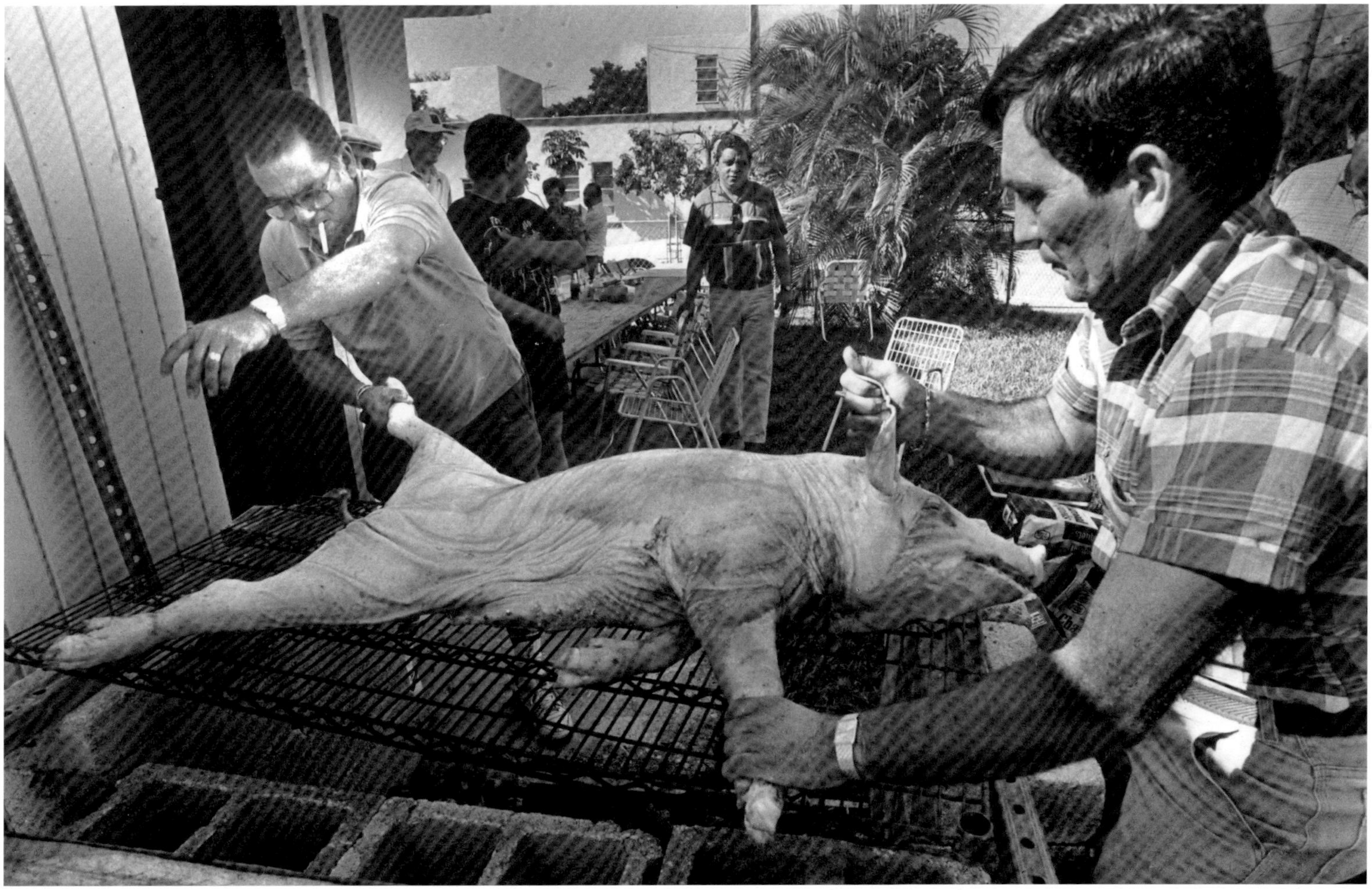

A *lechon* is laid out for roasting at a Cuban barbecue in Miami. It would likely be served with some form of plantain (*maduros,* known as sweet plantains, or *tostones,* known as fried plantains) or *congri,* which is rice cooked with black beans.

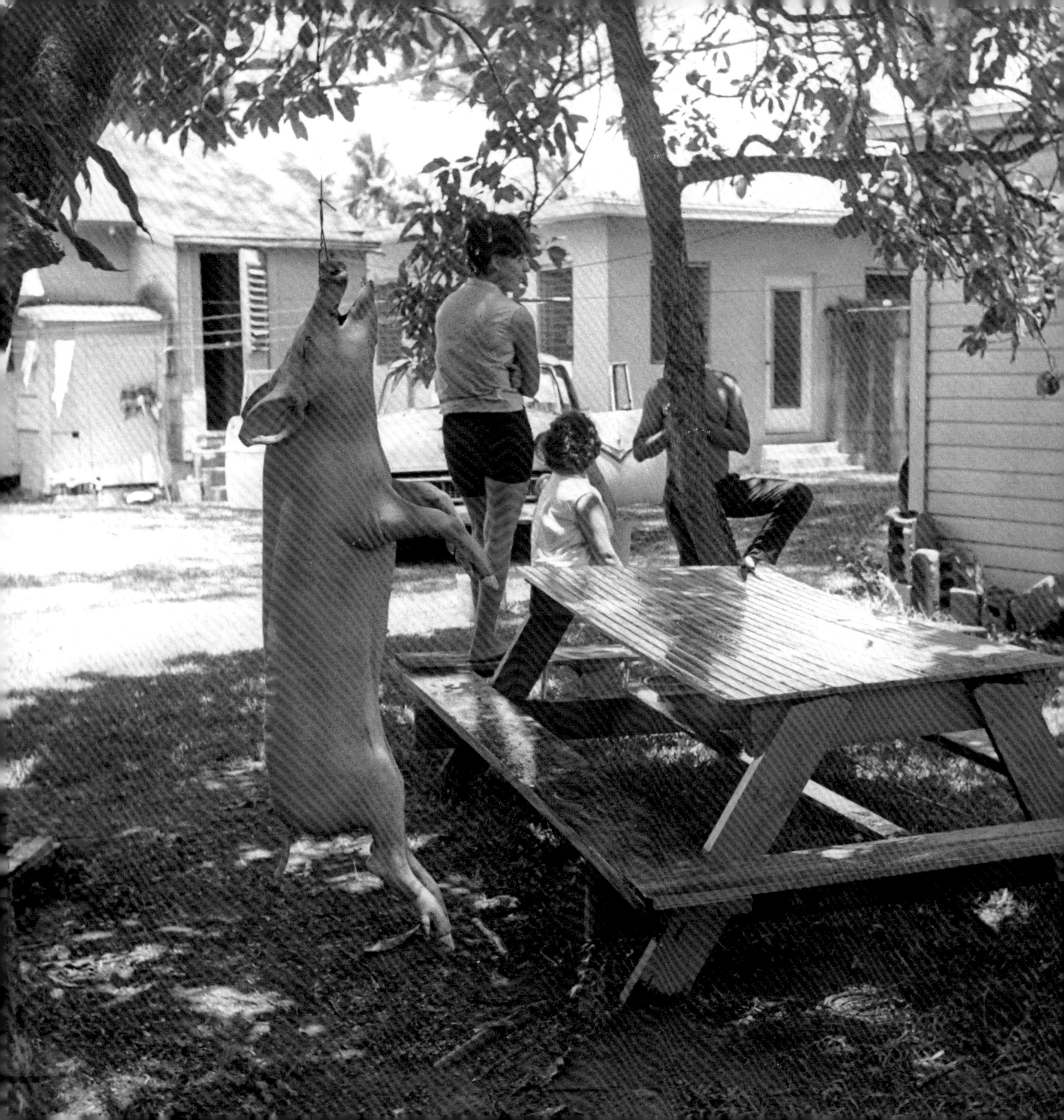

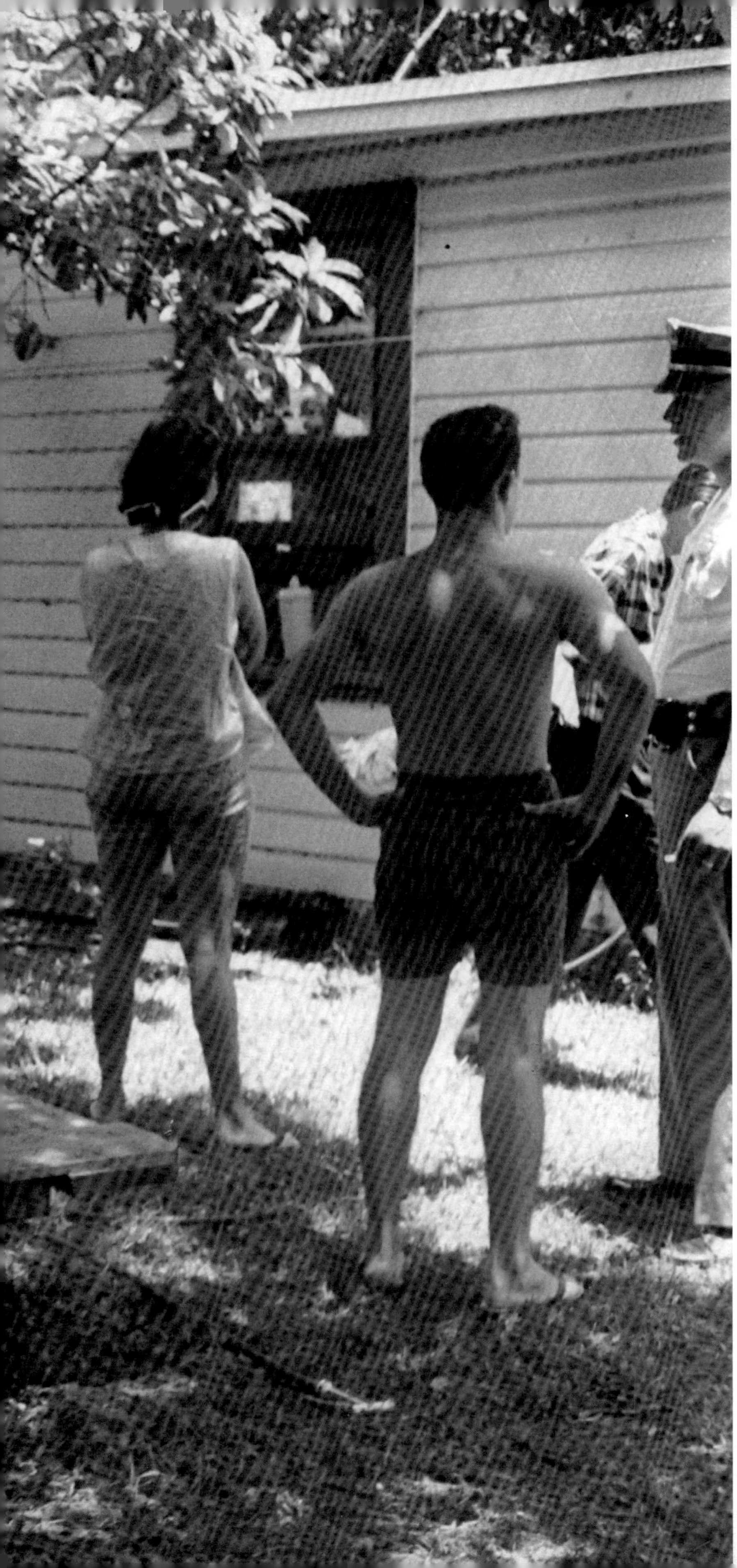

A *lechon* hangs in preparation for a Cuban-style dinner. Unacceptable at the time in Miami, but common practice in the rural areas of Cuba. A police officer stands to the right.

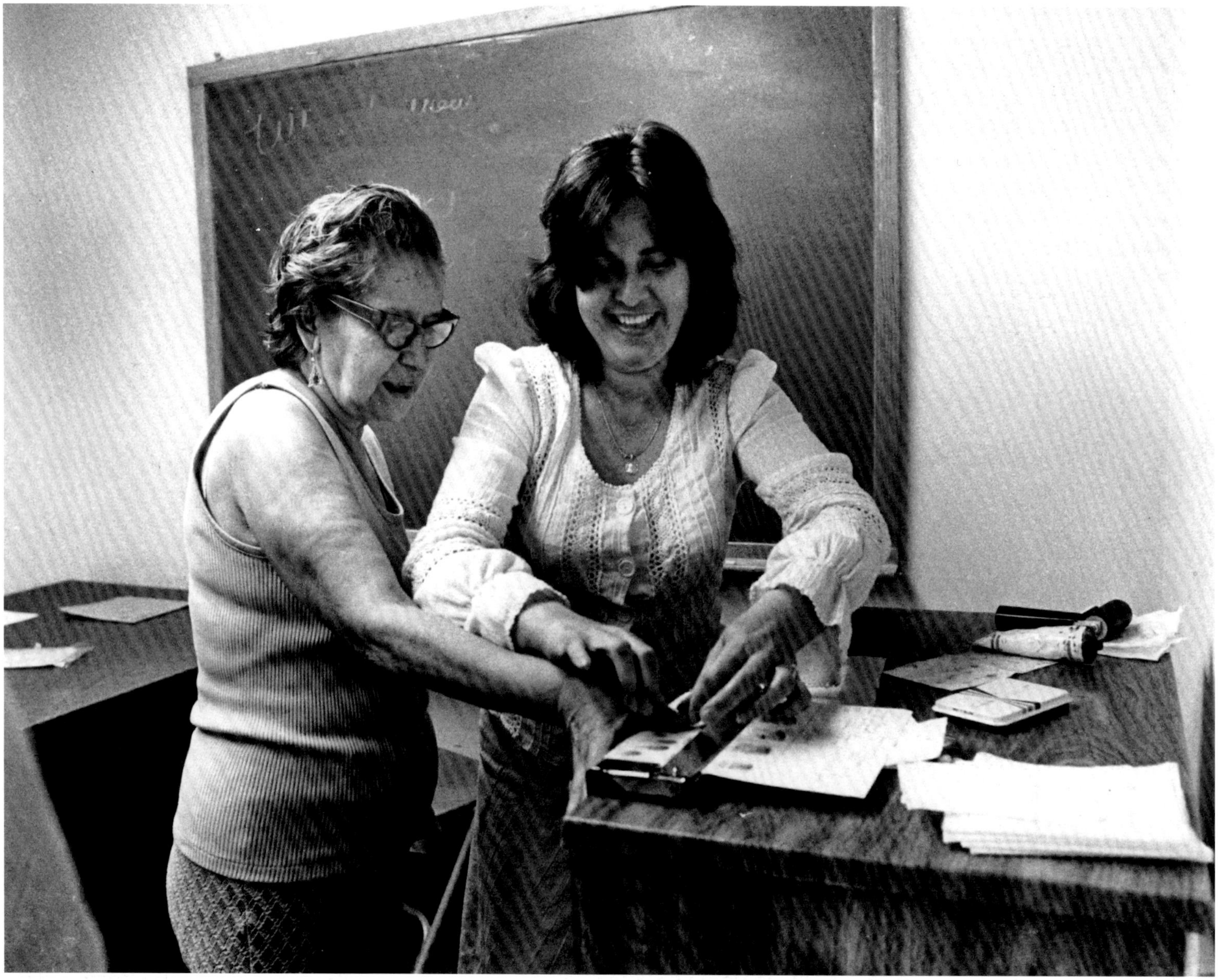

Emelina Rodriguez de Avila and Myriam Canas go through the process of fingerprinting and application for alien status on April 5, 1970.

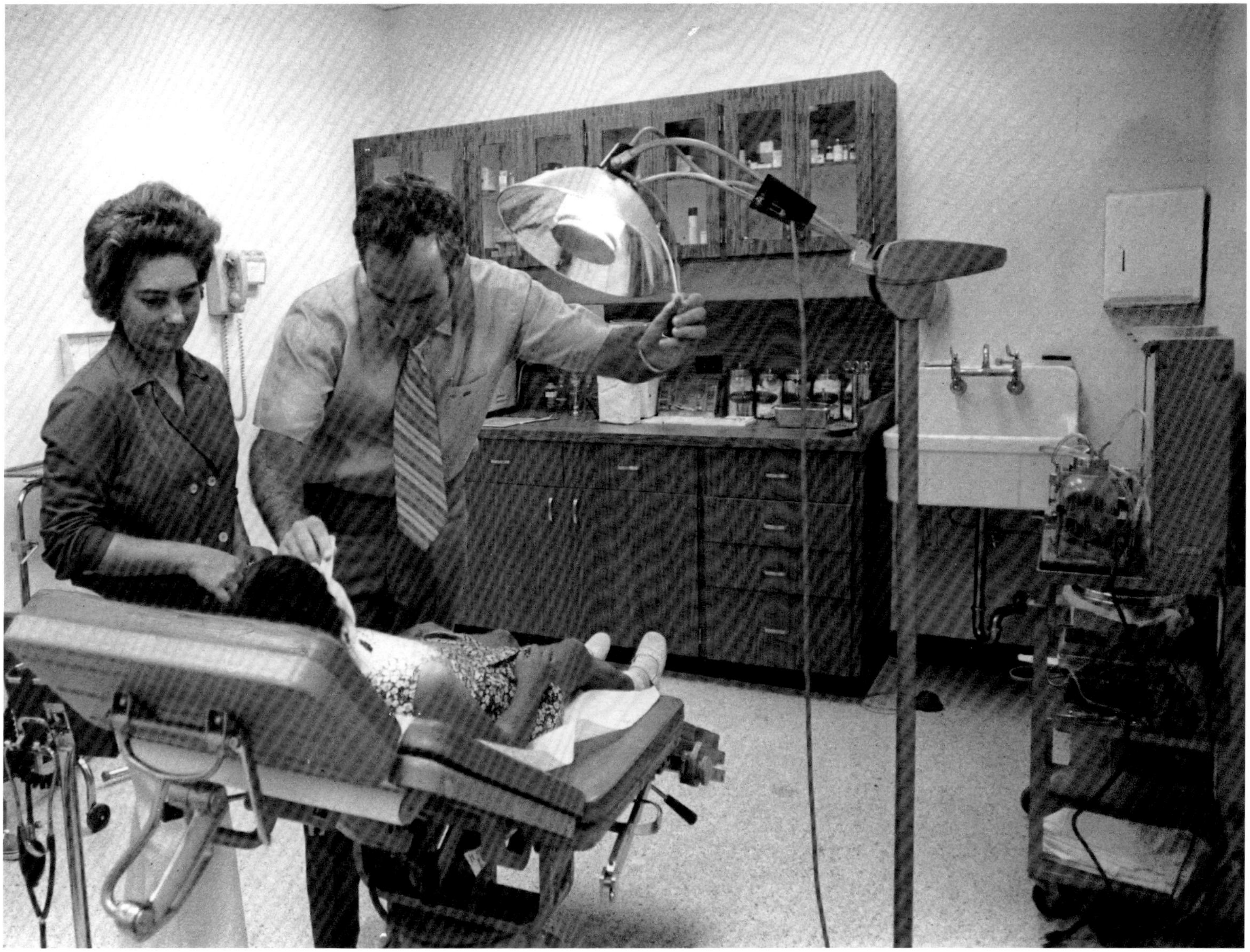

Cuban-born medical professionals treat Cuban patients at the Flagler Granada Clinic in 1971.

Women engage in crafts at the Little Havana Activities and Nutrition Center, established in 1971 to serve socially isolated and needy elderly.

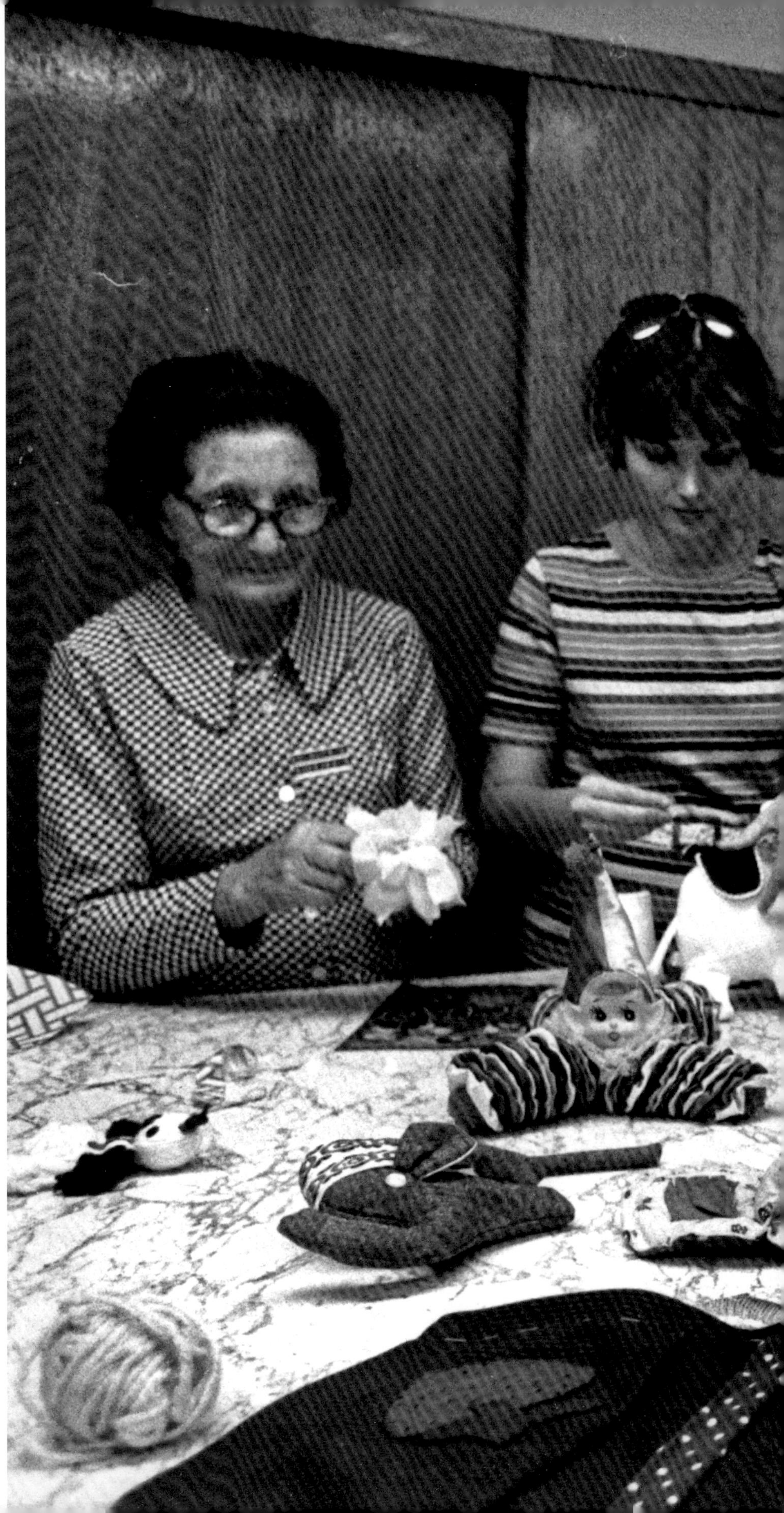

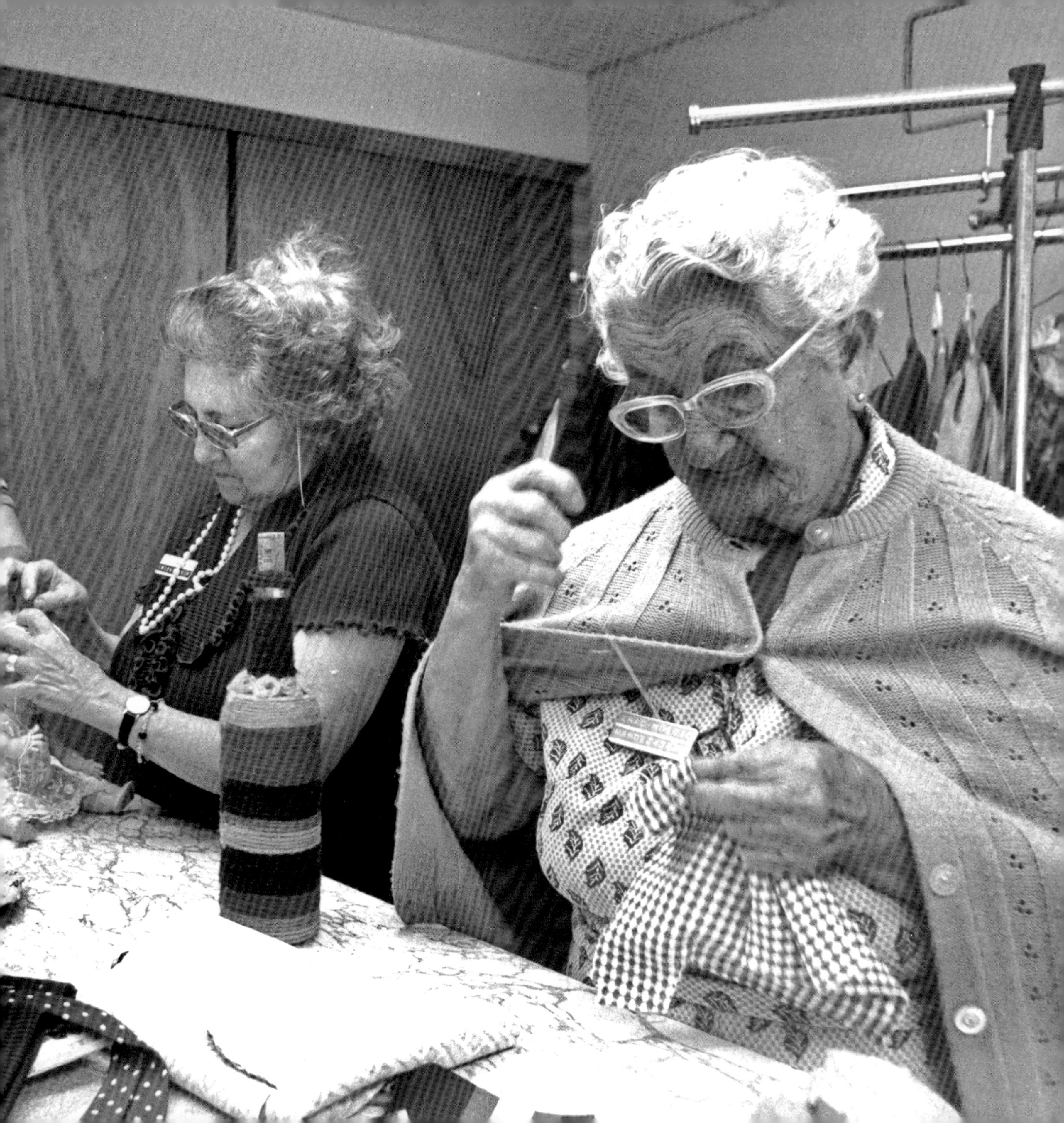

This storetop sign, Colon Supermarket, Carniceria y Pescaderia Latina, is an example of "Spanglish" in Cuban Miami.

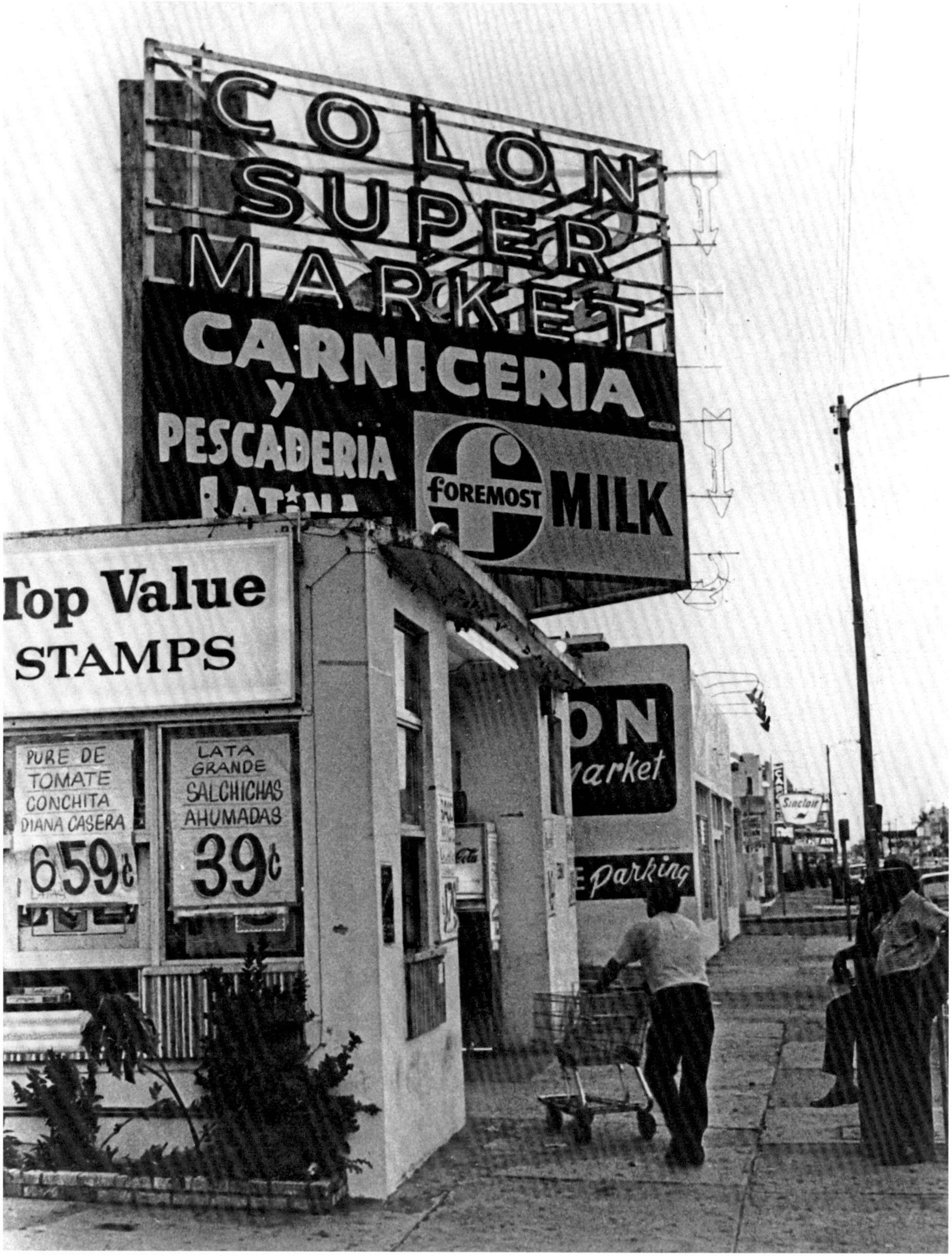

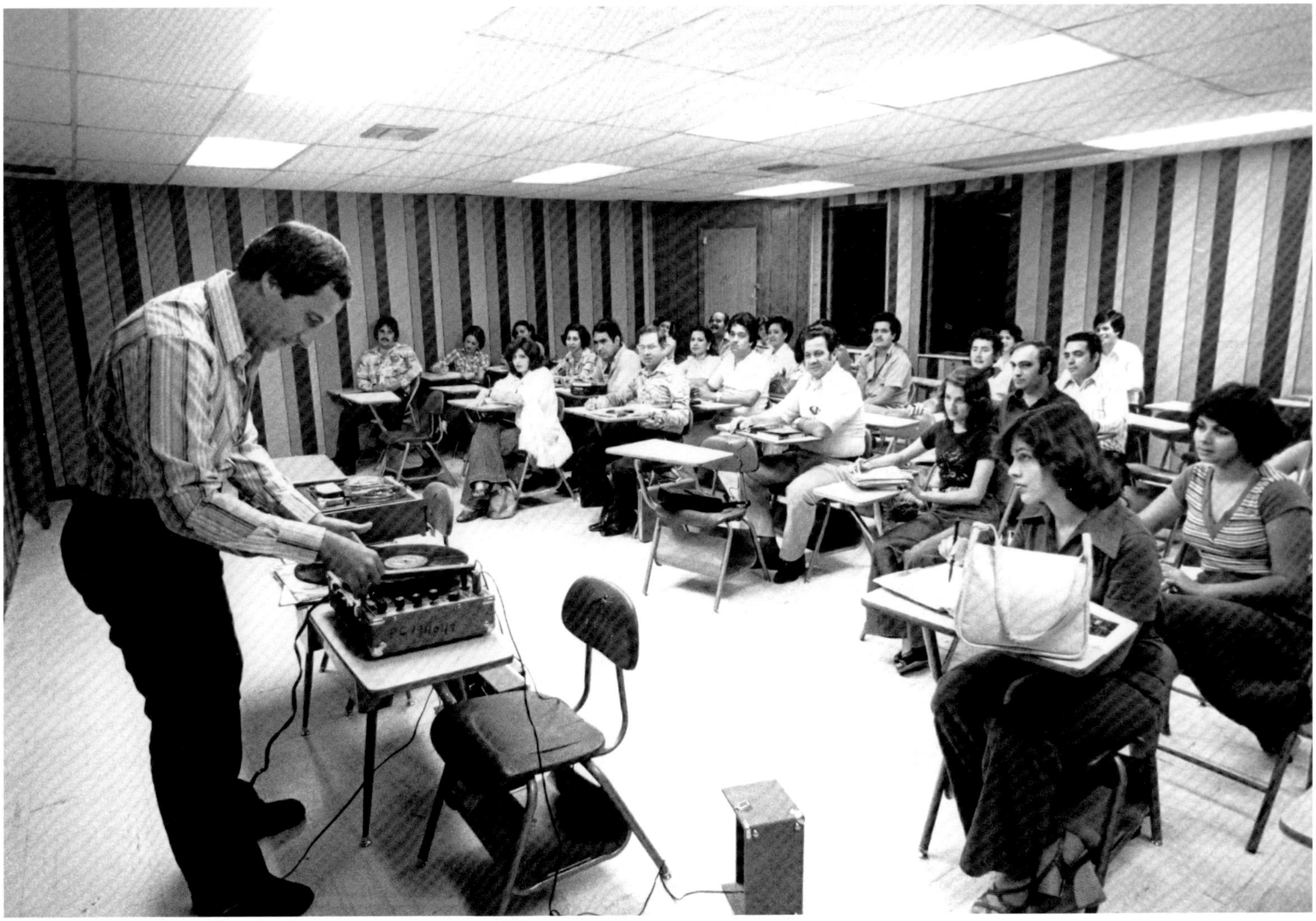

A class meets in the bilingual program at Miami Dade Community College's InterAmerican Campus. Bilingual education is extremely important to Cubans in Miami, and ESOL teachers are frequently in high demand.

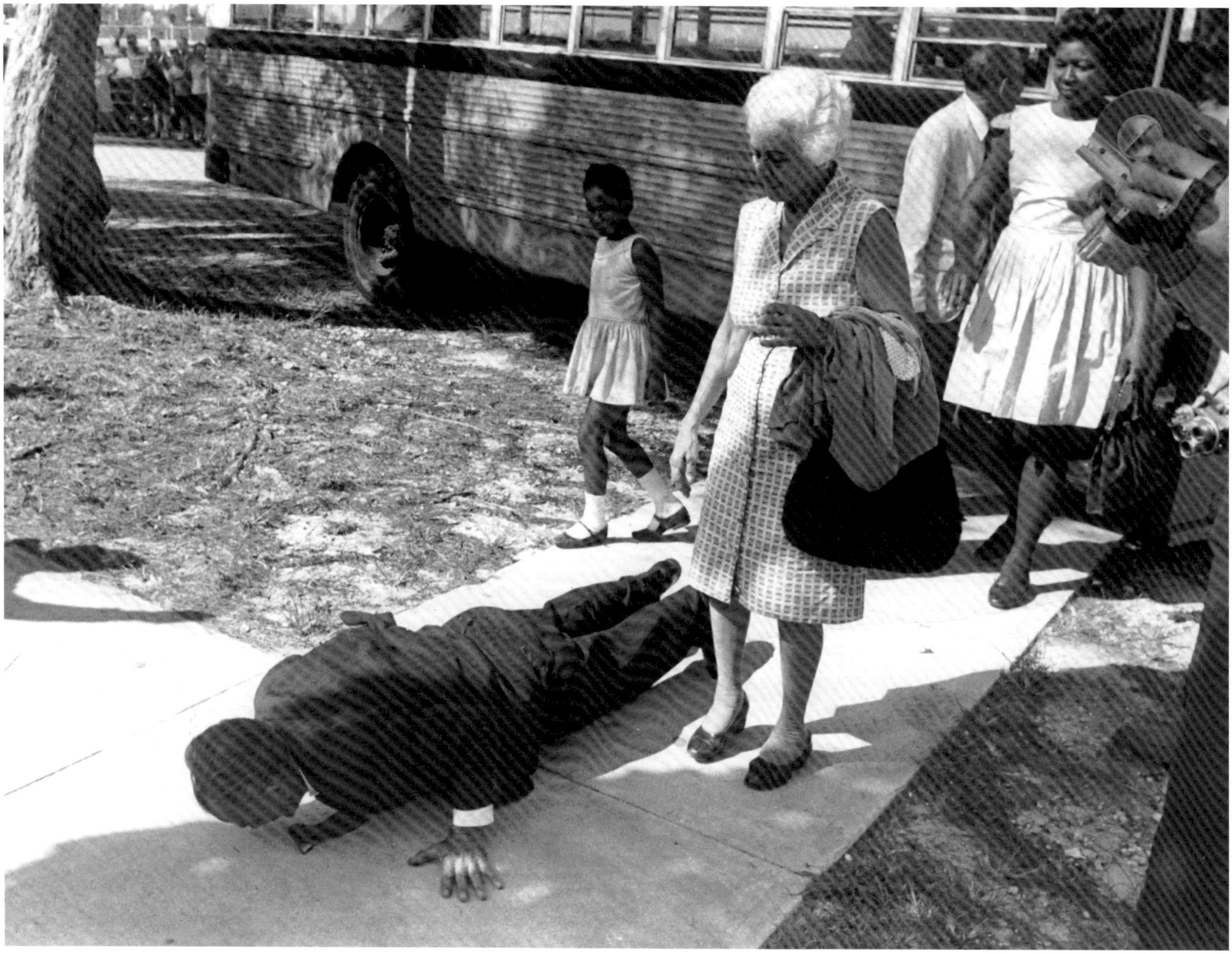

An airlifted exile kisses the ground after stepping off a bus in 1971.

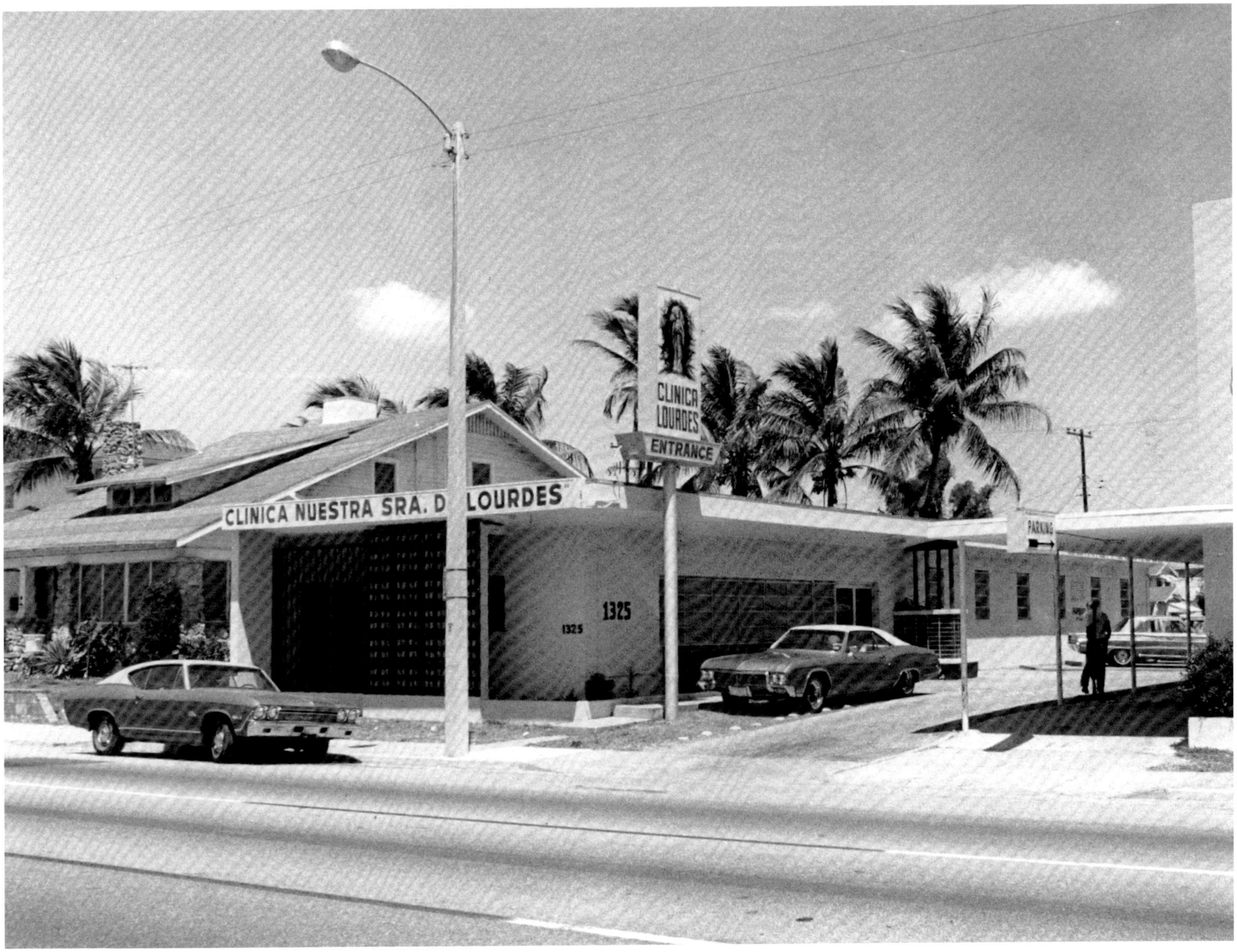

Clinica Nuestra Sra. de Lourdes. Many Cuban refugees enrolled in quintas, paying a predetermined fee each month to cover specified medical services. These clinics were not licensed or accredited, and therefore were not inspected or supervised by the state. In 1971, about 20 clinics were operating with memberships ranging between 400 and 14,000 persons per clinic.

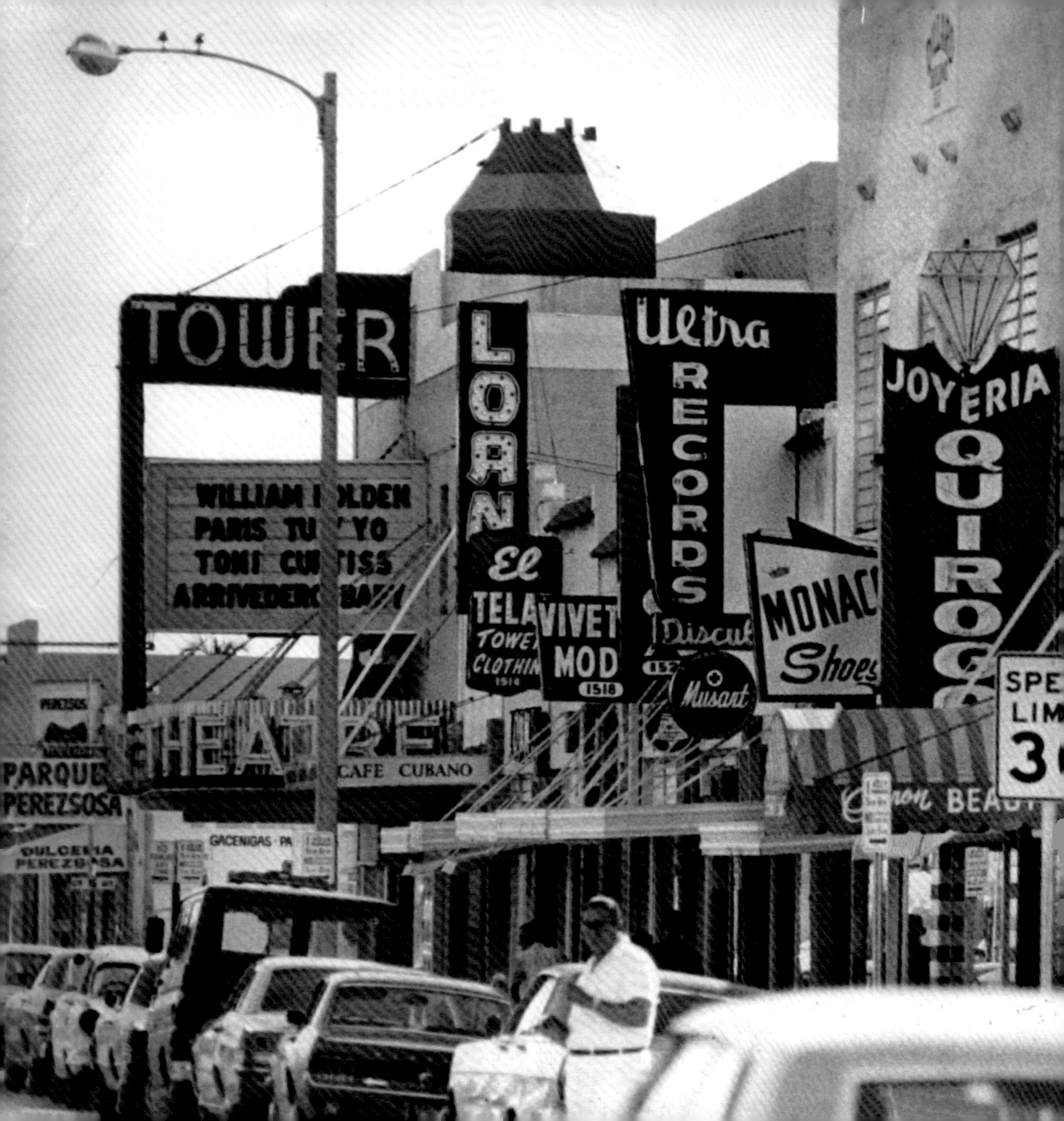
TOWER
WILLIAM HOLDEN
TONI CURTISS
LORAN
El
TELA
TOWER
CLOTHING
1514
VIVET
MOD
1518
Ultra
RECORDS
Musant
MONAC
Shoes
JOYERIA
QUIRO
CAFE CUBANO
PARQUE
PEREZSOSA
DULCERIA
PEREZSOSA
BEAU

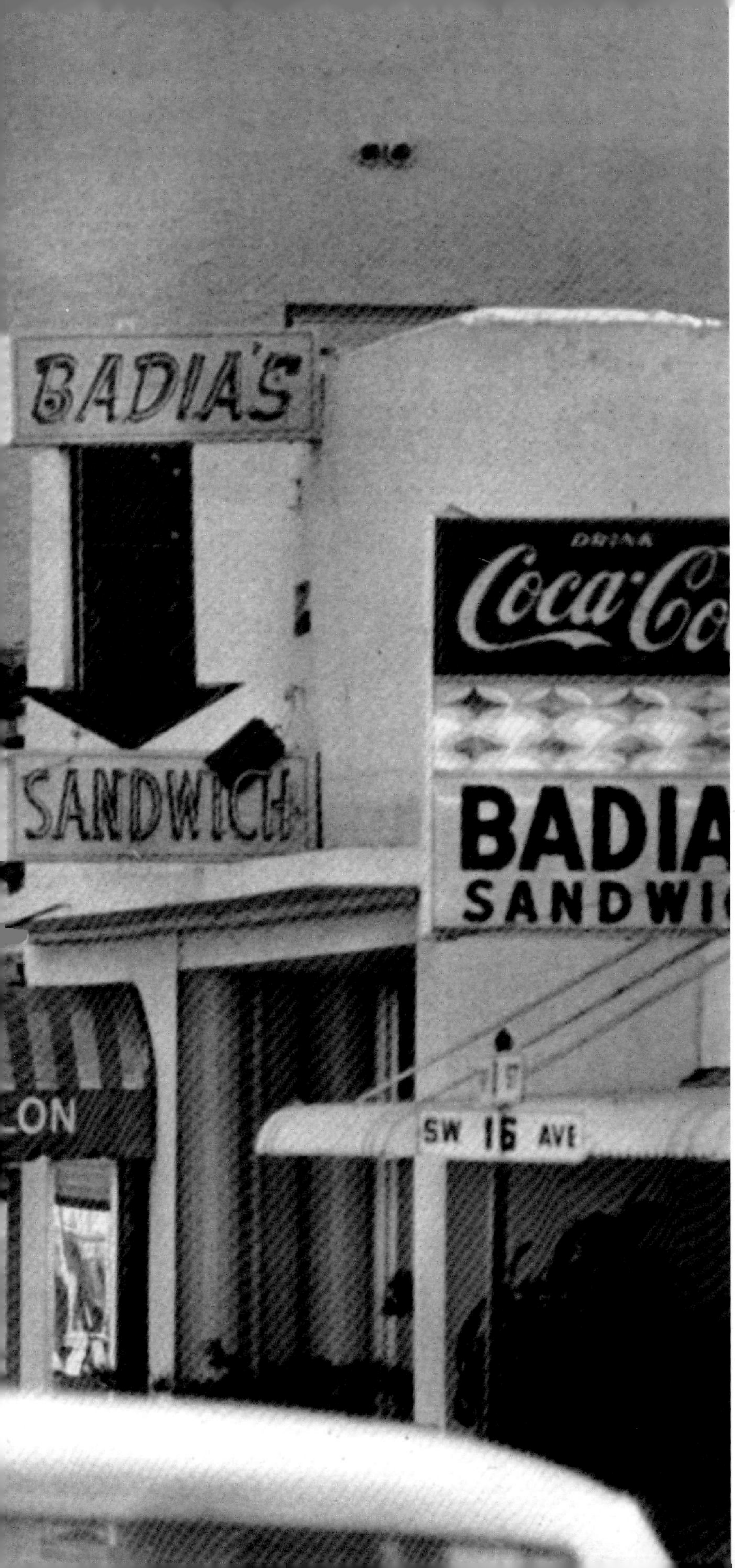

Cuban-owned shops and Spanish-language signs have proliferated in this view of the intersection at SW 8th Street and SW 16th Avenue.

This fashionable dog has joined the Nixon campaign, holding a sign protesting coexistence with Castro's Cuba and endorsing Richard Nixon for president.

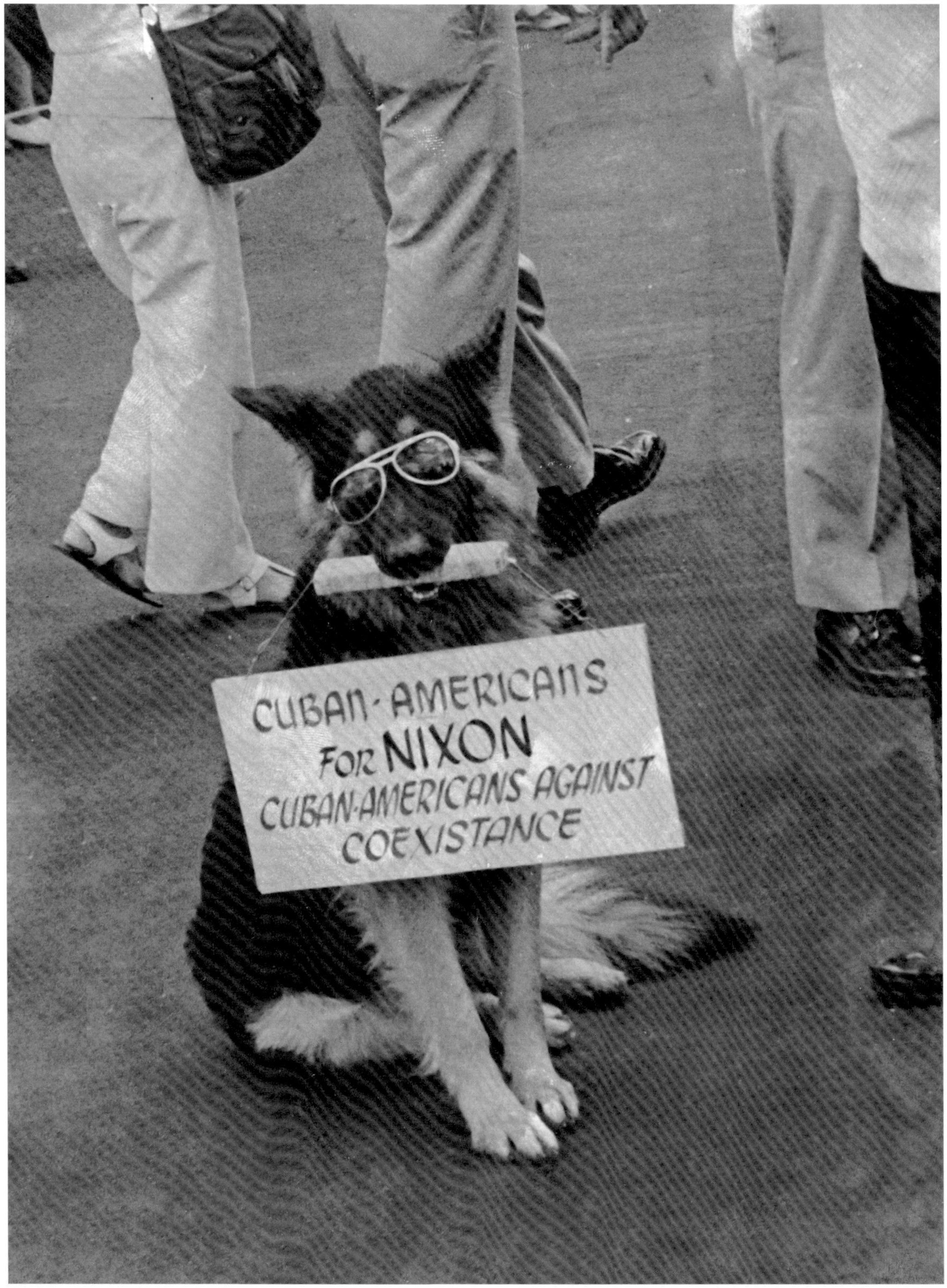

Turbulence and Prosperity

(1974–1979)

The 1970s were an especially turbulent time in Miami. There were several failed and successful bombings and assassinations. Terrorist groups popped up in Miami and other locations in the United States and internationally. Some of these groups were said to be sponsored by Castro. There were also radical anti-Castro Cuban exile groups, some rumored to be CIA-sponsored. There were frequent protests and riots throughout the city and suburbs of Miami. One violent episode took place in 1976, when Emilio Milian, a Spanish-language broadcaster, was targeted with a car bomb, which blew his legs off.

On a milder note, but surely not peaceful, several Cuban exile groups had formed in the past decade. They increasingly took to the streets to protest a variety of different issues. There were protests against coexistence with Cuba, anti-Castro protests, protests for the freedom of political prisoners, and many more. These groups had been forming since the 1960s, but the conflicts escalated greatly in the late 1960s and throughout the 1970s.

It wasn't all bombs and banners. There was plenty of progress made, and the first community celebrities began to emerge. Cubans like Manuel Carbonell, artist, and Luis Botifoll, banker, exemplified the success that the first wave of Cuban refugees had brought to Miami. It was obvious that the Cuban-American community was growing and thriving. They were here to stay, whether they knew it or not. Cuban-Americans entered the mainstream of pop culture through shows like *¿Que Pasa, USA?,* produced in Miami by federally funded WPBT, and through music, like that of Celia Cruz, the Queen of Salsa. Many Cuban-Americans also began to dip their feet in the pool of political office. Unfortunately, some of these political leaders had not learned the lessons of their kin back in Cuba, and allowed corruption to tarnish their reputations.

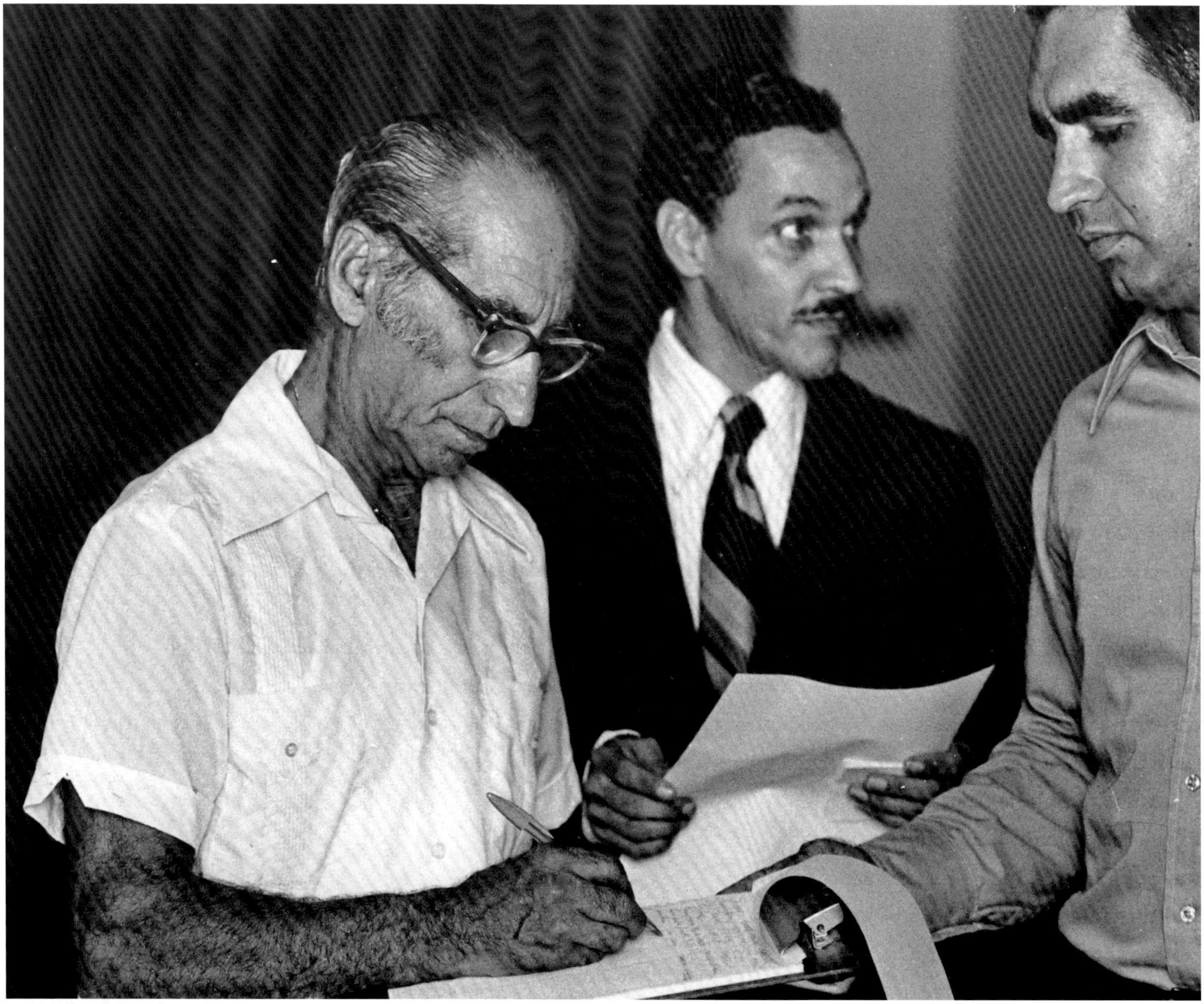

Joaquin Garcia signs a petition opposing coexistence at a Pro-Cuban rally. Also pictured are his son (at center) and Euripedes Riera, of the Cuban American Committee of Florida and Pan American Chamber of Commerce.

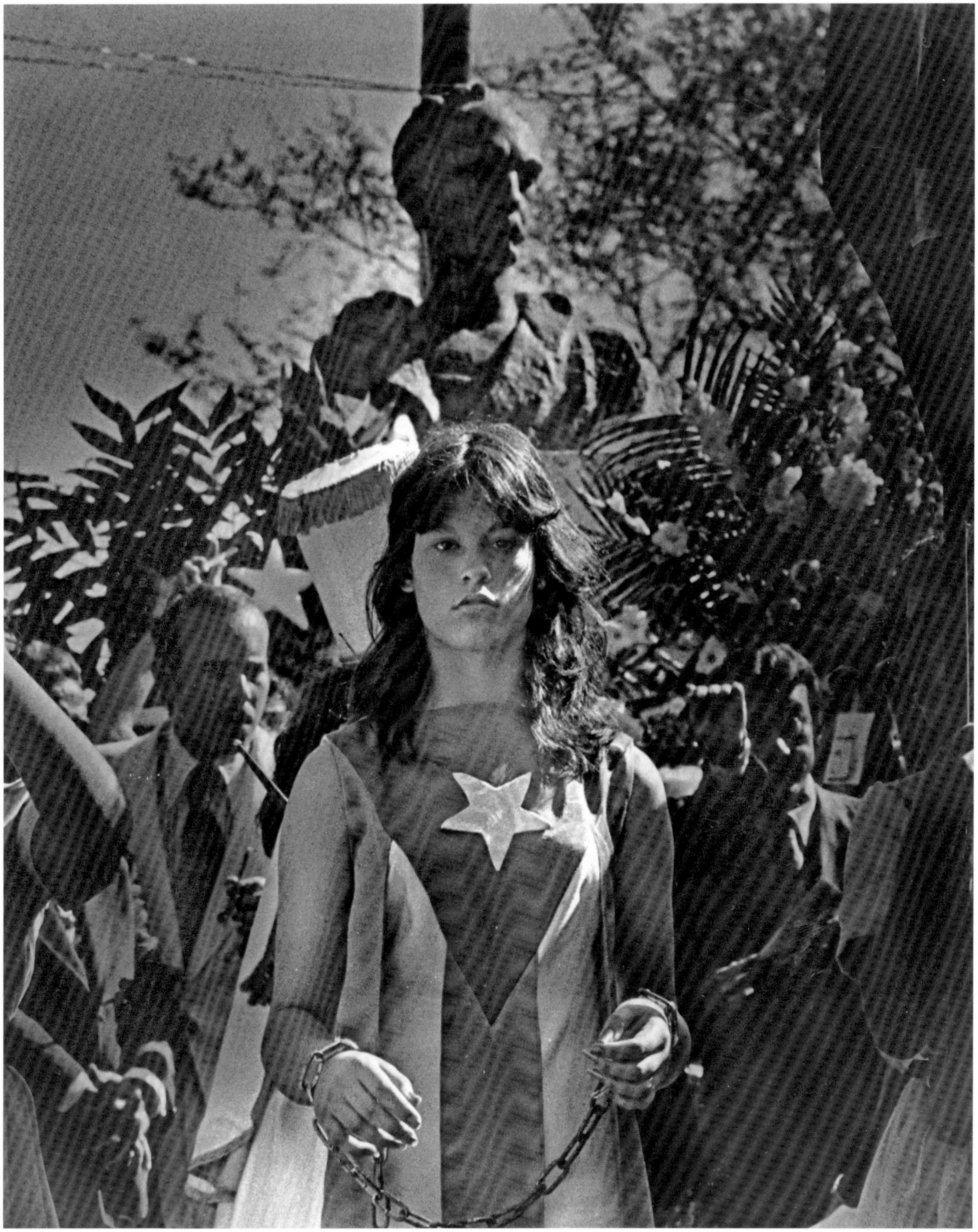

Lisset Verra wears chains in front of a statue of Jose Martí during a Jose Martí celebration, symbolizing Cubans in bondage. Jose Martí is a Cuban hero, for his tireless fight to gain Cuban independence from Spain and for his struggle to bring the rights and freedoms enjoyed and defended by Americans to Cuba. He would not live to see Cuban independence, achieved in the Spanish-American War a few years after his death, and Cuba would not achieve a democratic system of government, like that of the United States, in the twentieth century.

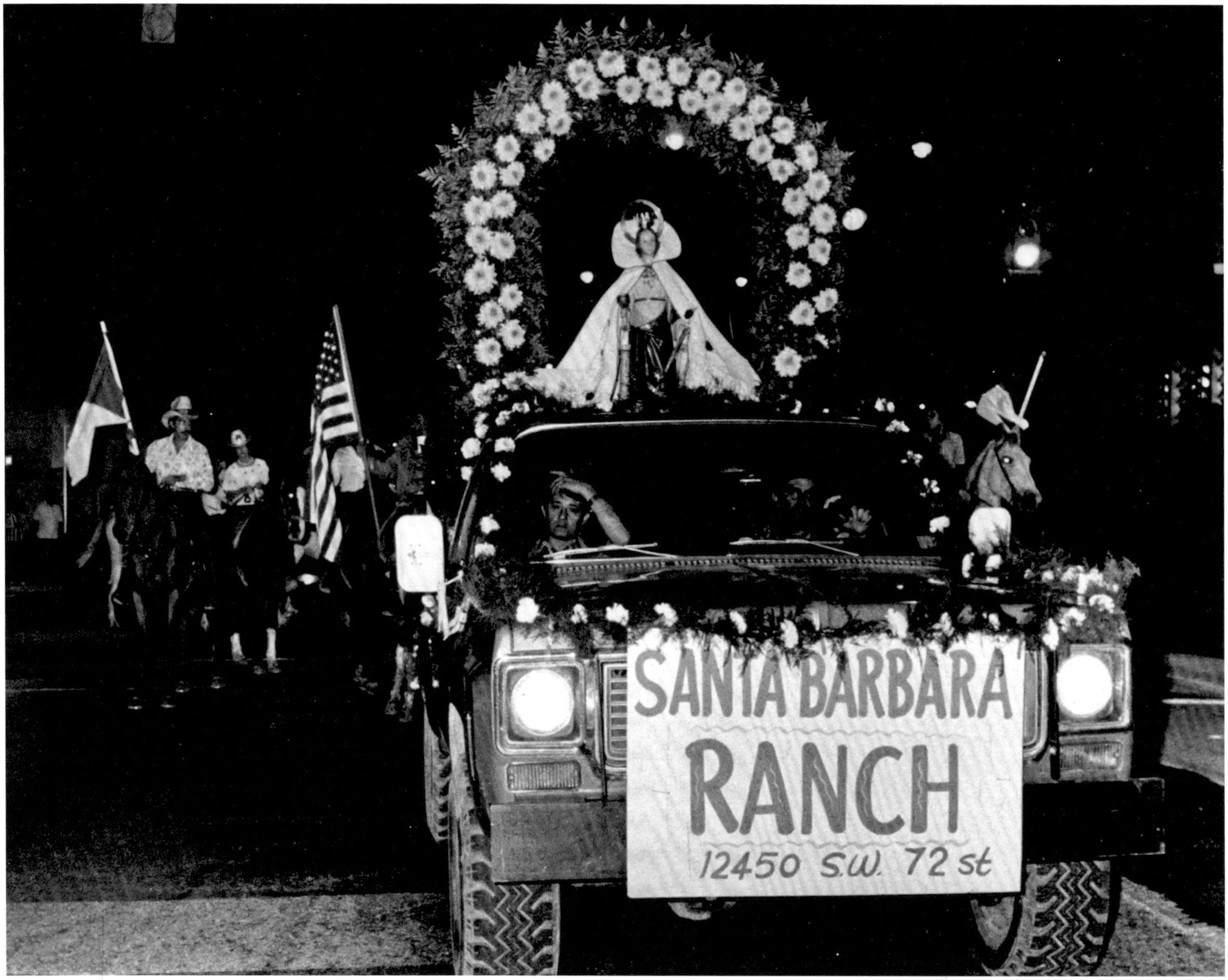

Cuban-Americans celebrate el Festival de Santa Barbara on December 5, 1975. Saint feasts are popular in both Santería and Catholicism. Santa Barbara is equated with Chango, since both carry swords.

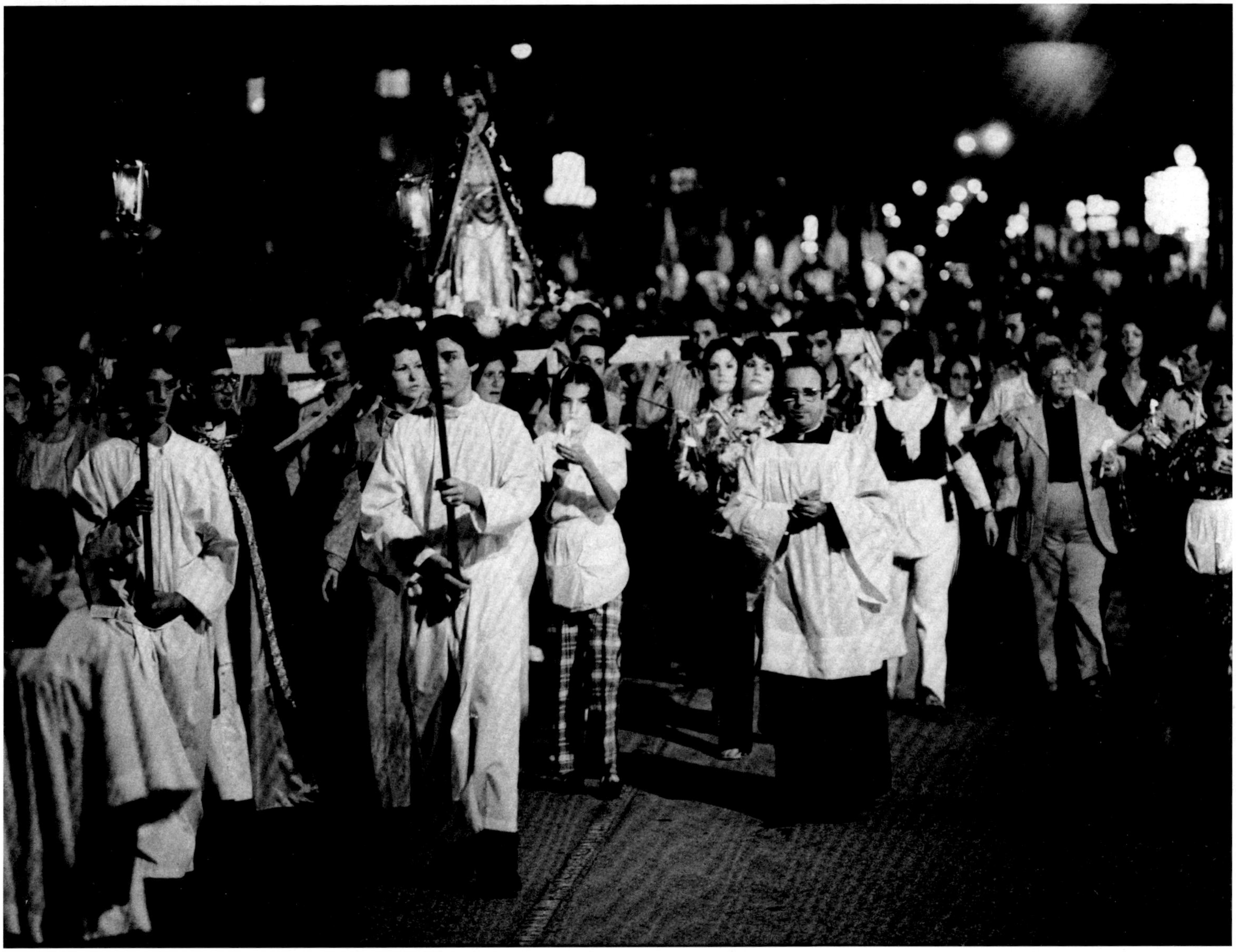

A candlelight procession in Little Havana honors Saint Lazarus on December 17, 1975. Saint Lazarus is equated with Babalu Aye by those who practice Santería. As is the case with la Virgen de la Caridad del Cobre, it is common to see the saint worshiped by a Cuban who practices either or both Catholicism and Santería.

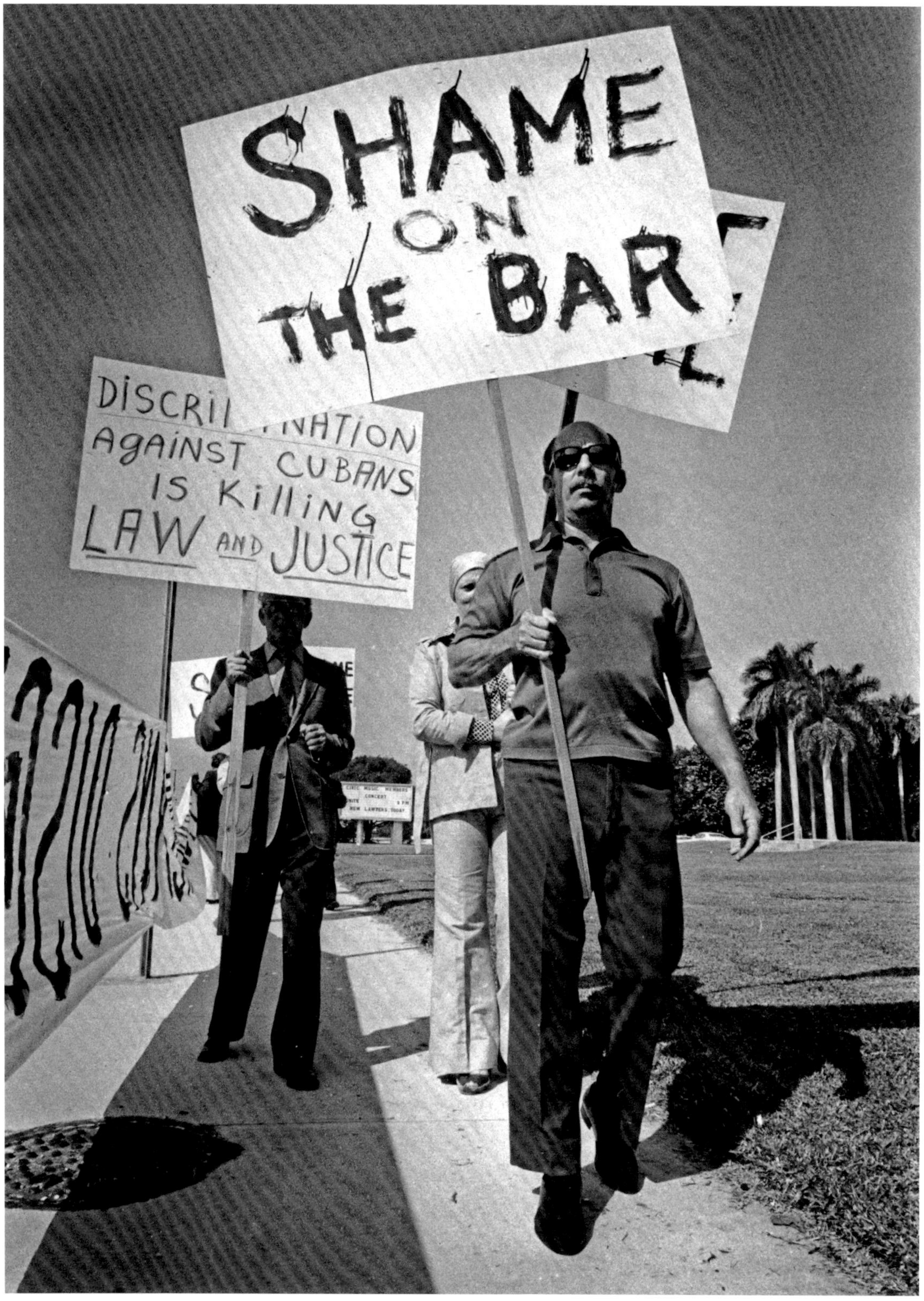

Cuban lawyers protest the bar exam at Dade County auditorium.

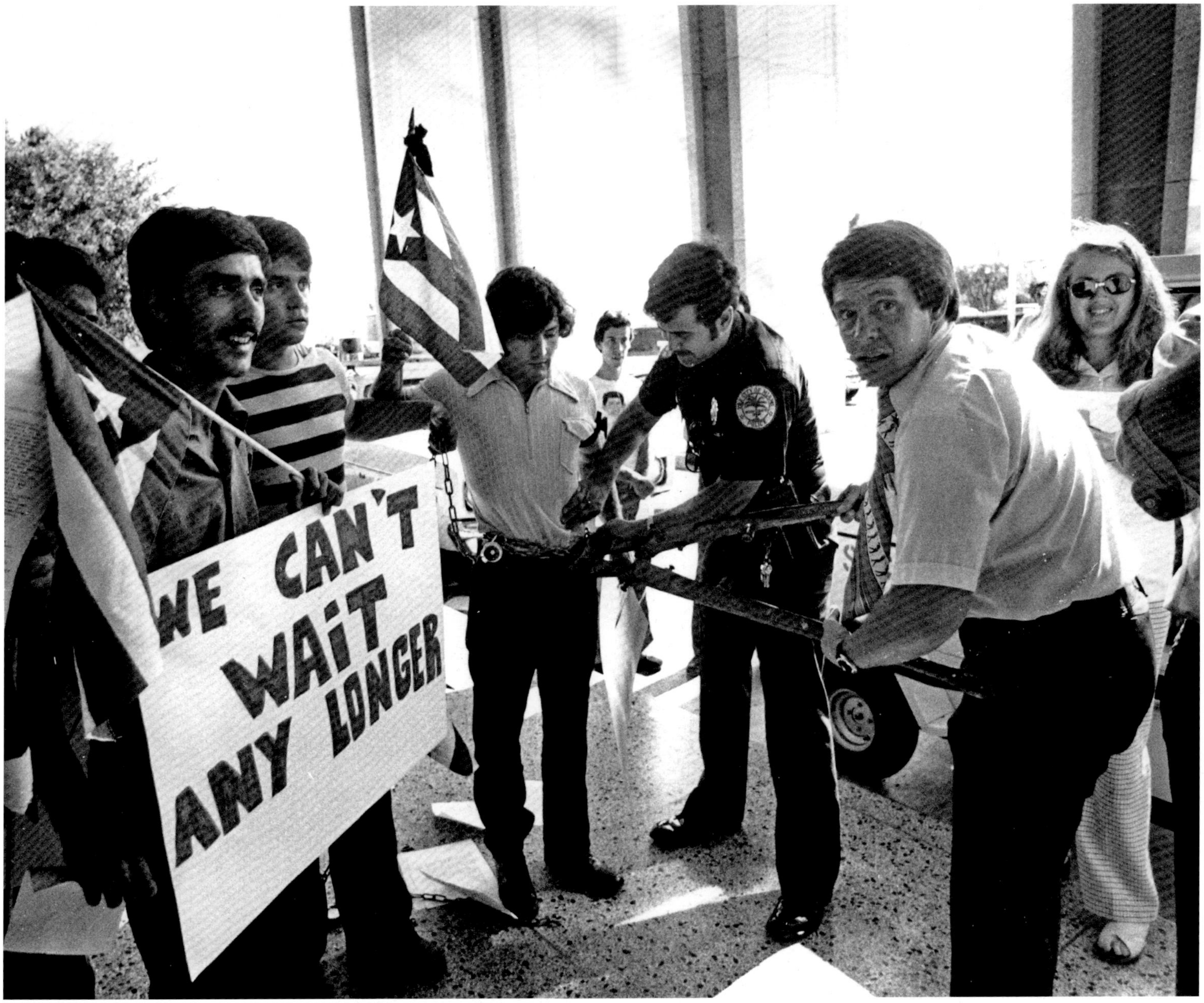

Cuban exiles protest in front of the Herald Building on April 5, 1976.

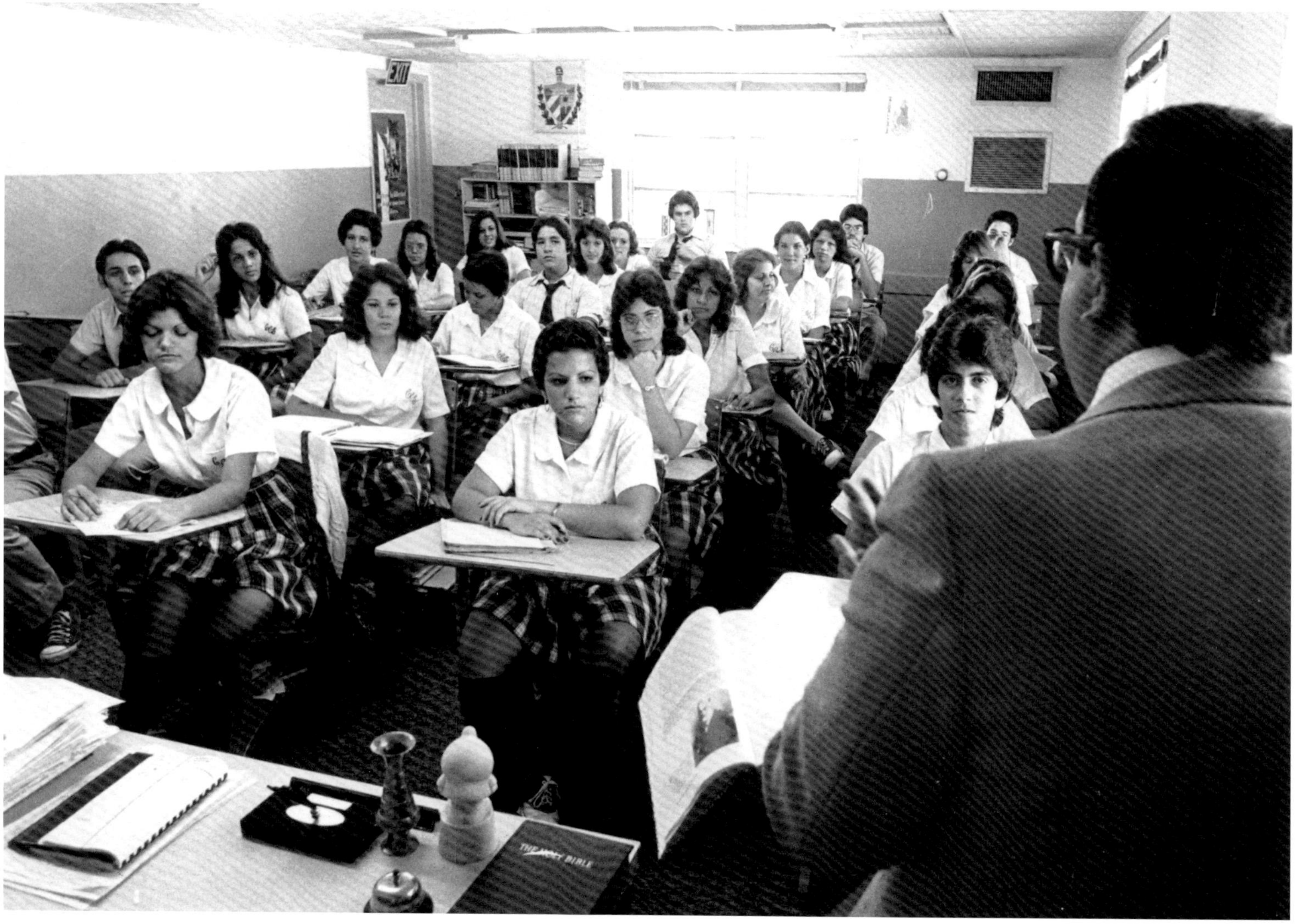

Students at the Champagnat Catholic School in a Miami-Dade community outreach program class. In the back of the classroom, a Cuban coat of arms hangs on the wall.

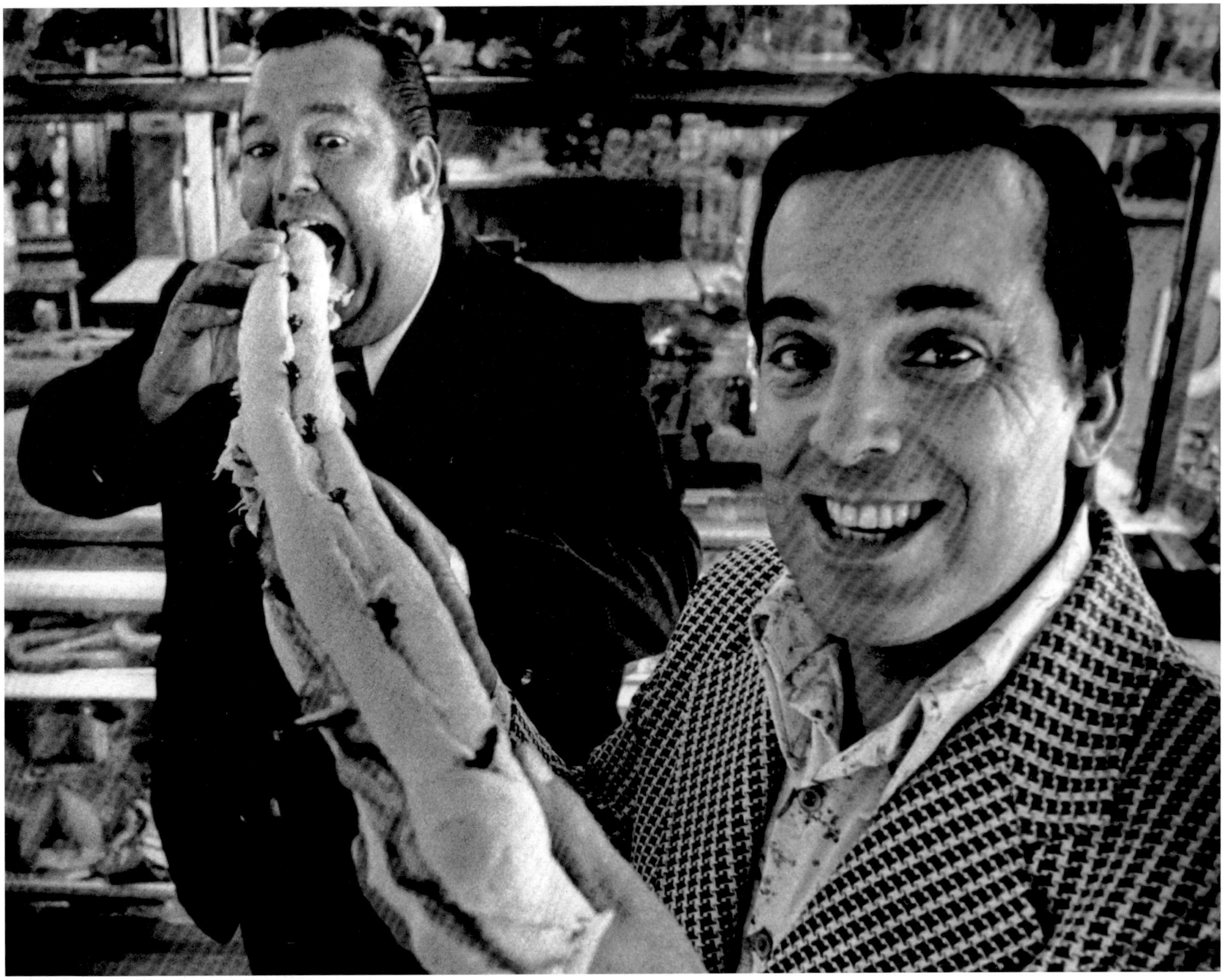

Felipe Angel Valls tackles an unusually long sandwich held by partner Arsenio Amadia. Felipe is the owner of the famous Versailles Cuban restaurant on Calle Ocho in Little Havana.

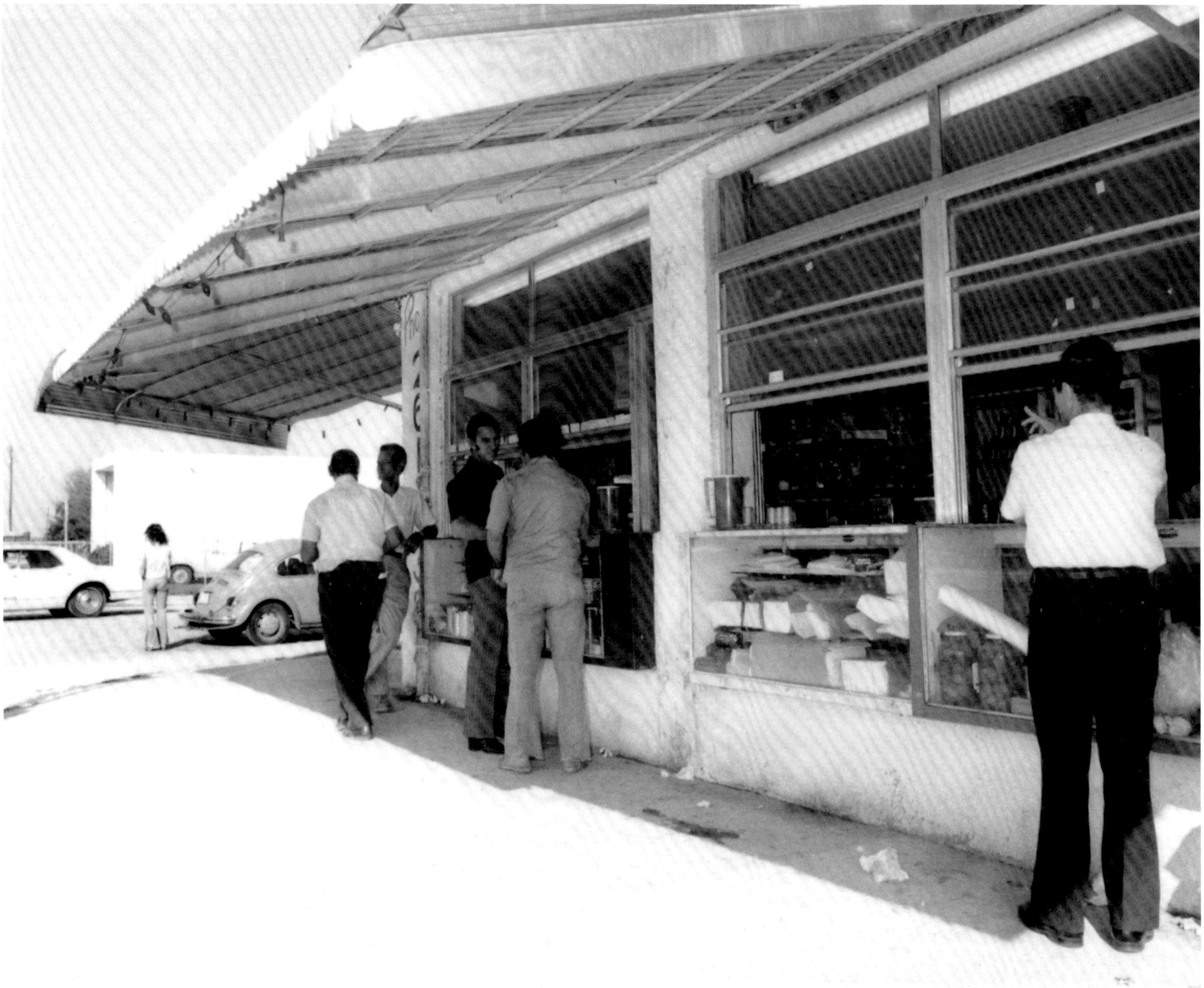

Walk-up service windows are typical of Cuban restaurants in Miami. Any patron can walk up and order cigars, a *cortadito,* or a *sandwiche Cubano* to go. However, most hang around and enjoy conversation with other patrons.

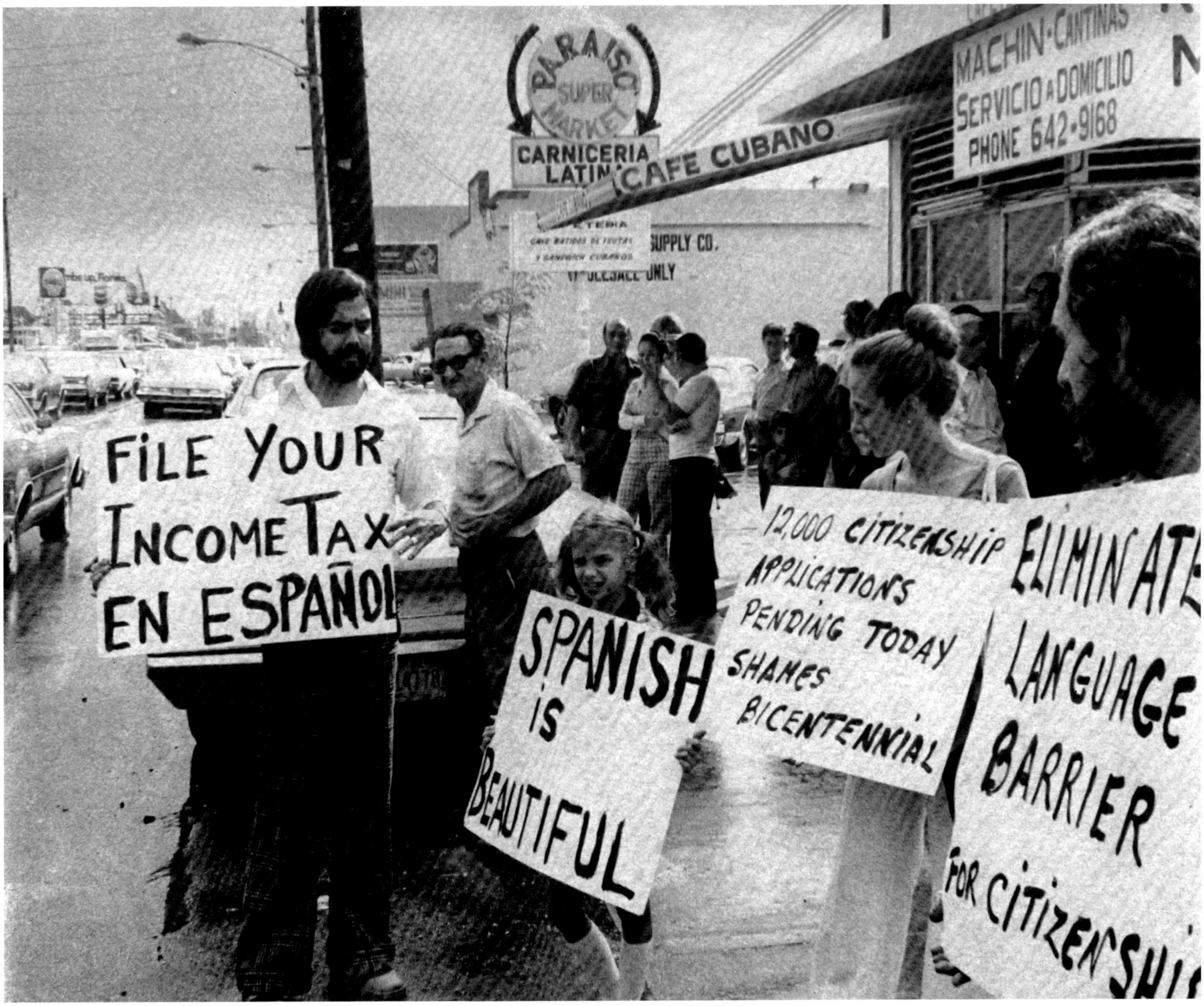

A protest in the 1970s encourages the use of Spanish in an effort to accommodate refugees, especially those seeking citizenship.

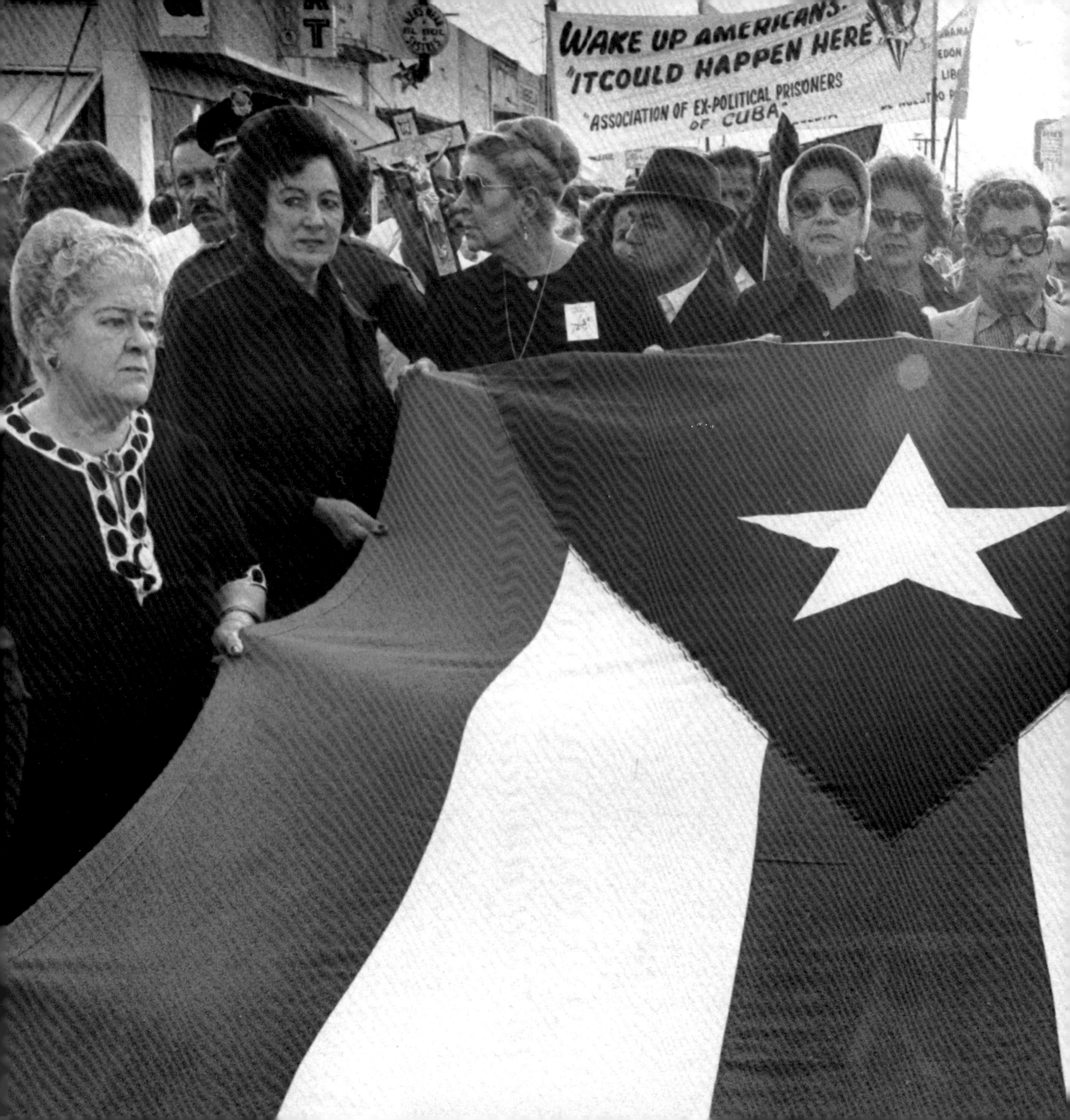
WAKE UP AMERICANS.
"ITCOULD HAPPEN HERE"
"ASSOCIATION OF EX-POLITICAL PRISONERS
OF CUBA"

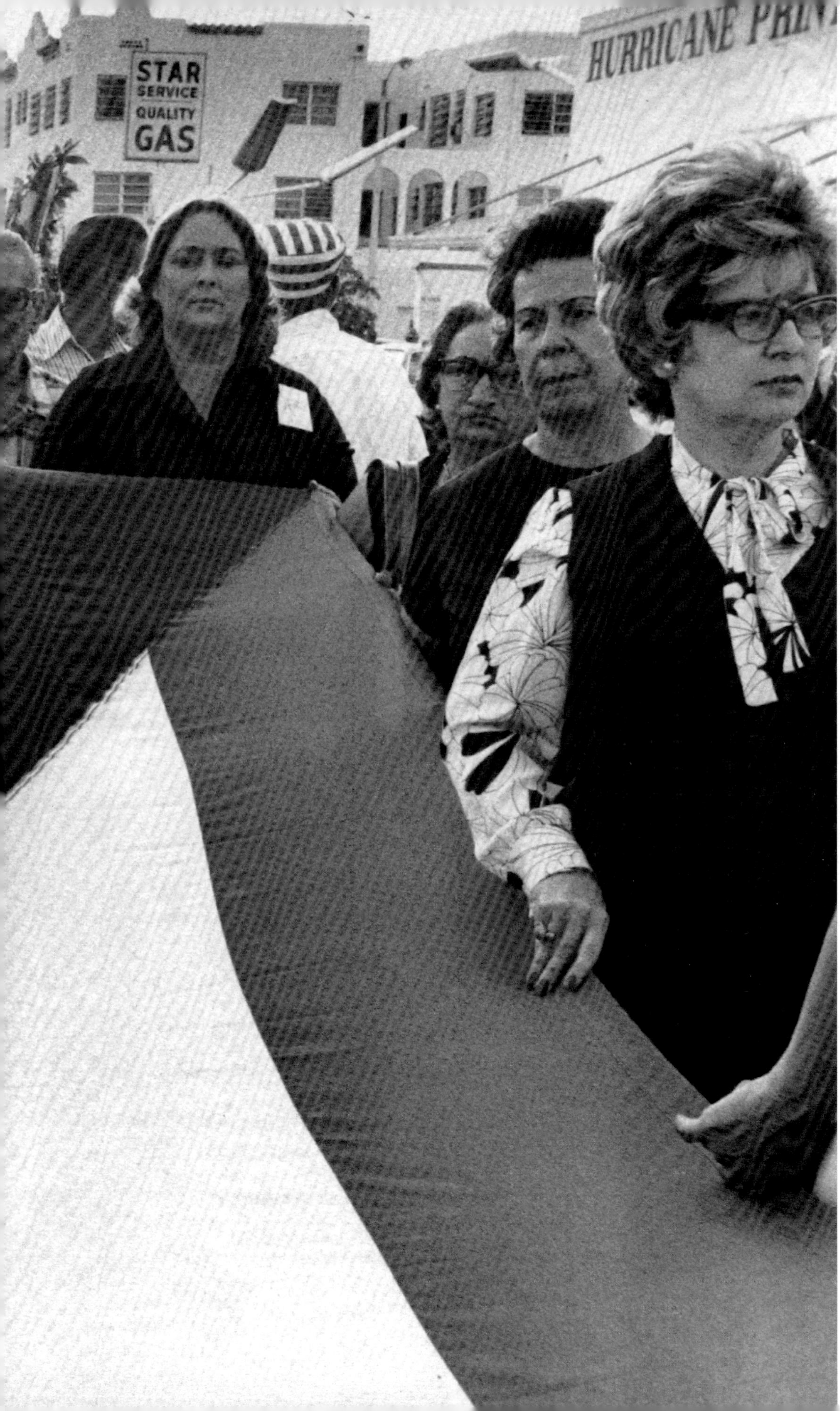

The Association of Ex-Political Prisoners of Cuba protests on behalf of political prisoners in Cuba on April 5, 1976. The banner in the distance proclaims in English, "Wake up Americans: 'It Could Happen Here.'"

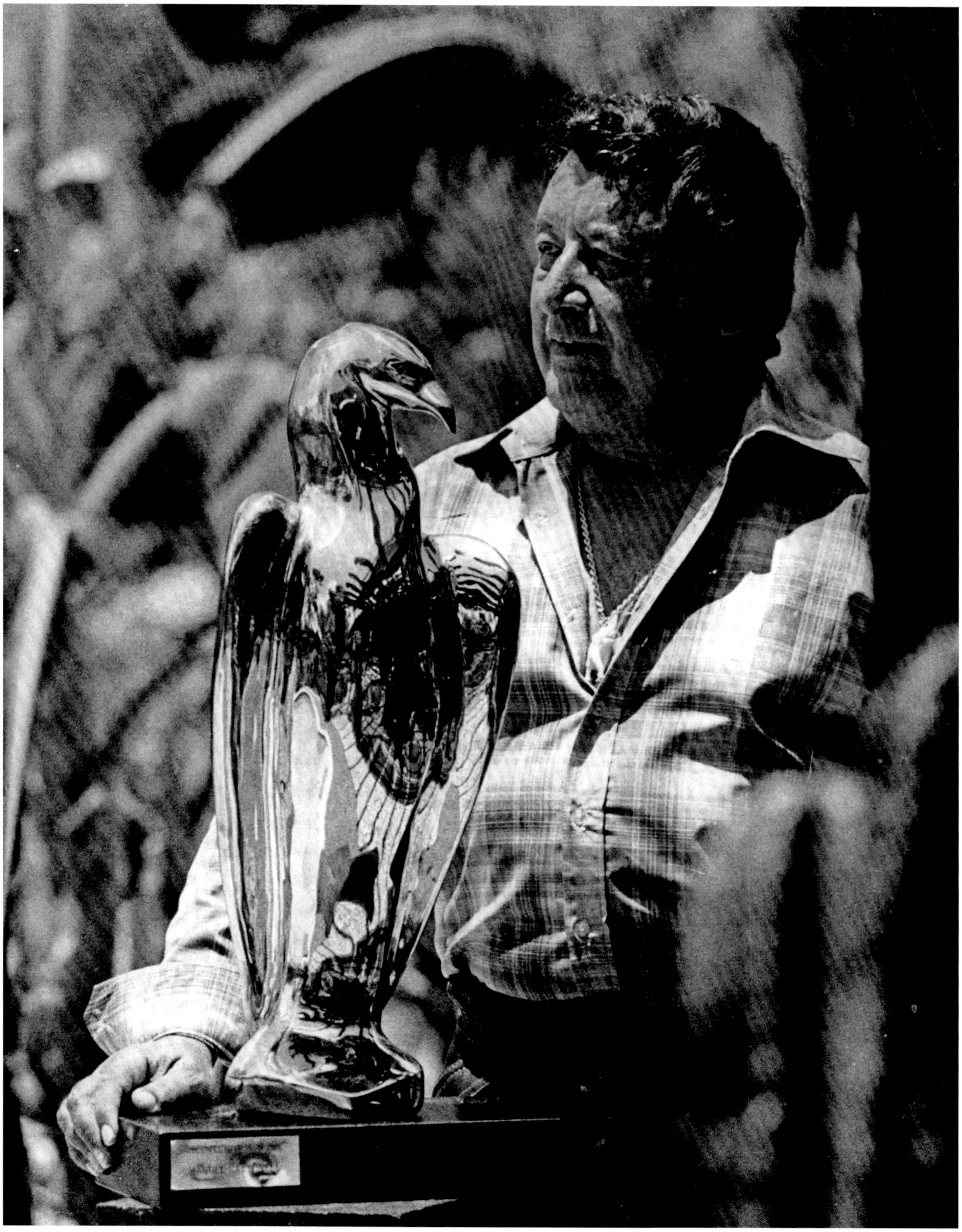

Artist Manuel Carbonell with his *Bicentennial Eagle.* In a formal ceremony at the White House, Carbonell presented the sculpture as his gift to the United States. It is currently part of the Smithsonian Collection. Carbonell is a resident artist at the Miami Beaux Arts Gallery.

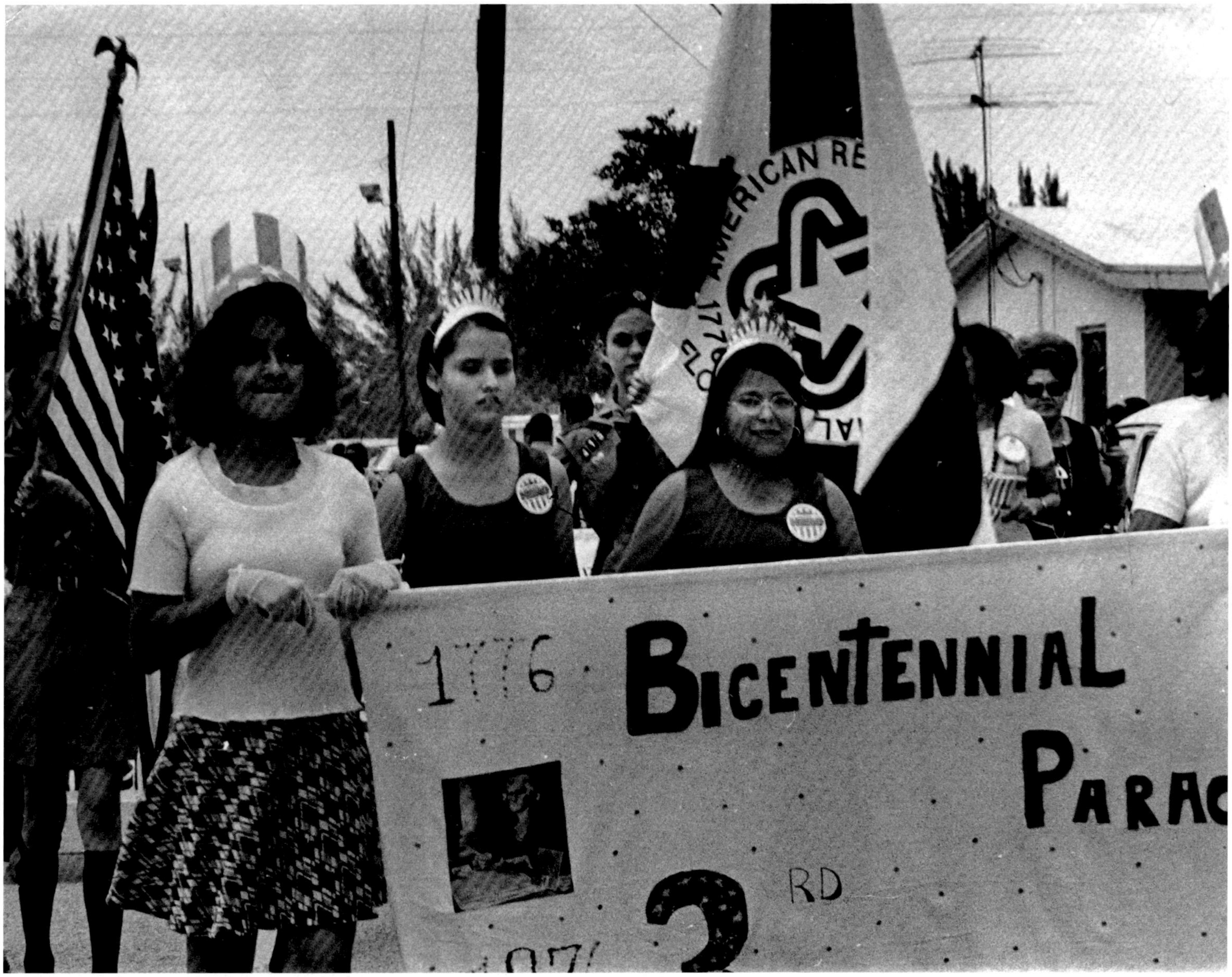

Cuban-American girls in a Bicentennial parade in 1976. Sometimes known as the "hyphen generation," these Cuban-Americans grew up between two distinct worlds.

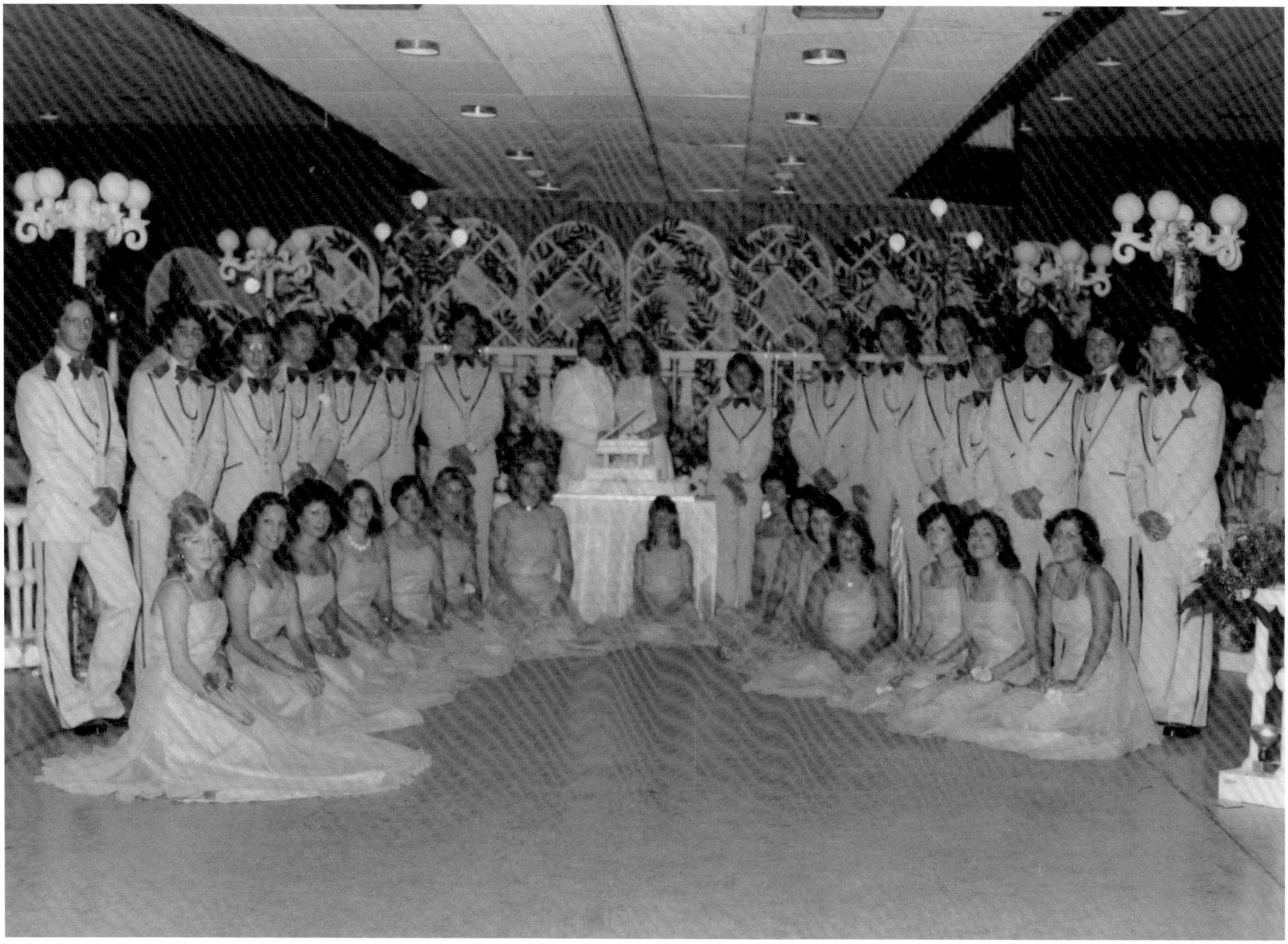

Sweet sixteens are popular throughout the United States, but in Miami, quinces are the society presentation of choice. *Quinceañeras* usually don white ball gowns and tiaras. It is traditional to have a "court" consisting of 15 couples, who dance during presentation of the *quinceañera.*

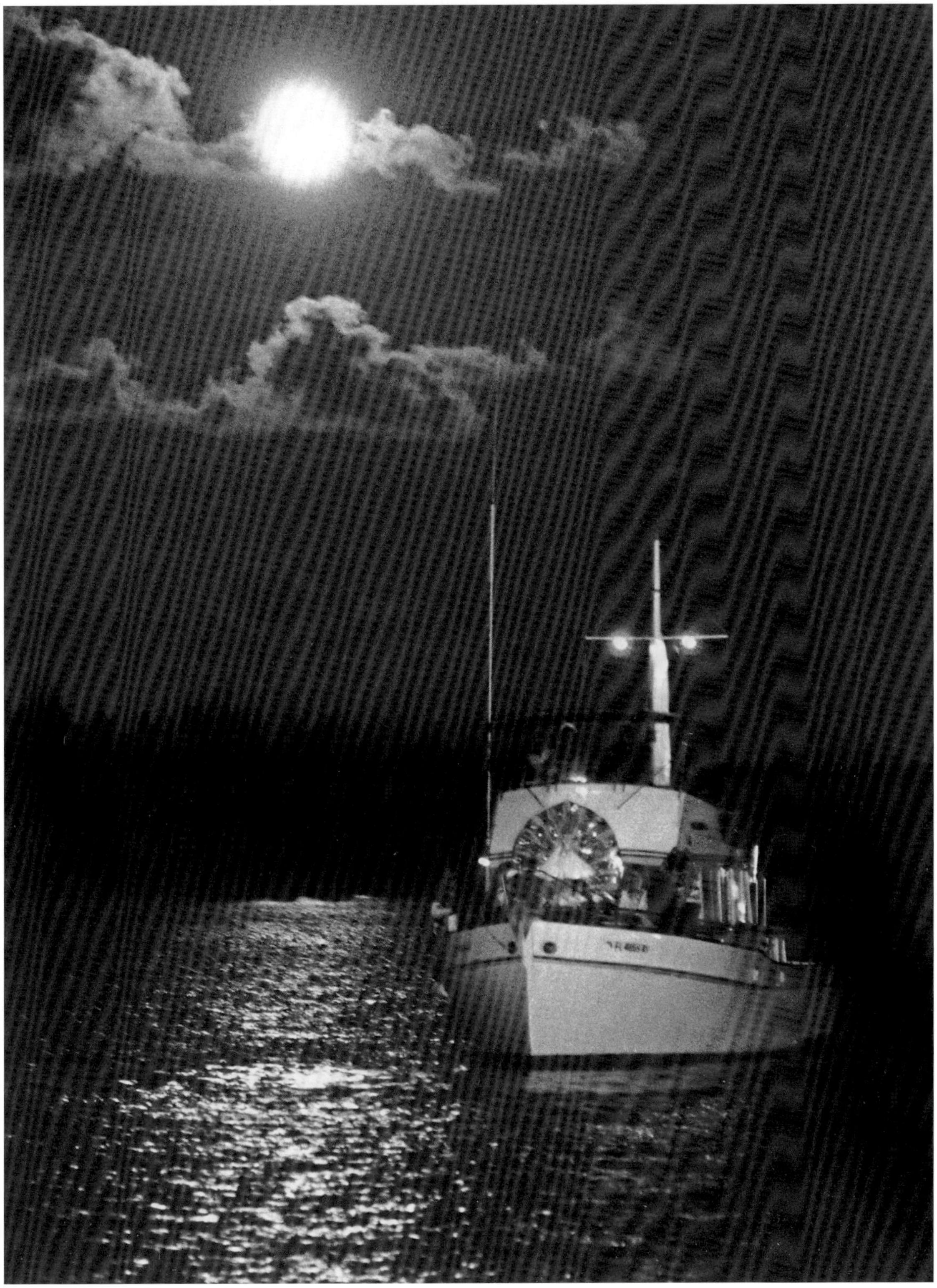

La Virgen de la Caridad del Cobre at the bow of a boat on the water in Miami. Tradition states that the Virgin appeared as a statue to three men, known as "the three Juans," who were caught at sea during a horrible storm. The statue remained completely dry, despite the storm. In Santería, the goddess Oshun has been syncretized with La Virgen de la Caridad del Cobre. To Cuban exiles, the Virgin means liberty and freedom, and was in their view the driving force in bringing them safely to the United States.

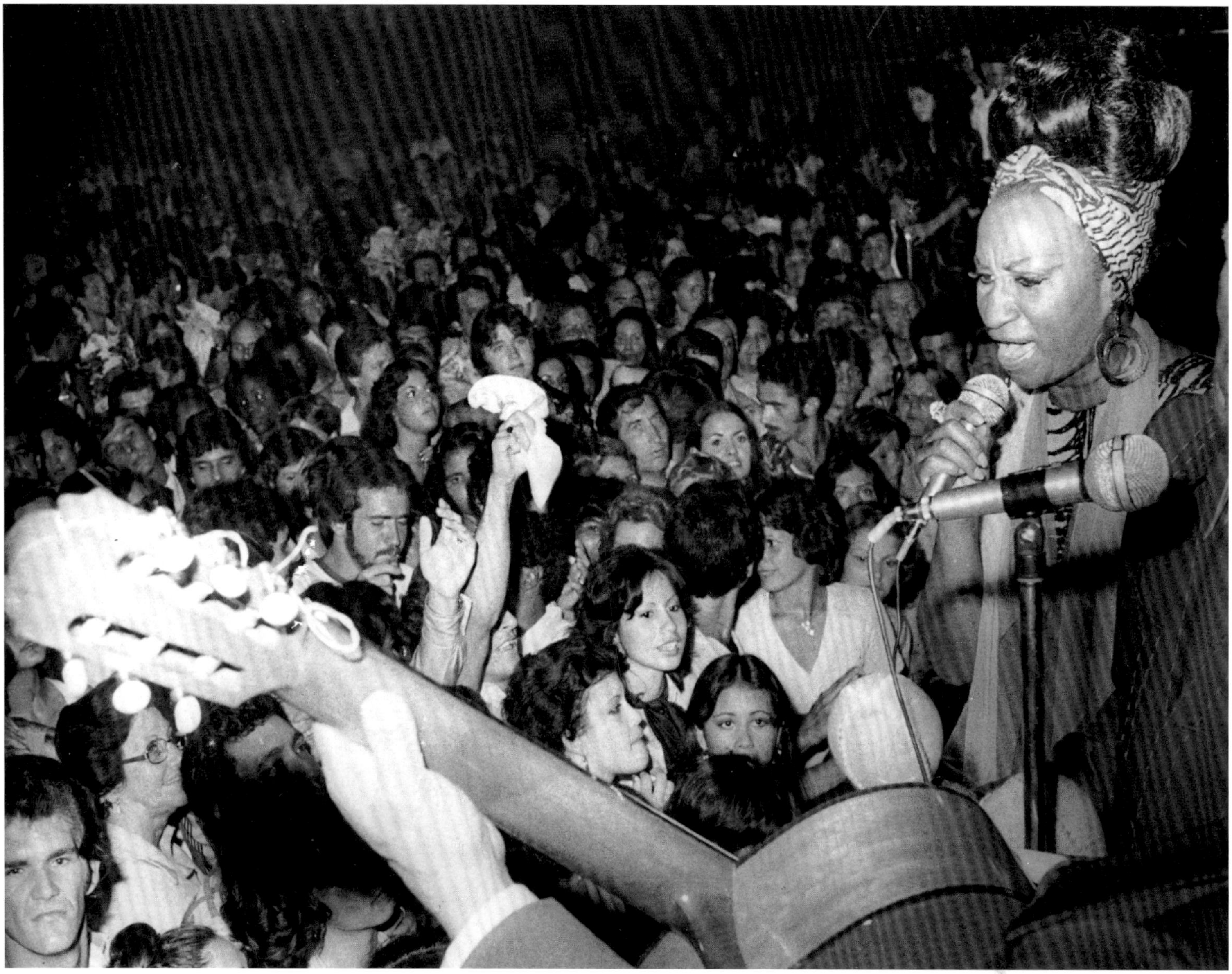

Celia Cruz (1924–2003) onstage July 15, 1976. Cruz is considered to be the most significant Cuban female singer to date. After her death in 2003, she was laid in state at the Freedom Tower, where more than 200,000 fans paid their respects. SW 8th Street is also known as Celia Cruz Way.

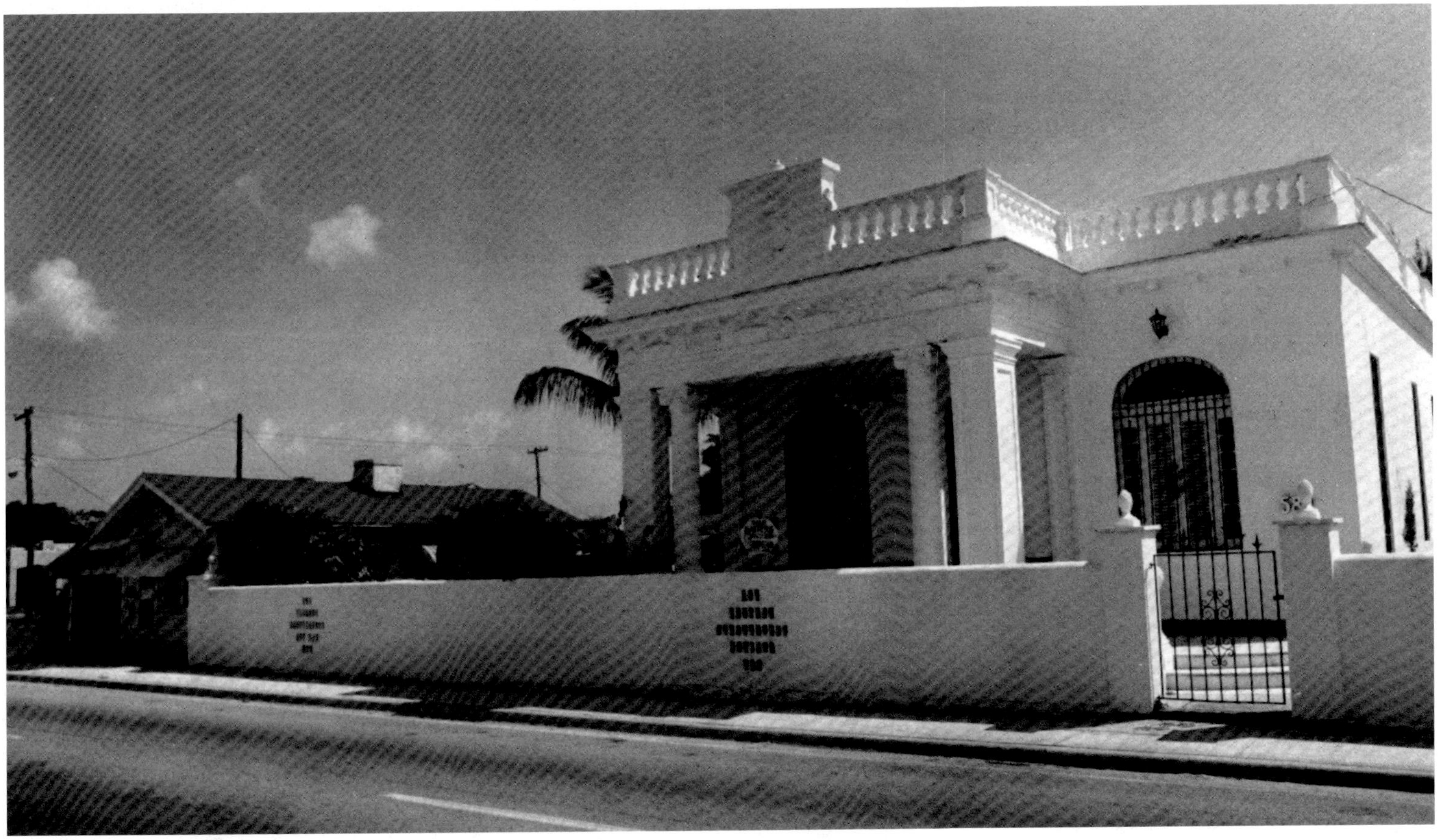

Villa Paula, located on North Miami Avenue, was originally built in 1926 as the Cuban Consulate. The building was constructed entirely of materials imported from Cuba. It was named for the wife of Cuban consul Douglas Milord. Milord's wife died of complications from a leg amputation and is said to have haunted the villa ever since.

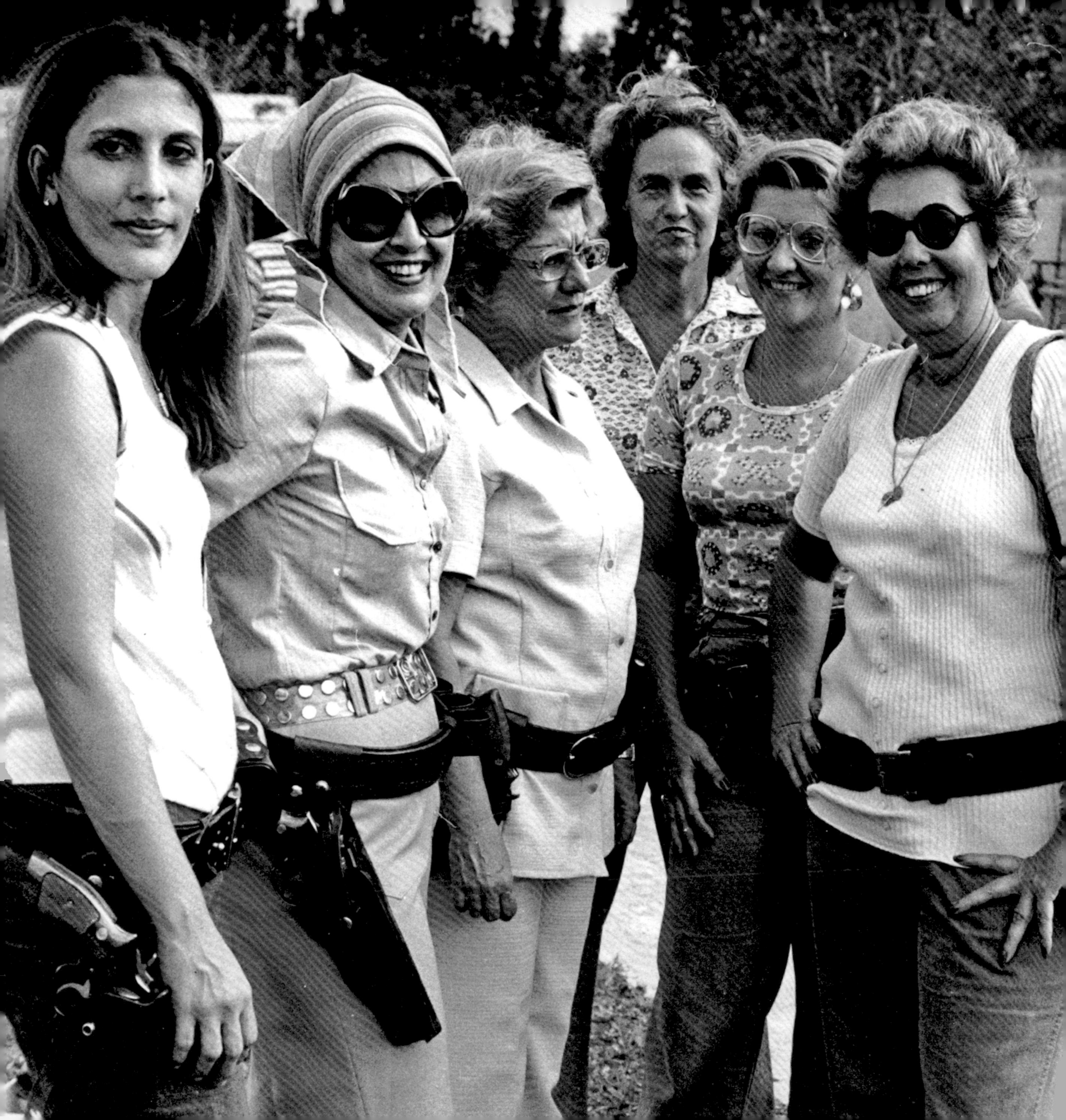

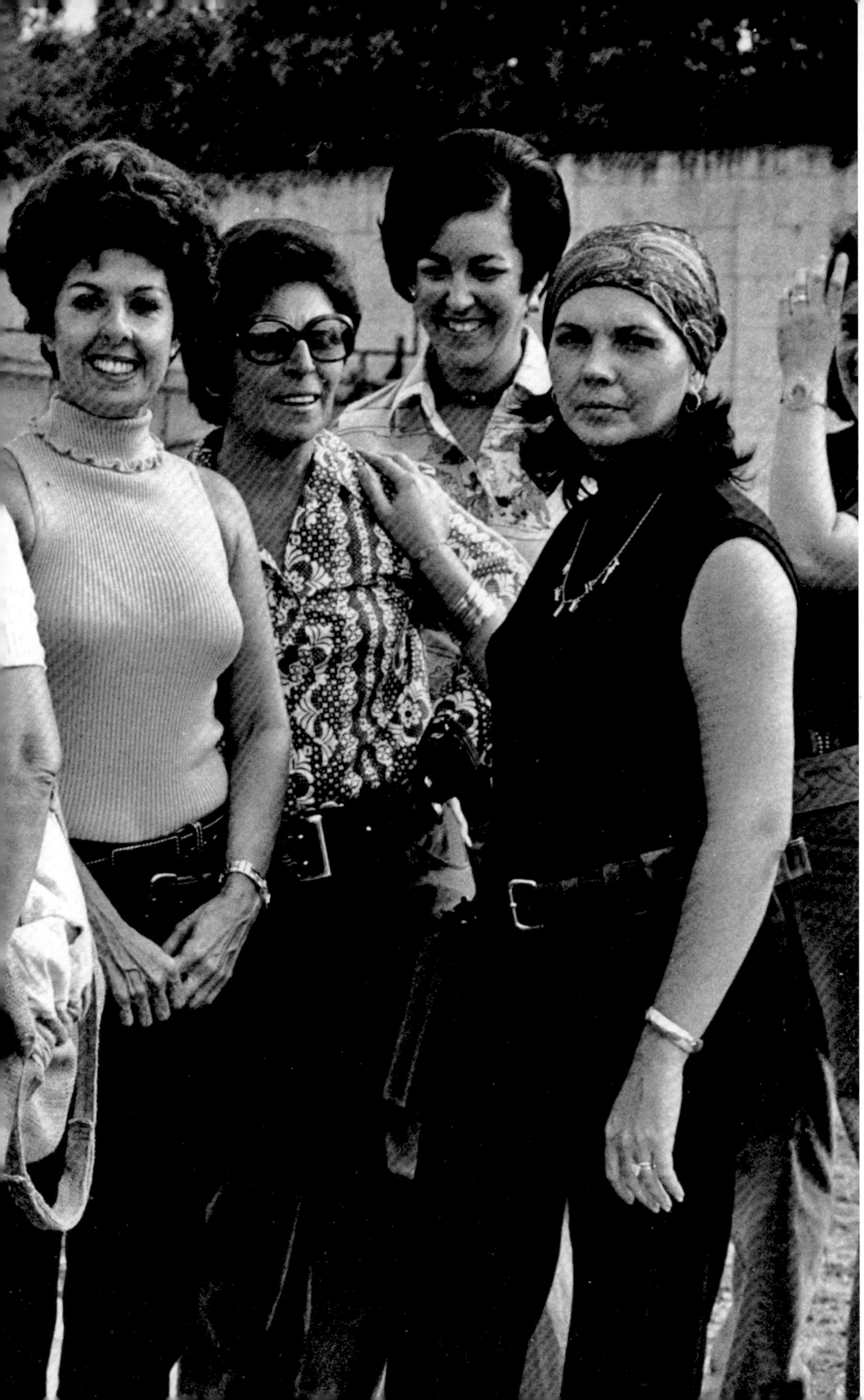

Sharpshooters at the Cuban-American Pistol Club in 1976 break for a group photo.

Balcony conversations at Westland Eden Apartments. It is a common joke among Cubans that they are very loud when communicating, and may even be partial to shouting.

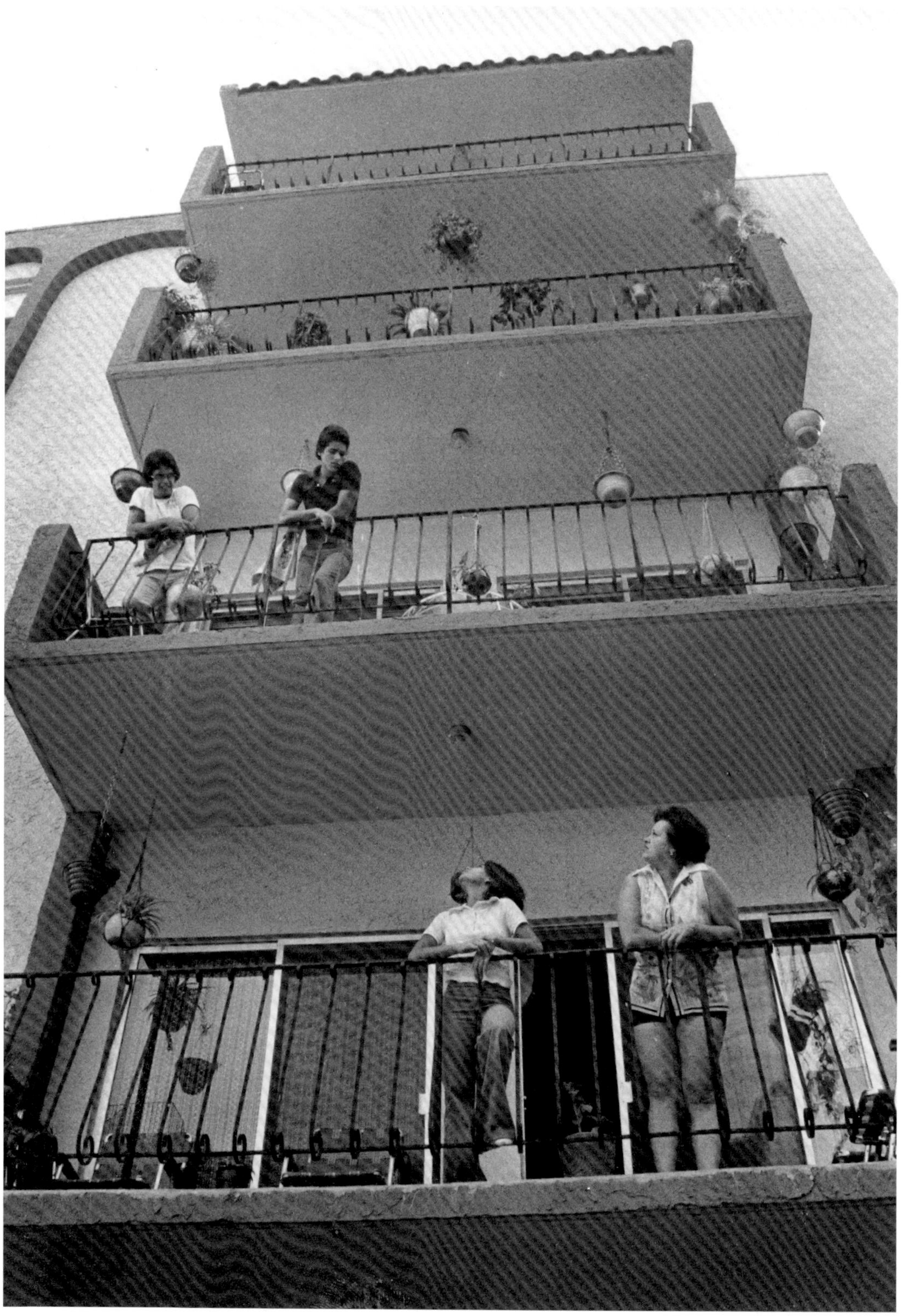

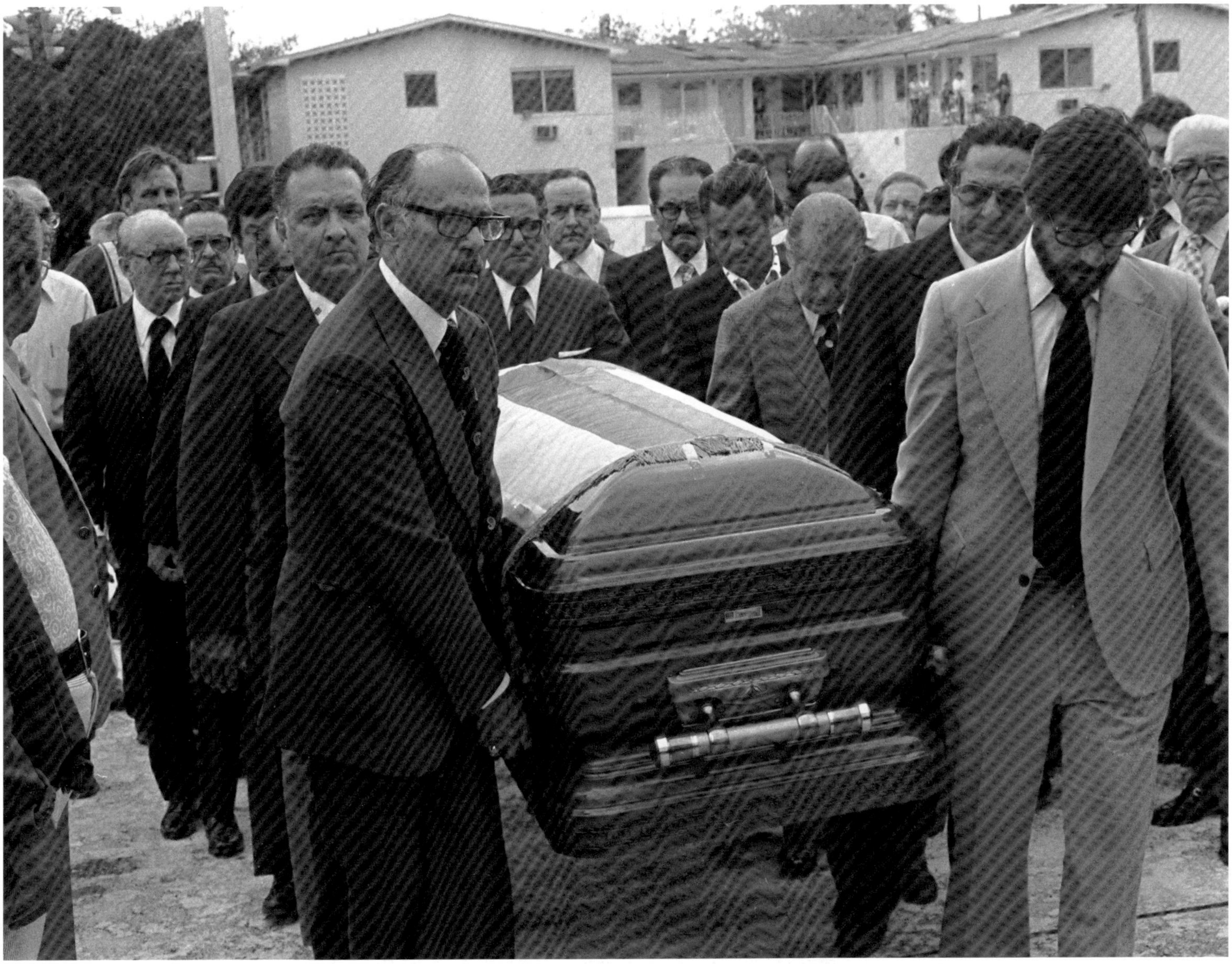

The funeral of Carlos Prio Socarrás, 16th president of Cuba, who died at age 73 of a self-inflicted gunshot wound in 1977. Like most other deceased Cubans in Miami, Prio Socarrás is buried at Caballero Rivero Woodlawn Cemetery.

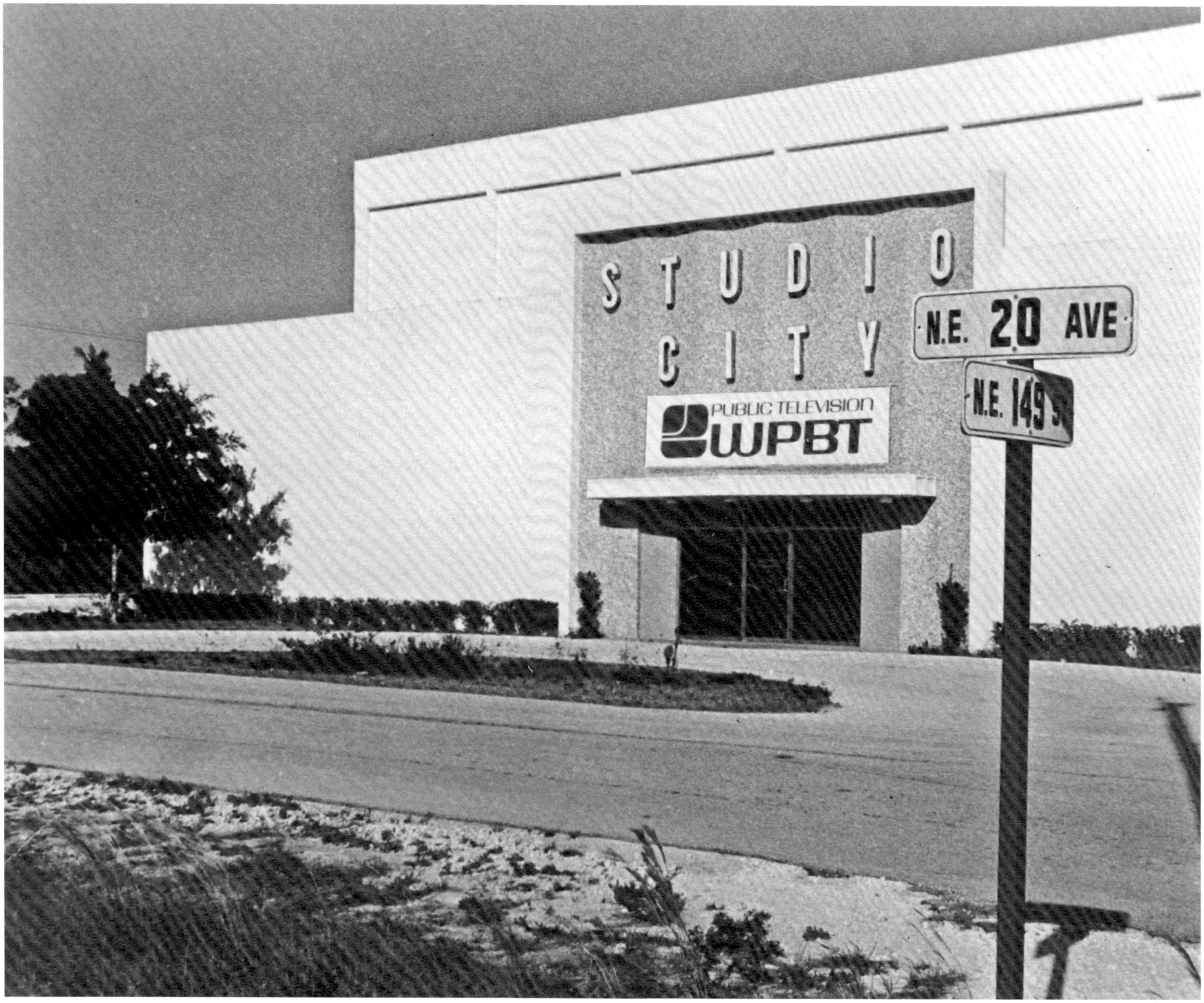

¿Que Pasa, USA?, the first bilingual TV show in the United States and the first sitcom produced for PBS, was filmed at WPBT studios in Miami. The show was a situation comedy based on a fictional Cuban family, the Peñas, living in Little Havana and the trials they faced in balancing the preservation of their culture with living in American society. The series aired 39 episodes from 1977 to 1980, and currently runs in syndication. PBS is largely funded by the Corporation for Public Broadcasting, a nonprofit corporation established by Congress and funded by the federal government.

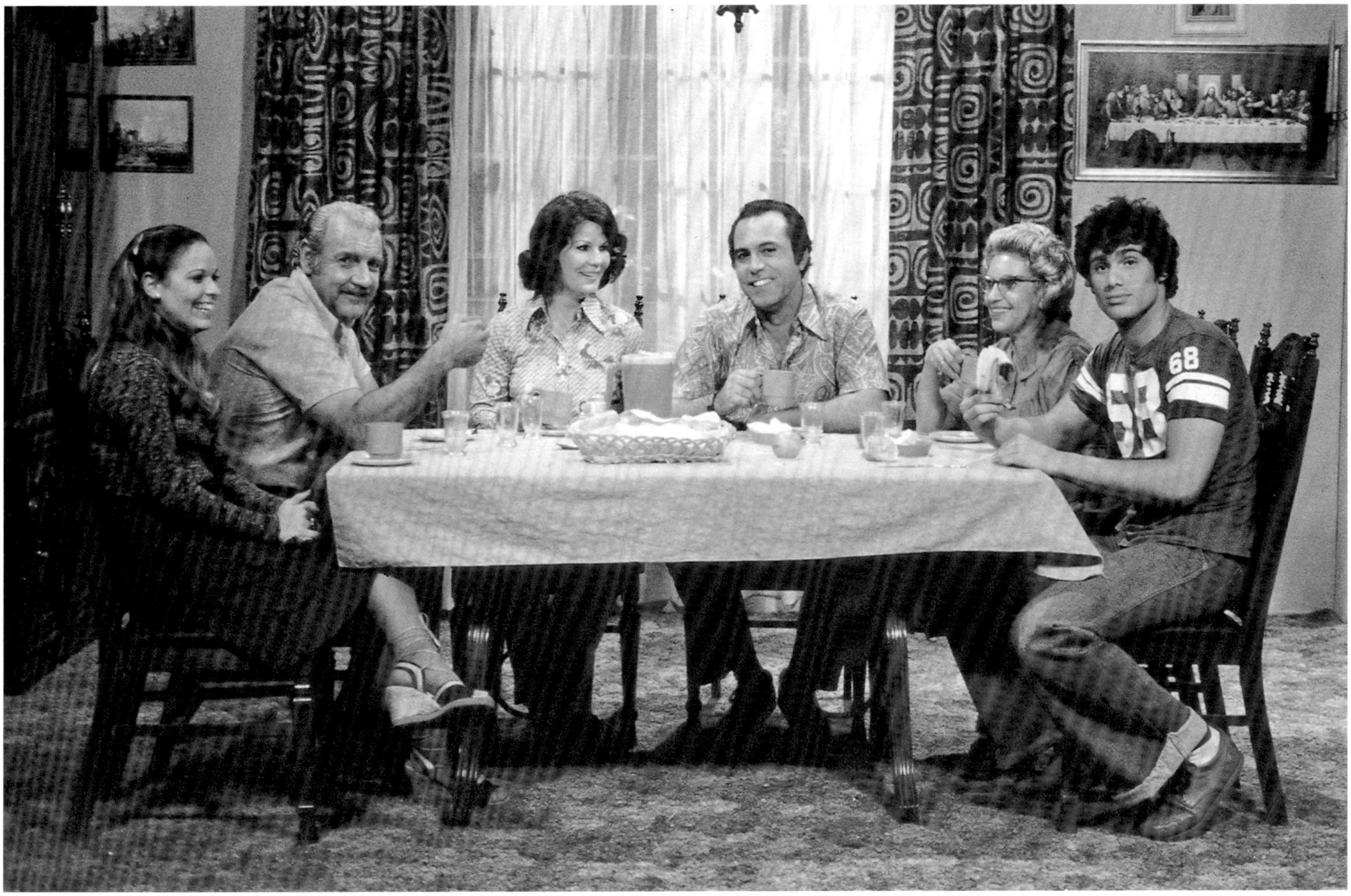

The Peña family seated around the table in their Little Havana home. Left to right are Violeta (Connie Ramirez), Abuelo Antonio (Louis Oquendo), Juana (Ana Margarita Martinez-Casado), Pepe (Manolo Villaverde), Abuela Adela (Velia Martinez), and Joe (Steven Bauer). The Peñas accurately portray the norm of a multigenerational Cuban family living under one roof, each generation having varying fluency in both languages. True to life, the show made frequent use of Spanglish and "code-switching."

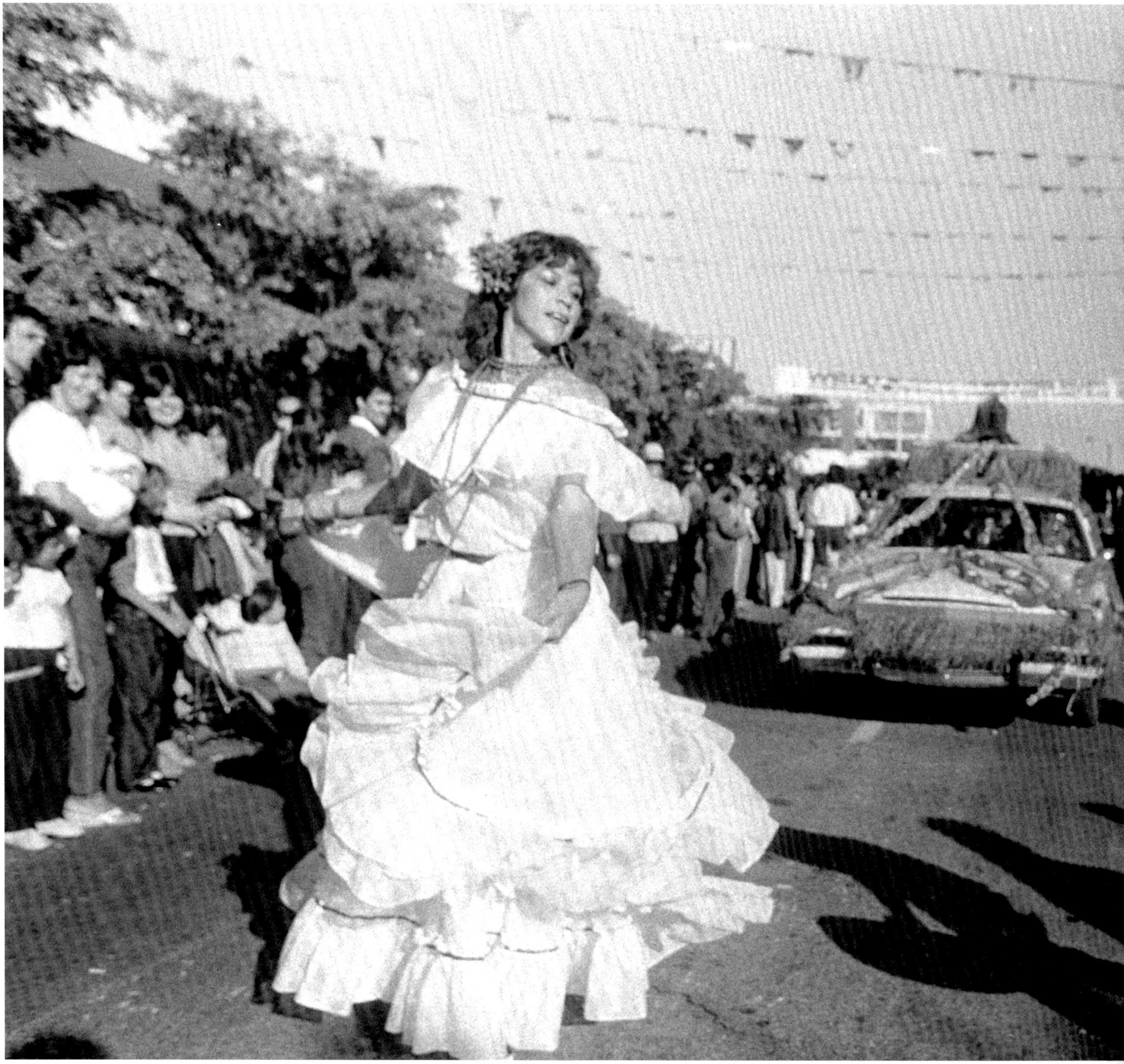

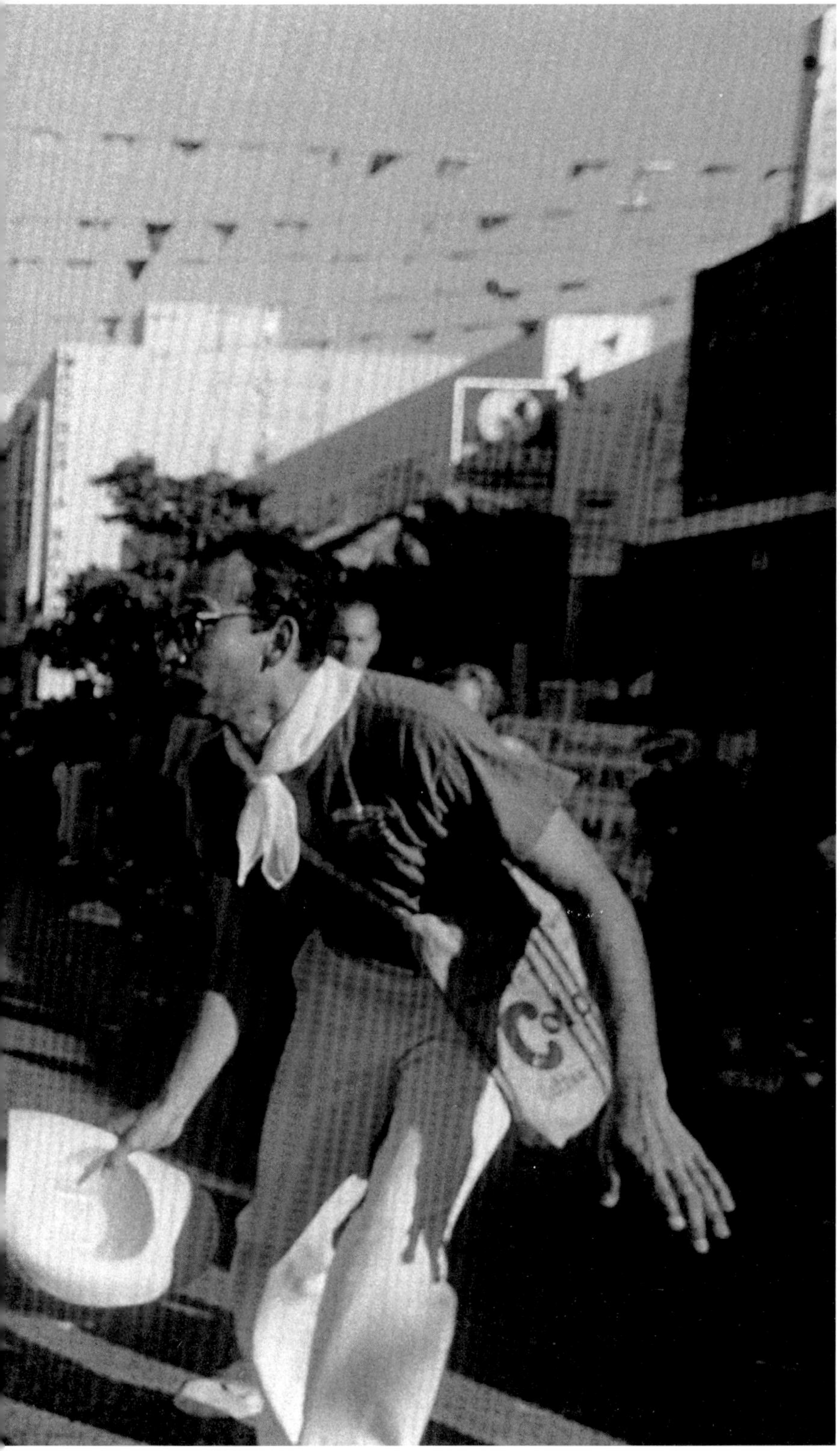

The first Calle Ocho festival was held in 1978 with more than 100,000 in attendance. It is held every year in Little Havana as a carnival celebration of predominantly Latino participants. In 1988, Calle Ocho went down in the *Guinness Book of World Records* for having the world's longest conga line—119,986 people linked up to participate in this Cuban dance. The festival now has attendance of more than a million each year.

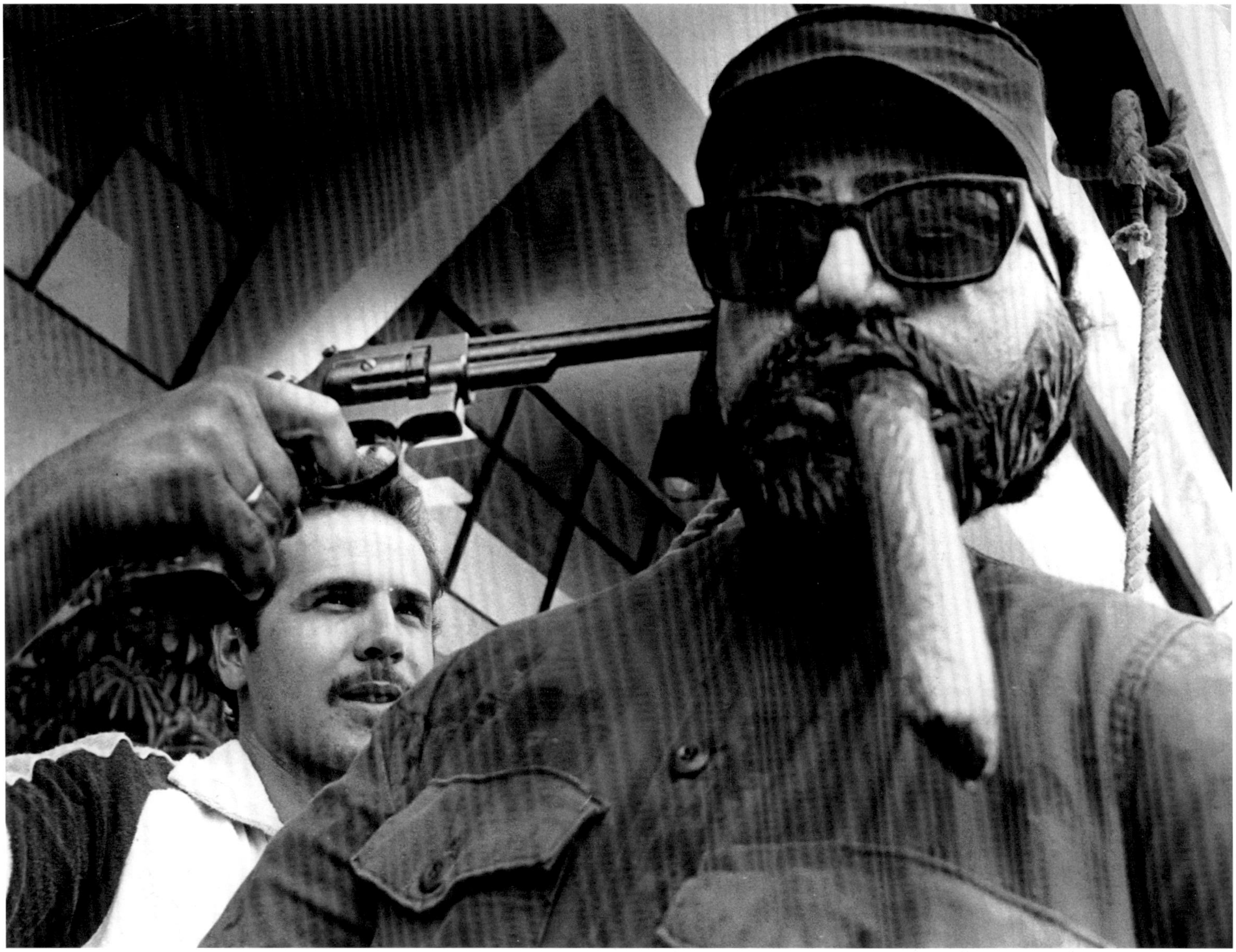

One Cuban demonstrates how most Cuban exiles feel about Castro by sticking a gun to the head of an effigy of the communist dictator.

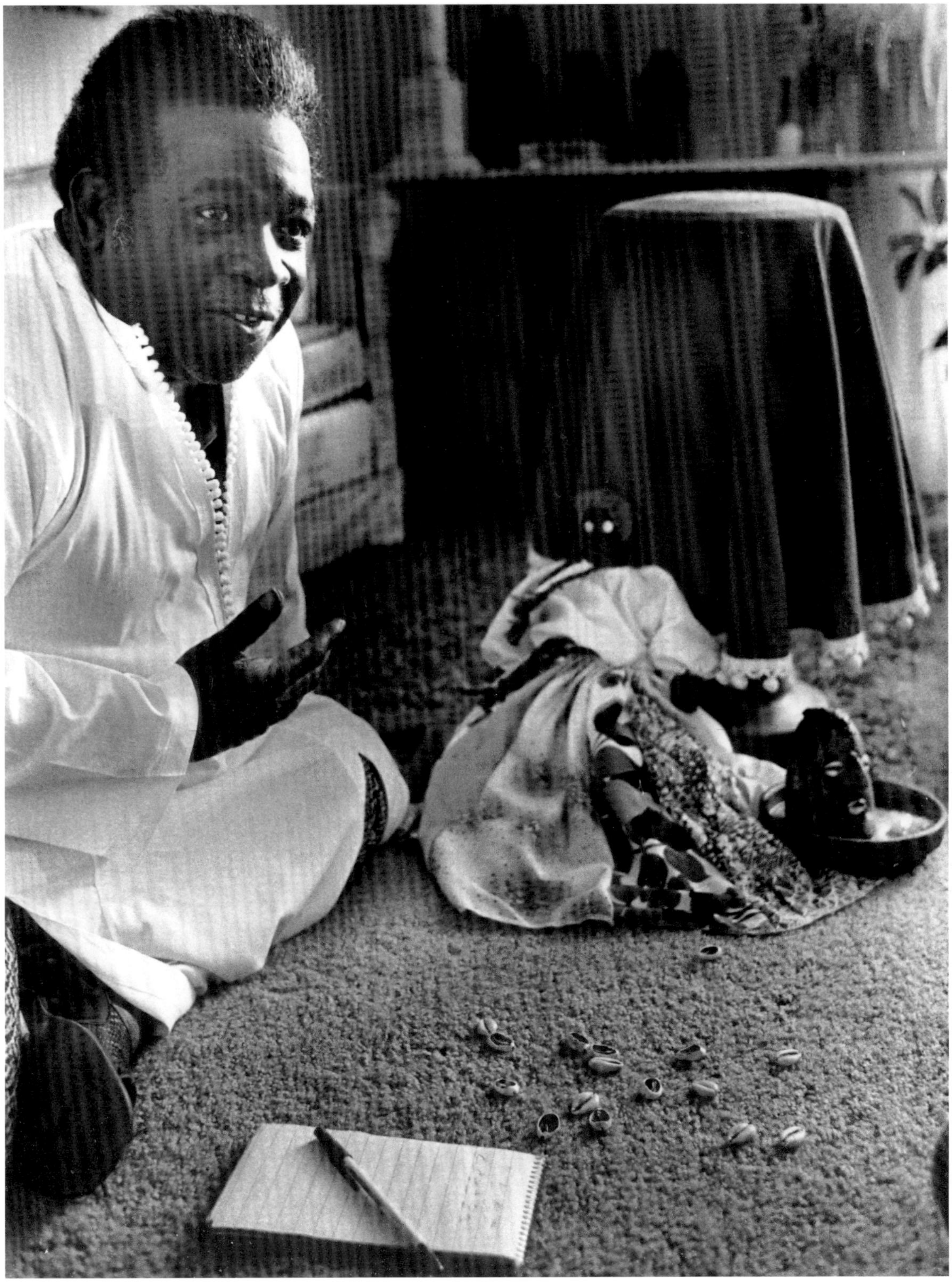

Ramon Martinez gives a Santería consultation. Cowrie shells, known as *caracoles,* are tossed and then read during consultations. It is thought to be the most precise method of divination in Santería. On the right is a figure of Ellegua.

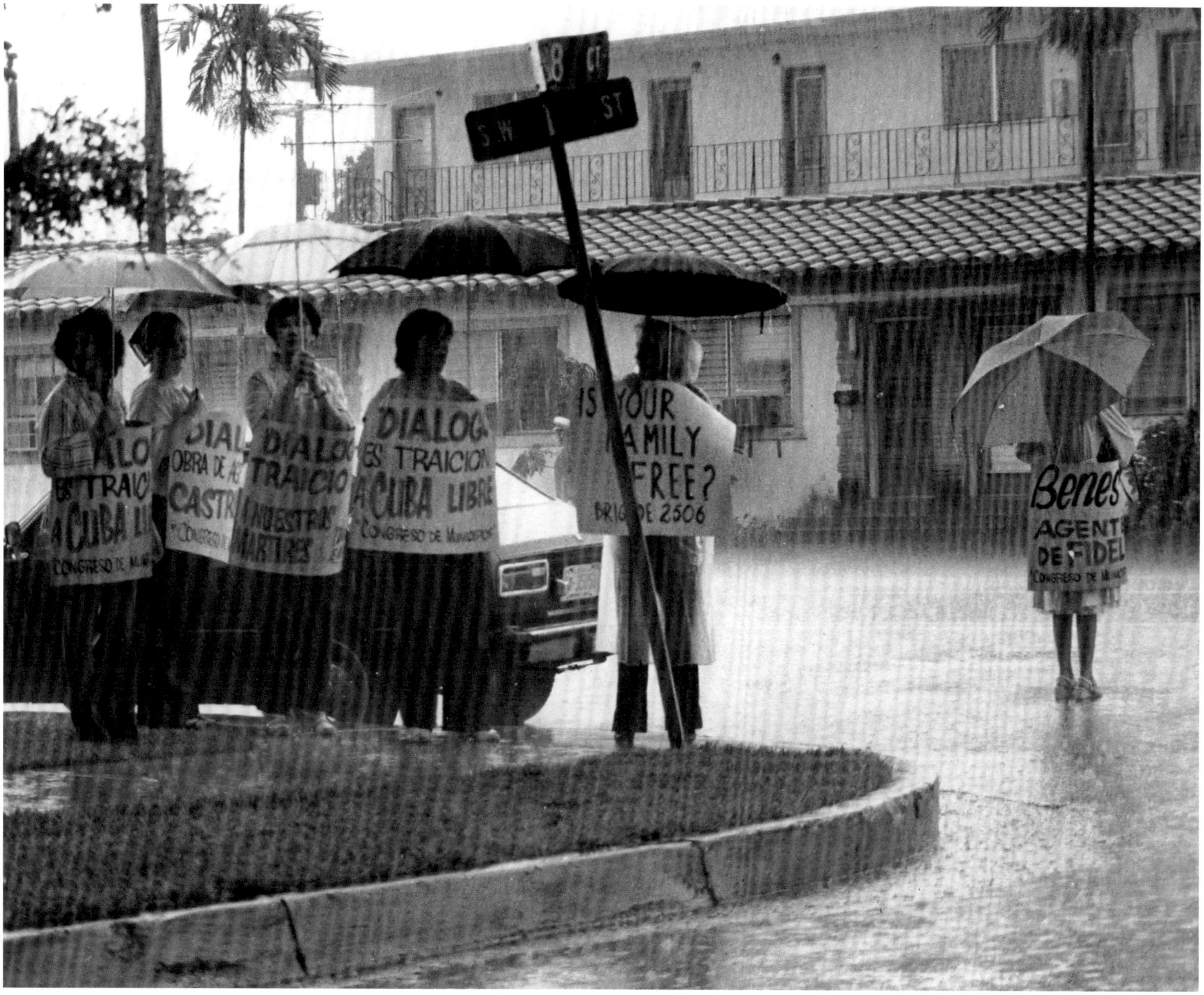

Members of Congresso de Municipios protest across from Continental National Bank of Miami, of which Bernardo Benes was vice-president. In 1978, Benes, a Jewish Cuban banker, became the first prominent exile to meet with Castro. That meeting, endorsed by President Carter and protested by anti-Castro Cubans in Miami, resulted in 3,600 political prisoners in Cuba being freed. Signs read: "Dialogue is treason to our martyrs," "Dialogue is treason to a free Cuba," and "Benes is an agent of Fidel."

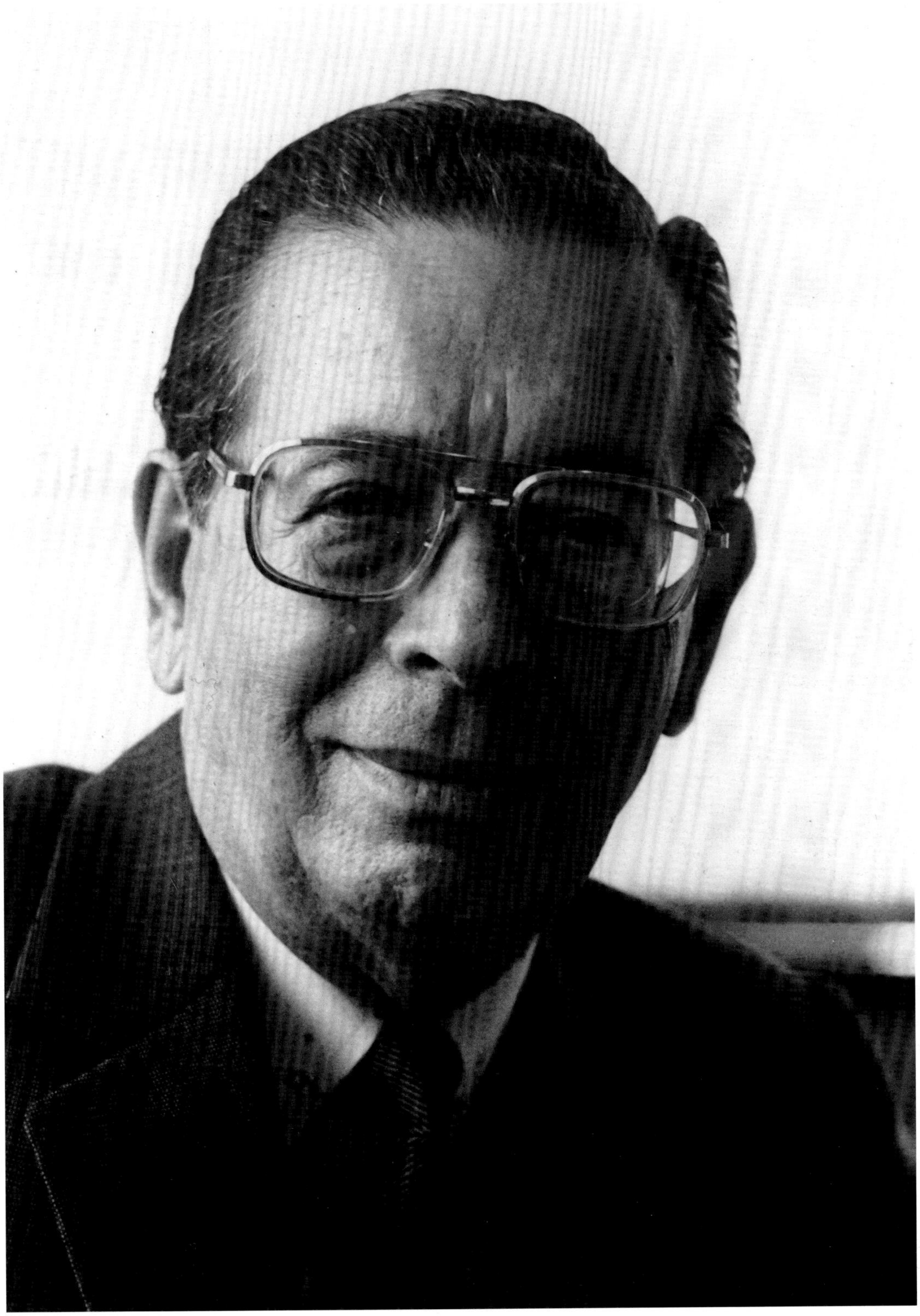

Luis Botifoll was a notable member of the Miami Cuban exile community and had become a well-known newspaper publisher and a lawyer before leaving Havana in 1960. In Miami, he became a successful banker known for giving loans to reputable Cubans who lacked sufficient credit history in the United States. Botifoll was a patron of the United Way and the University of Miami, where a collection of oral interviews is named for him.

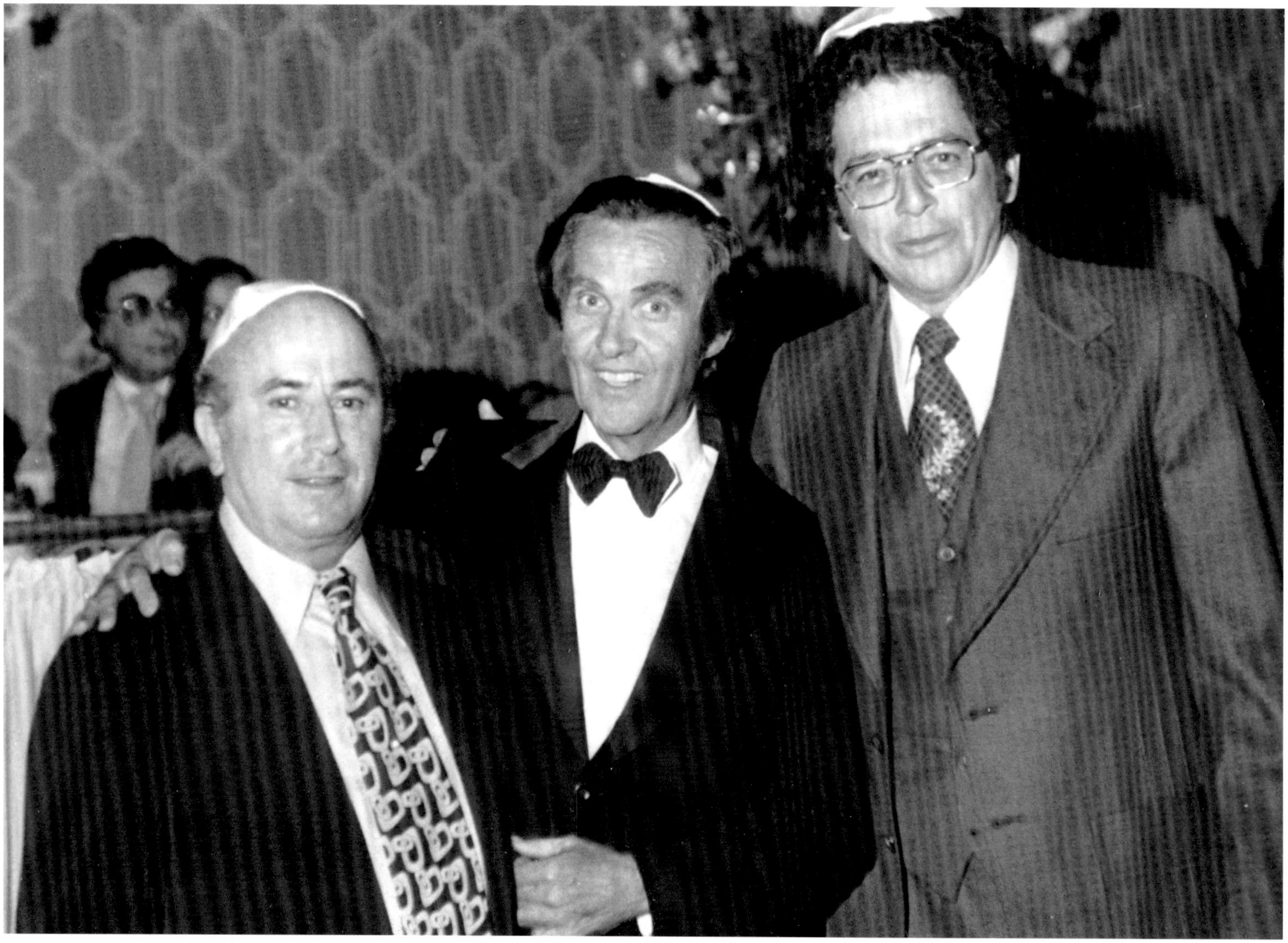

Jack Chester, Rabbi Mayer Abramowitz, and Raphael Kravic at the Jewish Federation award ceremony in 1978. Kravic was thrown in jail for opposing the revolution and came to Miami within a week of his release. Rabbi Mayer Abramowitz is a well-known rabbi in the Cuban community noted for having offered exiles free membership to synagogue.

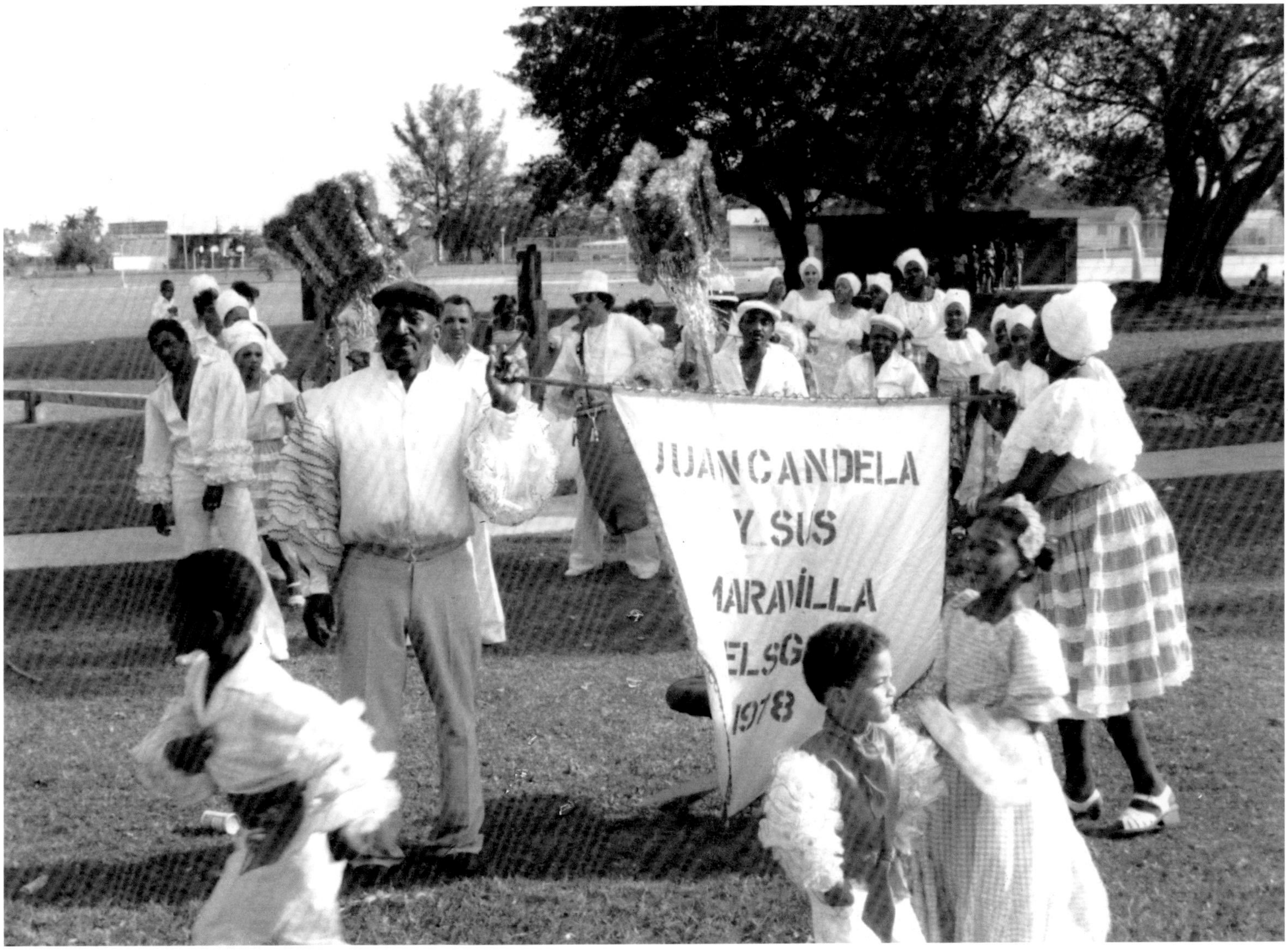

Juan Candela and his *comparsa* group in 1978. *Comparsas* are a team of dancers in uniform performing choreography in carnivals or with bands that play the conga. This Cuban tradition, like so many others, originated from African religious processions.

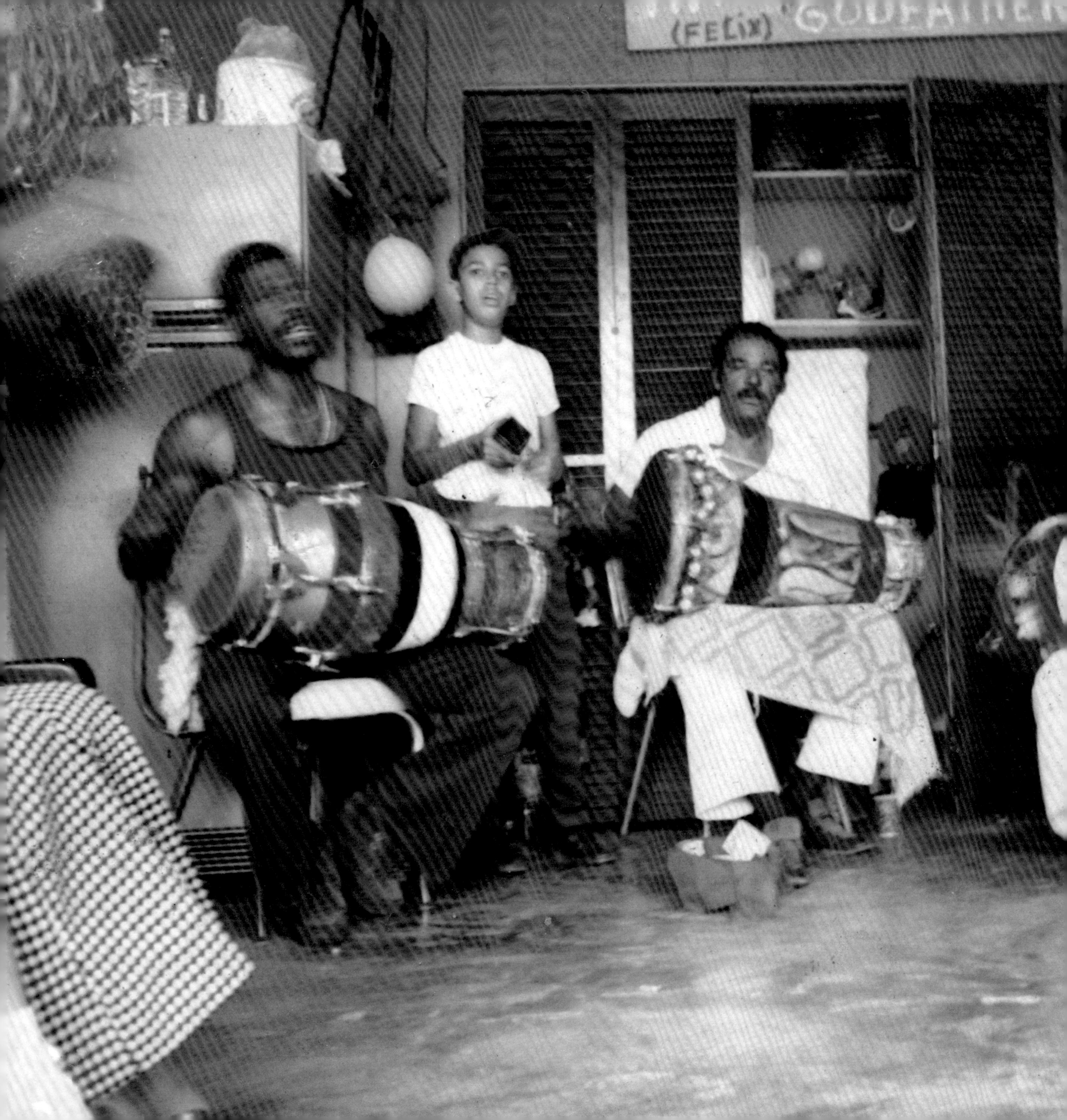
(FELIX)

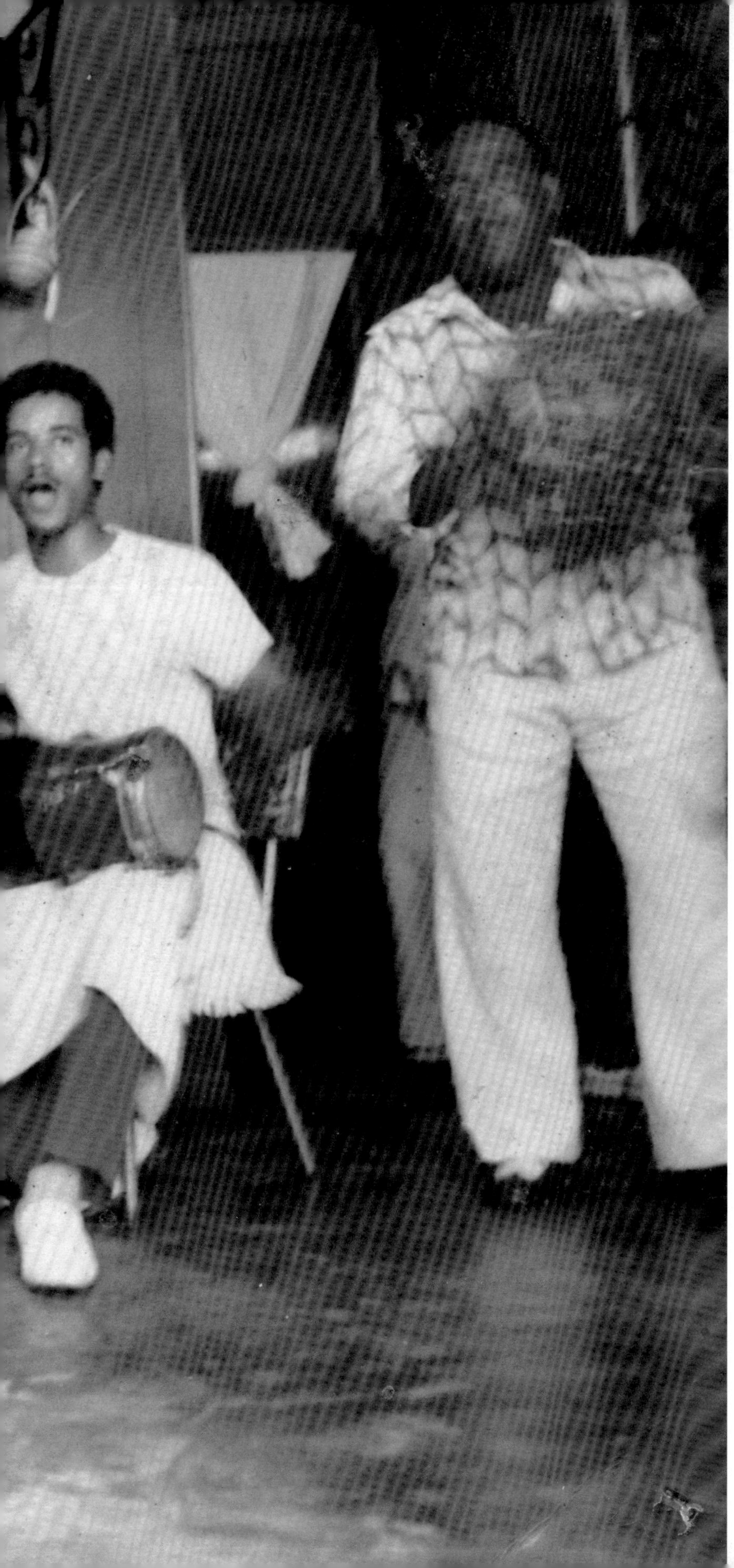

Comparsa conga musicians are shown performing in 1979.

Miami's first Kings Day Parade was held on January 6, 1976. El Dia de los Reyes Magos (known as the Day of the Magi or Three Kings Day) is traditionally more popular in Latin American countries than Christmas and Noche Buena. Most exiles celebrate both holidays, with an emphasis on Noche Buena, owing to America's observation of Christmas Eve and Christmas Day.

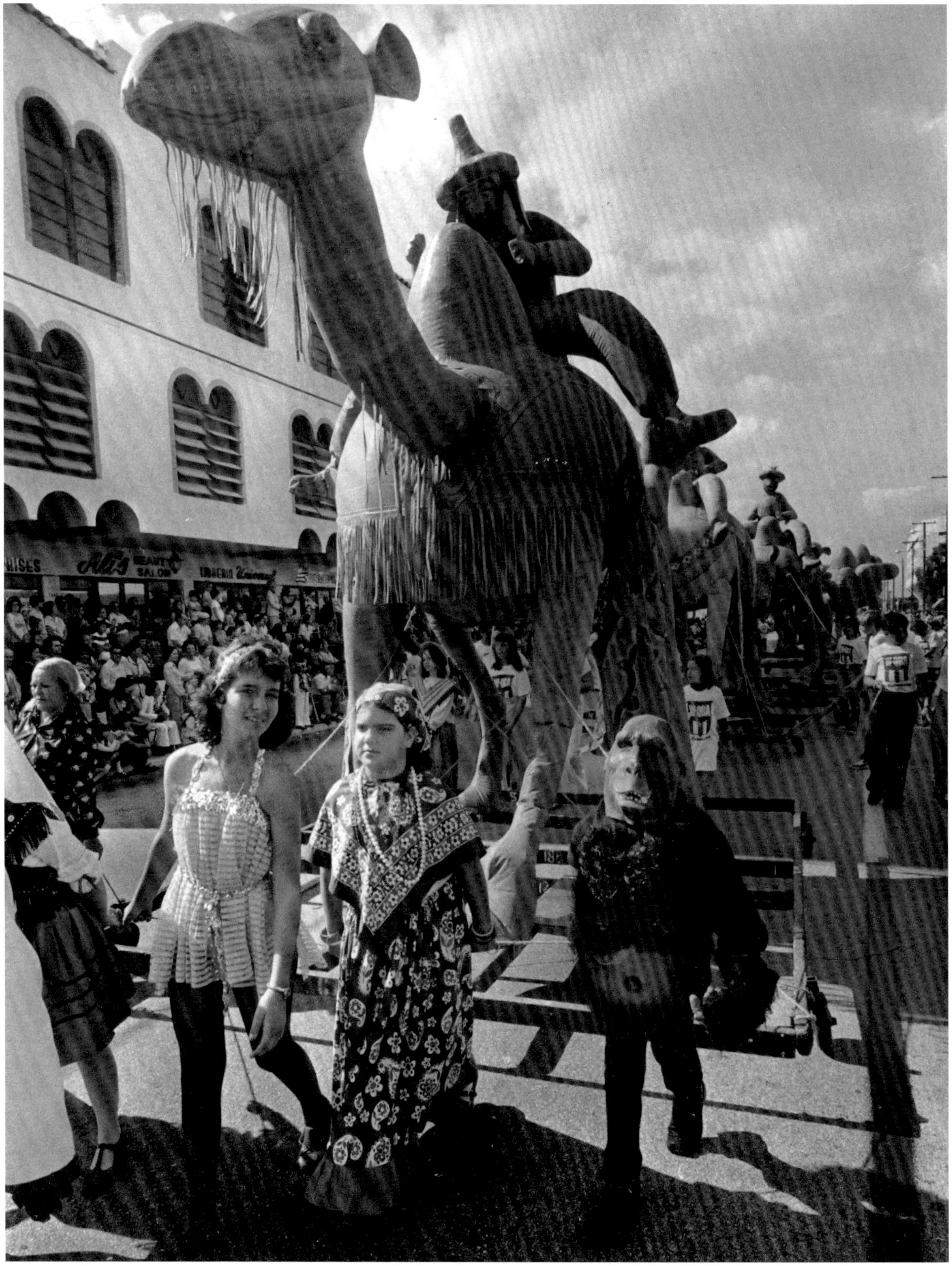

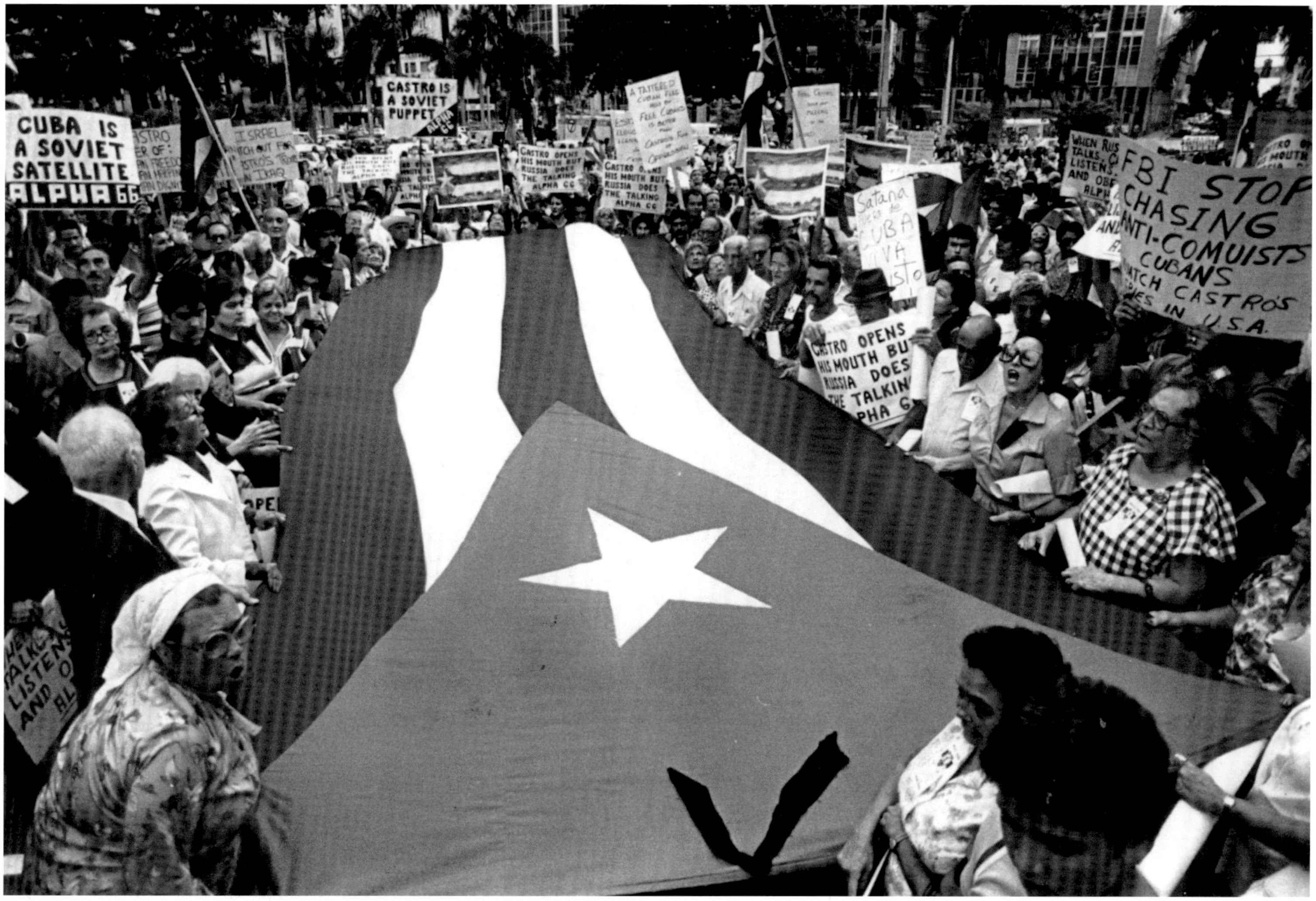

A huge anti-Castro protest takes place in Bayfront Park on October 12, 1979.

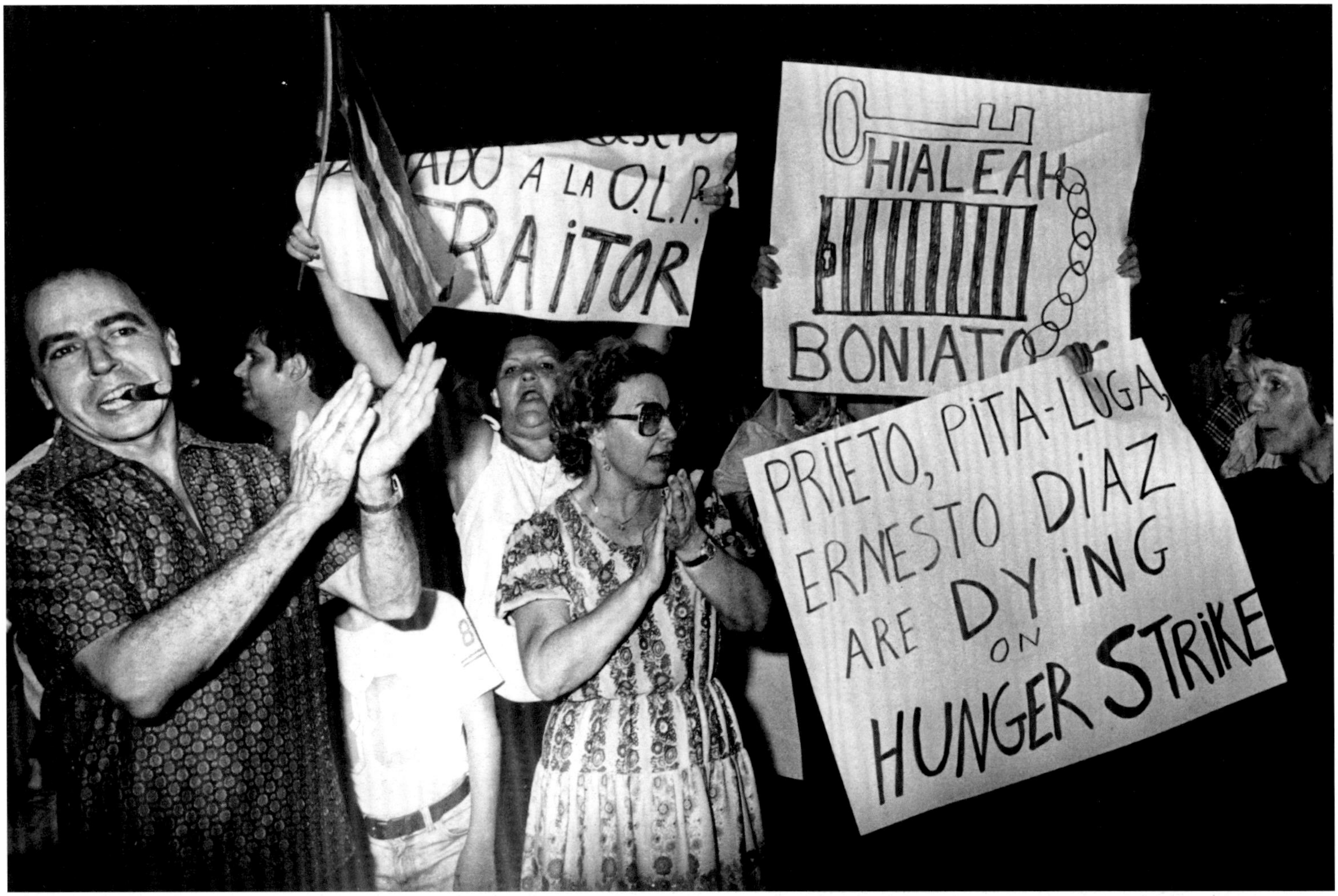

Cuban protesters march in Hialeah on August 28, 1979.

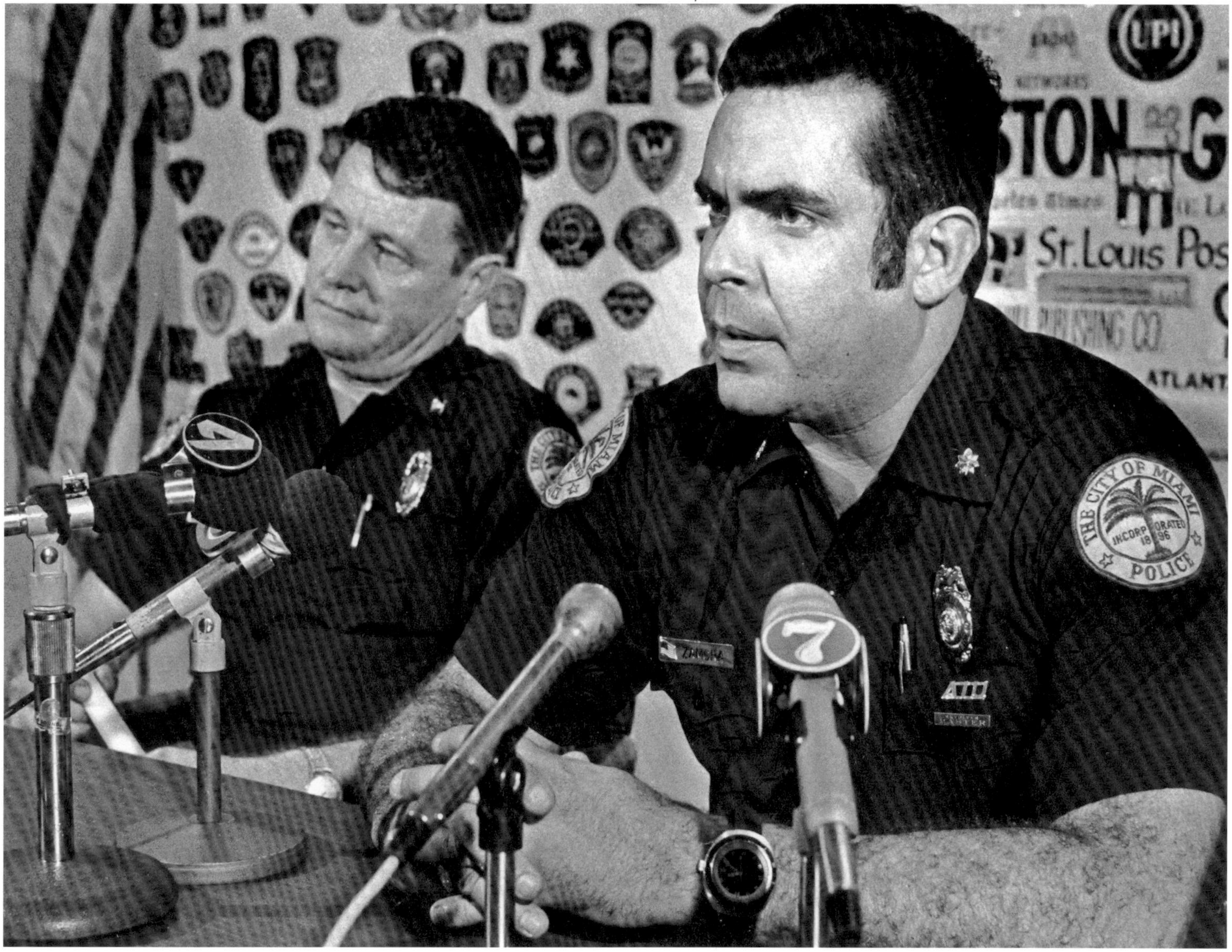

Major Guillermo Zamora, shown here with Chief Garland Watkins, was one of the first high-ranking Cuban-American officials on the Miami Police force. Zamora later resigned from the force during an investigation, after many years of service.

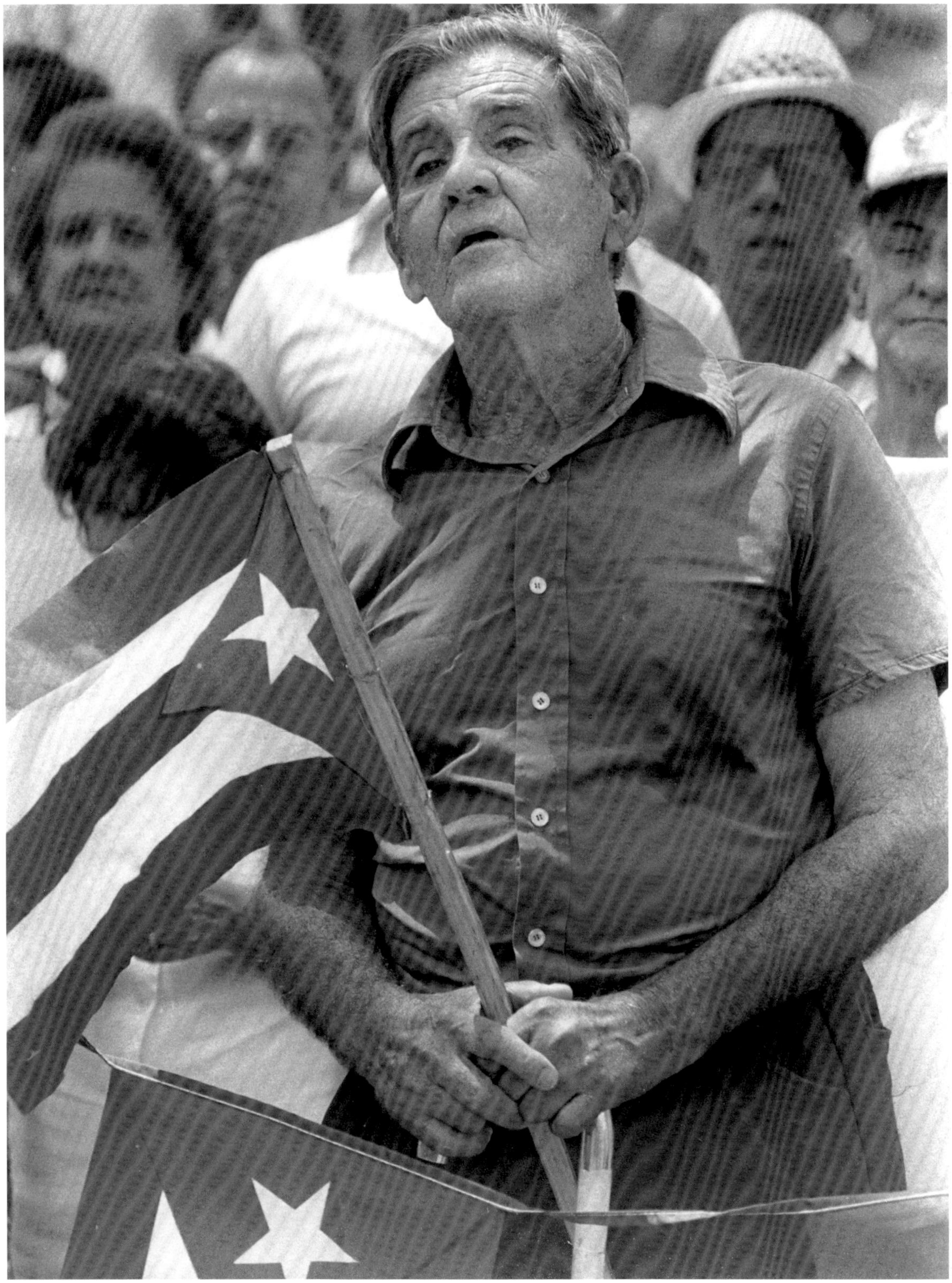

An elderly Cuban man holds a Cuban flag in a crowd at Antonio Maceo Monument on SW 8th Street and 13th Avenue in Little Havana.

The Mariel Boatlift

(1980–1985)

Around 1980, Cuba's economic malaise took a turn for the worse. More than 10,000 Cubans flooded the Peruvian embassy in Cuba with requests for asylum. In response, Castro opened the port of Mariel and announced that whoever wanted to leave could. The response was overwhelming, as more than 100,000 Cubans rushed to leave Castro's Cuba in a matter of months. The exodus was mostly organized by Cubans in Miami. Fully unprepared for the rush of new Cubans, Miami authorities decided to construct temporary housing in what was known as Tent City, under I-95. The U.S. Coast Guard had severe difficulties in properly transporting the "Marielitos" picked up offshore. A few of the refugee boats capsized and there were fatalities, owing to a lack of life jackets.

All the difficulties notwithstanding, the Cuban community in Miami happily welcomed long unseen family and friends. Even Castro must have been delighted. He had used his economic crisis as an opportunity to rid the island of "undesirables," opening up his jails and mental institutions to allow severely unstable and hardened criminals the freedom to leave Cuba. Unknown to the United States, until after they had come ashore, these undesirables were now America's problem. When the public got wind of what had happened, Miami's Cuban community and the Carter administration took a big hit. Miami was already suffering from drug wars and high crime, which only increased with the chaos of the Mariel. The entire ordeal tarnished the image of Cubans, since many of the Mariel refugees were among Castro's undesirables.

In a fortuitous turn of events, Miami would experience great financial prosperity despite the Mariel and the challenges posed by too many unexpected immigrants too soon. In the 1980s, Miami was serving as headquarters for the Latin American operations of thousands of multinational corporations. The growth of the Magic City would not slow, anytime soon.

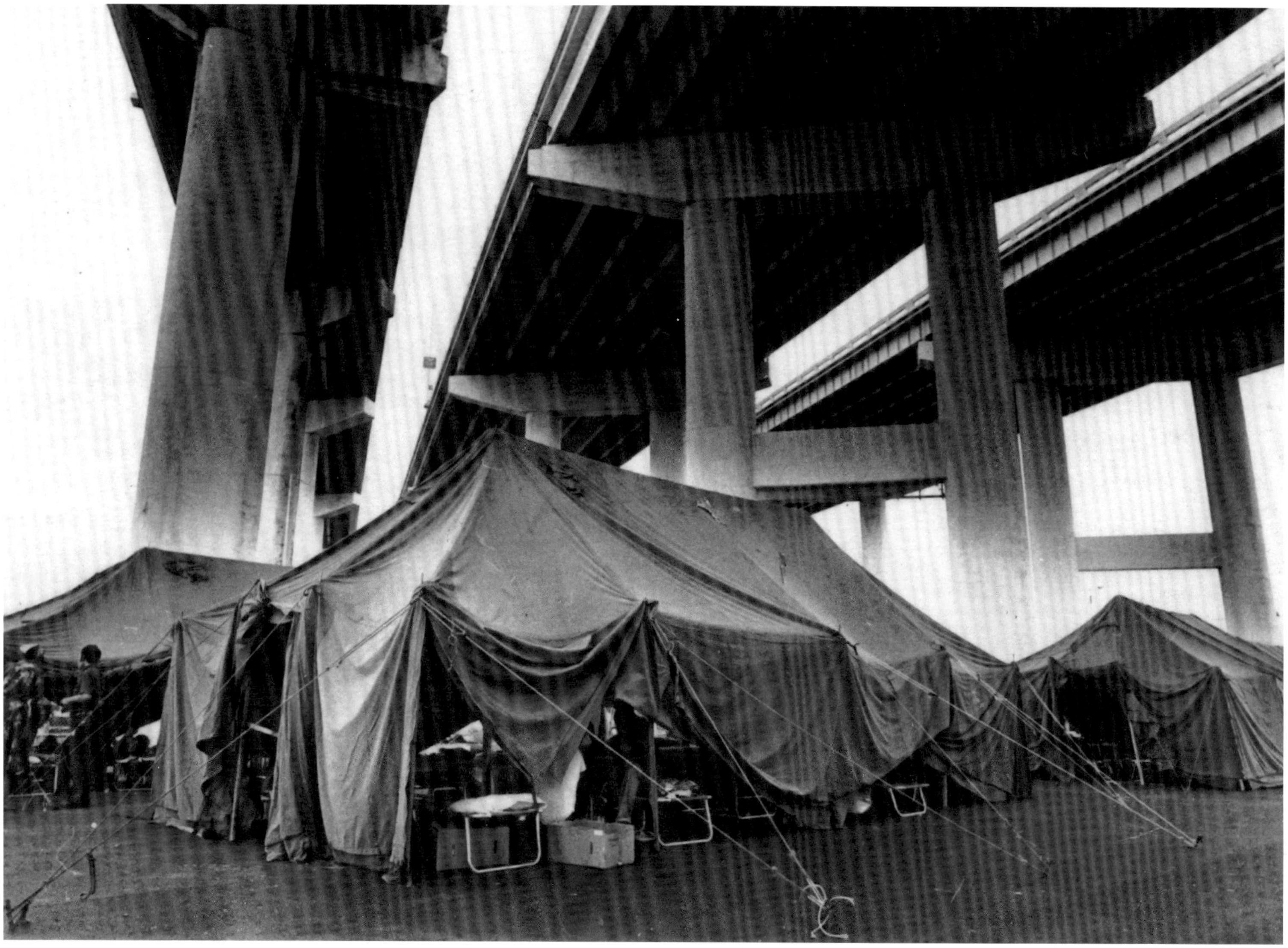

The Mariel boatlift began on April 20, 1980, and lasted until September 26 of that year. An estimated 125,000 refugees came to the United States by boat, overwhelming the U.S. Coast Guard. Castro used the Mariel as an opportunity to unload Cuba's prisons and mental institutions. The sudden influx of Cubans was so overwhelming that temporary refugee housing was set up under I-95. The shelters became known as Tent City.

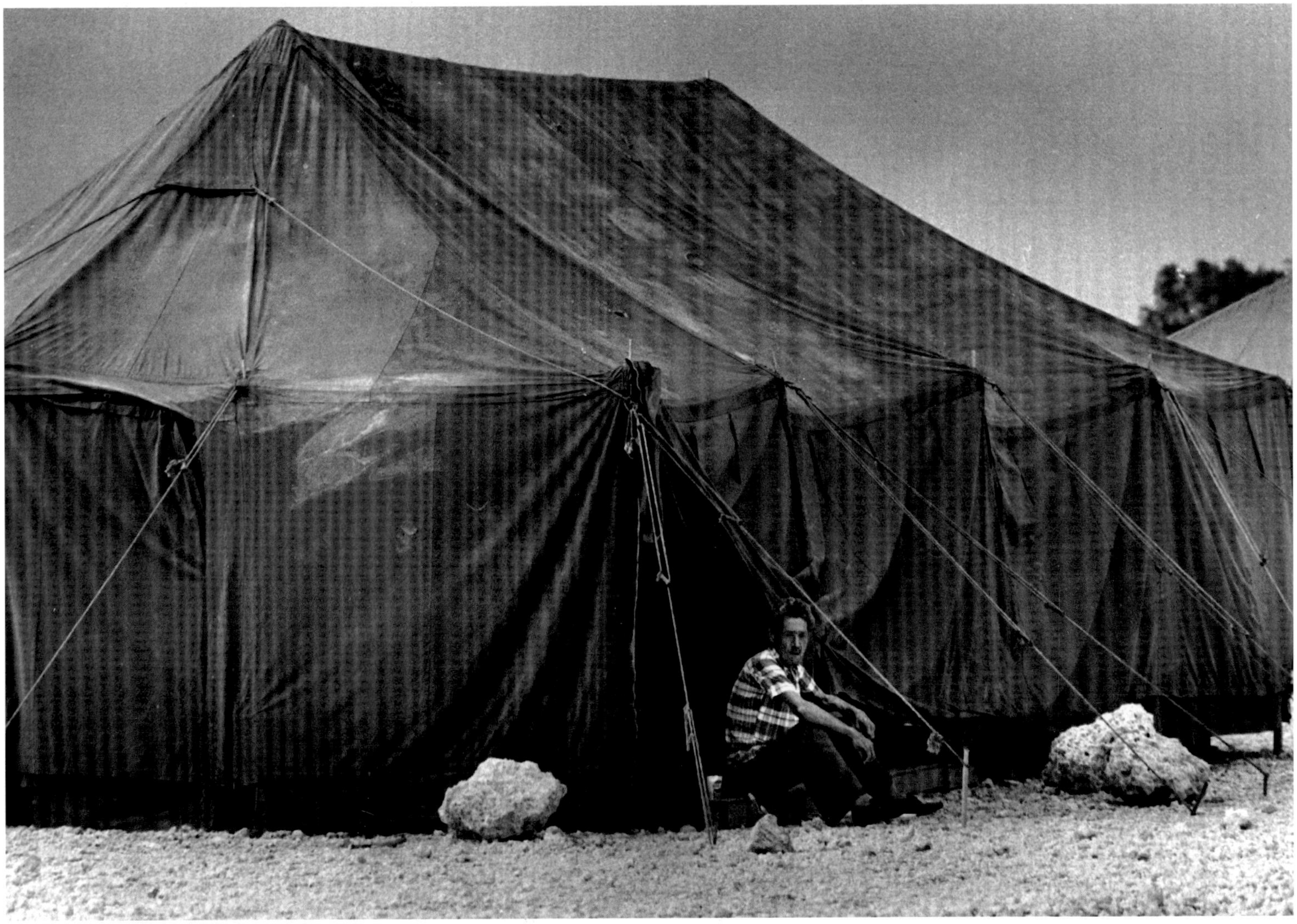

In 1980, a man waits to be claimed or placed in Tent City.

Refugee David Rodriguez at the Sunny Haven Hotel on Collins Avenue. He and other refugees were squatting on the abandoned property.

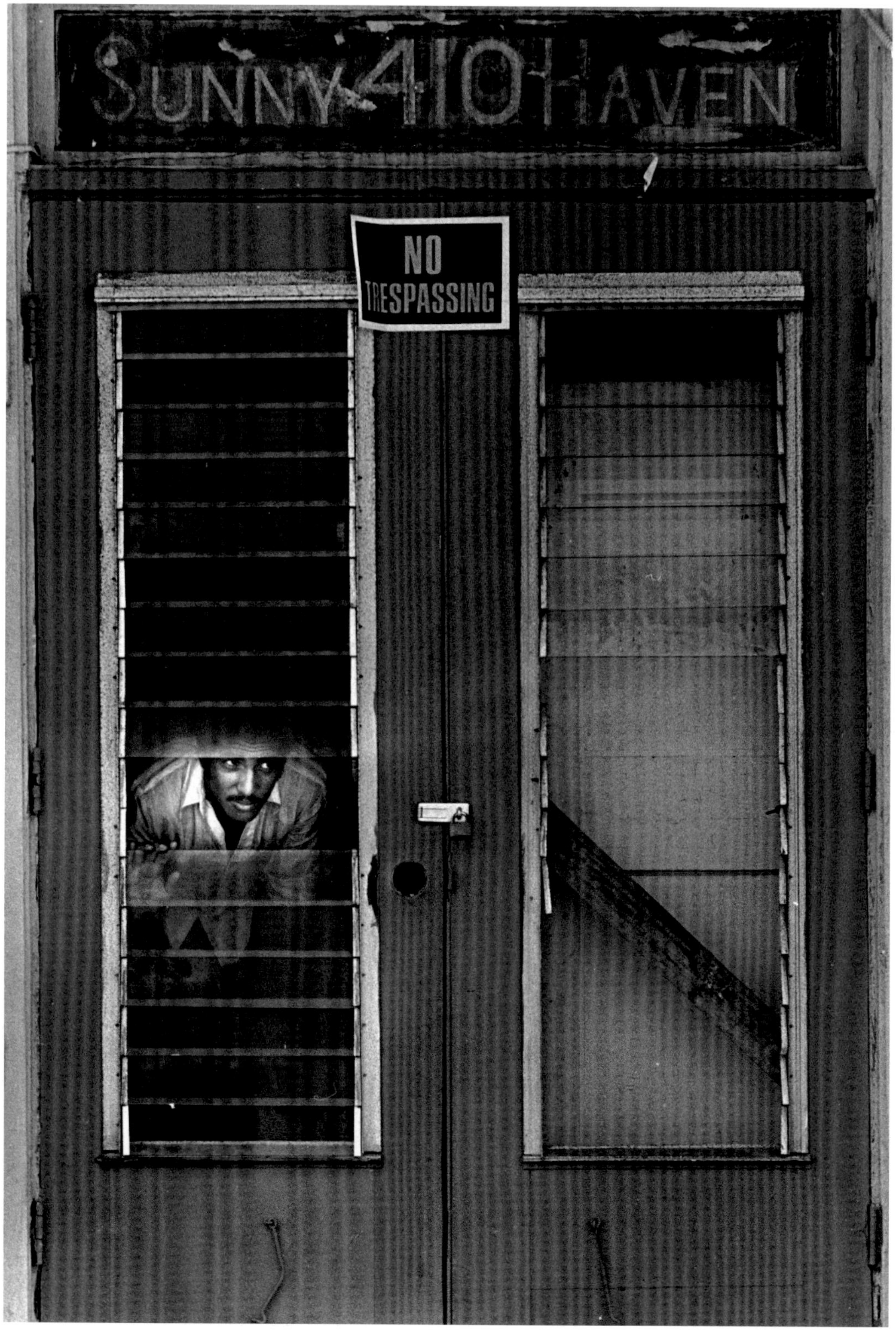

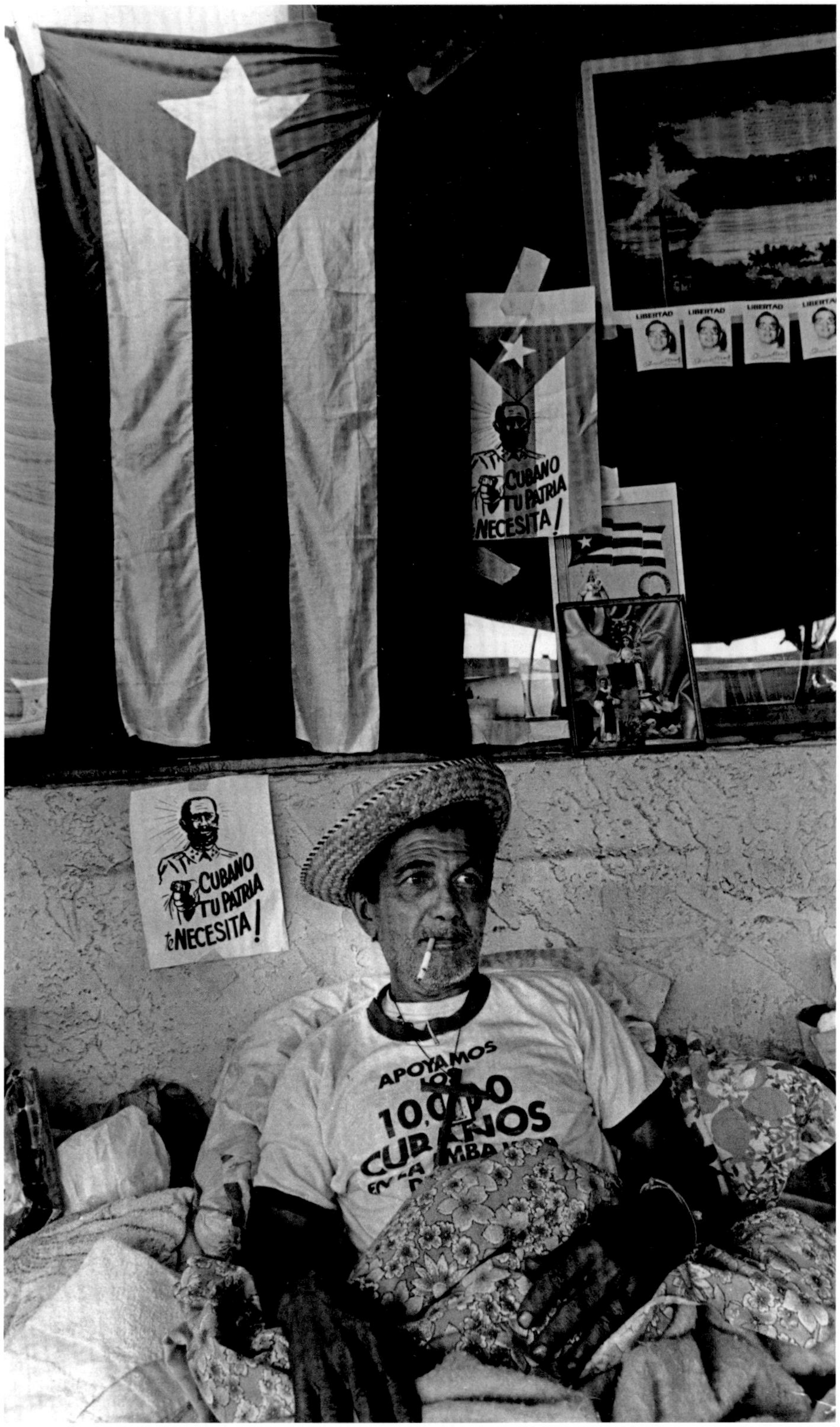

Concerned for other Cubans at the Peruvian Embassy in Havana, Angel Urquiola goes on a hunger strike under the Royal Trust Tower on SW 8th Street and 27th Avenue.

Ramon Puig at his shop, La Casa de las Guayaberas. A famous establishment and tourist attraction in Little Havana, Puig's shop sells *guayaberas,* many of which are locally or custom made.

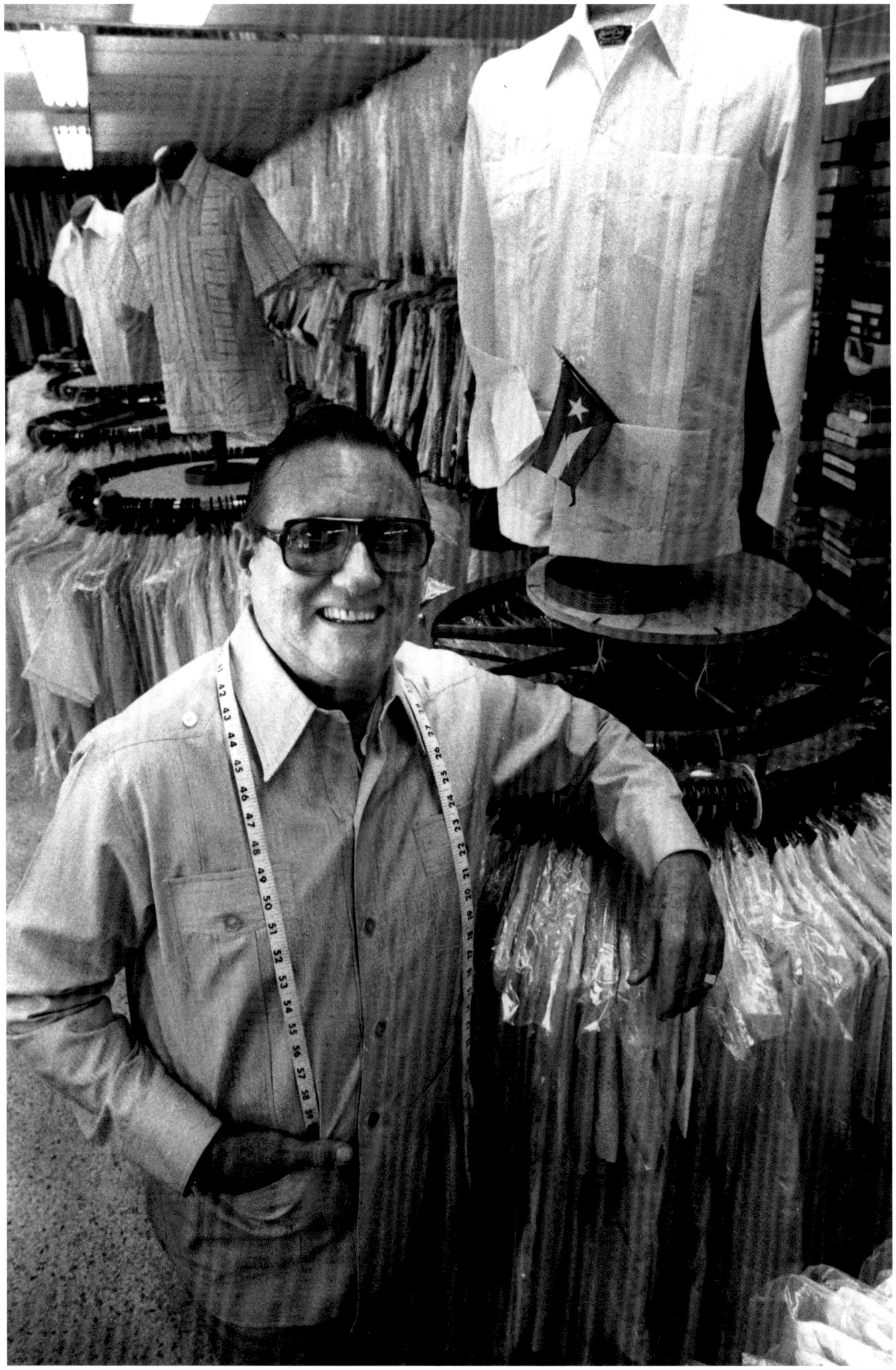

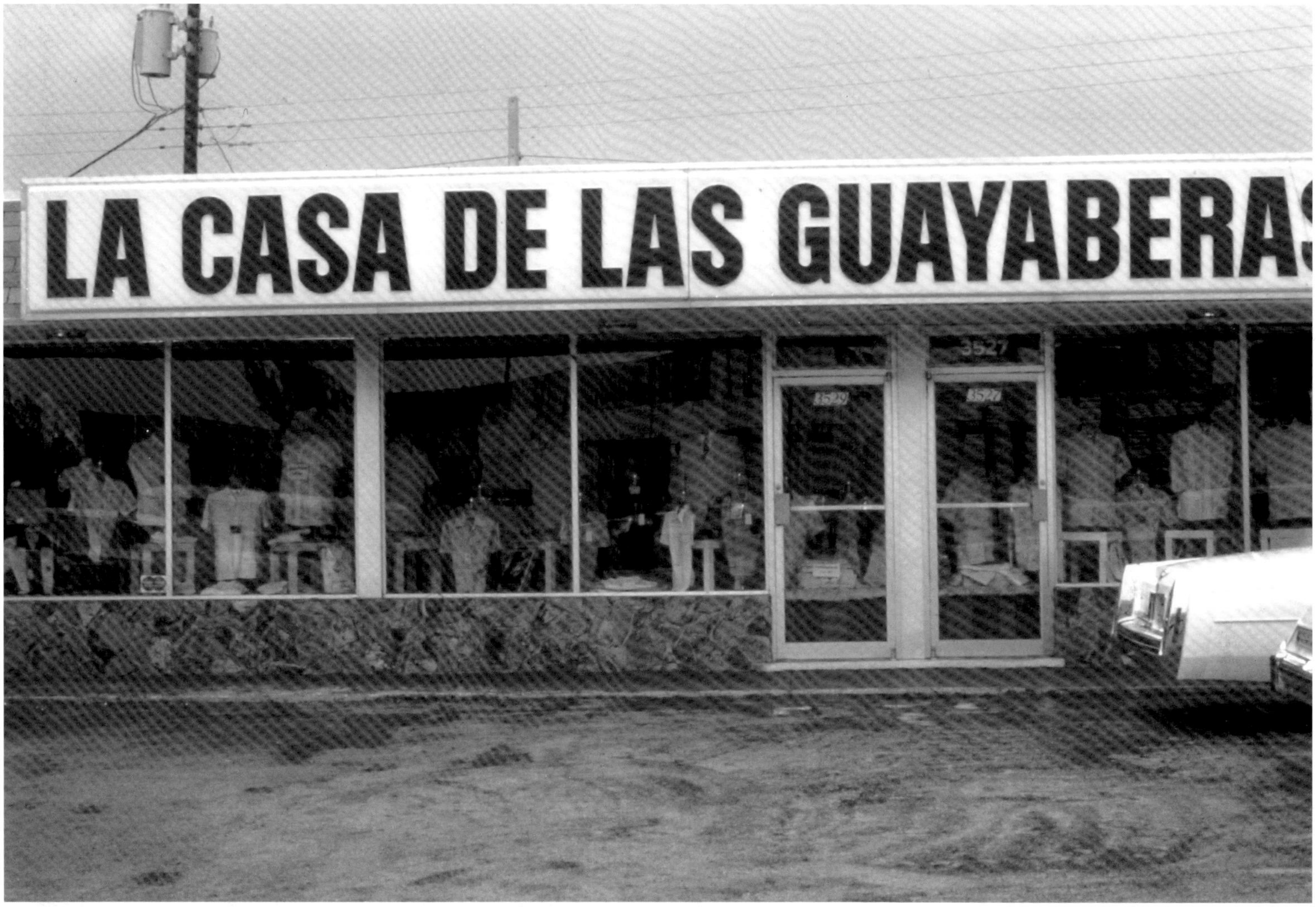

The exterior of Puig's shop, La Casa de las Guayaberas, in Little Havana.

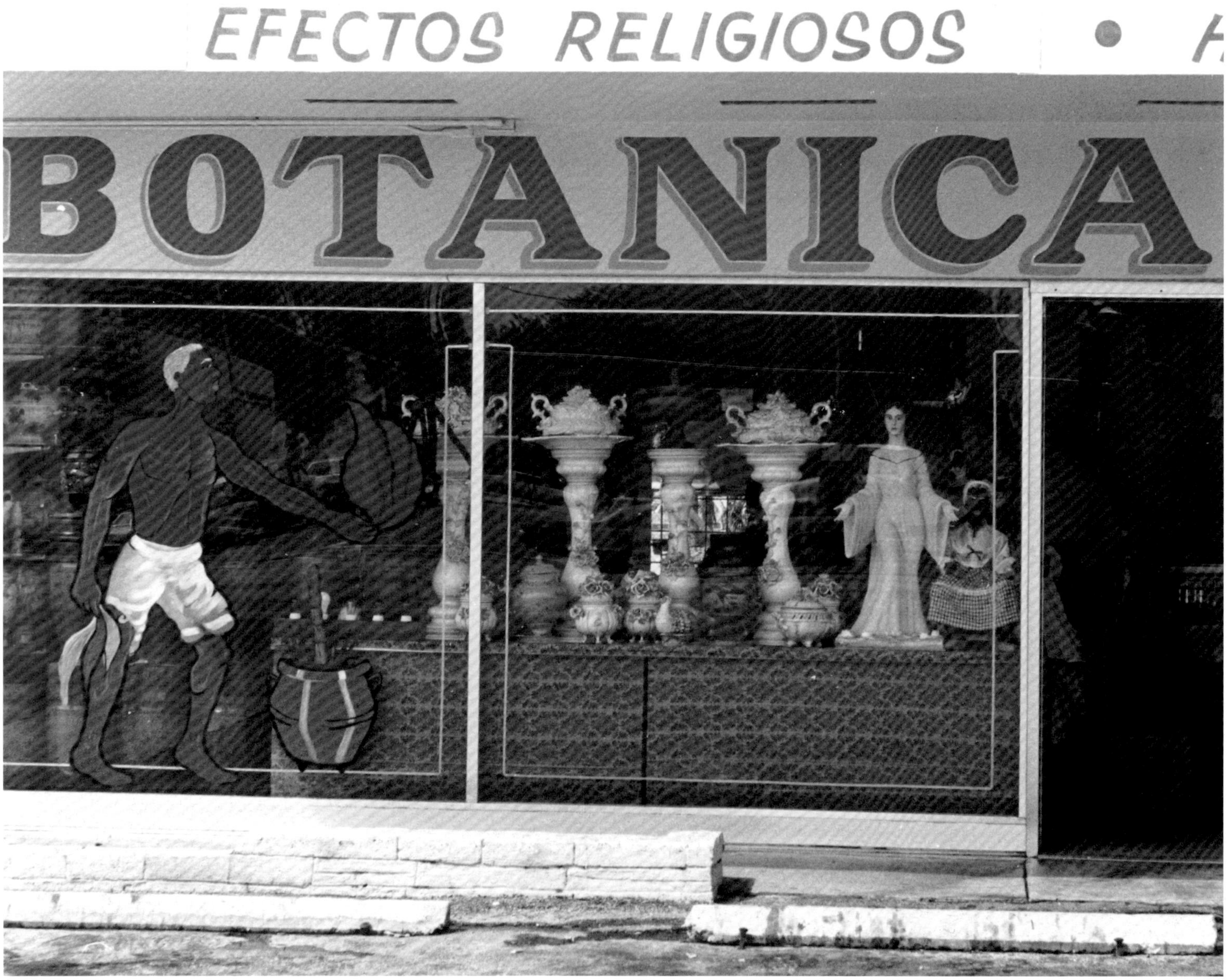

The Botanica Nena, one of many *botanicas* that sell herbs, charms, and other religious paraphernalia to the devotees of Santería in Miami.

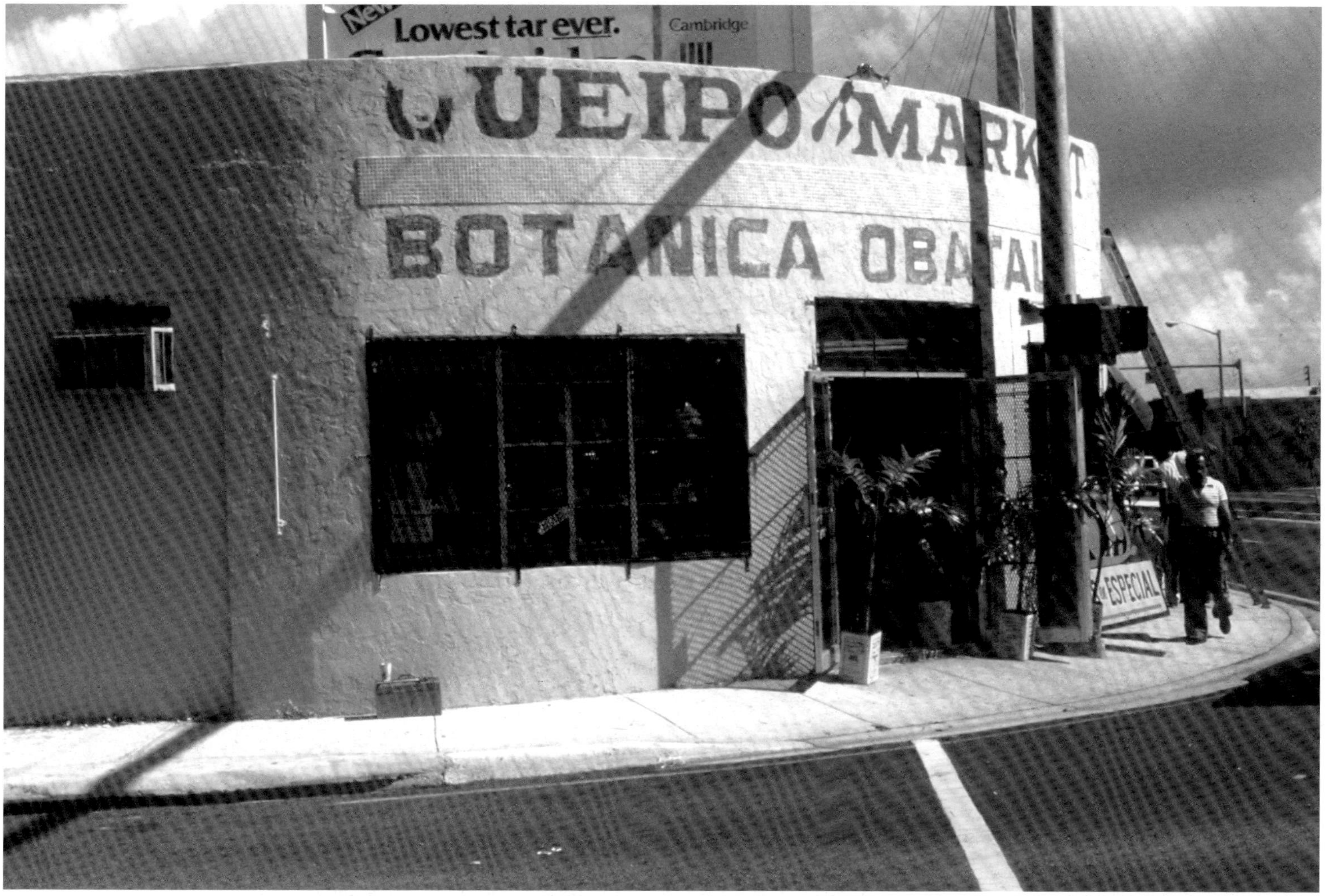

Queipo Market, in Little Havana, did business as a *botanica,* selling religious articles to be used in Santería rituals. Santería was brought to Miami by Cubans. Although similar to Voodoo, it developed as its own religion in Cuba, therefore becoming a separate religion.

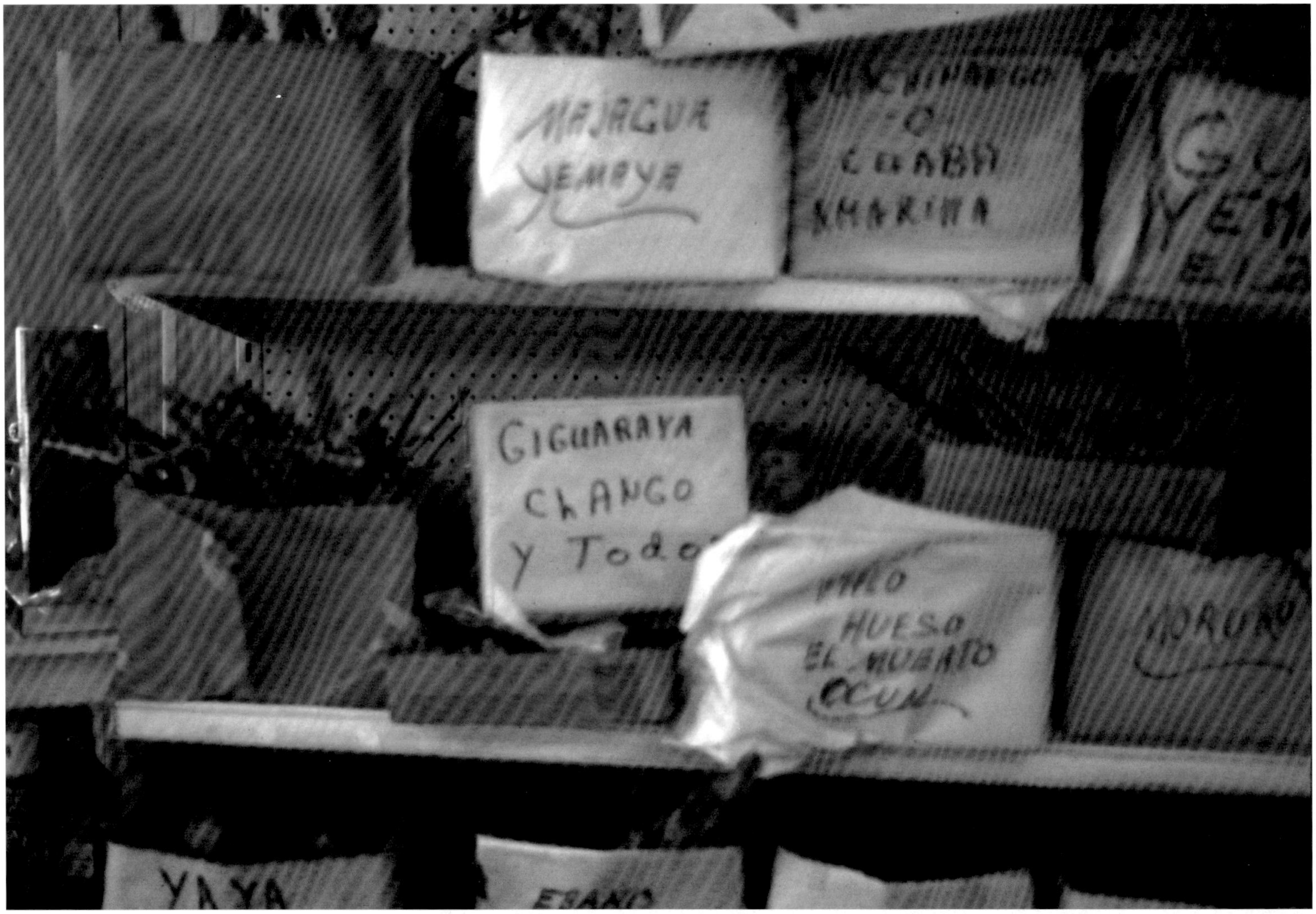

Palos for sale at the Queipo Market. Each one serves a separate purpose in Santería ritual.

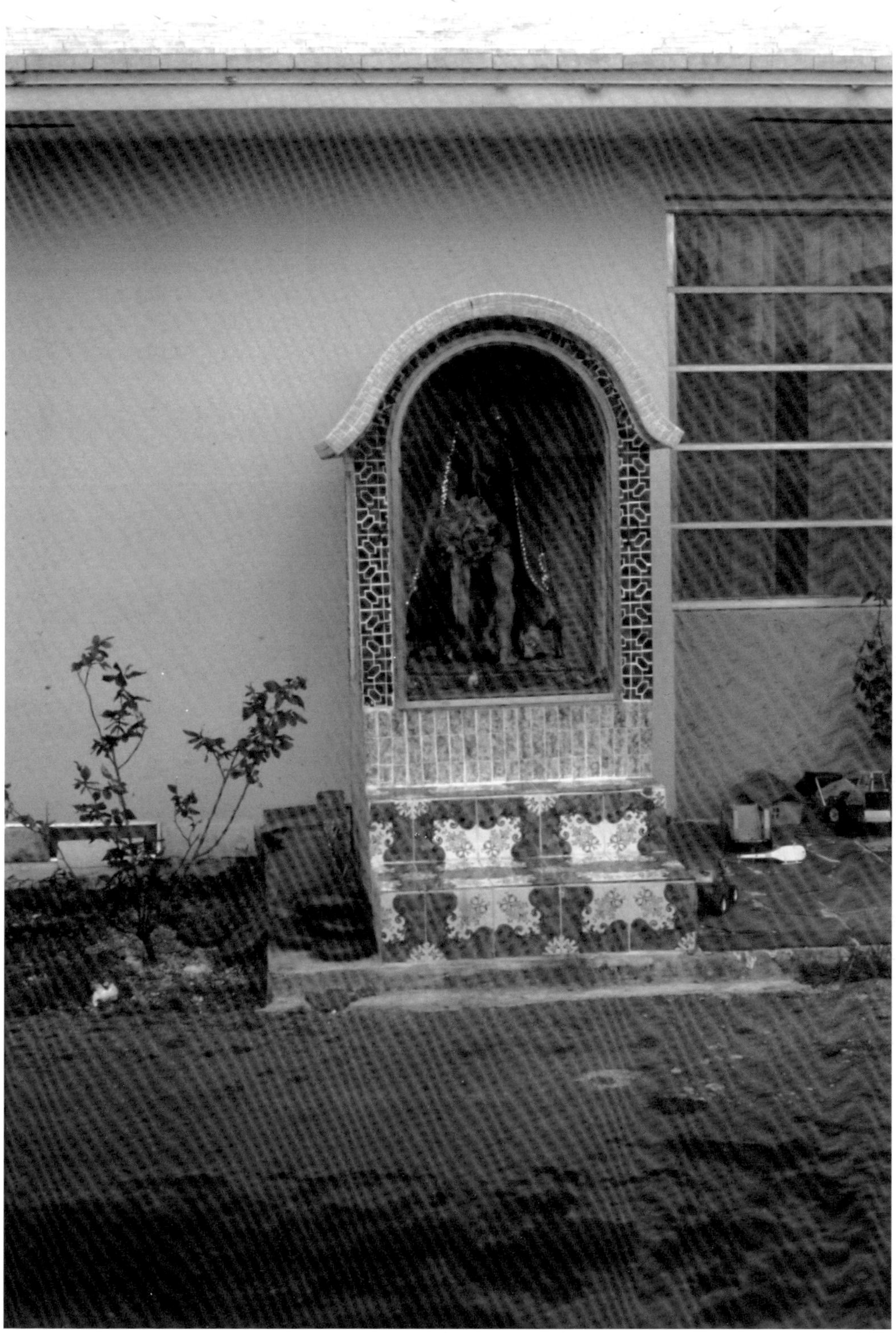

Altars like these are often seen in yards or in homes in Little Havana and other Cuban-American neighborhoods of Miami-Dade County. It is difficult to distinguish between the Catholic and Santero shrines.

Located in Little Havana, this monument is dedicated to those who gave their lives in the 1961 Bay of Pigs invasion of Cuba.

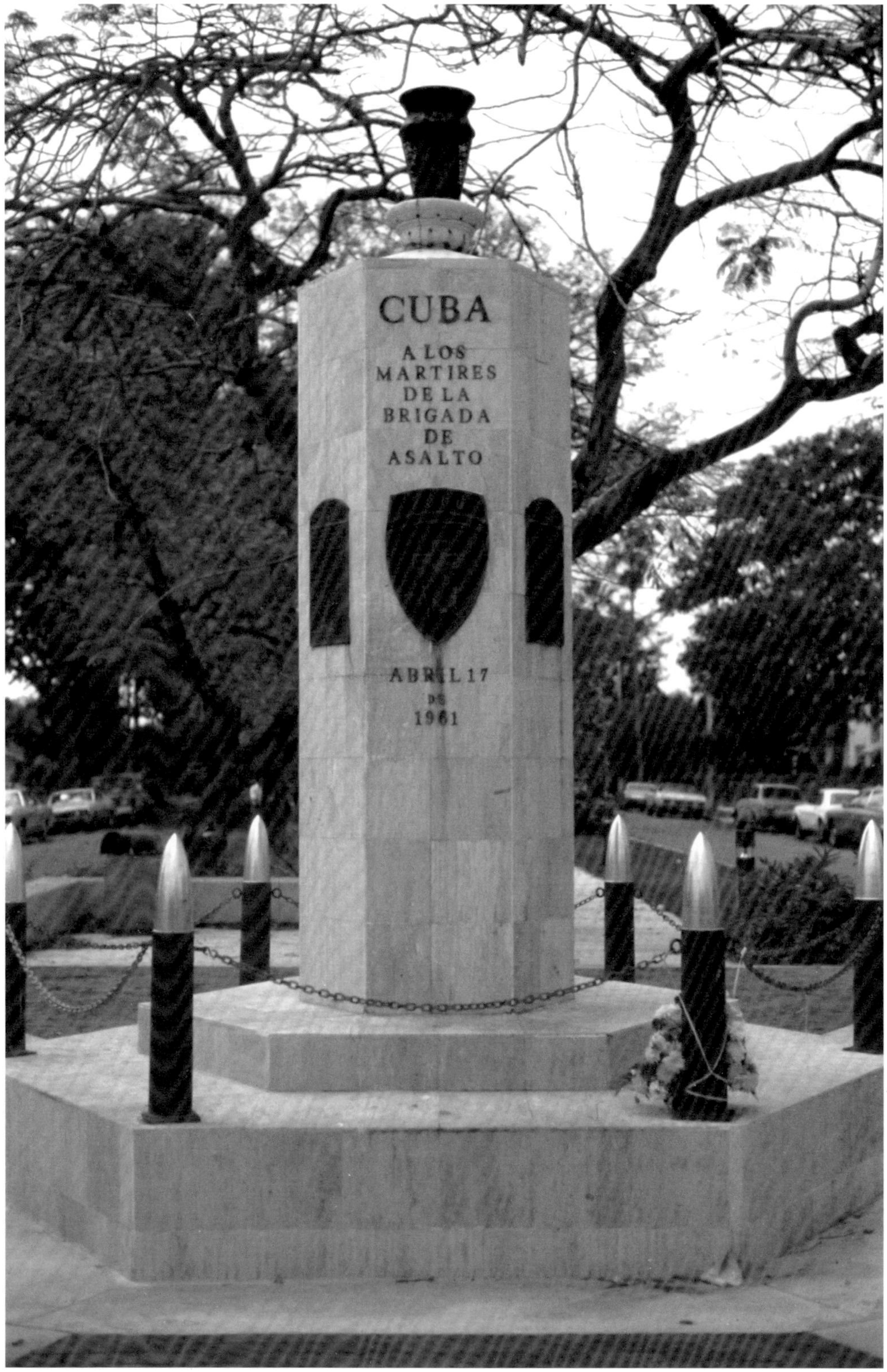

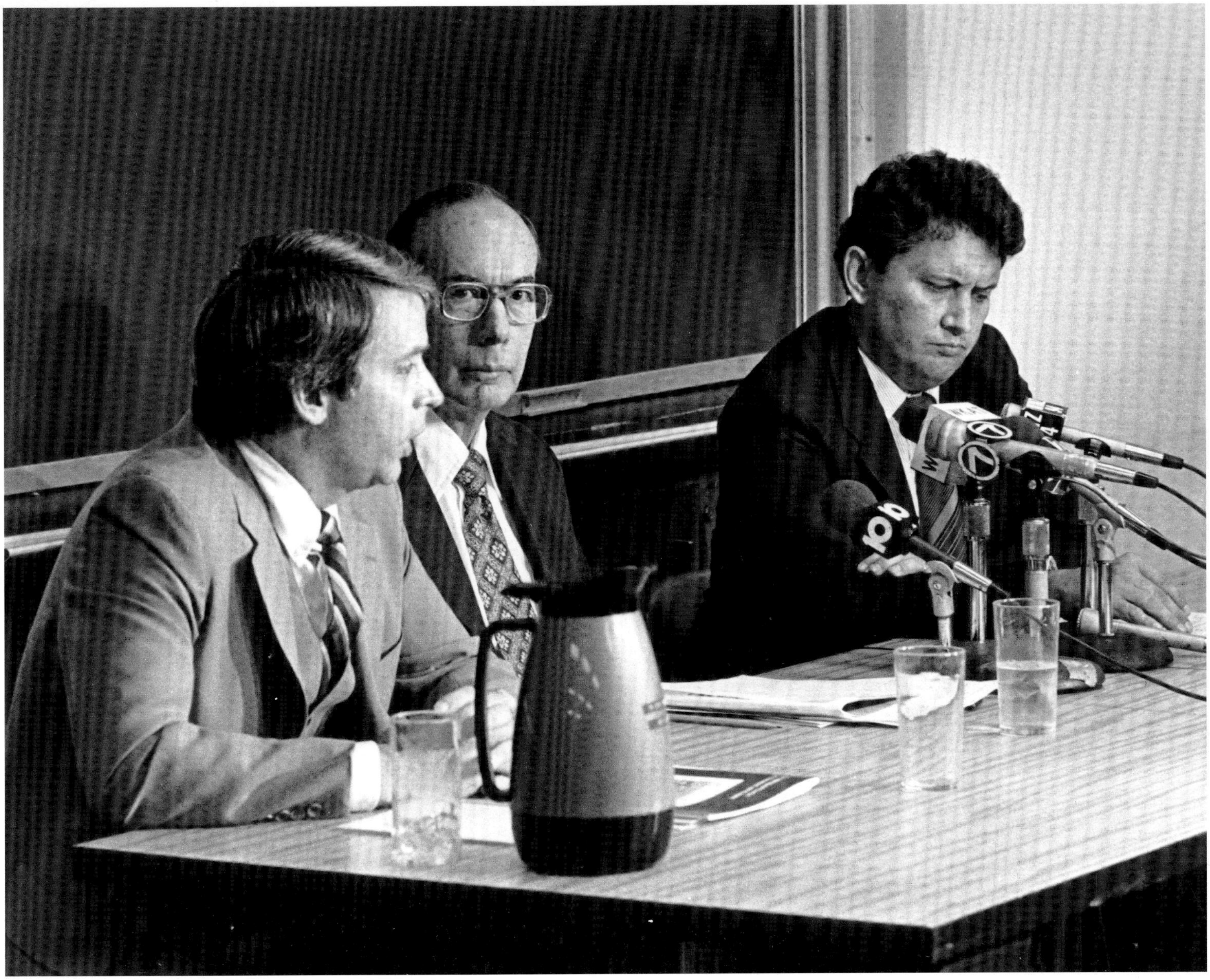

The 1980 Mariel Exodus Special Report at Miami Dade College.

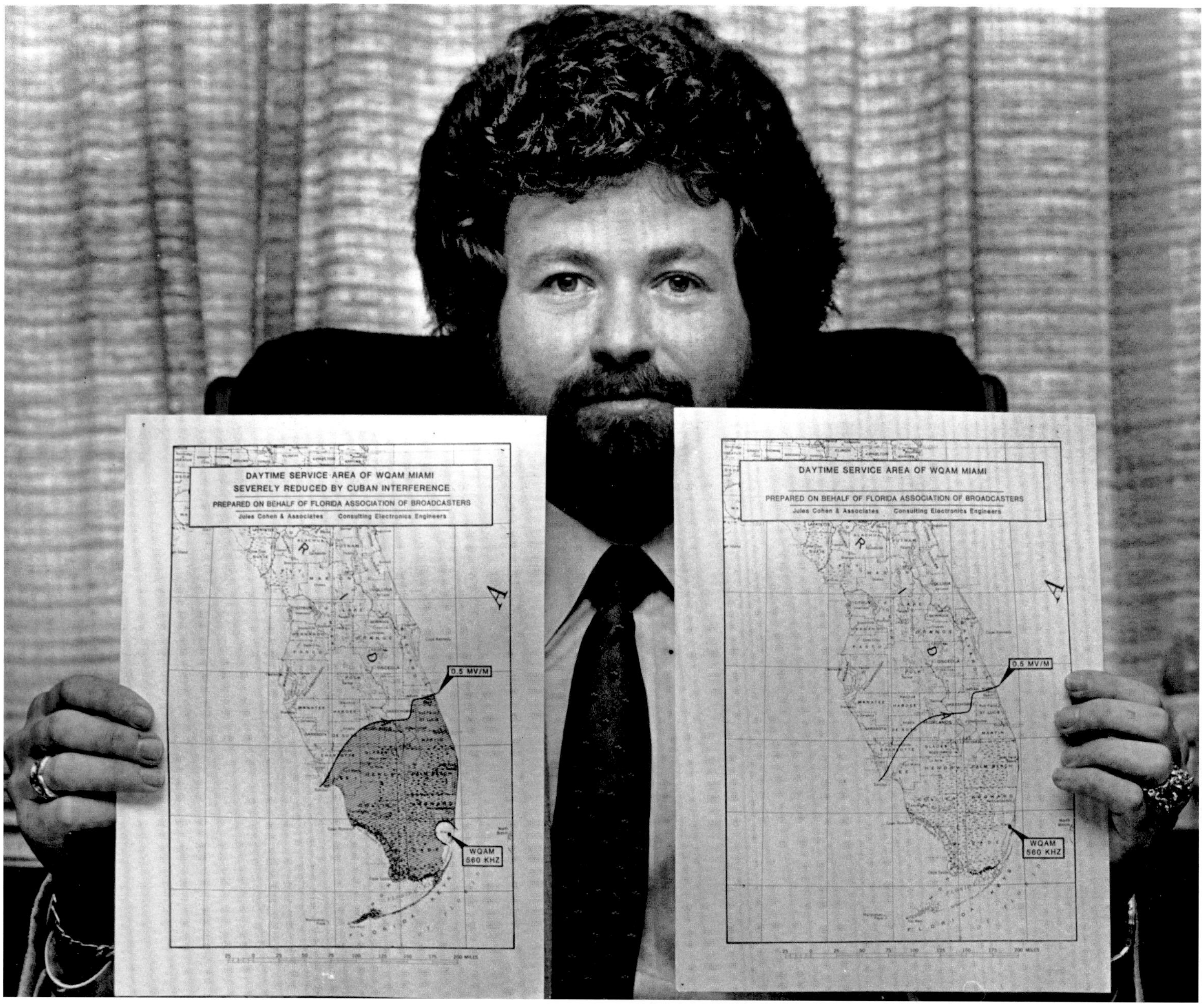

Matt Leibowitz displays maps revealing that Castro's radio stations would overpower WQAM's signal in 1981. Prior to that year, WQAM was easily found by Cubans living in Cuba from the 1960s forward, especially youths tuning in to listen to popular American music. By the time the interference began, WQAM was no longer a pop music station and now broadcasts as an all-sports station that still suffers from interference.

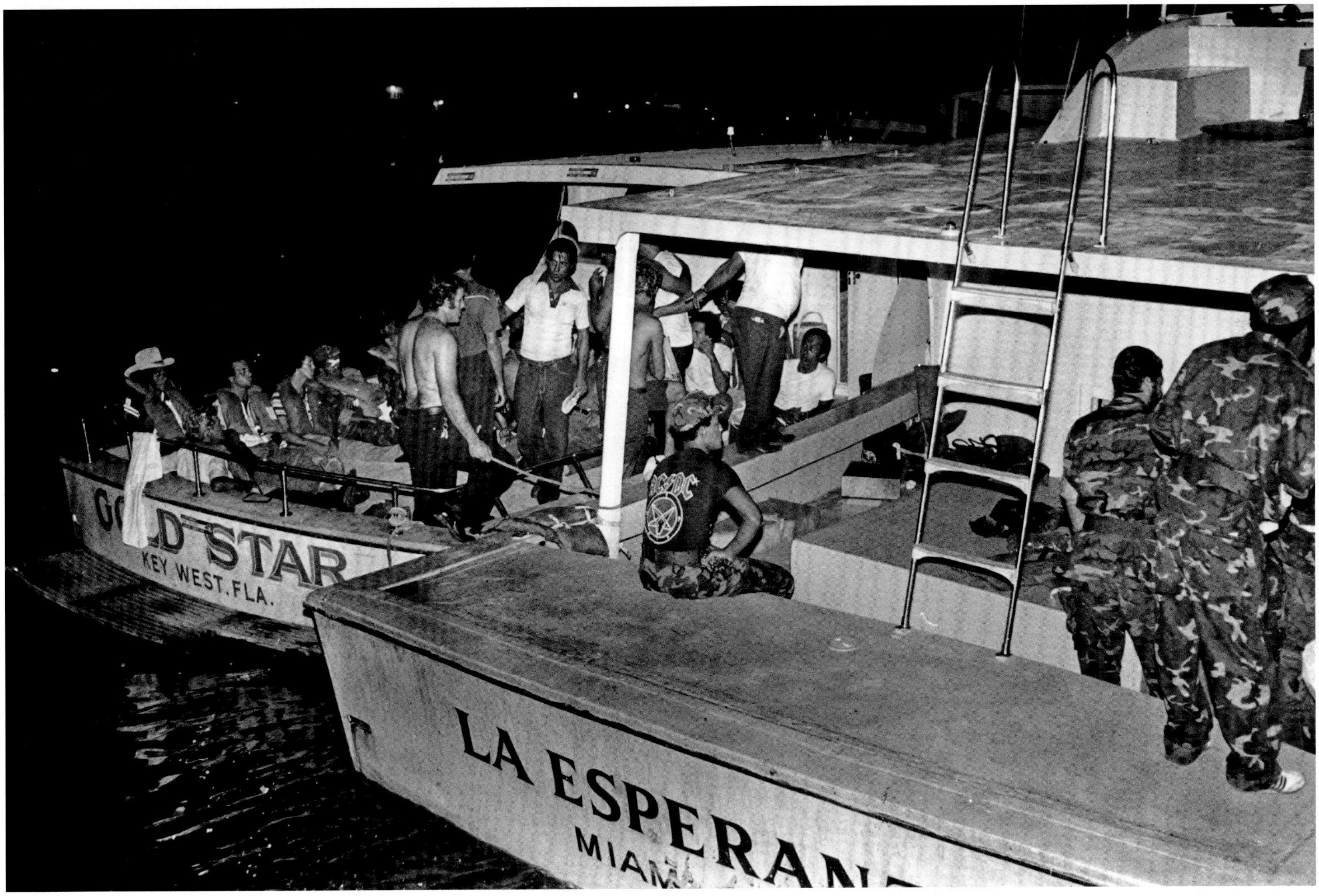

Members of Cubanos Unidos leave Miami to set up a new, free Cuban government in Guantanamo in 1981. Not surprisingly, the mission failed. Guantanamo, a U.S. Naval base, does not admit civilians, so the group would never have succeeded. That is, if they had gotten past the U.S. Coast Guard, which stated that they did not have enough life jackets.

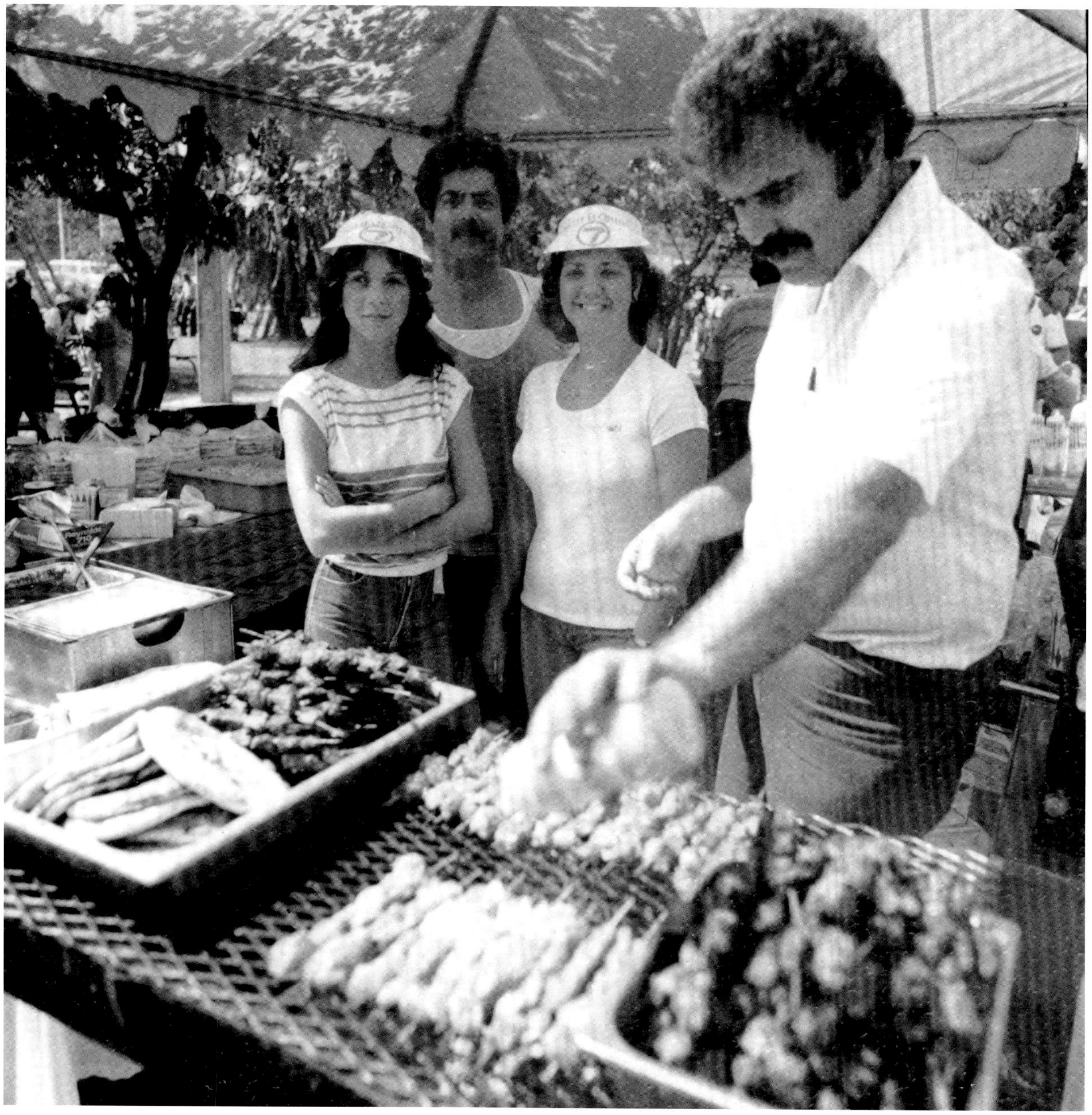

Kabobs are prepared at a Hispanic festival in Miami.

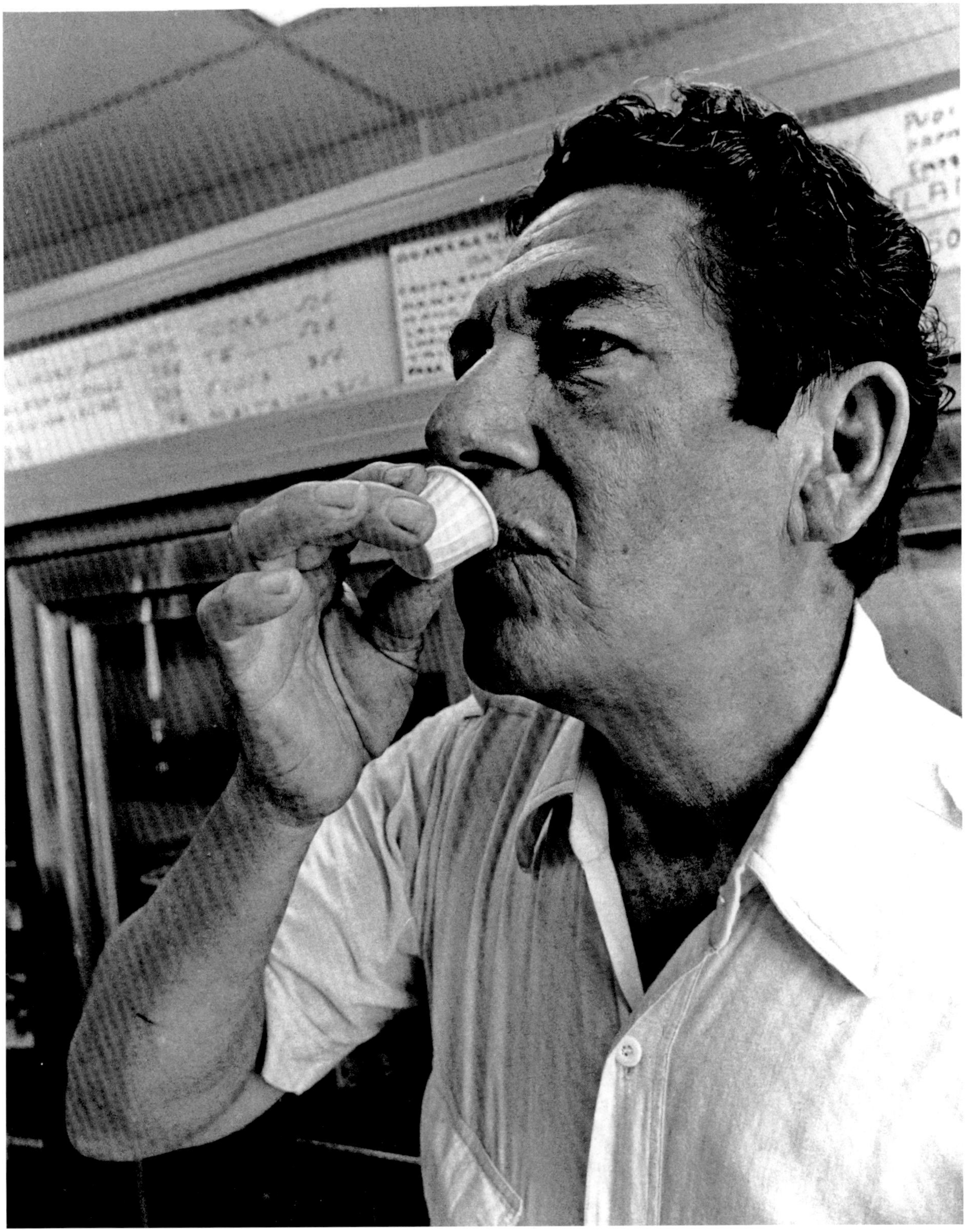

Jose Hernandez enjoys *café cubano* at Kantoray Coffee Shop located at 2200 SW 8th Street.

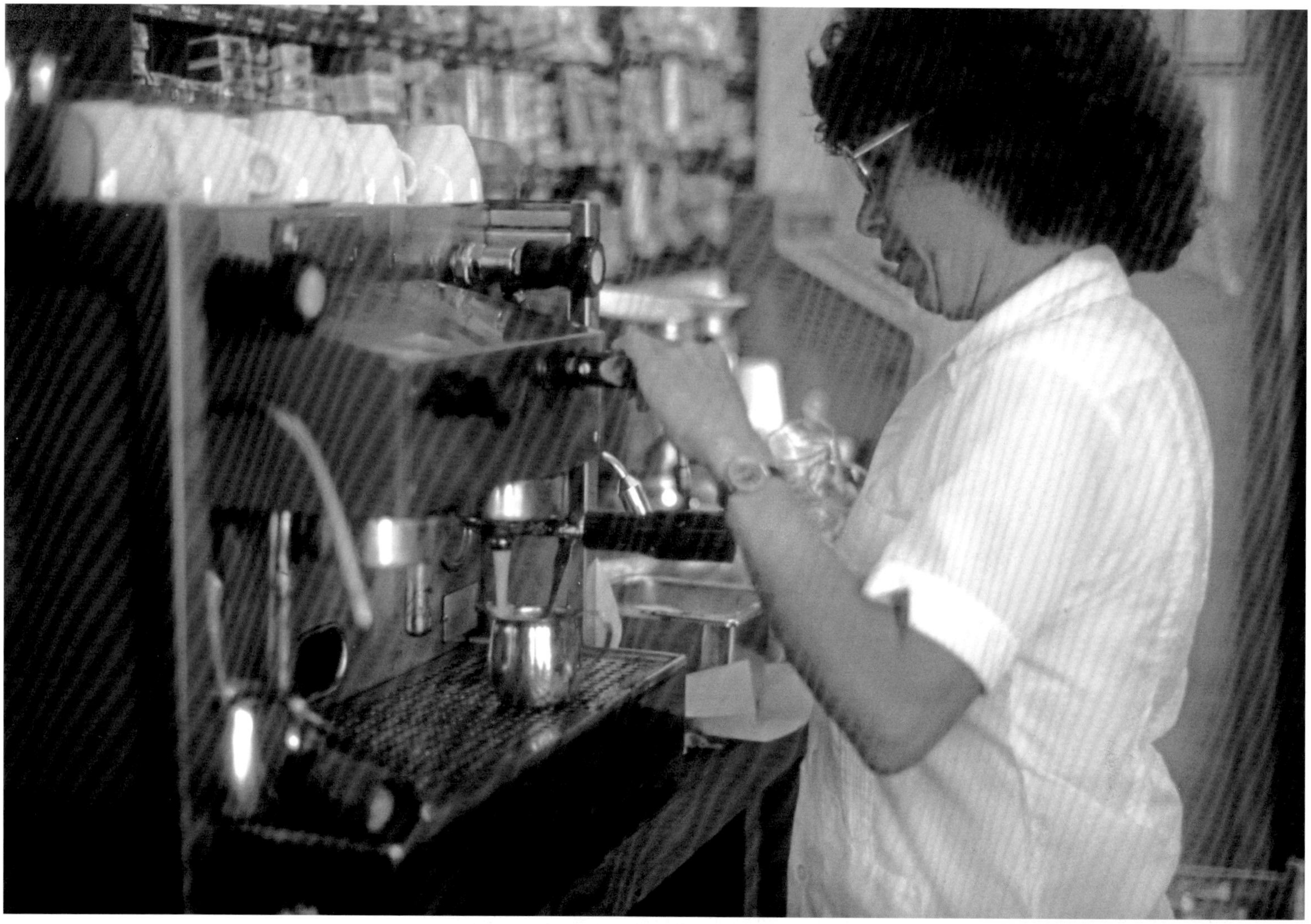

A woman prepares Cuban coffee—*café cubano*. Cuban coffee is known for being extremely robust and for being sweetened while brewed. It is served in very small portions because of its strength. Traditional preparations are *café con leche, cortaditos* (very strong shots cut or "cortado" with milk), and *coladas* (several shots of pure coffee meant to be shared).

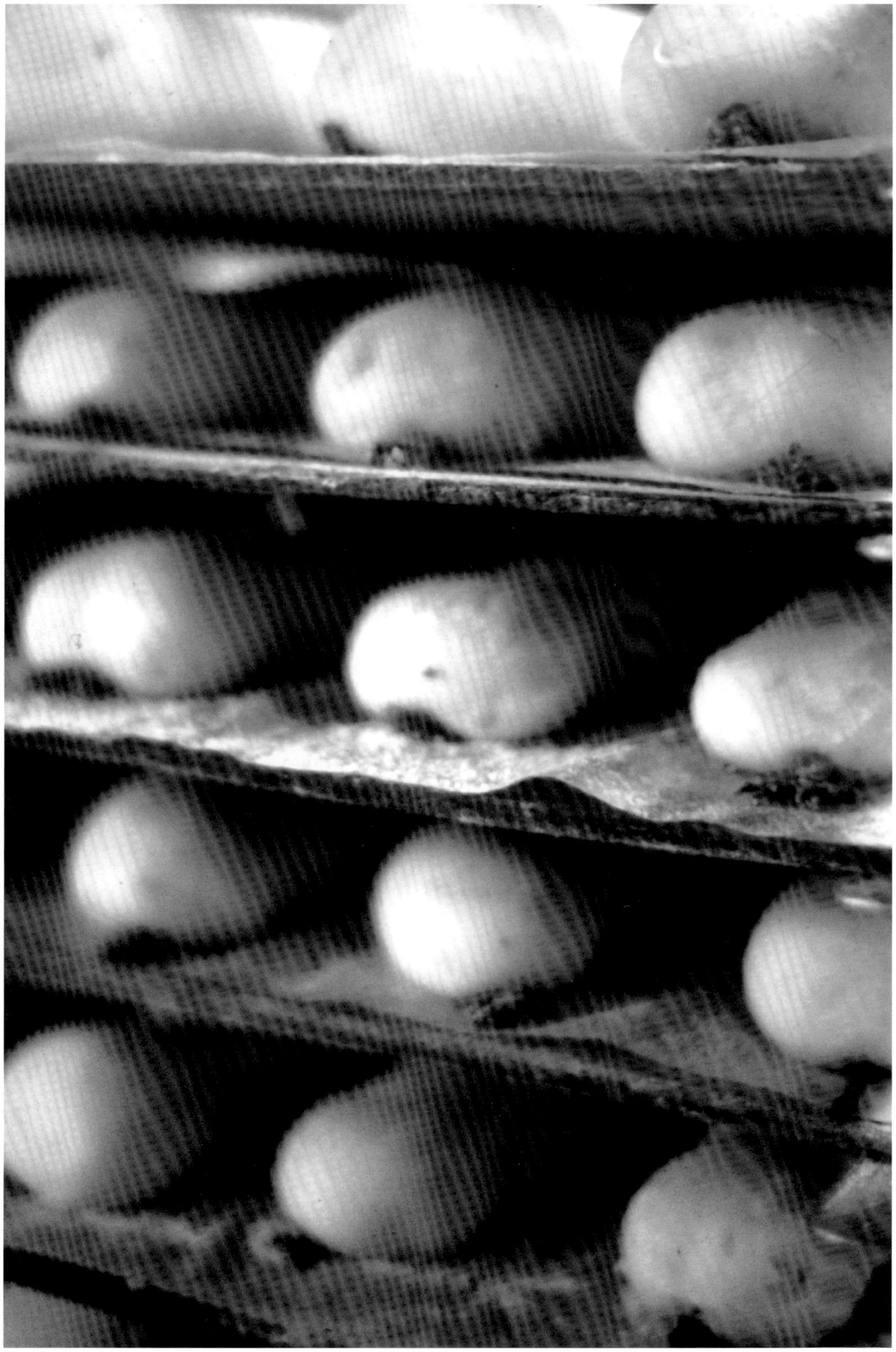

A good loaf of Cuban bread has a light, paper-thin crust and is airy and soft inside. It was traditionally baked with a palm frond on top, which was removed before serving, leaving an indention along the top of the loaf. The bread is known to grow stale quickly, usually within 24 hours. It is a staple of Cuban breakfasts, served with *café con leche,* and is the only acceptable bread used to make a *sandwiche cubano.*

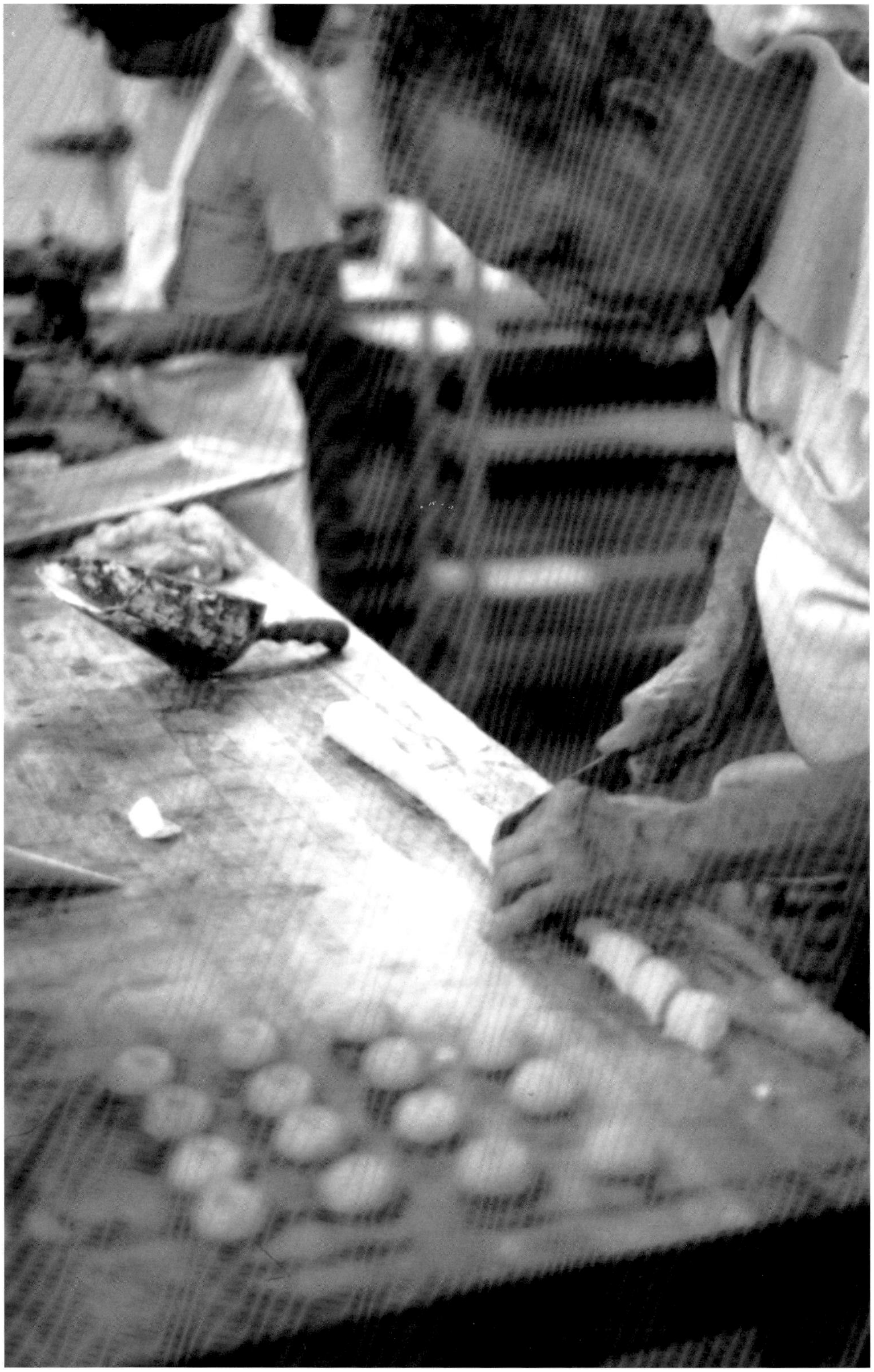

A chef makes cookies at Cafe Cubano in Little Havana. It is said that to find real Cuban food, one must visit Miami, since the scarcity of ingredients in Cuba has restricted the ability of locals to prepare traditional Cuban cuisine.

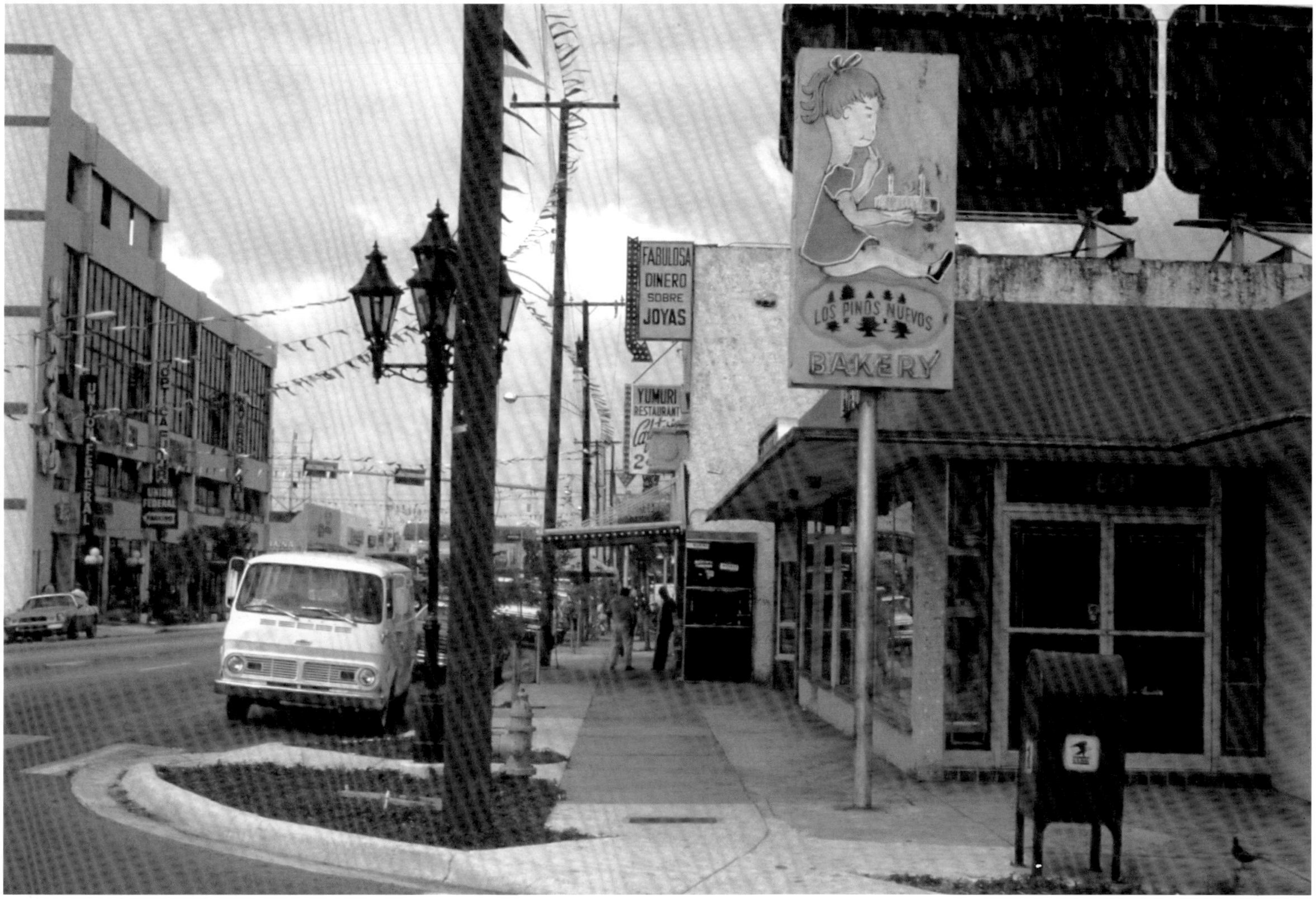

This street corner in Little Havana features a Cuban bakery. Cuban bakeries typically serve *croquetas, pastelitos, flan,* and *pan cubano.*

This sculpture in Little Havana of Antonio Maceo holding a machete is inscribed with Maceo's words "La Libertad no se Mendiga. Se conquista con el filo del machete." In translation, Maceo said, "Freedom isn't begged for. It is won with a blade."

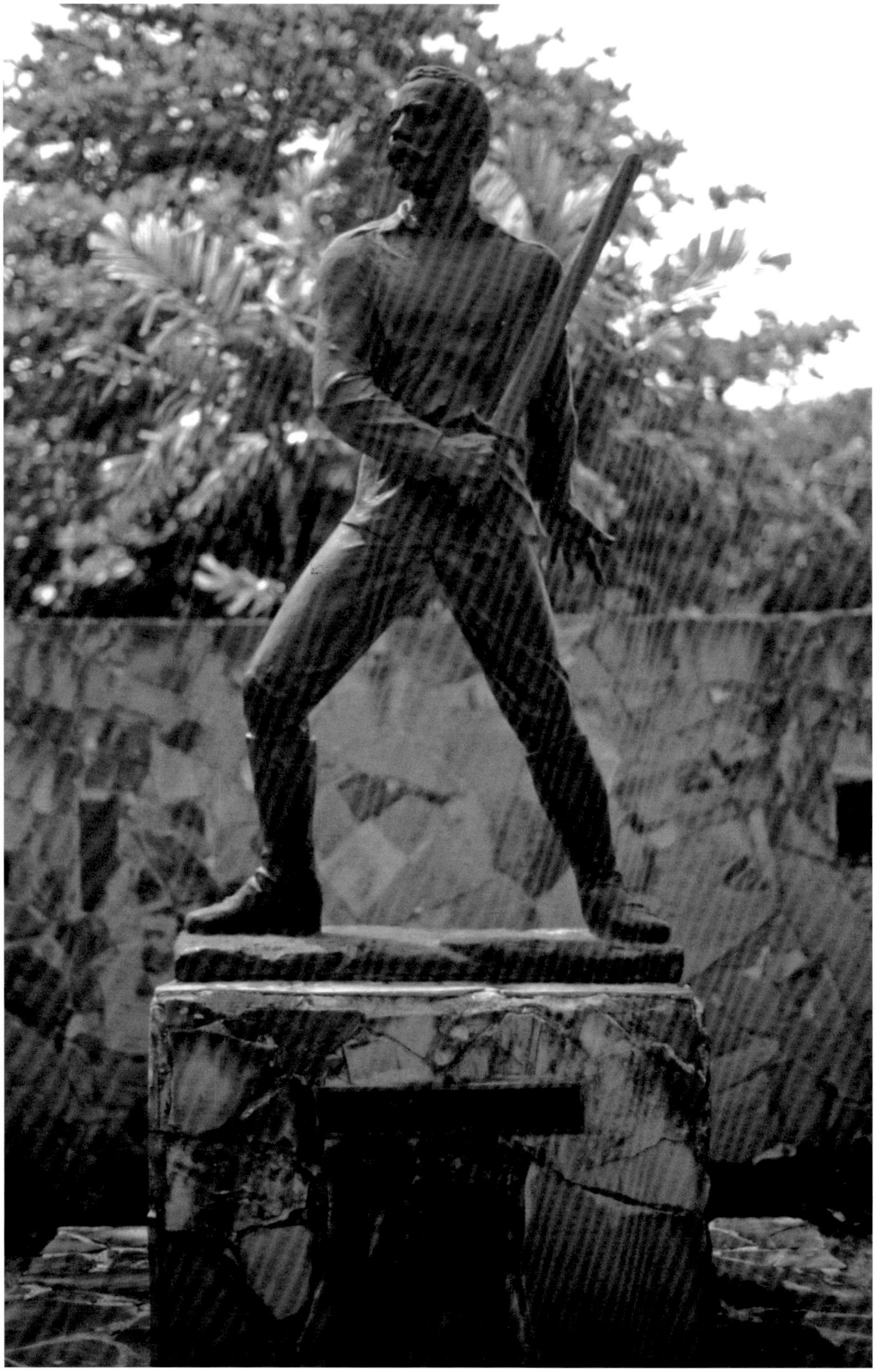

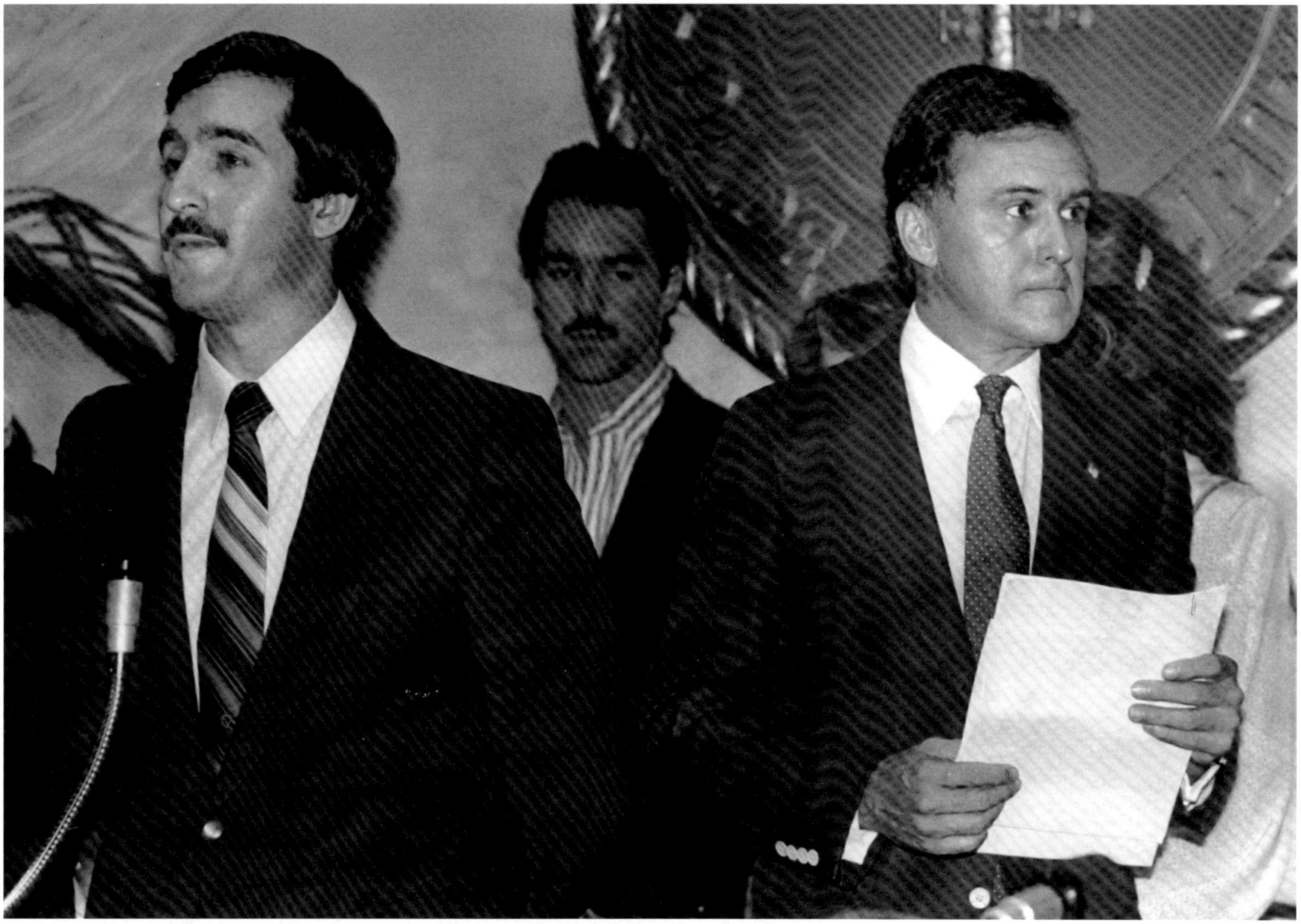

Future mayor of Miami Joe Carollo makes an appearance with then mayor Maurice Ferre, the first Hispanic mayor of Miami. Puerto Rican Ferre was mayor from 1973 to 1985. He was succeeded by Xavier Suarez, the first Cuban mayor of Miami, who served from 1985 to 1993 and 1997 to 1998. Carollo would serve as mayor from 1996 to 1997 and 1998 to 2001.

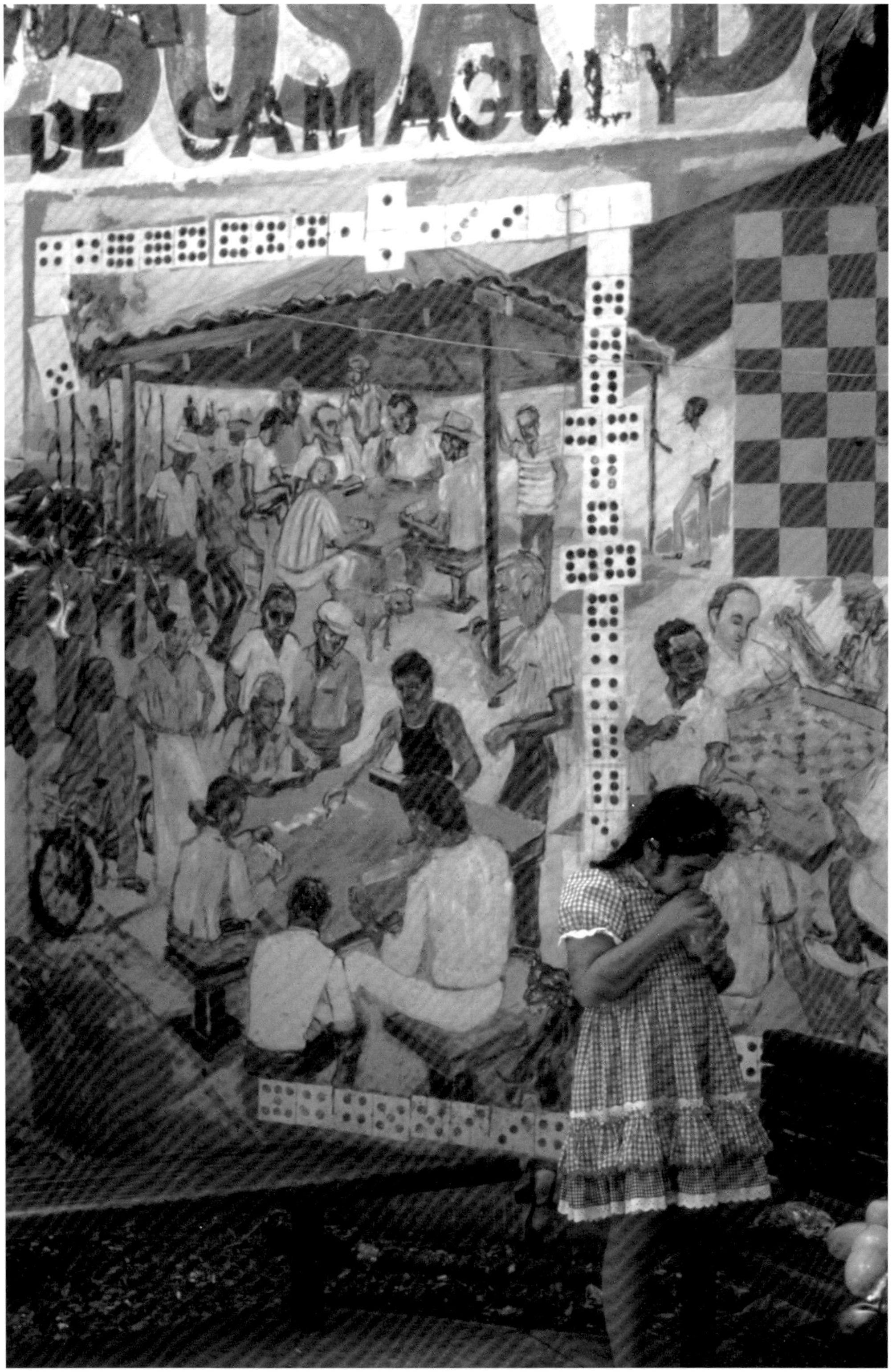

A mural of men playing dominoes in Little Havana. The little girl at lower-right is inflating a balloon.

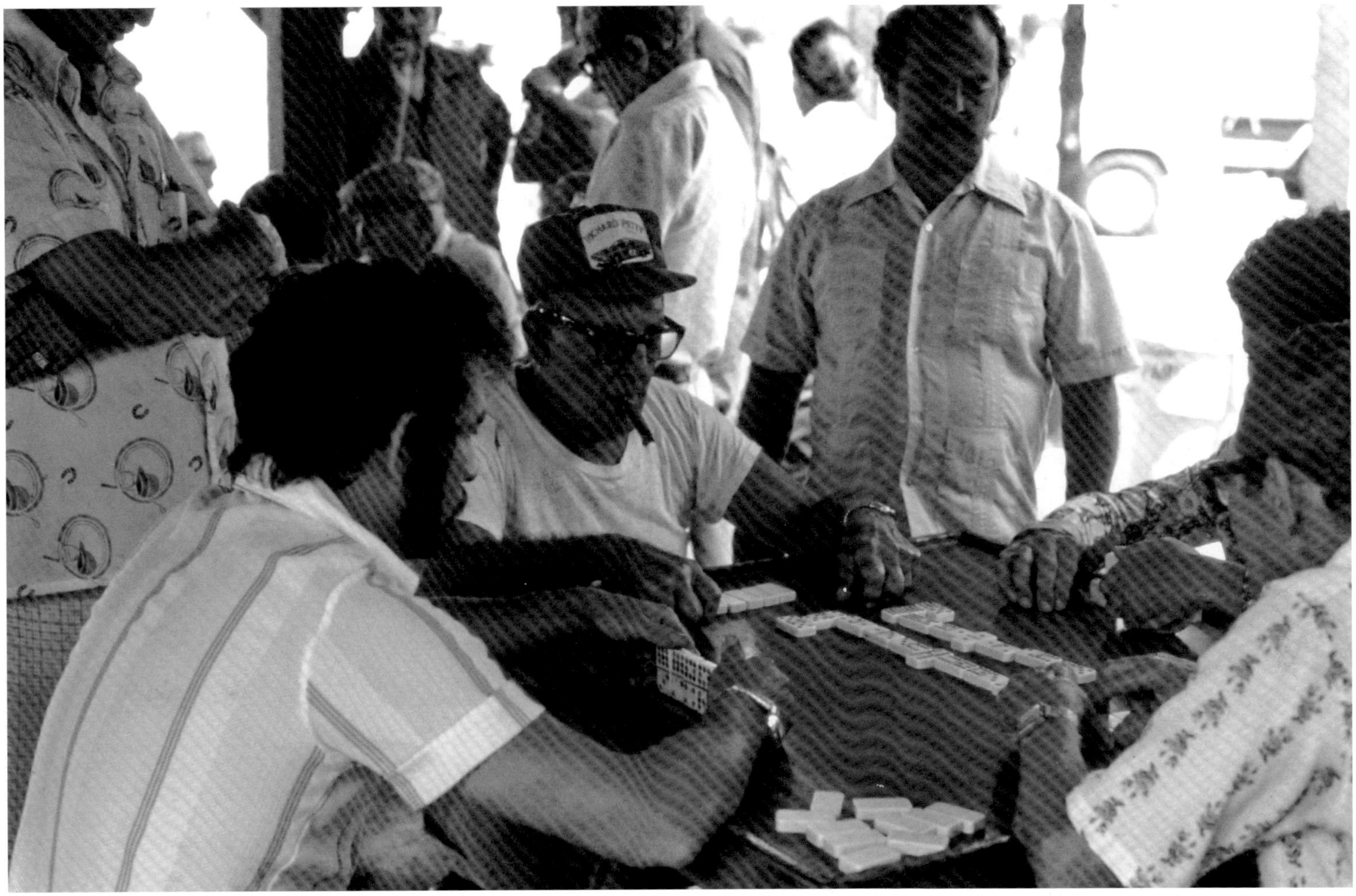

These men enjoy a game of dominoes at Domino Park in Little Havana.

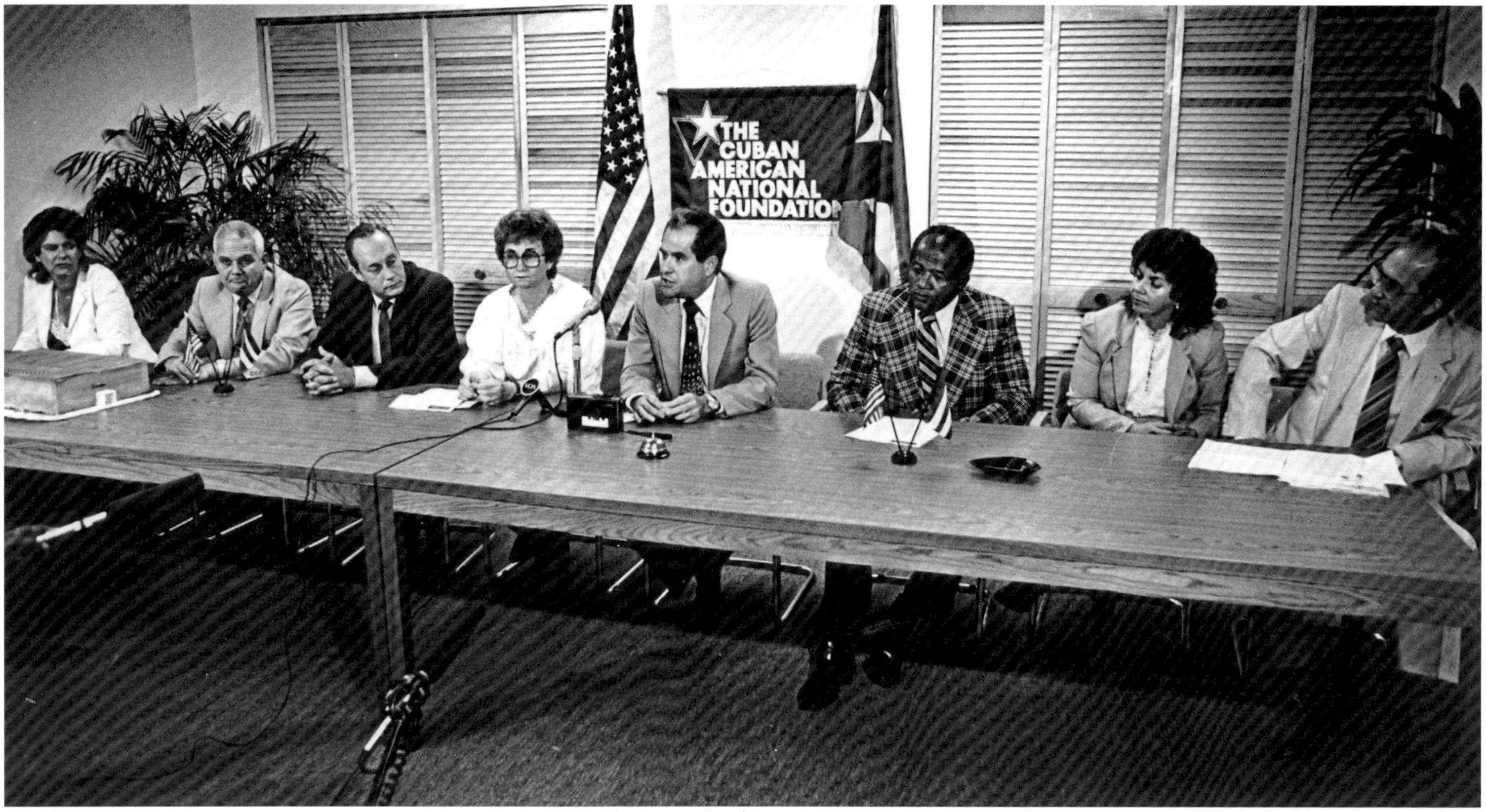

These members of the Cuban American National Foundation, from left to right, were Ada Perez Rodriguez, Eduardo Capote, Alfredo Izaguirre, Janita Castro, Jorege Mas Canosa, Sergio Bravo, Maria Oiva, and Jose Carreno.

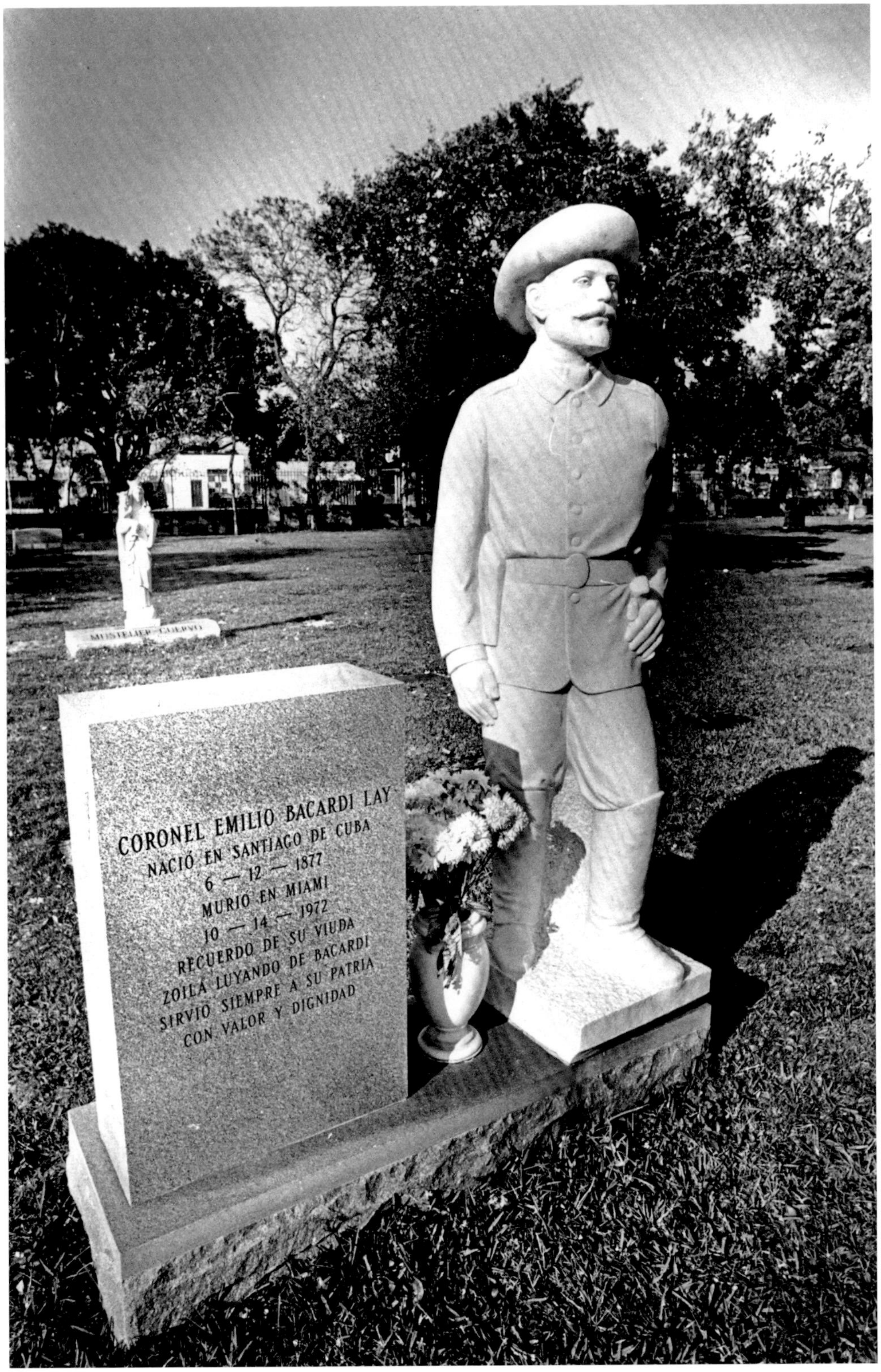

The statue and headstone of Emilio Bacardi Lay at Woodlawn Cemetery, the resting place of most Cubans in Miami. Bacardi was not native to Puerto Rico. The Bacardis were Cuban, as was their rum. Prior to Castro's rise to power, production of Bacardi rum had been moved to Puerto Rico and Mexico, imports were headquartered in New York, and trademarks were held in the Bahamas. When Castro made good on nationalizing industry, the Bacardis and their rum were long gone.

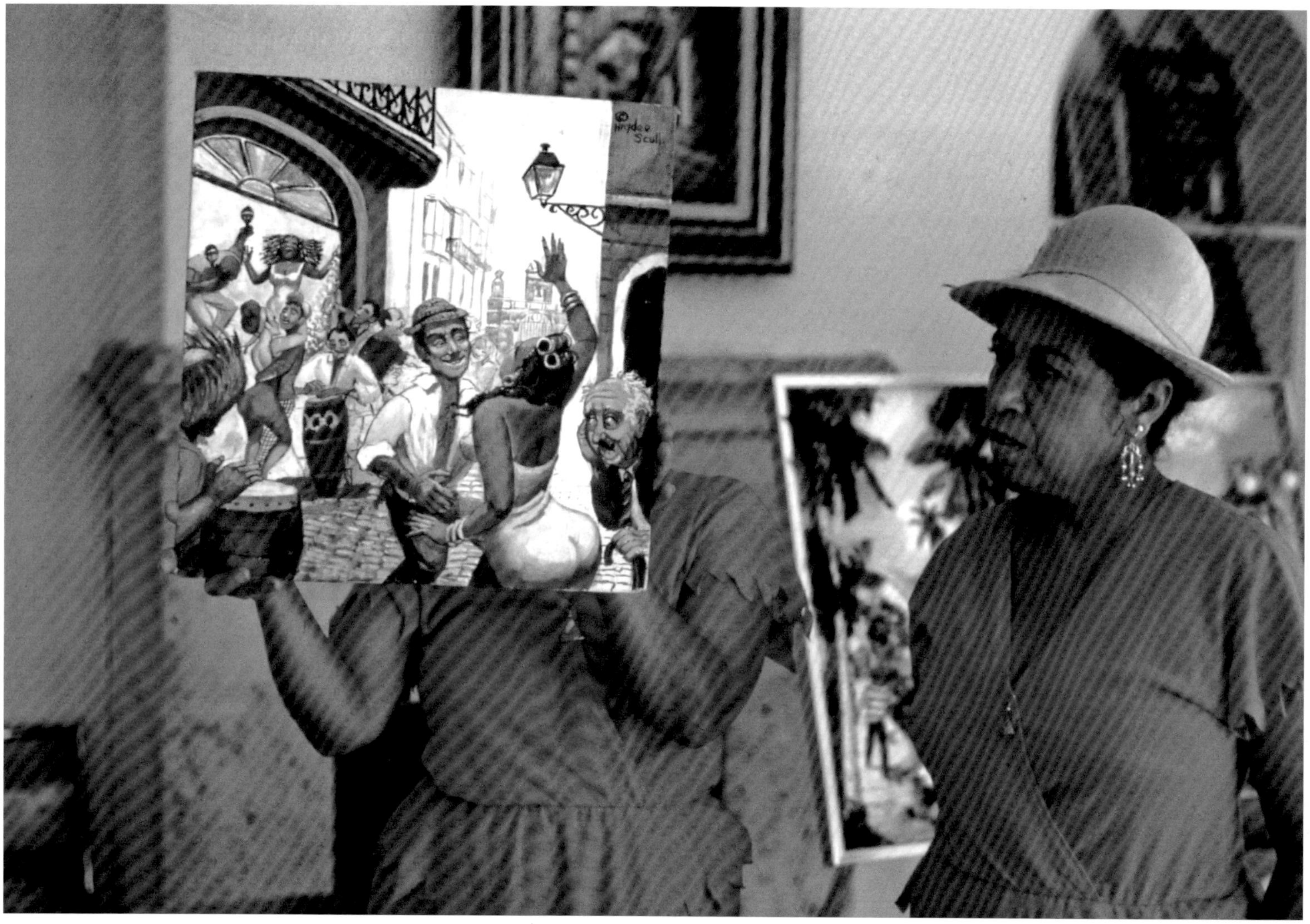

Haydee and Sahara Scull hold an album cover with their painting *New Miami* on it.

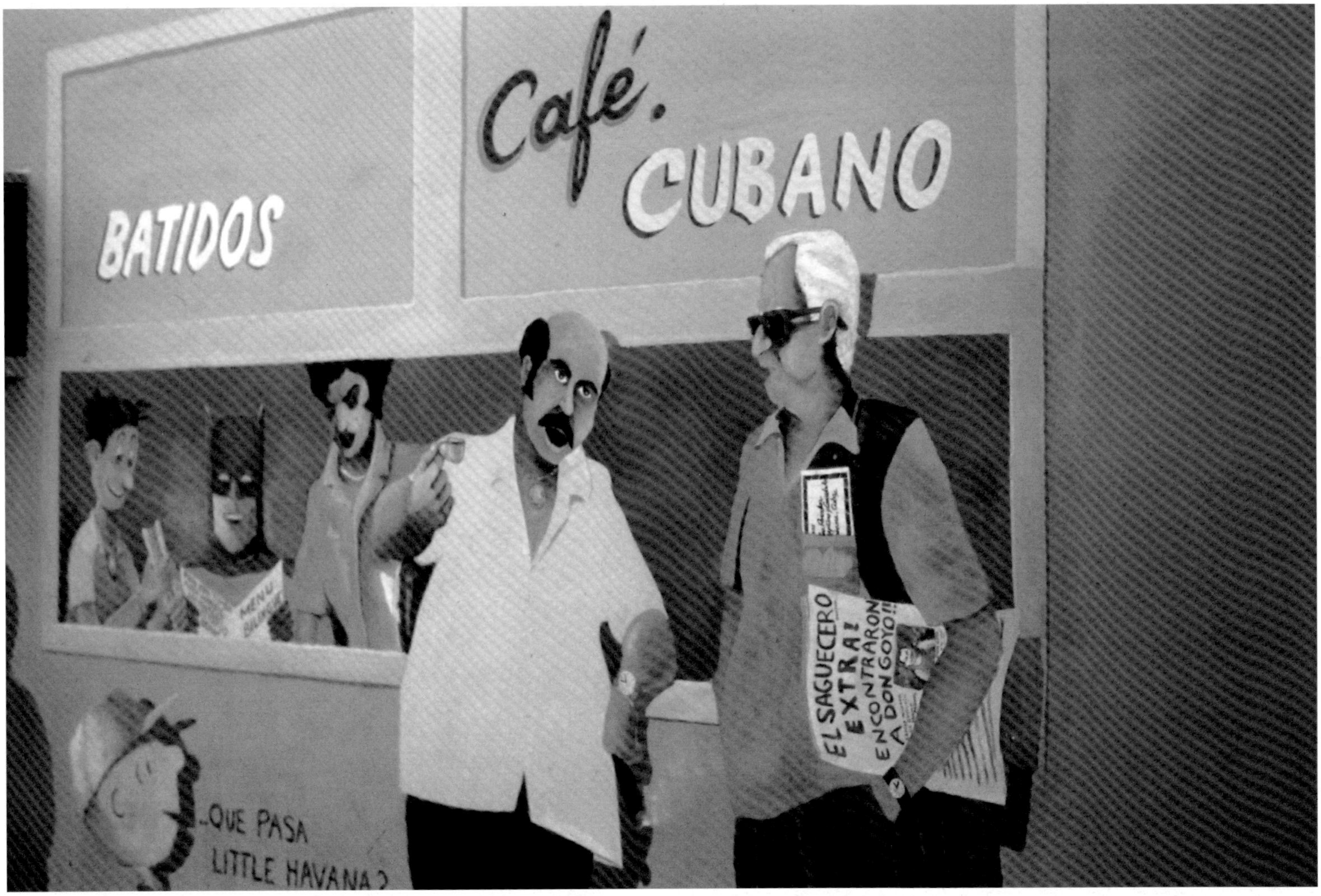

It is not uncommon to see symbols of American pop culture hand-painted on the exteriors of Cuban stores, on goods made by Cubans, and even on cars. These displays are almost always humorous or awkward, which lends a sort of charm that may be apparent only to locals in the community.

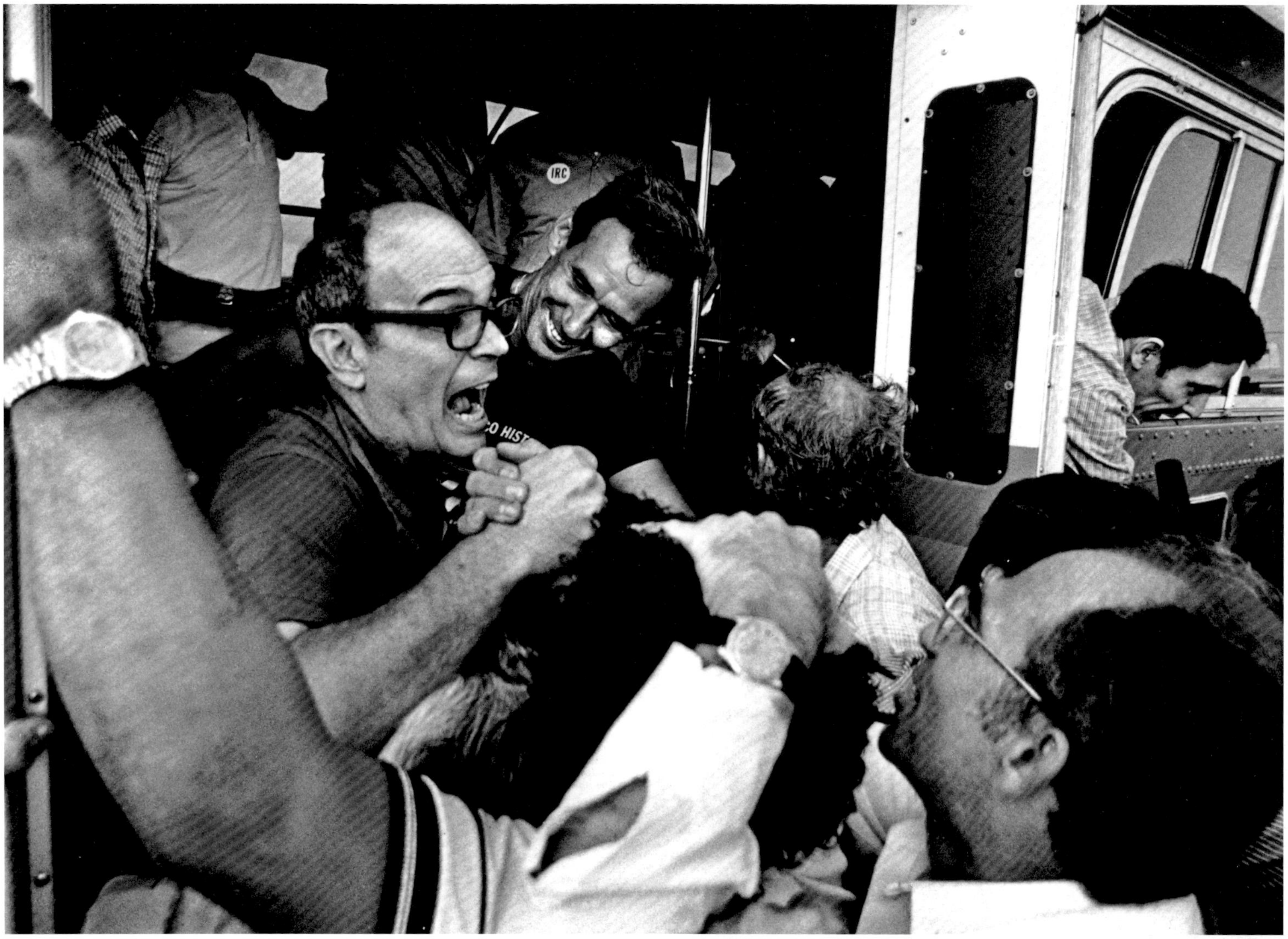

An ex-prisoner, just released from Castro's jail, is purely joyful as he comes off the bus to reunite with family and friends.

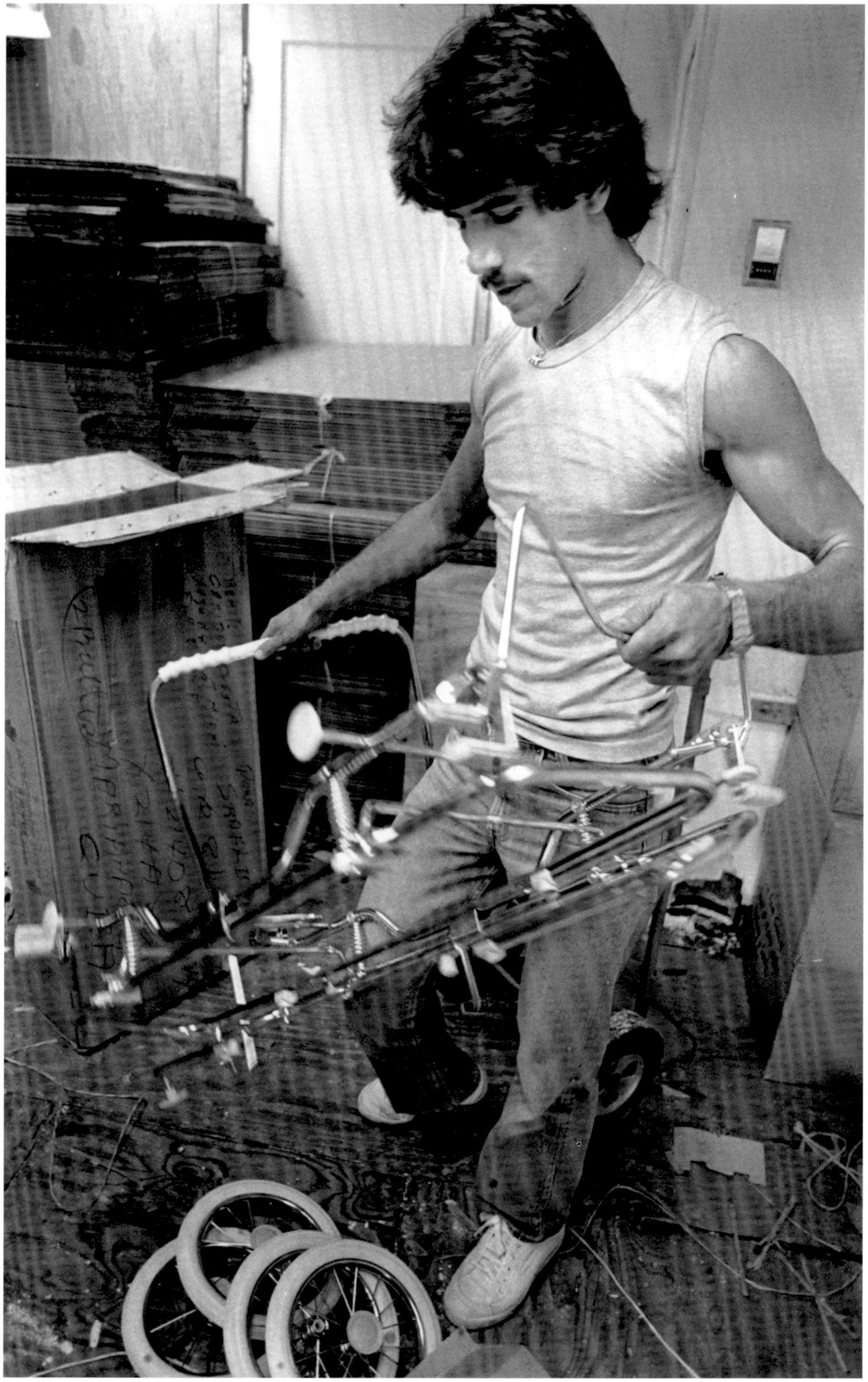

Arturo Lopez packs children's clothes and a baby carriage for a trip to Cuba.

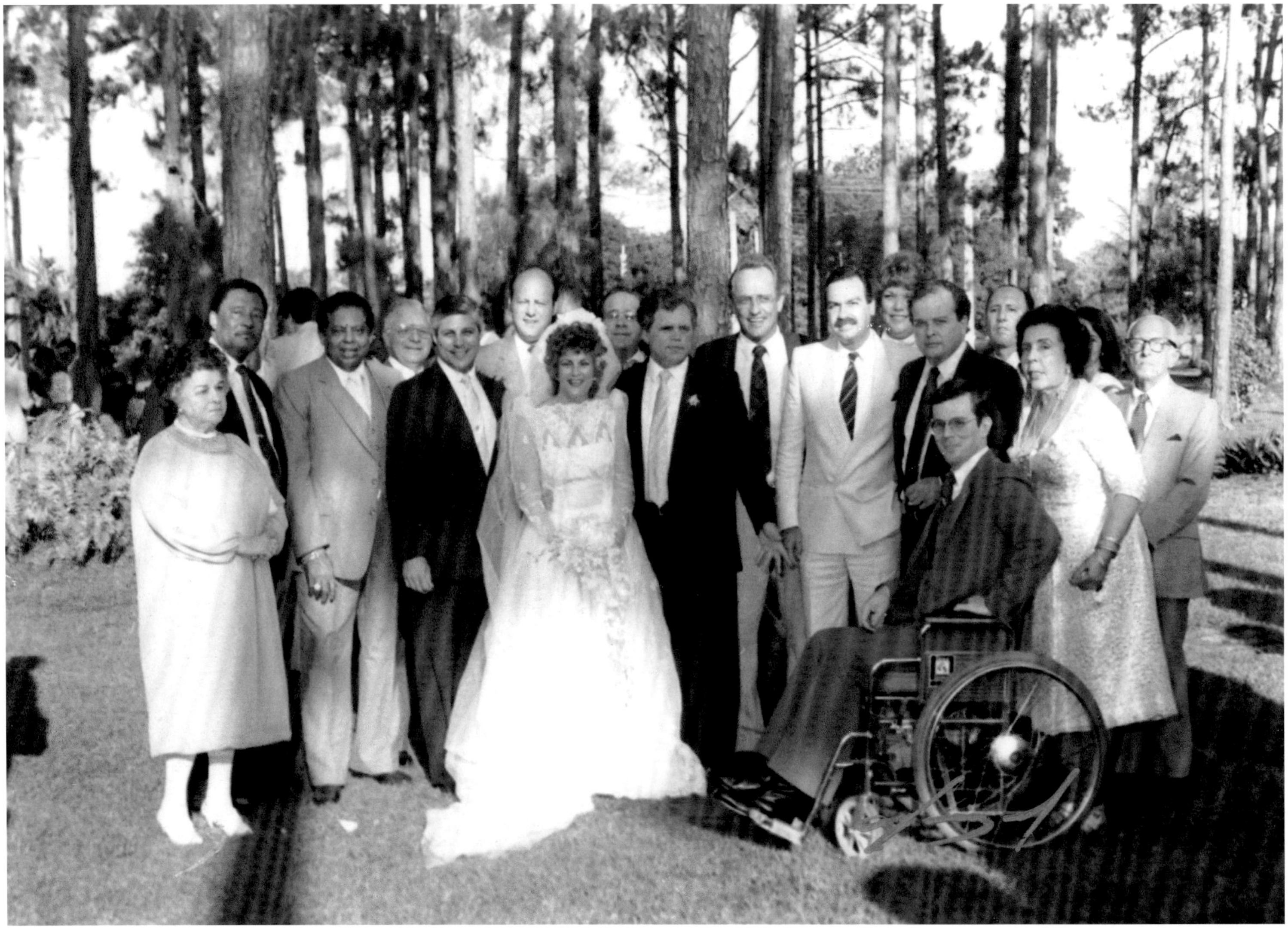

Illeana Ros and Dexter Lehtinen were married on June 9, 1984. Both have served in the Florida House of Representatives and the Florida Senate.

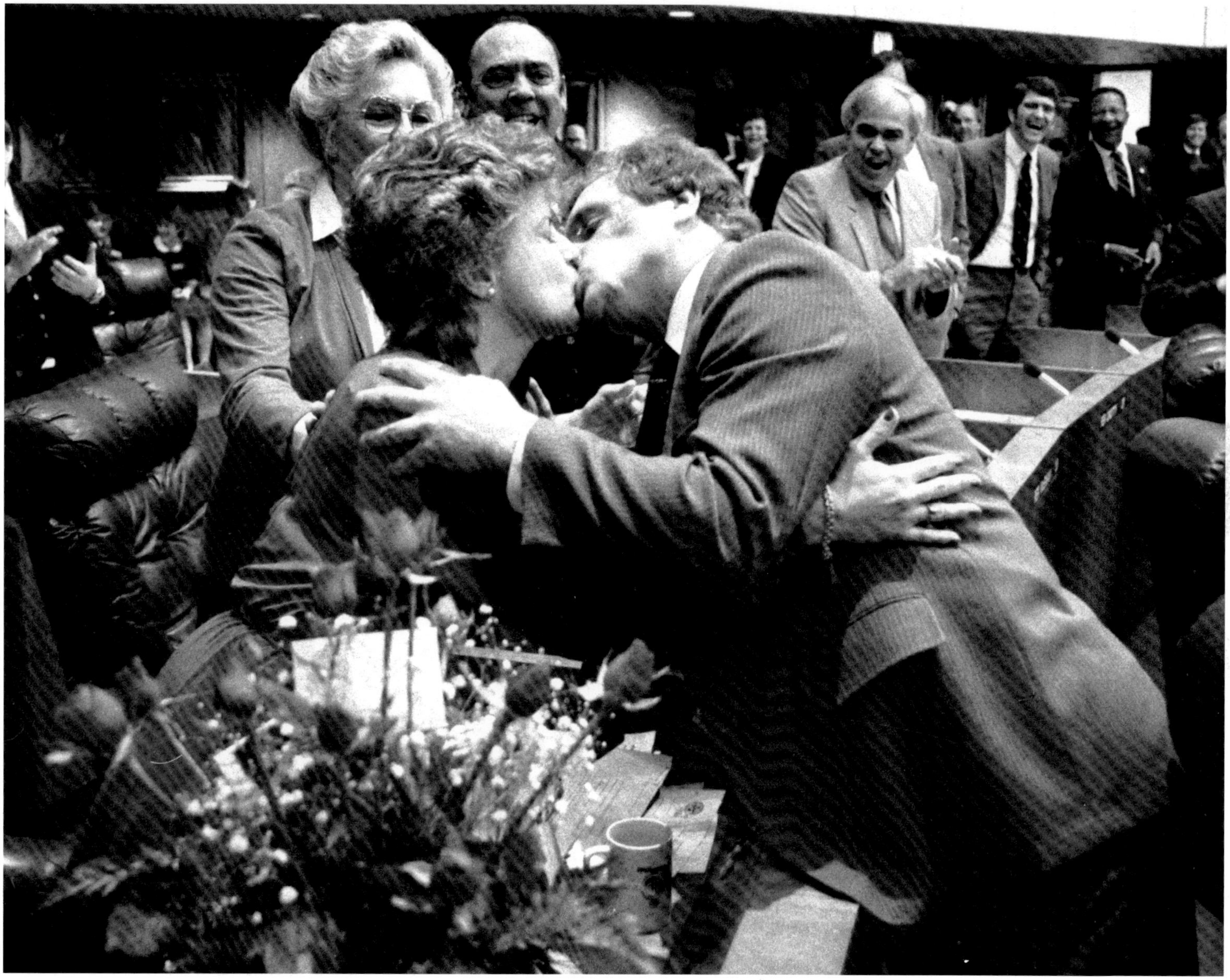

Cuban-American members of the Florida House of Representatives, Illeana Ros-Lehtinen and Dexter Lehtinen. Ros-Lehtinen is a Miami representative and a prominent member of the Cuban-American community in Miami.

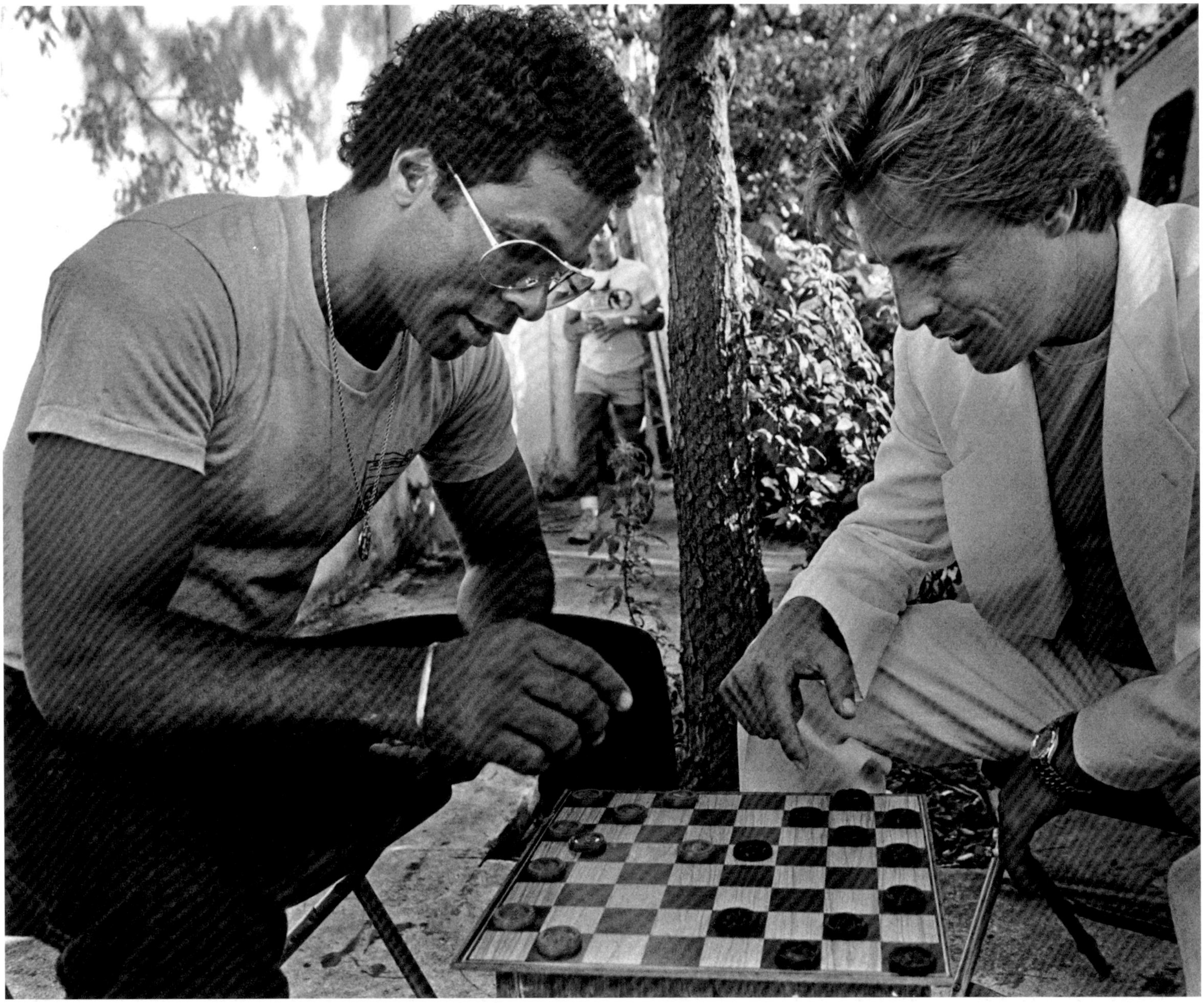

Produced by Anthony Yerkovich, *Miami Vice* was filmed on location, in most cases on Miami Beach. One episode of the show was called "Cuba Libre," which was based on a Cuba-Miami conspiracy.

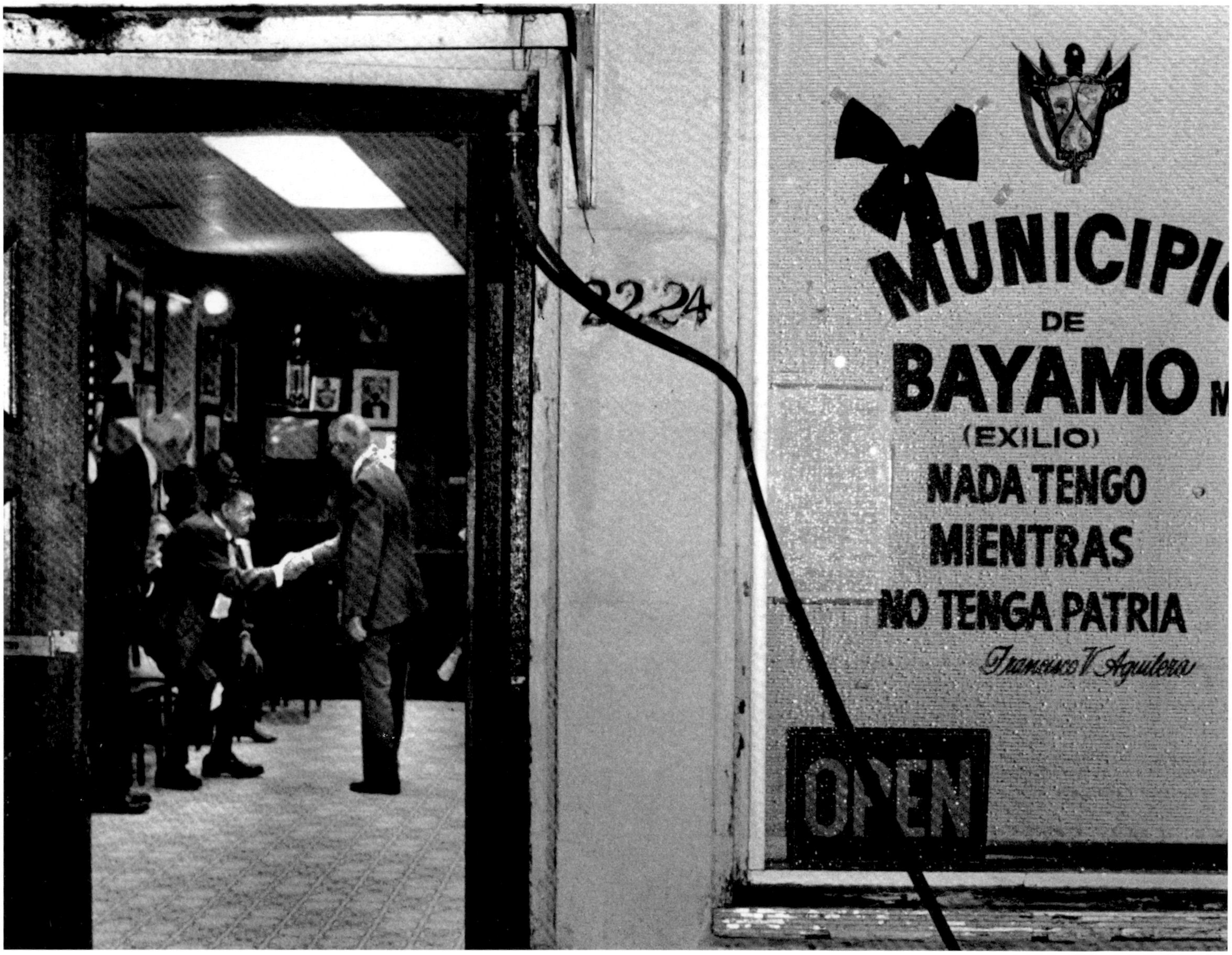

Cubans meet at the Municipio de Bayamo Exilio in Miami. The words on the exterior say, "Nada tengo mientras no tenga patria" (translation: I have nothing, if I don't have a country.)

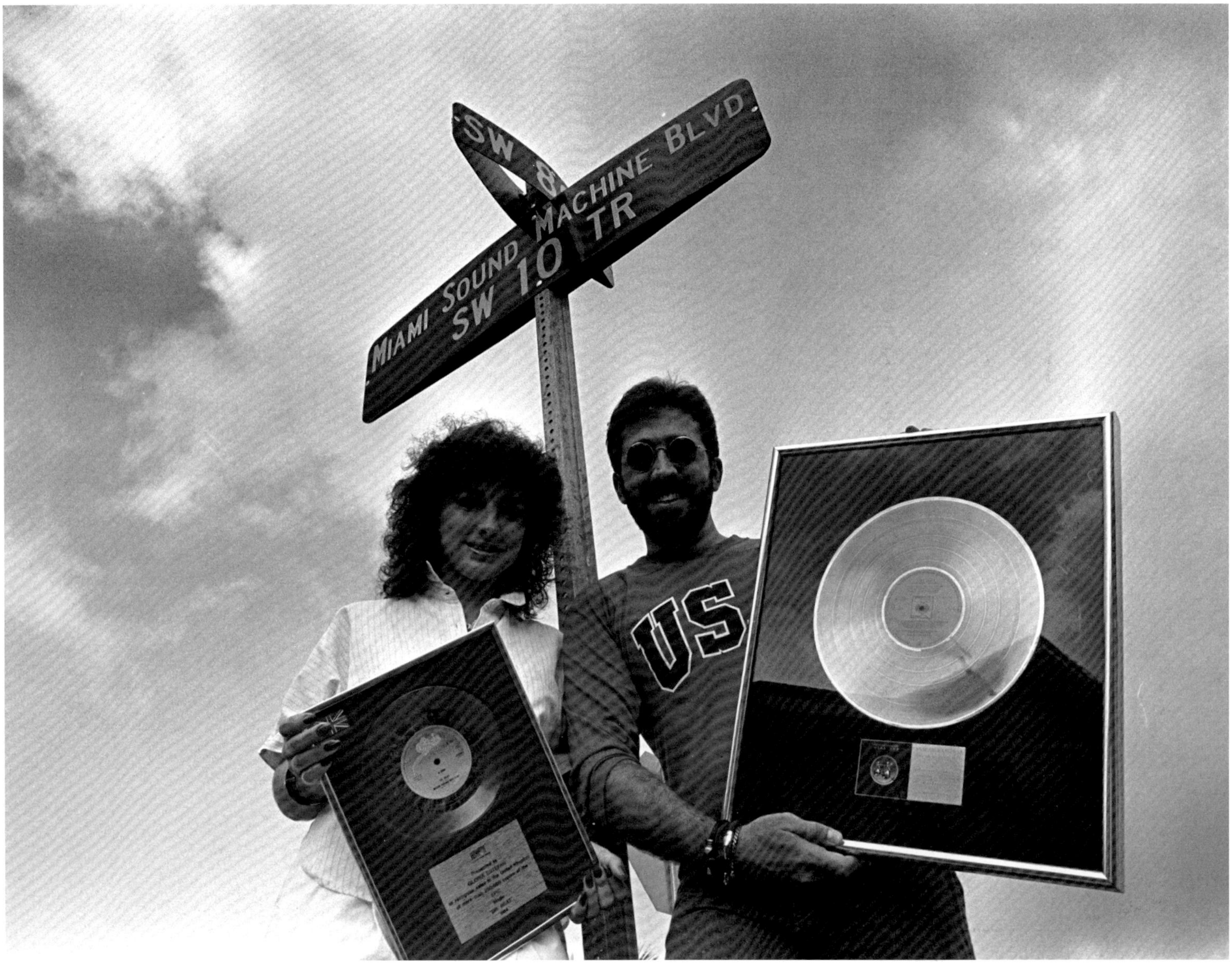

Two of the Miami Sound Machine's more famous members, Gloria and Emilio Estefan, stand on the street named after the group. Members include famous Cuban talk-show host, Cristina Saraluegi.

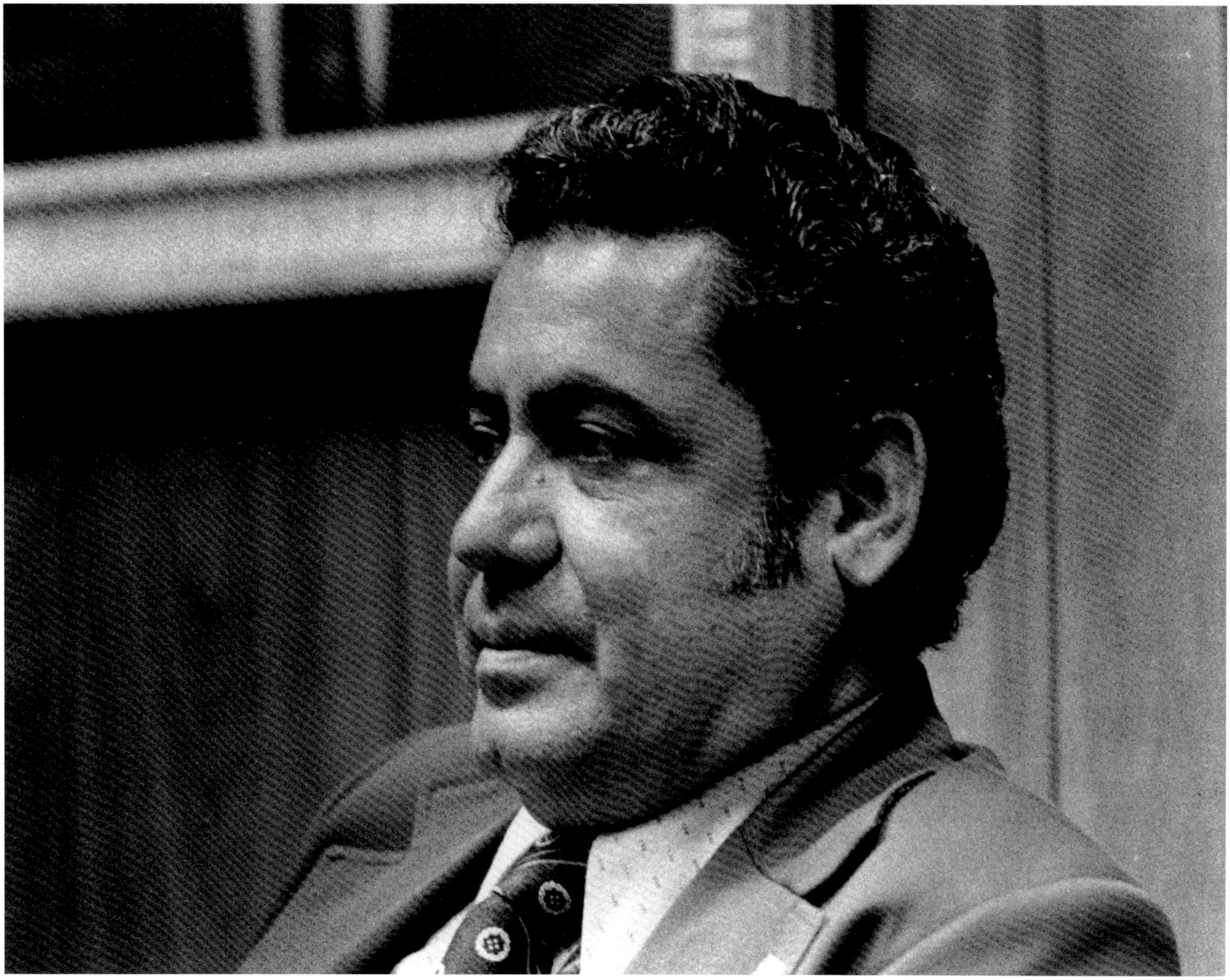

Hiram Gomez, a Bay of Pigs veteran, served the City of Miami for several years and was honored by House Representative Ros-Lehtinen for his service as the public relations specialist for Little Havana's neighborhood enhancement team. Gomez founded the Embrace our Elderly Program and has been involved in many other associations in Miami.

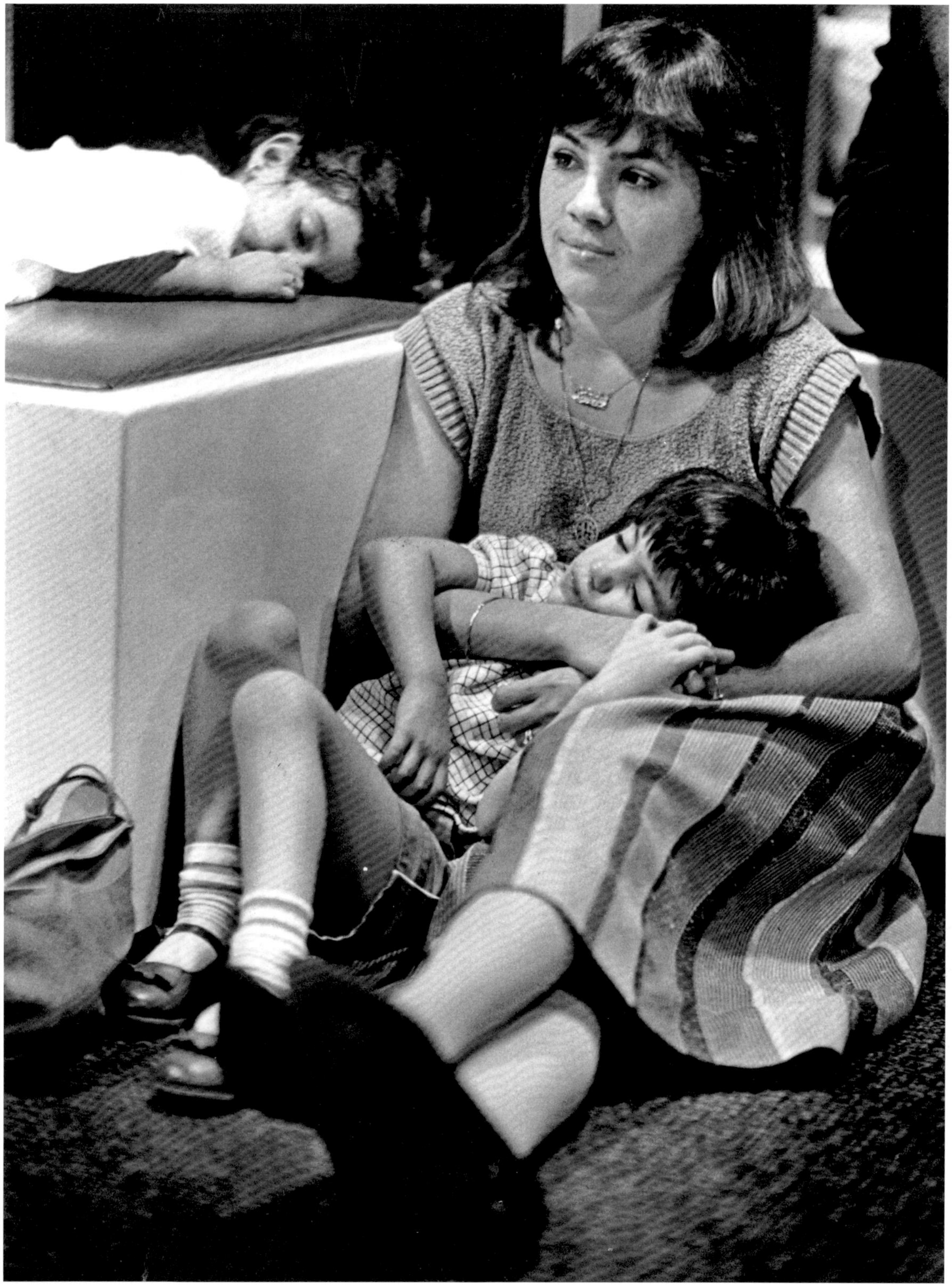

Odalys Soberon holds her niece Ydalis as her other niece Margarita sleeps. Soberon was waiting for her father, Raul Orellana, to return from Cuba.

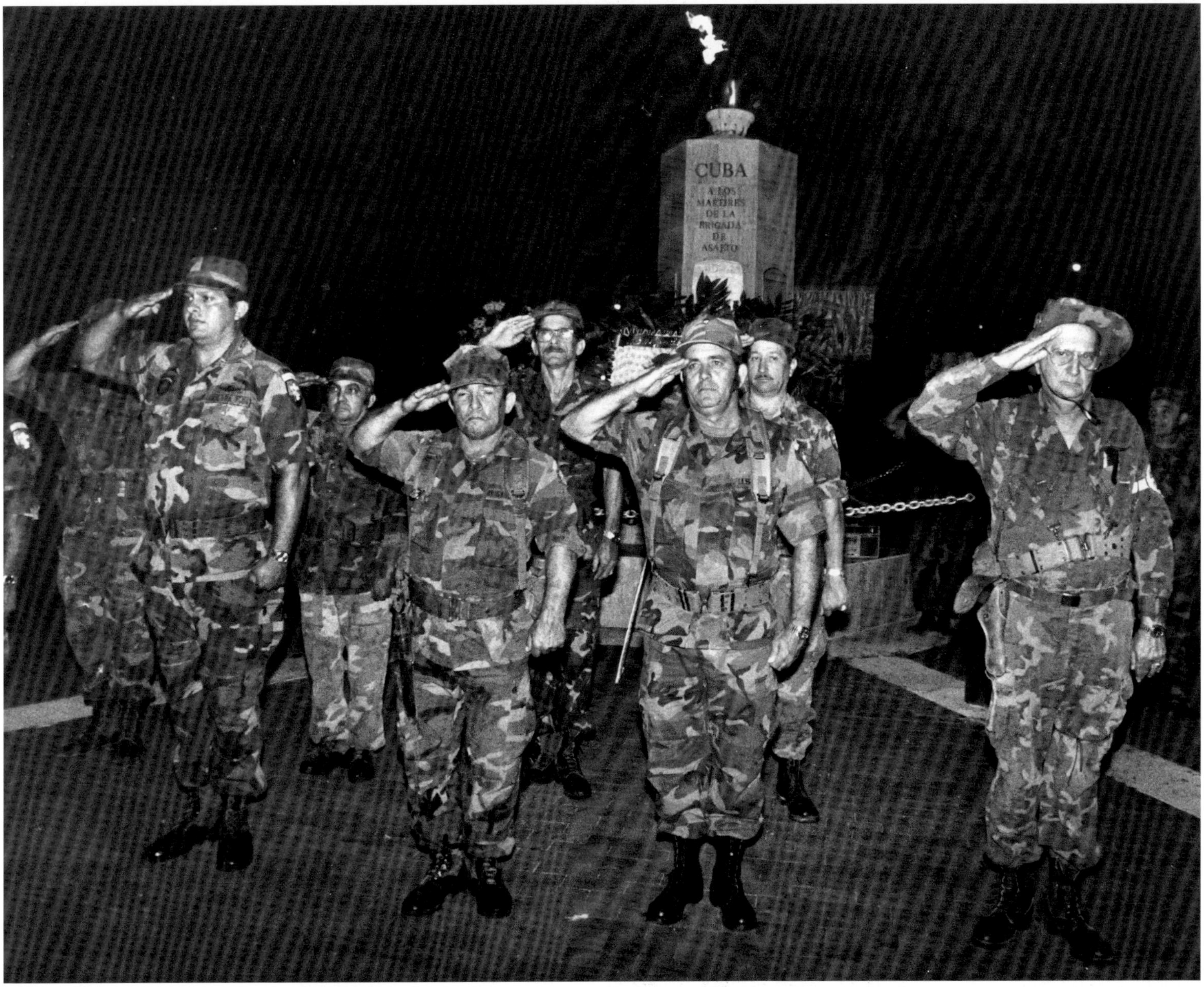

On April 16, 1985, Bay of Pigs veterans at SW 8th Street and 13th Avenue commemorated the 24th anniversary of their mission. They had not taken back Cuba, nor would they anytime soon. They could, however, continue to hope.

Hansel y Raul play *charanga* in the Infinites Club in 1985. *Charanga* is traditional Cuban dance music such as "Son" or "Danzon" played with an emphasis on strings and woodwinds, instead of the usual brass that typifies much of Cuban music. It was very popular in the 1940s, and like many things of old Cuba, has experienced a revival.

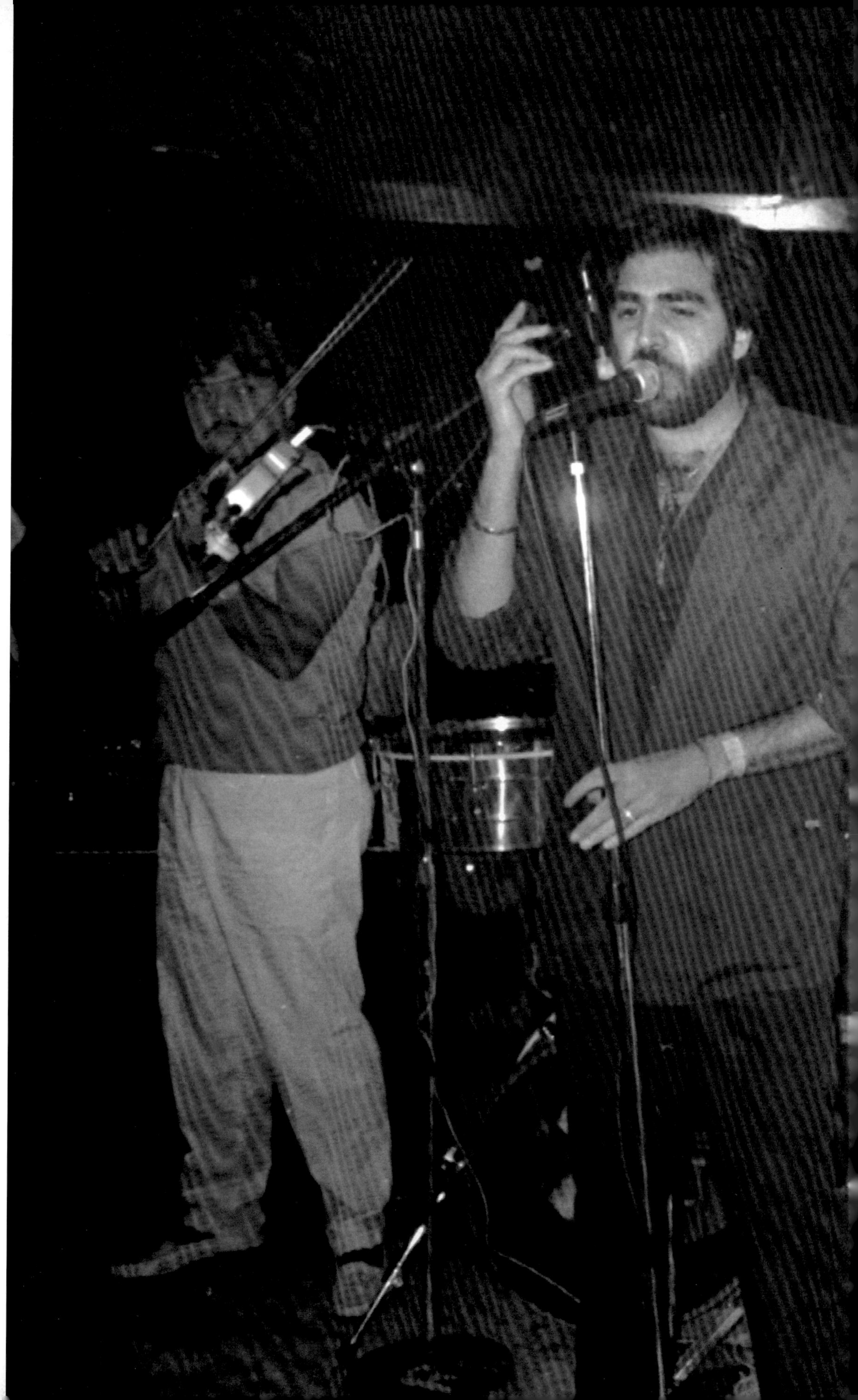

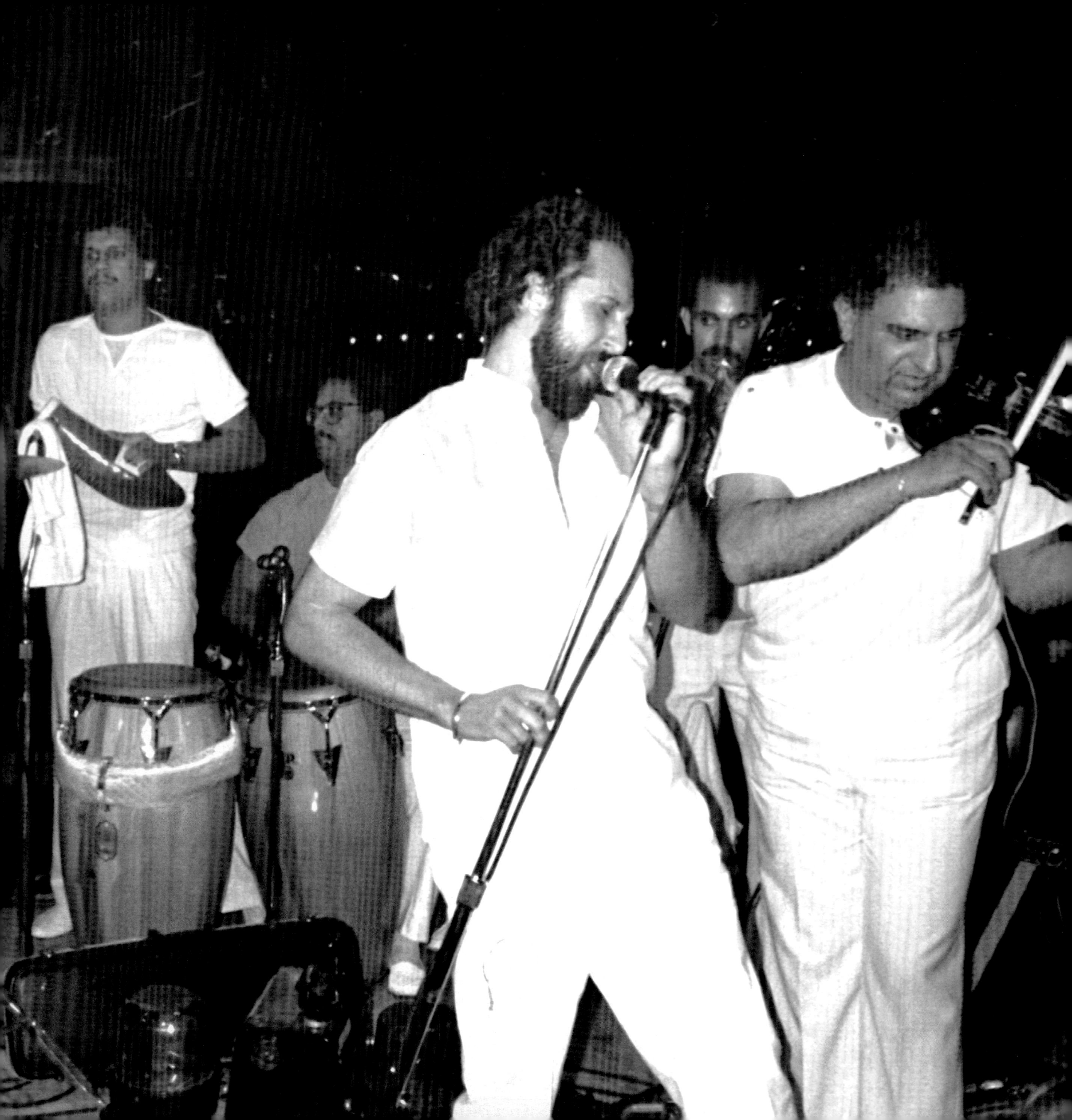

Xavier Suarez, the first Cuban mayor of Miami.

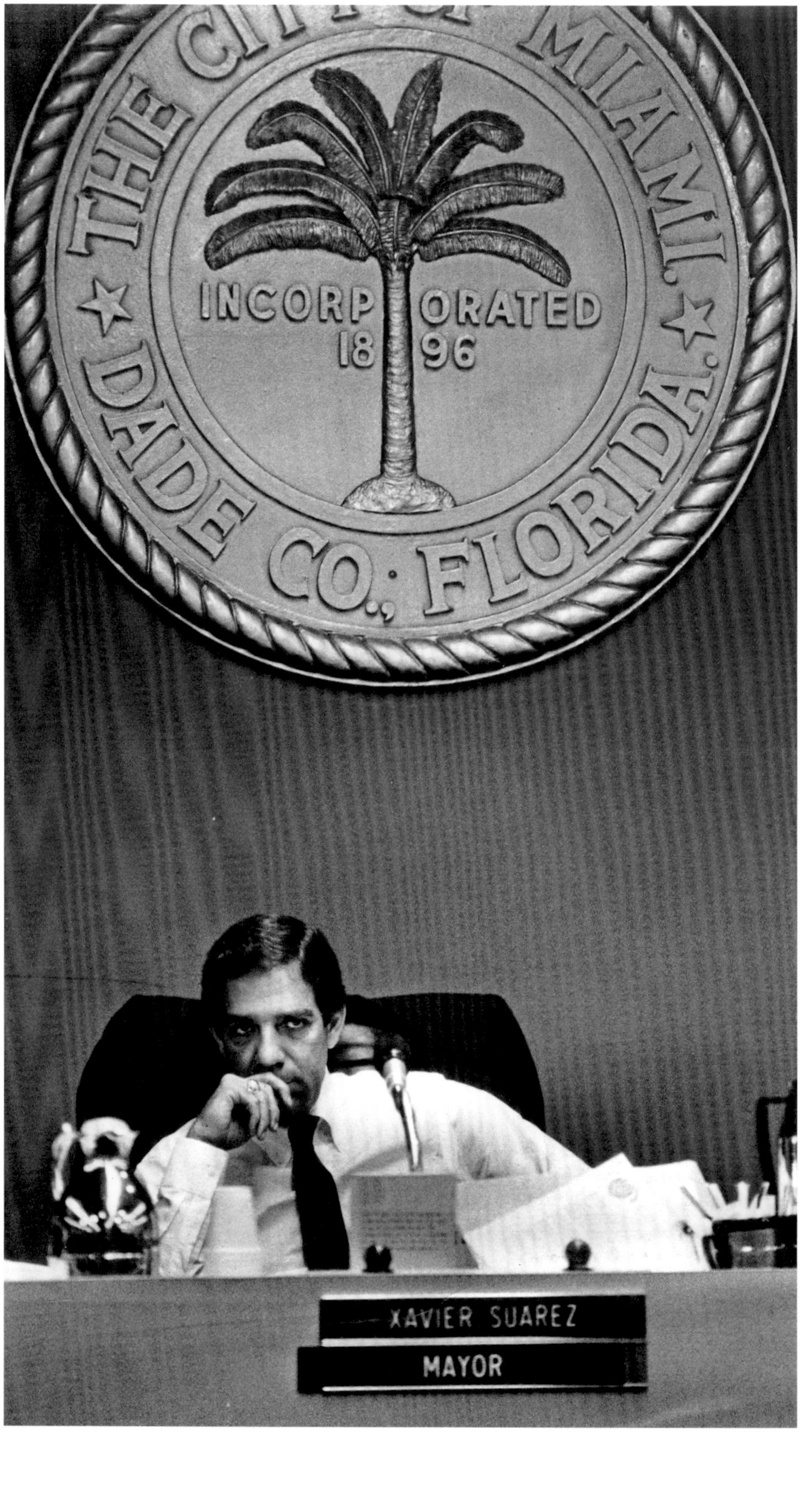

Notes on the Photographs

These notes, listed by page number, attempt to include all aspects known of the photographs. Each of the photographs is identified by the page number, photograph's title or description, photographer and collection, archive, and call or box number when applicable. Although every attempt was made to collect all data, in some cases complete data may have been unavailable due to the age and condition of some of the photographs and records.

II **Miami Waterfront**
Library of Congress
LC-USZ62-96369

VI **First Wave Arrivals**
Historical Museum of Southern Florida
1989-011-4514

X **Three New Arrivals**
Florida State Archives
MS26177

2 **Portrait of Henry Flagler**
Florida State Archives
RC02842

3 **Portrait of Julia Tuttle**
Florida State Archives
RC06560

4 **Jose Martí at Key West, 1891**
Historical Museum of Southern Florida
1976-139-1

5 **Incorporation of Miami, 1896**
Florida State Archives
NO38907

6 **First Passenger Train Arrival**
Florida State Archives
RC06062

7 **Metropolis Front Page**
Florida State Archives
RC05729

8 **Dade County's First School**
Florida State Archives
RC02970

9 **Early Office Buildings**
Florida State Archives
RC19966

10 **A Founding Family**
Florida State Archives
RC08601

11 **Aboard the Three Friends**
Florida State Archives
NO40916

12 **Tent Camp for the Troops**
Historical Museum of Southern Florida
X-1102-1

13 **Certificate for Disabled Veteran**
Florida State Archives
RC19551

14 **The Miami Skyline, 1910**
Florida State Archives
RC03600

15 **Entrance to the City, 1911**
Florida State Archives
RC20411

16 **Miami Herald Employees**
Florida State Archives
RC19545

17 **Deering Estate from the Water, 1919**
Florida State Archives
RC19091

18 **Carl Fisher**
Florida State Archives
RC03727

19 **Miami Beach Polo Fields**
Florida State Archives
WE186

20 **First U.S.-Cuban Polo Match**
Florida State Archives
RC01801

21 **Arrival of Steamship Hauley**
Florida State Archives
WE045

22 **Early Cruises**
Florida State Archives
CO16436

23 **West Flagler Street, 1921**
Florida State Archives
RC20456

24 **Real Estate Boom Tours**
Florida State Archives
RC03396

25 **Miami Studios Under Construction**
Florida State Archives
RC03738

26 **Petroleum Exports**
Florida State Archives
RC17589

27 **George Merrick**
Florida State Archives
RC16166

28 **Miami News–Metropolis Building**
Florida State Archives
RC08637

29 **The Miami News Tower**
Florida State Archives
PR06853

30 **Unloading Cuban Imports**
Florida State Archives
RC19904A

31 **Auction at the Almendares**
Florida State Archives
rc13444

32 **Pan American Fokker Airplane, 1927**
Florida State Archives
PR00579

33 **Departure for Havana Aboard Pan Am F-7 Flight**
Florida State Archives
PR00513

34 **Aftermath of 1926 Hurricane**
Florida State Archives
RC03744

35 **Aftermath of 1926 Hurricane no. 2**
Florida State Archives
RC08433

36 **Cuban Athletic Club in Miami**
Florida State Archives
RC04696

37 **Inauguration of New Pan Am Terminal**
Florida State Archives
PR00511

38 **Miami Bottling Works**
Florida State Archives
NO34904

39 **Gerardo Machado in Exile**
Historical Museum of Southern Florida
1995-277-17438

40 **Riverside Elementary School**
Florida State Archives
RC19881

41 **Airship Akron at All American Air Races**
Florida State Archives
RC12769

42 **Pan Am Transfer of Cattle to Cuba**
Florida State Archives
RC15237

43 **Mario G. Menocal with Companions**
Florida State Archives
NO35086

44 **SS Florida Bound for Havana**
Florida State Archives
PC21481

45 **Miami Daily News Tower at Night**
Florida State Archives
PR06809

46 **Early Cuban Flavor**
Florida State Archives
NO38732

47 **Pan Am Air Mail Commemoration**
Florida State Archives
MC0093

48 **Fulgencio Batista at Miami Depot, 1938**
Historical Museum of Southern Florida
1985-136-141

49 **Batista with Colonel Charles Metzler**
Florida State Archives
RC11511

50 **Aerial View of Hialeah Racetrack**
Florida State Archives
PR15236

52 **The Hialeah Park Flamingos**
Historical Museum of Southern Florida
1989-011-6899

53 **The Cape Florida Property**
Florida State Archives
NO45389B

54 **Aerial View of Tamiami Trail**
Florida State Archives
PR15241

55 **Castro at the Flagler Theater**
Historical Museum of Southern Florida
2004-281-1

56 **Palm Avenue in 1959**
Historical Museum of Southern Florida
1989-011-6872

58 **CARLOS PRIO SOCARRÁS WITH DAUGHTER**
Historical Museum of Southern Florida
1995-277-15621

59 **EMMA CASTRO DELIVERING A SPEECH**
Historical Museum of Southern Florida
1995-277-11879

60 **CUBAN EXILE BUSINESS FACADE**
Historical Museum of Southern Florida
1995-277-3040

62 **AIRLIFT REFUGEES AT MIAMI INTERNATIONAL AIRPORT, 1961**
Florida State Archives
PR04721

63 **OPERATION PEDRO PAN**
Florida State Archives
PR04712

64 **STANDARD X-RAY PROCEDURE**
Florida State Archives
NO31977

65 **NURSE WITH YOUNG CUBAN WOMAN**
Florida State Archives
NO31979

66 **THE SCHIADOSKI FAMILY WITH RABBI DOW ROZENCWAIG**
Florida State Archives
MS26192

67 **LYDIA CABRERA**
Historical Museum of Southern Florida
1995-277-11488

68 **DOWN WITH CASTRO**
Courtesy of Ortiz-Perez
Book Pictures 002

69 **LOYOLA SCHOOL FOR REFUGEES**
Historical Museum of Southern Florida
CM-5-00226-3

70 **CAFE AL MINUTO IN LITTLE HAVANA**
Florida State Archives
PR04696

71 **CUBA DAY PARADE ON FLAGLER STREET**
Historical Museum of Southern Florida
1995-277-2900

72 **ABEL HOLTZ**
Historical Museum of Southern Florida
1995-277-14949

73 **ALPHA 66 IN THE EVERGLADES**
Historical Museum of Southern Florida
1989-011-364

74 **THE CENTRO VASCO RESTAURANT**
Florida State Archives
C681043

75 **LA ROSITA SUPERMARKET**
Florida State Archives
RC12310

76 **FIVE CUBAN REFUGEES, 1962**
Florida State Archives
PR04710

78 **STORY OF CUERVO CASTILLO AND FAMILY**
Cuervo Castillo Family
Book Pictures 001

79 **HISTORICAL MUSEUM OF SOUTHERN FLORIDA**
Historical Museum of Southern Florida
1989-011-7027

80 **DEMOCRACY TRAINING**
Historical Museum of Southern Florida
1989-011-4458

81 **JOSE ALEMAN**
Historical Museum of Southern Florida
1995-277-9750

82 **KENNEDYS AT BAY OF PIGS CEREMONY**
Historical Museum of Southern Florida
1989-011-21744

83 **KENNEDY ORANGE BOWL COIN TOSS**
Florida State Archives
RC22878

84 **AN UNFAMILIAR CULTURE AND LANGUAGE**
Historical Museum of Southern Florida
1989-011-4416

85 **THE FIRST WAVE**
Historical Museum of Southern Florida
1989-011-4462

86 **ARCHITECT HILARIO CANDELA**
Historical Museum of Southern Florida
1995-277-11629

87 **CONCERT AT MIAMI MARINE STADIUM**
Florida State Archives
C671284

88 **LA LECHONERA RESTAURANT**
Florida State Archives
C681042

89 **CUBAN PROFESSIONALS AT WORK**
Historical Museum of Southern Florida
1989-011-4482

90 **COAST GUARD RESCUE OF CUBANS**
Historical Museum of Southern Florida
1989-011-4524

91 **CUBAN REFUGEE ASSISTANCE PROGRAM**
Historical Museum of Southern Florida
1989-011-4433

92 **ANTI-CASTRO MIAMI HEADQUARTERS, 1964**
Historical Museum of Southern Florida
1989-011-4241

93 **RADIO CENTRO A.K.A. THE FLAGLER THEATER**
Historical Museum of Southern Florida
1989-011-16164

94 One of the First Freedom Flights
Historical Museum of Southern Florida
1989-011-4510

95 Miriam Alonso and Daughter
Historical Museum of Southern Florida
1995-277-9785

97 Furniture Repair at Cuban Refugee Center
Historical Museum of Southern Florida
1989-011-4434

98 Aerial View of Interstate 95
Florida State Archives
RC17198

99 Suitcase Filled with Family Photos
Historical Museum of Southern Florida
1989-011-4516

100 Cuban Cigar Contraband
Historical Museum of Southern Florida
1989-011-4533

101 Cigar Maker in Little Havana
Florida State Archives
FS8085A

102 Cigars Ready for Pressing
Florida State Archives
FS8081A

103 Poder Cubano Brick
Historical Museum of Southern Florida
1989-011-4431

104 The Miami Stingers' Joe Zabala
Historical Museum of Southern Florida
1989-011-24203

105 Cuban Barbecue in Miami
Historical Museum of Southern Florida
1989-011-4485

107 Preparations for Cuban-style Dinner
Historical Museum of Southern Florida
1989-011-4441

108 An Application for Alien Status
Historical Museum of Southern Florida
1995-277-3042

109 Flagler Granada Clinic
Historical Museum of Southern Florida
1989-011-4481

111 Crafts at the Little Havana Center
Florida State Archives
PR23433

112 Colon Supermarket and Spanglish
Historical Museum of Southern Florida
1995-277-3041

113 Bilingual Program at Miami Dade College
Florida State Archives
PR23434

114 Grateful Exile Kissing the Ground
Historical Museum of Southern Florida
1989-011-4562

115 Cuban Refugee Clinic
Historical Museum of Southern Florida
1989-011-4480

117 Cuban Miami Shops and Signs
Historical Museum of Southern Florida
1995-277-3039

118 Cuban-Americans for Nixon
Historical Museum of Southern Florida
1995-277-3013

120 Petition Against Coexistence
Historical Museum of Southern Florida
1995-277-14155

121 Jose Martí Celebration
Historical Museum of Southern Florida
1995-277-3130

122 The Santa Barbara Festival, 1975
Historical Museum of Southern Florida
1995-277-3098

123 Candlelight Procession in Little Havana
Historical Museum of Southern Florida
1995-277-3100

124 A Bar Killing Shame
Historical Museum of Southern Florida
1995-277-3057

125 Herald Building Protest
Historical Museum of Southern Florida
1995-277-3082

126 Miami-Dade Outreach Class
Florida State Archives
PR23640

127 Versailles Sandwich Tackle
Historical Museum of Southern Florida
1995-277-16823

128 Walk-up Service
Florida State Archives
C681026

129 Language Protest
Historical Museum of Southern Florida
1995-277-3058

131 Wake Up Americans
Historical Museum of Southern Florida
1995-277-3060

132 Manuel Carbonell with Sculpture
Historical Museum of Southern Florida
1995-277-11667

133 Bicentennial Parade, 1976
Historical Museum of Southern Florida
1995-277-3011

134 A Miami Quince with Court
Historical Museum of Southern Florida
1995-277-3010

135 Our Lady of Charity on Bow of Boat
Historical Museum of Southern Florida
1995-277-3105

136 Celia Cruz Onstage, 1976
Historical Museum of Southern Florida
1995-277-12662

137 Villa Paula a.k.a. the Cuban Consulate
Historical Museum of Southern Florida
1995-277-2995

139 Sharpshooters at Pistol Club
Historical Museum of Southern Florida
1995-277-2993

140 Balcony Conversations
Historical Museum of Southern Florida
1995-277-3107

141 Carlos Prio Socarrás Funeral
Historical Museum of Southern Florida
MN_1970

142 WPBT Bilingual Sitcom
Historical Museum of Southern Florida
1989-011-15973

143 The Peña Family
Courtesy of WPBT 2
Peña Family (table)

145 The First Calle Ocho Festival, 1978
Historical Museum of Southern Florida
MN_5503

146 Shooting Castro in Effigy
Historical Museum of Southern Florida
1995-277-3210

147 Santería Consultation
Historical Museum of Southern Florida
1995-277-3183

148 Protesting Bernardo Benes
Historical Museum of Southern Florida
1995-277-3092

149 Luis Botifoll
Historical Museum of Southern Florida
1995-277-10861

150 Jewish Federation Award Ceremony, 1978
Florida State Archives
MS26345

151 Juan Candela and His Comparsas
Florida State Archives
FP79789

153 Comparsas Conga Musician Performance
Florida State Archives
FP79790

154 First Kings Day Parade
Historical Museum of Southern Florida
1995-277-9244

155 Anti-Castro Protest at Bayfront Park
Historical Museum of Southern Florida
1995-277-3053

156 Marchers in Hialeah
Historical Museum of Southern Florida
1989-011-6876

157 Guillermo Zamora with Chief Garland Watkins
Historical Museum of Southern Florida
1989-011-24246

158 Elderly Cuban with Flag
Historical Museum of Southern Florida
1995-277-3033

160 Tent City Under I-95
Historical Museum of Southern Florida
1981-099-113

161 Tent City Under I-95 no. 2
Historical Museum of Southern Florida
1995-277-3110

162 Abandoned Property Squatter
Historical Museum of Southern Florida
1995-277-3115

163 Hunger Strike for Cubans at Risk
Historical Museum of Southern Florida
1995-277-3047

164 Ramon Puig at His Shop
Historical Museum of Southern Florida
1995-277-17265

165 Exterior of Puig's Shop
Florida State Archives
FS80124A

166 The Botanica Nena
Florida State Archives
fp79807

167 Queipo Market
Florida State Archives
FS80133A

168 Palos for Sale at Queipo Market
Florida State Archives
FS80153a

169 Religious Shrine in Little Havana
Florida State Archives
FS80112a

170 **Monument to the Bay of Pigs Fallen**
Florida State Archives
fs80113A

171 **Mariel Exodus Special Report**
Florida State Archives
PR22026

172 **Revealing Castro's Radio Threat**
Historical Museum of Southern Florida
1995-277-3127

173 **Cubano Unidos Mission to Cuba**
Historical Museum of Southern Florida
1995-277-3005

174 **Hispanic Festival in Miami**
Florida State Archives
C820619

175 **Enjoying Café Cubano**
Historical Museum of Southern Florida
1995-277-3026

176 **Preparing Café Cubano**
Florida State Archives
FS8057A

177 **Good Loaves of Cuban Bread**
Florida State Archives
FS8068A

178 **Making Cookies at Cafe Cubano**
Florida State Archives
FS8066A

179 **Little Havana Street Corner**
Florida State Archives
FS80122

180 **Sculpture of Cuban with Machete**
Florida State Archives
FS80114A

181 **Hispanic Mayors of Miami**
Historical Museum of Southern Florida
1995-277-11750

182 **Mural of Dominoes Players**
Florida State Archives
FS80119

183 **Dominoes at Domino Park**
Florida State Archives
FS80117A

184 **The Cuban American National Foundation**
Historical Museum of Southern Florida
1995-277-2991

185 **Emilio Bacardi Lay Gravesite**
Historical Museum of Southern Florida
1995-277-2020

186 **The Sculls with Album Cover**
Florida State Archives
FS864853

187 **Symbols of American Pop Culture**
Florida State Archives
FS8059A

188 **Arrival of Jubilant Ex-Prisoner**
Historical Museum of Southern Florida
1995-277-3123

189 **Packing for a Trip to Cuba**
Historical Museum of Southern Florida
1995-277-3050

190 **Ros and Lehtinen Marriage**
Florida State Archives
PT01542

191 **Florida State Representatives**
Florida State Archives
PT01541

192 **Miami Vice Checkers**
Historical Museum of Southern Florida
1989-011-16025

193 **At the Municipio de Bayamo Exilio**
Historical Museum of Southern Florida
1995-277-3023

194 **The Miami Sound Machine**
Historical Museum of Southern Florida
MN_5379

195 **Hiram Gomez**
Historical Museum of Southern Florida
1995-277-14341

196 **Waiting for Cuban Family Member's Return**
Historical Museum of Southern Florida
1995-277-3154

197 **Bay of Pigs Commemoration, 1985**
Historical Museum of Southern Florida
1995-277-3020

198 **Hansel and Raul at the Infinites Club**
Florida State Archives
FA1181

200 **Mayor Xavier Suarez**
Historical Museum of Southern Florida
1989-011-24794